DISTRIBUTION OF POWERS AND RESPONSIBILITIES IN FEDERAL COUNTRIES

A GLOBAL DIALOGUE ON FEDERALISM
A joint program of the Forum of Federations and the International Association of Centers for Federal Studies which creates forums around the world through which experts exchange experiences, ideas, and academic research to identify emerging challenges and inspire new solutions.

www.forumfed.org
www.iacfs.org

Other publications in the Global Dialogue on Federalism Series include:
BOOK SERIES
Constitutional Origins, Structure, and Change in Federal Countries (2005), Volume I
BOOKLET SERIES
Dialogues on Constitutional Origins, Structure, and Change in Federal Countries (2005), Volume I
Dialogues sur les origines, structure et changements constitutionnels dans les pays fédéraux (2005), Volume I
Dialogues on Distribution of Powers and Responsibilities in Federal Countries (2005), Volume II
Dialogues sur la répartition des compétences et des responsabilités dans les pays fédéraux (2005), Volume II

A Global Dialogue on Federalism
Volume II

DISTRIBUTION OF POWERS
AND RESPONSIBILITIES
IN FEDERAL COUNTRIES

EDITED BY AKHTAR MAJEED,
RONALD L. WATTS, AND DOUGLAS M. BROWN

SENIOR EDITOR JOHN KINCAID

Published for

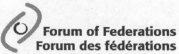
Forum of Federations
Forum des fédérations

and

iacfs
INTERNATIONAL ASSOCIATION OF
CENTERS FOR FEDERAL STUDIES

by

McGill-Queen's University Press
Montreal & Kingston · London · Ithaca

© McGill-Queen's University Press 2006
ISBN 0-7735-2974-8 (cloth)
ISBN 0-7735-3004-5 (paper)

Legal deposit first quarter 2006
Bibliothèque nationale du Québec

Printed in Canada on acid-free paper that is 100% ancient forest free
(100% post-consumer recycled), processed chlorine free.

This book was produced with the generous financial support of the
Swiss government.

McGill-Queen's University Press acknowledges the support of the Canada
Council for the Arts for our publishing program. We also acknowledge
the financial support of the Government of Canada through the Book
Publishing Industry Development Program (BPIDP) for our publishing
activities.

Library and Archives Canada Cataloguing in Publication

Distribution of powers and responsibilities in federal countries /
   edited by Akhtar Majeed, Ronald L. Watts and Douglas M. Brown;
   senior editor John Kincaid.

(A global dialogue on federalism; v. 2)
Includes index.
ISBN 0-7735-2974-8 (bnd)
ISBN 0-7735-3004-5 (pbk)

   1. Federal government. 2. Comparative government. I. Brown, Douglas M.
(Douglas Mitchell), 1954– II. Kincaid, John, 1946– III. Majeed, Akhtar
IV. Watts, Ronald L V. International Association of Centers for Federal Studies
VI. Forum of Federations VII. Series: Global dialogue on federalism; v. 2

JC355.D58 2006   321.02   C2005-905815-3

This book was typeset by Interscript in 10/12 Baskerville.

Contents

Preface

This volume on the distribution of powers and responsibilities in federal democracies is the second contribution to a series of practical books on federalism being published as a part of the program entitled "A Global Dialogue on Federalism." The goal of this Global Dialogue is to engage experts from around the world in comparative conversations and debates about core themes and issues of federalism, the point being to build an international network that enables practitioners, students, scholars, and others to learn from one another, to share best practices, and to enhance their understanding of the prospects as well as the problems of federalism as a mode of governance in today's world, especially in relation to democracy, freedom, prosperity, and peace.

The Global Dialogue is sponsored jointly by the Forum of Federations and the International Association of Centers for Federal Studies (IACFS). The Forum is an international network on federalism that seeks to strengthen democratic governance by promoting dialogue on and understanding of the values, practices, principles, and possibilities of federalism. The IACFS is an association of centres and institutes throughout the world that maintains a research and teaching focus on political systems that have federal features.

The work of the Forum of Federations and the IACFS is part of a broader endeavour to build and strengthen democracy through federalism when and where appropriate. As a mode of governance that seeks to combine self-rule for regional and minority interests with shared rule for general and common purposes, federalism is necessarily of interest to advocates of democracy. This is particularly true in a world in which the vast majority of nation-states are multinational, multilingual, multireligious, and/or multicultural. Indeed, there has been a tremendous upsurge of interest in federalism since the emergence of a new wave of democratization in the late 1980s. This worldwide interest in federalism is directly linked to movements promoting greater democracy and decentralization and to the simultaneous trends towards globalization and regionalization evident throughout today's world.

Given the dominance of statist ideologies during the past two centuries, however, federalism has often been viewed as a stepchild less worthy of attention and cultivation than the seemingly natural children of modern nationalism. Consequently, while there is a long history of federal-democratic experience in a few countries, such as Australia, Canada, Switzerland, and the United States, there is little practical experience with democratic federalism in most countries, and there are problematic experiences in a number of fledgling federal democracies. In turn, there is a paucity of accessible literature and information on comparative federalism and a dearth of intel-lectual capital available for investment in research and teaching about the many varieties of federalism worldwide.

This series of books, being published as one important product of the Global Dialogue program, seeks to create informational capital and to fill gaps in our comparative knowledge by providing as balanced a view as possible of theories and practices of federalism in various countries around the world. It does this by exploring comparative and contrasting theoretical and practical perspectives, with each volume focusing on a particular aspect of federalism through the examples of selected countries that reflect federalism's diversity, including its strengths and weaknesses.

Our aim is to produce books that are accessible to interested citizens, political leaders, government practitioners, and students and faculty in institutions of higher education. Each chapter, therefore, seeks to provide an overview of its country's distribution of powers in a way that covers all relevant, important information without overwhelming the reader in detail. It also seeks to provide an analysis of the rationales and workings of the system and to indicate how well or poorly the latter functions in relation to its constitution and its society.

The first volume of the series, *Constitutional Origins, Structure, and Change in Federal Countries*, offers an exploration of the constitutional systems of twelve federal countries. Future volumes will be devoted to legislative and executive governance in federal systems, fiscal federalism, foreign affairs in federal countries, and other important themes, with a somewhat different mix of countries being represented in each volume. The Global Dialogue program also produces a booklet series that provides an entry point to each book by highlighting the insights, key issues, and items of international interest that arose at the country and international roundtables. In keeping with their educative and accessible format, the booklets also include a glossary of country-specific terminology. The booklet for this second volume, *Distribution of Powers and Responsibilities in Federal Countries*, is available; indeed, the limited scope of the booklet allows it to be published quickly, in multiple languages, and reproduced as changes in the federal countries warrant.

The conceptual framework of the program can be found in Volume 1, edited by John Kincaid and G. Alan Tarr and published in 2005. The key idea of the Global Dialogue is to draw on the wealth of others' experiences and to learn from them. The program entails a comparative exploration of a dozen core themes in federal governance. Through a series of themed roundtables, participants representing diverse viewpoints in a representative and diverse sample of federal countries search for new insights and solutions. The new information emanating from the roundtables is used to produce comparative materials for worldwide distribution.

The exploration of each theme entails a multiple-staged process. First, a "theme coordinator" is chosen, who makes use of the most current research to create an internationally comprehensive set of questions covering institutional provisions and how they work in practice. This set of questions, or "theme template," is the foundation of the program as it guides the dialogue at the roundtables and forms the outline for the theme book. The theme coordinator also selects a representative sample of federal countries and recommends a "country coordinator" for each. Each of these coordinators is the author of a country chapter.

Next, each country coordinator invites a select and diverse group of expert practitioners and scholars to participate in a roundtable in his or her country, guided by the theme template. The goal is to create the most accurate picture of the theme in each country by inviting experts with diverse viewpoints and experiences who are prepared to share with and learn from others in a non-politicized environment.

At the end of the day, the coordinators are equipped to write a short article that reflects the highlights of the dialogue from each country roundtable. The booklet articles have been generated from such exchanges.

Once each country has held its roundtable, representatives gather at an international roundtable. The representatives are experts who share their varied experiences and perspectives, as well as the knowledge gained from their country's roundtable, to identify commonalities and differences and to generate new insights.

To ensure that the knowledge gained at these events does not end with only those who participated in them, the final stage integrates the reflections from the country roundtables and new insights from the international event into book chapters, thus building on the progress already made and creating opportunities to use the material for further events. The chapters reflect the fact that their authors were able to explore the theme from a global vantage point, resulting in a more informed comparative analysis of the topic.

Given the extent of the Global Dialogue program, we have many people to thank. We offer thanks to Akhtar Majeed, Ronald L. Watts, and Douglas M. Brown, the editors of Volume 2, for their invaluable help in launching this work. We wish to acknowledge the contributors to this volume and their institutions for their dedication in hosting events, writing chapters, and helping us to uphold the excellence of the program. Thanks are due also to participants in the eleven country roundtables and in the international roundtable, whose input helped to shape the content of the chapters.

We wish to thank, as well, colleagues who read and critiqued drafts of the chapters contained in this book: Brian Dollery, University of New England, Australia; Martin Painter, City University of Hong Kong, China; Maureen A. Covell, Simon Fraser University, Canada; Patrick Peeters, Katholieke Universiteit Leuven, Belgium; Celina Souza, Universidade Federal da Bahia, Brazil; Robert H. Wilson, University of Texas at Austin, United States; Anthony Careless, University of Toronto, Canada; Guy Laforest, Universite de Laval, Canada; Susan P. Phillips, Carleton University, Canada; Christopher S. Allen, University of Georgia, United States; Franz Gress, Johann Wolfgang Goethe Universität, Germany; M. Govinda Rao, National Institute of Public Finance and Policy, India; Sandeep Shastri, visiting at the International Academy for Creative Teaching, MATS University, Bangalore, India; Peter M. Ward, University of Texas at Austin, United States; José M. Serna, Instituto de Investivaciones Juridicas, Universidad Nacional Autónoma de México, Mexico; Alvin Magid, State University of New York at Albany, United States; Ladipo Adamolekun, formerly of The World Bank, Nigeria; Robert B. Agranoff, Indiana University, United States; Eva Desdentado Daroca, Universidad de Alcalá de Henares, Spain; Max Frenkel, *Neue Zürcher Zeitung*, Switzerland; Sonja Wälti, Georgetown University, United States; G. Alan Tarr, Rutgers University, United States; Joseph F. Zimmerman, State University of New York at Albany, United States; and Keith E. Whittington, Princeton University, United States. The assistance of these individuals is much appreciated, although they are, of course, not responsible for any deficiencies remaining in the chapters.

We also thank our colleagues and associates at the Forum of Federations and at the International Association of Centers for Federal Studies. The program and the present book could not exist without their assistance and expertise. We wish to acknowledge the work of the entire Forum of Federations staff and, in particular, Barbara Brook, former Program Manager, Global Dialogue; Abigail Ostien, Program Manager, Global Dialogue; and Rhonda Dumas, former Program Assistant. Thanks are due also to Brandon Michael Benjamin, undergraduate EXCEL Scholar, and Terry A. Cooper, Administrative Assistant, for their work on behalf of this volume at the Robert B. and Helen S. Meyner Center for the Study of State and Local

Government at Lafayette College, Easton, Pennsylvania. Finally, we thank the staff at McGill-Queen's University Press for all of their assistance in producing the volume and working with us to ensure the success of *Distribution of Powers and Responsibilities in Federal Countries.*

On behalf of the Global Dialogue Editorial Board
John Kincaid, Senior Editor

DISTRIBUTION OF POWERS AND RESPONSIBILITIES IN FEDERAL COUNTRIES

Distribution of Powers
and Responsibilities

AHKTAR MAJEED

Distribution of Powers and Responsibilities in Federal Countries presents an objective and balanced description and analysis of the distribution of powers and responsibilities in the federal constitution and actual federal practice of eleven countries: Australia, Belgium, Brazil, Canada, Germany, India, Mexico, Nigeria, Spain, Switzerland, and the United States of America. For each federation there is an in-depth examination of such themes as (1) the distribution of governmental, political, monetary, fiscal, administrative, and policy responsibilities; (2) symmetry and asymmetry in the distribution of responsibilities; (3) the reasons and ways in which powers and responsibilities are explicitly and implicitly exclusive, concurrent, or shared in the constitution; (4) the reasons and ways in which responsibilities become divided and shared in actual governmental practice; (5) current controversies over the division and/or sharing of powers and responsibilities; and (6) assessments of the exclusive and concurrent exercise of powers and responsibilities.

This volume identifies similarities and differences among these federal polities with regard to intergovernmental distribution of powers and responsibilities. In all eleven countries the system is part of the constitutional structure; yet there is a wide range of variations among these systems. Whereas the United States and Australia present one type of distribution system, Canada and India present another. Belgium's system of double symmetry, which involves two different kinds of federating units that cut across, and overlap, each other, presents still another. In addition, European federations such as Germany and Switzerland exhibit a division between the allocation of legislative and executive authority in particular areas. Thus, in view of differences in forms and scope of various distributions of powers and responsibilities, it can be surmised that there is no pure model of federalism but, rather, several practical variations within the common framework of federal systems.

Interdependence in governance necessitates shared governance. The philosophical foundations of some federal polities stipulate that a government is best when it governs the least and, therefore, only limited functions are given to the central or federal government at its founding. In other places, in view of historical traditions of centralization of power and authority, the operative principle is that a government is best when it is able to bring about social transformation. Hence, the framers of these federal constitutions and subsequent law makers consciously ensured that the overwhelming authority was kept with the federal government. Sometimes what was overlooked were the cardinal federal principles that good governance is no substitute for self-governance and that, even if a function is conducted better by a central rather than a regional government, power should not necessarily be assumed by the centre. In other words, constantly rationalizing in order to keep functions at the centre is not only against an accepted federal norm but also against the democratic principle of self-rule. Moreover, the sharing of powers between the federal government and the state or provincial governments often evolves to a point at which federal powers became exclusive but state/provincial powers remain shared. This has created serious problems for many federal systems.

The question of distribution of responsibilities and assignment of resources is also linked to political culture. It is not as if it is only now that we have started thinking about whether a federal distribution of powers is generally compatible with a society's political culture and economy. For example, in some societies there are concerns that some planned development is needed to remove regional disparities. In other societies maintenance of unity and national integration is a major concern. In yet other countries the federalization of the party system has altered the basic premises of intergovernmental relations and has created new mechanisms that are distorting the federal structure. This has led to the development of new ways of organizing interstate and centre-state relations. In some societies newly evolved structures are informal, even ad hoc and para-constitutional. All this has affected the nature of political coalitions and alliances, intergovernmental relations, and, consequently, the nature of the distribution of responsibilities among different orders of government.

However, in federal polities the reallocation of authority has been going on along two planes. On the one hand, decision making is no longer the concern of core central representative institutions alone; on the other hand, such central institutions have been forced to disperse formal authority, both up (to supranational institutions) and down (to subnational governments). Many developing countries are decentralizing authority, as are most European countries. Thus, the economic integration of Europe means that decision makers in federal countries have less legal flexibility than they had before.

This volume identifies policy areas and assesses how authority over each of them is allocated. Power over resources, and over taxing and spending, vitally affects governance in virtually all policy areas. It is here that this study asks how different jurisdictions interact with one another. Their relationships may be characterized by hierarchy, mutual dependence, asymmetrical dependence, or relative independence. To understand these distinctions one has to understand both the formal and informal institutions of the country in question. In addition, any discussion about the distribution of powers and responsibilities must encompass the constitutional mechanisms that have been used for that end. Structural changes have been introduced in many federal countries, and any debate on a distribution of responsibility and of resources remains incomplete if the constitutional position of the federal structure remains blurred.

A number of images emerge in the chapters that follow. There is the image of the "divided federalism" of Canada as a contrast to the "integrated and shared federalism" of Germany, with the "quasi-federalism" of India lying in between. The U.S. system underscores a delegation of powers to the national government rather than a distribution of powers between the national and the state governments – but not without an often strongly coercive centralism. Whereas Canadian fiscal federalism is one of the most decentralized forms of federalism, India's is one of the most centralized.

Nevertheless, what is common is the ever-continuing debate about "who does what" in socioeconomic policy areas. There are variations in the degree to which policy areas are handled by different orders of government. Overall, though, the impression is that intergovernmental relations need to focus more on the needs of the citizens – particularly in welfare policy – and less on questions of turf and jurisdiction. Constituent units are generally at a disadvantage if they are responsible for social policy and programs because the financial powers are concentrated in the national government. It is clear, however, that if the constituent units want some cultural autonomy, then they have to have control over their own economy as well.

The liberalization and deregulation of national economies have transformed government from a regulator into a facilitator. No doubt even a federal state would have to regulate, but a facilitating state regulates differently. It is in this context that the issue of a supposed paradigm shift needs to be analyzed. This paradigm shift appears to involve a move from the principle of dual federalism (with each order of government exercising its own powers) to cooperative federalism (with the federal and state governments interacting with each other in the formulation and implementation of public policy).

In most of the federal countries the appraisal of the cost effectiveness of redistribution policies is now focused selectively. This is especially so in developing countries, which do not have many resources to spare for social welfare programs and where centralized federal leadership has historical suspicions about the "wasteful use of social programs" undertaken by the constituent units.

Federalism is also seen as a method of good governance in which political accommodation and understanding become sound practices in the midst of conflicting ideologies, disparate groups, and seemingly irreconcilable positions. Given that a decline of the legitimate political order results in a decline of the moral authority of the nation-state, the link between the need for good governance and federal power-sharing is obvious. The federal system is a device of shared governance, and the constitutions of federal polities usually envisage a "creative balance" between the need for an effective federal centre and the need for effectively empowered constituent federal units. There is also a need to balance the factors promoting a federal-institutional model of self-rule with those promoting shared rule. The notion of power-distribution and power-sharing arrangements must be addressed by both the national and regional constituents of a federation. In this volume the relationship between the substructures of a federal centre and its constituent units is examined in light of the notion of competence – the division and sharing of a government jurisdiction.

Thus, as is shown in *Distribution of Powers and Responsibilities in Federal Countries*, the responsibilities of various orders of government are determined by the functions that are assigned to them. However, the ability to perform these functions depends on the earmarking of sources of finance. In theory, any efficient demarcation of functions and finances is possible if there has first been an adequate cost-effective analysis of the ability of different orders to undertake certain functions. Moreover, the functions of government – allocation, distribution, and stabilization – are not independent of each other. It is federalism that makes it possible for different groups in different constituent states to have different preferences for public services, thereby creating differences in levels of taxation for public services. Of course, there are also differences in preferences regarding the degree of taxation and practical fiscal capacity. This tax differentiation, in turn, affects the distribution of resources. Thus, intergovernmental transfers are instruments for resolving horizontal imbalances. Fiscal imbalances are resolved or alleviated when the federal government offsets the fiscal disabilities of the constituent units. This gap between resources and needs has been continuously increasing in many federal systems. Disharmony between the federal centre and the constituent units regarding fiscal matters is systemic, and the major cause of this is interdependence in fiscal operations.

Finally, this book focuses on the principal philosophical, historical, cultural, and political bases for the distribution of powers and responsibilities in federal democracies, and it considers such issues as:

- What is the fundamental logic behind the distribution of powers and responsibilities in federal democracies?
- What, if anything, is unique or different about any system of constitutional distribution of powers as compared to the distributions found in other federal constitutions?
- How is a system of distribution of powers and responsibilities generally compatible with a country's society, political culture, and economy; and how is the distribution of powers supported by an underlying federal society or political culture?
- How effectively autonomous are the states in performing functions that are constitutionally assigned to them? Does the system of distribution of powers and responsibilities represent a system of shared powers and responsibilities?
- What mechanisms do federal democracies use to maintain symmetry or asymmetry between federating units? Also, what mechanisms are utilized for resolving differences and conflicts over competencies, powers, and responsibilities?
- What are the major reasons for the success, partial success, or failure of a system of distribution of powers and responsibilities? Where is the debate, if any, about the distribution of powers going, and what are the likely future trends for the allocation and sharing of powers in federal constitutions and federal practices?

The country chapters that follow are the result of a collaborative effort between the author and other academic experts and practitioners in each country represented. This has led, among other things, to clear explanations regarding distinctions between policy making and policy implementation. Thus, a key feature of the following chapters is the analysis not only of formal constitutional structures but also of the degree to which, over time, practice has been consistent with such structures or has varied from them. It is this aspect of the volume that makes it a reference point for academics and practitioners who seek to understand the working of the federal polity in a comparative context.

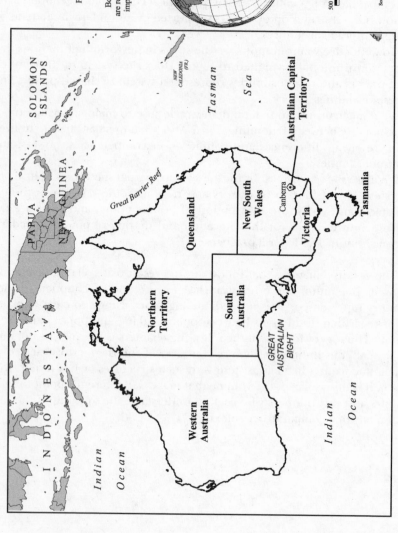

Australia

Capital: Canberra
Population: 20 Million
(2004 est.)

Boundaries and place names
are representative only and do not
imply any official endorsement.

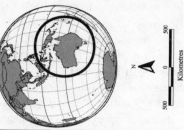

N

500   0   500

Kilometres

Sources: CIA World Factbook; ESRI Ltd;
Times Atlas of the World

SOLOMON
ISLANDS

*NEW
CALEDONIA
(FR.)*

Tasman

Sea

Australian Capital
Territory

Great Barrier Reef

PAPUA

NEW GUINEA

Queensland

New South
Wales

Canberra

Victoria

Tasmania

I N D O N E S I A

Northern
Territory

South
Australia

*GREAT
AUSTRALIAN
BIGHT*

Western
Australia

Indian

Ocean

Indian

Ocean

Commonwealth of Australia[*]

JOHN M. WILLIAMS
AND CLEMENT MACINTYRE

The constitutional distribution of powers and responsibilities in the Australian federation has proved to be exceptionally flexible. Originally conceived as a decentralized federation with the bulk of powers remaining in the hands of the states, in fact there has been a steady accretion of power to the Commonwealth government since shortly after federation in 1901. Although formal amendment of the constitution has been limited, changing interpretation by the High Court and the exercise of financial control by the Commonwealth[1] have resulted in growing power and responsibility being exercised by the Commonwealth government.

The Constitution of the Commonwealth of Australia came into force on 1 January 1901. The creation of "one indissoluble Federal Commonwealth under the Crown of the United Kingdom of Great Britain and Ireland" was the result of protracted negotiations throughout the 1890s between the framers of the Constitution, the colonial parliaments, the people, and, ultimately, the Imperial Parliament.[2] The result was a constitution that brought together the two themes that have since dominated Australian governance: responsible government and federalism. These twin aspects of the Constitution captured Australia's comfortable constitutional inheritance from the United Kingdom together with the less familiar constitutional solution of a federal system. The latter dimension was an obvious solution to the need to retain the political integrity of the Australian colonies. The system was informed by comparative constitutional research that focused primarily on the United States and, to a lesser degree, on Canada and Switzerland.[3]

As Cheryl Saunders has made clear, the "distinctive characteristic" of the Constitution's growth, including the development of the powers and responsibilities within the federal structure since 1901, has been one of evolution *not* revolution.[4] To achieve the union, the Constitution built on what was largely known, and what was needed, in 1901. Not surprisingly, the imperatives for federation – defence, uniformity of economic policy, freedom of interstate trade, and uniformity in immigration policy – form central parts of the constitutional compact. In a way that was consistent with their understanding of extant models, the framers trusted in parliamentary government and thus saw no need to adopt a bill of rights.

Since federation, the development of the Constitution has continued along an evolutionary path. In the 105 years since the Constitution's adoption, there have been only eight formal amendments, of which only three relate directly to the distribution of powers.[5] This is a reflection of both the procedural difficulty to effect such change and the cautious approach with which Australian electors approach reform. Yet, notwithstanding the lack of formal change, the Constitution, inasmuch as it relates to the distribution of powers and responsibilities between the states and the Commonwealth, is now read in different terms than it was in 1901. Several factors account for this. The assertion of Australia's legal sovereignty vis-à-vis Great Britain shows an incremental shift despite the formal links to the British monarch still in place.[6] More significantly, it is the High Court, rather than formal constitutional amendment, that has presided over the significant centralization of authority in the hands of the Commonwealth. The role and function of the states have, consequently, reflected this change.

Moreover, an overview of the drafting, management, and development of the distribution of powers and responsibilities in the Australian system is reflective of a federal system founded on concurrency. Despite the limited number of expressly exclusive powers of the Commonwealth, contemporary governance has seen the Commonwealth come to dominate the states. This has been the result of changing interpretation and national sentiment.

THE FEDERAL CONSTITUTION
IN HISTORICAL-CULTURAL CONTEXT

In the 1890s, on the eve of the federation of the colonies, a popular slogan for proponents of the union was "a nation for a continent, and a continent for a nation."[7] The Commonwealth of Australia is now one of the world's oldest parliamentary democracies and is the only nation-state that occupies the whole of a continental landmass. Australia comprises a land area of 7,692,024 square kilometres and has a population of approximately 20 million people.[8] The bulk of the population is concentrated in the five state capital cities on the coastal regions of the mainland: Sydney (capital of New South Wales), Melbourne (Victoria), Adelaide (South Australia), Brisbane (Queensland), and Perth (Western Australia). The other principal cities are Hobart (capital of the island state of Tasmania), Canberra (Australian Capital Territory), and Darwin (Northern Territory).

The predominant language of the Australian population is English. A feature of contemporary Australia is a multicultural population that is a result of a large influx of immigrants from Continental Europe after the Second World War and subsequent waves of migration from Asia and Africa since the 1970s. The indigenous Aboriginal and Torres Strait populations are estimated to be about 2.2 percent of the overall population. Christianity is the predominant religion in Australia.

Historically, the Australian economy was based on primary production, supplemented after the Second World War by a manufacturing industry supported by high external tariffs. These traditional industries have declined in more recent times. Today's economy, now relatively free from tariffs and other trade barriers, is largely based on services. The GDP in 2002 was US$411.9 billion and the GDP per capita in 2001 was US$18,900.[9]

The process of federation had its origins in the colonization of Australia. The settlement of Australia by the British began in 1788 with the establishment of a penal colony at Sydney in New South Wales. The British Crown's audacious claim was for title of more than half of the landmass of the continent.[10] The story of the European settlement of Australia and movement to federation by 1901 is well known and does not need to be retold in detail. In short, the federation of the Australian colonies progressed slowly through a number of stages. The development of the colonies' self-government and greater legislative independence was a crucial part of this process. By the late nineteenth century the social and political identity of the colonies matured to a point where their federation as a union (the purpose being to overcome disparate policies and administrative inconvenience) became irresistible. Moreover, the importance of uniformity of immigration, defence, customs, and tariff policy had become a pressing political issue.

The final stage of federation was completed at a convention elected to draft the Constitution. The convention met in Adelaide, Sydney, and Melbourne during 1897–98. By mid-1898 a draft constitution was put to the electors in each of the participating colonies. While receiving majority support in each colony that voted, the bill failed to reach a threshold of 80,000 affirmative votes in New South Wales. A further round of negotiations between the premiers saw a number of concessions made to New South Wales, and a second vote, this time with Queensland participating, was held in 1899. By the close of 1899 all the colonies except Western Australia had passed referenda in support of the proposal, which was then forwarded to the British Parliament in London for consideration. Given the fact that the Australian Constitution required passage as an act of the Imperial Parliament, a delegation was sent from Australia in 1900 to assist in the passing of the bill. In July 1900 Western Australia also voted to be included in the federation.

New Zealand made submissions to London to be allowed to keep open the option to join the federation as an "Original State." This was not granted, though New Zealand is still mentioned in covering clause 6 in the definition of a "colony." Ultimately, distance, racial policy, New Zealand nationalism, and domestic politics precluded a broader Australasian federation.[11]

The negotiations in London were protracted, with the ultimate stumbling block being the retention of appeals to the Judicial Committee of the Privy Council in the United Kingdom (hereafter "Privy Council").[12] The resulting compromise retained appeals to the Privy Council but qualified the grounds upon which they were to be made. So-called "inter se" questions, involving the interpretation of the distribution of constitutional powers between the Commonwealth and the states, were to remain with the High Court (unless the Court certified the appeal to the Privy Council). However, the compromise did not prevent appeals from state supreme courts or limit, at that time, the prerogative of the Crown to grant special leave. The ending of these appeals was completed in a number of stages starting in 1968 and ending in 1986.[13]

The federation has been remarkably stable, with only one threatened secession. In the early 1930s a secession movement established itself in Western Australia. Dissatisfied with the Commonwealth Constitution and, in particular, with the perceived economic disadvantages that it had brought to their state, Western Australians voted to leave the Commonwealth.[14] They petitioned the Imperial Parliament, which referred the matter back to the Commonwealth. Ultimately, there was no secession, though low-level discontent with Canberra remains a feature of Western Australian politics.

The other significant development has been the evolution of the Northern Territory towards statehood. At federation, the Northern Territory formed part of South Australia. In 1908 South Australia surrendered the Northern Territory to the Commonwealth and it was accepted.[15] The Northern Territory was granted self-government in 1978, and in 1999 there was an unsuccessful referendum on statehood, with the defeat being attributed to dissatisfaction with the proposed constitutional arrangements.[16] The issue remains a live one and is likely to be revisited within the decade.

CONSTITUTIONAL DISTRIBUTION OF POWERS AND RESPONSIBILITIES

As with all federal systems, there are tensions between the constituent parts. This tension is most evident in the distribution of rights and responsibilities. As is the case with the United States Constitution, the Australian Constitution clearly articulates the powers of the Commonwealth Parliament (Sections 51 and 52).[17] The residue is left for the states. In practice, as a result of shifting financial and political authority and constitutional interpretation, the Commonwealth has come to dominate the federal landscape. This situation was predicted by one of the framers, Alfred Deakin, who was later to become the second prime minister of Australia, when he said:

As the power of the purse in Great Britain established by degrees the authority of the Commons, it will ultimately establish in Australia the authority of the Commonwealth. The rights of self-government of the States have been fondly supposed to be safeguarded by the Constitution. It left them legally free, but financially bound to the chariot wheels of the central Government. Their need will be its opportunity.[18]

Under the express terms of the Constitution, it can be reasonably said that Australia is best described as a "cooperative" federal system, although the academic literature has seen some debate as to whether or not this provides an accurate description. There is further debate over the precise meaning of phrases such as "coordinate," "concurrent," and "cooperative" federalism.[19] Indeed, in Australia the literature on federalism has generally tended towards highlighting its perceived inefficiency.[20] As Brian Galligan notes, the literature is based on "old prejudices and presuppositions about federalism being an immature, transitional, inefficient and even perverse form of government."[21] Notwithstanding its bad press, the federal system in Australia is predicated on the ability of the states and the Commonwealth to enter into cooperative schemes such as uniform consumer-credit codes and aspects of corporation law. Before leaving this point, it should be noted that at least one member of the High Court is adamant that "cooperative federalism" is not a "constitutional term" but, rather, a "political slogan," and it is clear that a number of constitutional limitations to cooperation do exist.[22] This, however, does not diminish the operative concurrency of Australian federalism.

Structurally, the federal system is "cooperative," but it also exhibits both vertical and horizontal "competitive" attributes; that is, there is competition between the states and territories to secure comparative advantages in the areas of policy settings. The most conspicuous of these competitions have been the enticing, or sometimes bidding for, investment from neighbouring states or from overseas. This has occurred when states have offered taxation holidays for investment or paid for infrastructure costs. This competition may also take the form of competition with the Commonwealth for policy settings. This is seen in such areas as industrial relations, where competing policies have been evident during a decade of reform. For instance, in 1995, with a conservative state government in Victoria restructuring the workforce, many unions sought to bring themselves within the more advantageous Commonwealth system of industrial regulation (based on the existence of interstate industrial disputes).[23]

The drift of political authority to the centre has significantly departed from the outcomes envisioned by the framers. For example, the growth of the Commonwealth's scope, seen especially in the added responsibilities after the First and Second World Wars, changed the relative authority of the states as the Commonwealth increasingly funded major welfare and infrastructure programs and also increased regulation of the economy.

The Constitution gives few exclusive powers to the Commonwealth Parliament (see Sections 51 and 52). These include aspects of defence, external affairs, coinage, and Commonwealth places. The external affairs power allows the federal government to enter into treaties and conventions and allows the Commonwealth Parliament to introduce into domestic law the terms of those international instruments. The bulk of the legislative authority under the Constitution is held concurrently between the Commonwealth and the states. In practice, however, once the Commonwealth has determined to exercise its capacity, it will have coverage of the area to the extent of the scope of the legislative power. For instance, the Commonwealth has established comprehensive legislative schemes in the areas of citizenship, immigration, and telecommunications, thus leaving very little, if anything, for determination by the states.[24] Due to the express limitations on some Commonwealth powers, for instance the limitation of "interstateness," the states have authority over purely intrastate activities such as trade and commerce, "state banking," and "state insurance" (Sections 51 [I, xii, xiv]).

Historically, several powers have been exercised predominantly by the states. They include land management, agriculture, the environment, health care, education, and criminal law. In recent years, the Commonwealth has come to play an increasingly significant role in shaping policy and legislative regimes in these areas. Primarily, this has been either a product of the implementation of Australia's international obligations (such as the protection of world-heritage areas) or the result of the direct financial support of the Commonwealth. In the latter category, the Commonwealth, through its grant power (Section 96 of the Constitution), has, arguably, dictated policy outcomes in the areas of education, health, competition policy, and housing. At federation, the Constitution included the power of the Commonwealth to provide "invalid and old-age pensions." As part of the country's post-Second World War reconstruction, the Commonwealth Constitution was amended to include a new section dealing with a broader range of pensions and benefits.[25]

Aboriginal Rights

The Aboriginal (and Torres Strait Islander) populations, like the populations of all colonial societies, suffered with the arrival of Europeans. The latter's advances were too often at the cost of the former. At federation the drafters of the Constitution held a distinctly Darwinian sentiment: they assumed that the indigenous population would die out. The Constitution, in a provision dealing with "people of any race," expressly excluded the "people of the Aboriginal race," thus leaving the latter's affairs to the states. In 1967 Australians voted to amend this section of the Constitution by removing reference to Aboriginals and Torres Strait Islanders together with one other discriminatory section. The legal effect of the change may be open to argument,[26] but it is clear that its intention was to secure the rights and interests of indigenous Australian peoples.

Representation and Federal Institutions

The Australian federation allows for a large degree of autonomy in the operational powers of the two spheres. Parliamentary representation is the province of each jurisdiction. In the Commonwealth realm, the Senate is representative of the states to the extent that an equal number of senators is elected from within the boundaries of each state. Originally, six senators were elected, though due to population growth this number has since grown to twelve. The Constitution draws a nexus between both houses of the Parliament, whereby it is required that the number of members from each state in the House of Representatives be as "nearly as practicable" twice the size of the number of members in the Senate (Section 24). The elected senators are not representatives of the state government but, rather, of the electors of that state. Moreover, in practice, with the advent of major political parties, the Senate does not really represent the states as such, although senators may be effective, at least in the party room and in government deliberations, in protecting the smaller states from discrimination. When they occur, casual vacancies in the Senate are filled with the approval of the state parliament or the governor on the advice of the government of the relevant state. Since a 1977 amendment to the Commonwealth Constitution, vacancies must be filled by persons "publicly recognized by a particular political party as being an endorsed candidate of that party."[27]

The people of the Australian states remain united "under the Crown of the United Kingdom." The enduring monarchical link to the British Crown means that Her Majesty now appoints the governor general and the state governors on the advice (given in accordance with the conventional rules relating to responsible government) of the Australian prime minister and each of the state premiers, respectively. Formerly, they were appointed on the advice of British ministers advising the monarch on matters relating to the British Empire. In the case of the appointment of the governor general, this change has had the effect of increasing the independence of the Commonwealth government.[28]

Within the architecture of the Constitution, the governor general and the state governors have important roles. The governor general or the governors make judicial appointments on the advice of the governments of the respective jurisdiction. There is a statutory requirement that the states be consulted about the appointment of judges to the High Court.[29] The vesting of federal judicial power by the Commonwealth Constitution in the courts of the states means that there is a degree of judicial oversight of the ability of the states to regulate the jurisdiction of the state courts.[30]

The Constitution includes a mechanism for the establishment of new states or the changing of the boundaries of existing states (Sections 121–124). Depending on the particular change, this requires the approval of the parliaments and/or the electors of the states concerned. In fact, the constitutional landscape has been remarkably stable since federation, and while two mainland territories have been created, no new states have been established since federation in 1901.

Fiscal Powers

The fiscal arrangements in the Constitution were one of the key aspects of the movement towards federation. The economic union created by the Commonwealth Constitution has, as the framers envisaged, allowed the Commonwealth to establish a single, uniform tariff policy (Section 90). This policy prevents the states from imposing protectionist burdens on interstate trade and commerce.[31] Although the Commonwealth and states both have power over taxation, the former has exercised its authority in a manner that has come to effectively prevent the latter from levying an income tax.[32] This was a result of the emergency of the Second World War. Despite an invitation by the Commonwealth to re-enter the field in the 1970s, the states have shown no interest in imposing a state-based income tax. As it has been famously stated, the "only good tax is a Commonwealth tax."[33] Thus, a hallmark of Australian fiscal federalism, likely more severe than in most federations, is the so-called "vertical fiscal imbalance," whereby the states have the legislative responsibility for the regulation of such things as hospitals and schools without the financial capacity, while the Commonwealth holds the effective powers of revenue but lacks the legislative authority to implement policy.[34]

The overall taxation situation has changed quite profoundly since federation. The states have generally seen their tax base eroded through a combination of the abandonment of certain tax streams (e.g., death duties)[35] and a declaration of unconstitutionality (e.g., levies on tobacco and alcohol) due to the fact that the Commonwealth has exclusive powers over taxation on goods.[36] This has left the states highly dependent on a limited number of tax sources, including the stamp duty, land taxes, registration fees, payroll taxes, and (increasingly) gambling taxes. In 1999 the Commonwealth Parliament passed a goods and services tax act that levied a consumption tax at 10 percent. The proceeds of this tax are distributed to the states in return for which they eliminated several minor, but inefficient, transaction taxes.

At the time of federation financial settlement proved to be one of the most difficult issues on which to find agreement.[37] The concerns of the framers related to both the ultimate economic settings of the new Commonwealth and the relinquishment of certain income that the colonies had derived from their own taxes. Coupled with this was an added concern that related to the level of debt that the colonies had accumulated for the provision of large infrastructure, such as railways. A significant proposal at the time was for the Commonwealth to take over some of the debt of the new states. Although this proposal was not agreed to, by the mid-1920s it had become clear that a measure of national control was appropriate. In 1928 the Constitution was amended by referendum to give effect to this change, and a subsequent intergovernmental agreement established the Loan Council to coordinate and oversee national borrowings (Section 105A). The agreement provided for Commonwealth borrowing on behalf of the states in accordance with the Loan Council's decisions. By the end of the century a combination of new international financial arrangements, and changes in the means by which states funded investment, meant that revisions were made to the scheme.[38] Since 1995 each government has had the authority to borrow in its own name (subject to disclosure and surveillance by the Loan Council). Beyond these formal requirements, it must also be recognized that the capacity of government to borrow is tempered by the rigorous scrutiny of money markets and the international ratings agencies.

As noted above, the major revenue of the states (customs and excise duties) was yielded to the Commonwealth at federation. At that time transitional provisions enabled the return of any surplus to the states on the basis of what was deemed "fair" by the Commonwealth Parliament. This requirement was effectively rendered meaningless by the ability of the Commonwealth to structure its financial arrangements in such a way as to avoid generating a surplus and, consequently, to avoid the substance of the provision.[39]

Federal Grants (Spending) Power

Chapter 4 of the Commonwealth Constitution contains the financial sections. The Constitution requires that all federal revenues or money raised or received form one Consolidated Revenue Fund and that all appropriations must be by law (Sections 81 and 83). Because the Commonwealth

Parliament may appropriate monies for the "purposes of the Commonwealth," there is no limit to which it may appropriate funds; however, the expenditure of those funds *is* limited. The High Court has held that the expenditure must be for the enumerated heads of the legislative power in the Constitution or, in addition, those things that are for the "national" benefit (such as scientific research).[40]

The limitation on the Commonwealth's spending power does not affect the ability of the Commonwealth to make available to the states grants to undertake certain activities. These grants, made under Section 96 of the Constitution, can be on such terms and conditions as the Commonwealth sees fit. The Commonwealth thus has the authority to offer conditional funding to the states.

It is clear that the legislative limits on the Commonwealth have not prevented it from playing a significant role in the formation of policy outcomes in areas historically seen as within the province of the states. Section 96 is the basis of this power. The use of tied grants in the areas of health and education has provided the Commonwealth operational authority in areas within which it lacks legislative authority. For instance, Australian universities (with the exception of those in the territories) owe their legislative existence to the states,[41] yet it is the Commonwealth and not the states that funds their operation. Under Section 96, however, the Commonwealth is required to use the states as a conduit through which it may provide funding. In recent times, this has been achieved by the Commonwealth bypassing the states and making direct grants to the universities through Section 81 of the Constitution. Using this example, the Commonwealth has proposed changes to the size and composition of university governing councils, their fee structures, their industrial-relations practices, the numbers of students placed, and the courses taught. In short, through the use of almost irresistible fiscal control the Commonwealth can drive its policy agenda in a myriad of areas where it lacks formal legislative authority.

Beyond the use of tied grants and intergovernmental agreements, there are few areas where the Constitution expressly requires one order of government to undertake specific operational or functional duties on behalf of the other. Indeed, there may be certain constitutional limits to such schemes.[42] There are provisions allowing the states to refer their legislative authority over certain matters to the Commonwealth, with the latter's agreement.[43] In particular, in Section 51 (xxxvii), the Commonwealth Parliament may legislate on matters referred to it by the parliament of a state or states. Similarly, the Constitution makes provision for the vesting of federal judicial power in any court of a state (Section 77 [iii]). Section 119 places an obligation on the Commonwealth to "protect every State against invasion and, on the application of the Executive Government of the State, against domestic violence." Perhaps the most commonly exercised obligation of the states is that they "shall make provision for the detention in its prisons of persons, accused or convicted of offences against the laws of the Commonwealth" (Section 120).[44]

The Constitution does have an approximation of the "necessary and proper" power expressed in Article I, Section 8, Para. 19 of the United States Constitution. The Commonwealth Constitution provides for an "incidental" power to facilitate the execution of the executive, legislative, or judicial powers of the Commonwealth (Section 51 [xxxix]).[45] In combination with the express executive power of the Commonwealth, it is said to give rise to an implied "nationhood power."[46] This power has been held to empower the Commonwealth "to engage in enterprises and activities peculiarly adapted to the government of a nation and which cannot otherwise be carried on for the benefit of the nation."[47]

The Evolution of Constitutional Interpretation

The interpretation of the Constitution has, not surprisingly, changed over time. The concept of "reserve powers" belonging to the states had currency in the first two decades of the federation. Influenced by U.S. jurisprudence, the High Court developed twin implications that limited the reach of the Commonwealth and the states and their ability to interfere with each other. Consistent with this view of federalism, the High Court highlighted the common assumption that certain areas of authority were reserved to the states.[48] Coupled with this implication was the express structure of the Constitution that limits the Commonwealth to the legislative power mentioned in Sections 51 and 52. Since 1920 the High Court has abandoned a fulsome view of this implication.[49] The states' constitutional existence is guaranteed by the Commonwealth Constitution (Sections 106 and 107). Relying on this guarantee, the High Court has prevented the Commonwealth from taking legislative actions that would discriminate against the states or place burdens on them that would curtail or destroy their capacity to operate as polities.[50] However, it has not protected all those areas that have traditionally been seen to be within their jurisdiction. For instance, the Commonwealth's entrance into the Convention for the Protection of the World Cultural and Natural Heritage empowered the Commonwealth Parliament to legislate using the external affairs power to prevent Tasmania from building a dam.[51]

A feature of recent constitutional litigation has been the determination that Australia has a single common law. The Constitution provides that the High Court is not only the final court of appeal in constitutional disputes but also the final arbiter (since the ending of appeals to the Privy Council) of the general law of Australia. Thus, unlike that of the United States of America, the Australian legal system is said to incorporate a

single common law, with the High Court at its apex as the final interpreter of this law. Thus, for example, in the area of defamation law, the
common law, as applied in the states, must conform to the Commonwealth Constitution.[52] Also, as noted above, the federal government is
limited to enumerated legislative powers, with areas such as civil and criminal law generally not being seen to be within its ambit. However, recent
pressures in the area of tort law have prompted the Commonwealth to
seek greater intervention as a means of lowering costs to the health-care
system and insurance.[53]

LOGIC OF THE CONSTITUTIONAL DISTRIBUTION OF POWERS AND RESPONSIBILITIES

The distribution of powers in Australia's federal system does not exhibit an
immediate logic. In 1987 the Advisory Committee to the Constitutional
Commission on the Distribution of Powers noted that the "division of
powers in any federal country is likely to depend upon historical factors, judicial interpretation and what tends to represent the greatest measure of
agreement between the conflicting political interests which exist in that
country at any given time."[54] These general parameters provide what logic
there is for the distribution of powers in Australia.

The drafting of the Australian Constitution was (in effect) based on concessions made by colonial politicians and, ultimately, by colonial voters to
the new Commonwealth. During these negotiations in the 1890s there
were framers who were vigilant to restrict the authority of the Commonwealth. Even those framers who were more favourably disposed to a national authority disagreed with the minimalists over democratic issues
rather than over the powers of the Commonwealth.[55]

The historical context is significant. The framers were well aware of the
distributions within the United States Constitution and the British North
America Act (1867). The fact that the Australian Constitution has many of
the same powers as does the U.S. Constitution is indicative of the influence
that the latter document had on the Australian drafters and the deliberate
decision not to adapt the Canadian constitutional model, which they felt to
be too centralizing.

Likewise, many of the powers reflect what could be seen as the minimum
requirements for the establishment of the Commonwealth. Defence, interstate trade and commerce, quarantine, immigration, naturalization, and
currency, for instance, were obvious national powers and were seen as such
by the drafters. Other powers were those that any government must have –
powers to create courts, to establish and control a public service, to impose
taxation, and so on. Further powers were, on the balance of convenience,
deemed to be granted to the federal Parliament. These included telecommunications, postage, weights and measures, and similar matters.

In short, the basic logic behind the Constitution is seen in those things that prompted the colonies to federate: national security, economic union, immigration control, and the convenience of uniformity of regulation. Not included in this list is the imperative to secure basic human rights or place limits on the Commonwealth Parliament. Such limitations are a product of a general distrust of a government not known to the political culture within which the framers operated. Thus, the Constitution, with very few exceptions, does not contain a bill of rights.[56]

The Australian Constitution is an example of a symmetrical distribution of powers. At the establishment of the federal polity the "original states" included all of the current six states of Australia. These original states now have the same relationship to the Commonwealth and with each other. In the first five years after federation Western Australia was granted some customs concessions (Constitution, 1901, Section 95).[57]

Presently, there are two mainland territories, the Northern Territory (NT) and the Australian Capital Territory (ACT). Since 1927 the ACT has been the seat of the federal government. Currently, statehood is being considered for the Northern Territory. The Constitution provides for the admission of new states on such terms and conditions as the Commonwealth may impose. This extends to representation in either house of the Commonwealth Parliament. It is unclear whether this would include the exclusion of those plenary functions held by the original states, and to this date it remains a hypothetical issue.

The Commonwealth, through both express and implied limitations on its authority, must legislate uniformly with respect to the states in such areas as taxation and the granting of bounties (other than on mining for gold, silver, and other metals) as well as being required not to place a discriminatory burden on them.[58] Thus, the Commonwealth and the states, as with the distribution of generally concurrent powers, share responsibilities in many areas of policy delivery. This, of course, is subject to a paramountcy granted to the Commonwealth within its enumerated powers. There remains some debate as to the extraterritorial powers of the states and to what degree they can bind each other and the Commonwealth.[59]

As noted above, the modern welfare state was in its infancy in Australia at the time of federation. Thus, the Constitution contains few powers that can be classified within this area. The assumption in 1901 was that welfare provision was to be left to the states. At federation one of the framers, James Howe, was insistent that the Commonwealth should have the power over invalid and old-age pensions.[60] Similarly, the convention narrowly endorsed the inclusion of a power over industrial "conciliation and arbitration beyond the limits of one State."[61] After the Second World War the Constitution was amended to empower the Commonwealth to legislate for "maternity allowances, widow's pensions, child endowment, unemployment, pharmaceutical, sickness and hospital benefits, medical and dental services (but not so as to authorize any form of civil conscription), benefits to students and family allowances" (Section 51 [xxiiiA]).

With regard to welfare (i.e., direct assistance to the poor) responsibilities are shared. Within their respective jurisdictions, there is plenary authority, though in many policy areas (such as child protection, guardianship, mental health, and hospitals) the states have the principal legislative authority.[62]

An amendment that has had profound importance in terms of race relations is the 1967 amendment to Aboriginal power, noted above. Until that year the Commonwealth power, which was included to deal primarily with races that the framers saw as inferior, expressly did not include "the aboriginal race in any State." In 1967 the Australian electorate voted overwhelmingly to remove those words and thus provided a moral imperative for the Commonwealth to take over the area of Aboriginal affairs.[63]

EVOLUTION OF THE CONSTITUTIONAL DISTRIBUTION OF POWERS AND RESPONSIBILITIES

The amendment provision in the Constitution is contained in Section 128 and provides for initiation of amendments by the Commonwealth Parliament by way of legislation. The proposed amendments are then submitted to the electors of the states and territories for their consideration. If a majority of the voters overall, and a majority of voters in a majority of the states (i.e., four of the six), agree, then the amendment is presented to the governor general for assent. Since 1901 there have been forty-four attempts at change, with only eight being successful. The Constitution was last amended in 1977. The complex process of double majorities has been seen as an overly burdensome mechanism. Yet rarely has a proposal secured "one of the majorities" but then been rejected because it failed to achieve both.

The lack of formal amendment of the Constitution has been the subject of much commentary.[64] Generally, those amendments that attempt to increase the power of the Commonwealth at the expense of the states have been unsuccessful. Similarly, those amendments that do not have bipartisan political support have not been approved by the electorate. For example, the 1988 amendments that proposed, among other things, fair elections and the extension of certain basic rights to the states, and to a lesser degree the 1999 republican referendum, became subjects of partisan political debate and were each defeated at a referendum.[65]

Of the eight changes that have been made, the majority of them have been procedural in substance. In brief, they changed the date of the rotation of senators (1907),[66] authorized the Commonwealth to take over and manage state debts in existence after federation (1910) and (1928), extended social-security legislative power to the Commonwealth (1946), extended the direct legislative power of the Commonwealth with respect to Aboriginal people (1967), amended the filling of casual vacancies in the Senate (1977), set a compulsory retirement age of seventy for the federal judiciary (1977), and included the citizens of the NT and the ACT in voting for constitutional amendments.

By far, the more significant changes in the distribution of responsibilities have come as a result of judicial interpretation of the Constitution. The High Court has been responsible for the interpretation of the Constitution and, since 1986, has been the ultimate final court of appeal.[67] At federation, as a result of a compromise between the Colonial Office in London and the Australian delegation, the Privy Council was the initial final court of appeal in non-constitutional matters. This situation was ended by a series of legislative actions by the states, the Commonwealth, and the United Kingdom starting in 1968 and concluding in the passage of the Australia Acts, 1986 (Cth and UK).[68] There has also been a change in the relationship with the Imperial Parliament. The move towards Australia's legal sovereignty saw a diminution, leading to the ultimate extinction, of the authority of the Parliament in London.

The general approach of the High Court to constitutional interpretation has involved a concentration and focus on textualism.[69] In this form of analysis, the text and structure of the Constitution, viewed in light of its history and logic, are deemed to provide a foundation for its application to legal controversies. However, this has not prevented the Court from developing the Constitution over time. The change in the distribution of powers has been realized by constitutional jurisprudence that, after the *Engineers'* case of 1920, placed an emphasis on the text of the Constitution and eschewed any implication that limited the reach of the Commonwealth Parliament or that upheld a notion of federalism.[70] While the High Court was to revive certain implications based on federalism, the pre-*Engineers'* methodology of protecting states' rights was not to return.[71] The emphasis on the text meant that the Commonwealth Parliament was to be given greater reach in areas such as industrial relations, corporations, and taxation.

This trend to centralization became especially pronounced in fiscal matters, for example during the Second World War when the High Court held valid a scheme that allowed the Commonwealth to take over the income taxation power of the states.[72] Similarly, the Court's interpretation of the meaning of "excise" in Section 90 of the Constitution has dramatically undermined the finances of the states – depriving the latter of levying the most important forms of consumption taxes.[73]

Australia's relationship with the world, first through the Empire and then as an independent nation, has also had an impact on the distribution of powers and responsibilities in the federal system. Through the external affairs power, the Commonwealth has been able to increase its legislative capacity in a way that is seen to be at the expense of the states. As the Commonwealth took its place in the community of nations, the implementation of treaty and convention obligations into domestic law allowed it to legislate in areas that were traditionally seen as being within the jurisdiction of the states (e.g., the environment, industrial relations, and race relations). While some members of the High Court saw this as unsettling the "federal balance," the majority of the Court was not prepared to rely on such an imprecise and static implication.[74]

In general, the changes in the distribution of powers have been the result of a number of factors. Specifically, the emergence of a greater political role for the Commonwealth after the First World War, as Justice Victor Windeyer noted, meant that "the Constitution was read in a new light, a light reflected from events that had, over twenty years, led to a growing realization that Australians were now one people and Australia one country and that national laws might meet national needs."[75] More generally, there has traditionally been a centralizing tendency within the Australian Labour Party (ALP), which has historically had a platform that sought to involve the Commonwealth in state policies (though this tendency is not limited to the ALP).

In summary, the High Court interpretation post-1920 has in general terms profited the Commonwealth over the states. In particular, certain sections, such as the external affairs power, the corporations power, taxation power, and Section 90 (covering excise taxes), have allowed the Commonwealth to exploit its already dominant constitutional position.

MAINTENANCE AND MANAGEMENT OF THE DISTRIBUTION OF POWERS AND RESPONSIBILITIES

The maintenance and management of the distribution of powers and responsibilities in the Australian federal system is one of collective responsibility. Lines of responsibility are rarely clear and, indeed, are often deliberately blurry. There remain various descriptors that may be used to understand the nature of federal relations in Australia; however, these terms may only have meaning in a comparative sense. Consequently, it may be meaningful to say that the Australian federation is more "cooperative" or "collusive" than are the American and Canadian federal systems but that it is perhaps more "competitive" than the German federation. Yet even that analysis may be very much dependent on the political cycle, on history, and on the policy issue at hand.

Like those of many federations, Australia's constitutional structure is based on cooperative assumptions. The limited legislative power of the Commonwealth presupposed that, in many areas, national schemes would only be created with the states and the Commonwealth acting in concert. The Constitution expressly allows for cooperative schemes and joint programs;[76] that is, where the Commonwealth and the states, acting in concert, focus their respective legislative, executive, and judicial powers on a particular joint policy.

Notwithstanding the sharing of authority, it is also the case that there are conflicts between the Commonwealth and the states. The Commonwealth, with its legislative paramountcy, has used its authority to invalidate state schemes and policy. For instance, in the areas of industrial relations and environmental protection, the Commonwealth, pursuant to international obligations, has displaced state policy.[77] These conflicts are not limited to areas where the Commonwealth has direct legislative capacity. Another example is that, through the use of Section 96 grants, the Commonwealth can, to the point of coercion, "buy" the compliance of the states with the offer of funding.[78] Thus, in competition policy and in health policy, the Commonwealth fiscal muscle has been used to establish Commonwealth views.[79]

The fact that responsibility vis-à-vis policy formation and service delivery is rarely clear results in accountability problems. It is open to speculation whether the Commonwealth and the states are in fact anxious to define with certainty the lines of authority and responsibility, and a corollary of this is ambiguity: it is often difficult for the citizens to determine accurately where policy authority lies and to ensure the accountability of the appropriate order of government. Even beyond such areas as health and education there are public policy matters where responsibility is diffuse. For instance, transport matters may be seen as having aspects that are Commonwealth, state, and local in jurisdiction. Although the Constitution does not mandate cooperation, common practice has seen a level of cooperation sufficient to facilitate appropriate policy outcomes.

Where conflicts do exist over the distribution of powers and responsibilities, they emerge over the application of policy to particular instances. For example, in recent years the Commonwealth has sought to assert authority over such matters as industrial-relations practices. The effect of this has been to provoke jurisdiction "shopping" on the part of employees and, alternatively, legislative responses by the Commonwealth and the states. Such disputes over policy have been regularly determined by recourse to litigation that have often raised constitutional points.[80]

While the discussion above has outlined a picture of accountability that is obscured by concurrent and overlapping jurisdiction between the Commonwealth and the states, it should be acknowledged that there is a hierarchy in the practical (as distinct from solely legal) means of resolving issues arising from ambiguity. In the first instance, recourse is made to the executive government in the Commonwealth and state arenas. Beyond this, in diminishing order of importance, are the courts, political parties, interest groups, and established intergovernmental institutions. Ironically, legislative bodies (because of the dominance of the executive in the Westminster system) are often the weakest actors when it comes to resolving disputes within the federation concerning where responsibilities and powers lie.

There are two types of formal intergovernmental agencies to be found in the Australian governmental system. The first type has certain statutory obligations and independence. For example, the Australian Securities Investment Commission and the Australian Competition and Consumer Commission have limited authority to oversee the distribution of powers and responsibilities. While independent and largely free of day-to-day government influence or pressure, they have no binding authority beyond that which is granted by the establishing government.[81] A second form of intergovernmental agency is found in the informal cooperative executive agencies. The preeminent example of such agencies is the Council of Australian Governments (COAG), comprising the prime minister, the state premiers, the chief ministers of the two self-governing territories, and the president of the Australian Local Government Association. This body, which has no express constitutional standing, nevertheless plays a significant role in maintaining and managing the distribution of powers and responsibilities in the federation, providing, as it does, a forum for negotiations between the political leaders of the Commonwealth. In addition, and reporting loosely to the COAG, there are more than twenty Commonwealth-state ministerial councils that deliberate and consult on specific policy areas.[82]

Despite the existence of a range of collaborative and cooperative agencies, there are no formal constitutional mechanisms for one government to monitor the operations of another. That being said, the Commonwealth can, through the operation of Section 96 grants, place stringent reporting regimes upon the receiver of the grant. Similarly, there are no formal means by which the federal executive or Parliament can give binding directions to any of the state governments or parliaments. Indeed, there is constitutional authority to suggest that there are implied limitations on the manner to which the Commonwealth and the states may each bind the other in their operations.[83]

Finally, the High Court has original jurisdiction over a variety of specified matters, including the actions of officers of the Commonwealth and legal proceedings involving the Commonwealth. It also has original jurisdiction in some proceedings where a state is a party. In such proceedings, the Court may make binding orders upon the Commonwealth and the states and their officers.[84] The High Court also has general appellate jurisdiction from federal and state courts and is at the apex of the Australian judicial system. The Constitution provides for the vesting of federal judicial power in state courts. The result, with some qualification, is a coordinated and largely unified judicial system involving both federal and state judicial power. In Australia, the separation of judicial power from executive and legislative usurpation is constitutionally entrenched in the Commonwealth's governmental structure. Thus, the federal government or Parliament cannot order courts to perform their functions in ways inconsistent with the exercise of judicial power.[85]

ADEQUACY AND FUTURE OF THE DISTRIBUTION OF POWERS AND RESPONSIBILITIES

One of the pitfalls of discussing the adequacy of, and future distribution of, powers is that it tends towards idealization, towards the projection of a perfect federal arrangement. With regard to Australia, the actual distribution of powers and responsibilities reflects the assumptions about the appropriate role of government held by the framers in the late 1890s.

From the perspective of the twenty-first century, the adequacy of the Constitution should not be seen solely in terms of its original design. Modification, usually by judicial interpretation and the changing national focus, has meant that lines of responsibility and accountability are not always clear. For some observers, this is a criticism not only of Australian federalism but also of federalism in general. Others see the constructive ambiguity more positively in that it allows for the flexibility needed to adapt to changing economic and social circumstances.

In short, questions of the adequacy of the distribution of powers and responsibility will often depend on the perspective of the participants and policy makers. Australia has made spasmodic attempts (especially over the past thirty years) at what has generally been described as "new federalism"[86] – that is, at attempting to refocus the role of the states in the federal compact. Notwithstanding the rhetoric, very little may be said to have come out of this.

One of the enduring features of Australian federalism, and one that helps to facilitate the intended coordination of the two spheres, has been regular premiers' and Commonwealth-state ministerial meetings. These gatherings, which have no express formal constitutional basis, are intended to facilitate coherence in national policy development. In terms of the premiers' conferences (renamed the Council of Australian Governments), the main debate has frequently been focused on the distribution of revenue. Since the introduction of the Goods and Services Tax, there has been a change of emphasis, with a more predictable share of revenue coming to the states.

As noted above, Australian federalism has witnessed a dramatic movement towards the centre in terms of fiscal authority. Through the operation of the Grants Commission, the states and the territories are provided with funding by the Commonwealth for the provision of significant services. Vertical fiscal imbalance remains a hallmark of the Australian system. Thus, while the states do have the administrative capacity to execute their constitutional responsibilities, it remains the case that the Commonwealth has the economic power.

Australia is one of the oldest democratic federal systems in existence. Its success may be assessed not only by its longevity but also by its ability to meet unforeseeable challenges and changing circumstances. As we have seen, the history of the Australian Constitution is one of shifting authority. In 1901 the fledgling Commonwealth came into existence with the states being the predominant site of political and financial authority. A century later the tables have turned. Through a procession of gradual and, at times, imperceptible shifts, the authority of the Commonwealth has come to the fore.

While formal constitutional amendment has proved to be an elusive achievement, this has not stopped many proposed initiatives. Of these, the most notable recent example was a sustained campaign to replace the Queen as the head of state and to reconstitute the Commonwealth as a federal republic. Although this proposal was defeated in 1999, it is inevitable that it will return to the political agenda.

Another likely amendment within the next decade will concern the conferring of statehood on the Northern Territory. This would make it the first new state in the history of the Commonwealth. The terms and conditions of its admission, especially in relation to political representation in the Commonwealth Parliament, are likely to be asymmetrical – that is, not equal to the original six states. At present, there is no realistic move towards the creation of a new state from the existing states.

Unlike many democracies, Australia has no statutory or constitutional bill of rights. There will continue to be debate on the need for such an addition to the constitutional architecture. If such a change is made at the Commonwealth level, it will inevitably have the effect of revising the existing distribution of powers and responsibilities. Despite the limited formal constitutional guarantee, it should be noted that many legislative protections, such as anti-discrimination laws, have been brought into Australian domestic law as a result of Australia's international obligations.[87]

In common with other nation-states, Australia's formal constitutional distribution of powers and responsibilities is also increasingly subject to the informal demands of global pressures. For instance, the World Trade Organization, the United Nations, and even the U.S. financial rating agencies all challenge the autonomy of the constituent parts of the Australian polity. Australian governmental institutions and Australian citizens have experienced difficulties in understanding the competing challenges and objectives of globalization, of nationalism, of federalism, and of regionalism.[88]

The Australian federal system has been dynamic in its evolution. Through economic crises and two world wars the Constitution has evolved to meet the changing needs of the social, economic, and political circumstances. The realignment of federal relations would astonish its framers, who conceived of a stronger federal instrument. Yet, overall, the Constitution has served Australia well. The past century has seen a centralization of power at the expense of the federal principle. Whether or not this trend continues, or whether there is a return to a more dispersed federal structure, is unclear. One thing, however, *is* clear: at present, there is no evident call for radical change or for abandoning the federation. If nothing else, this can be seen as a measure of its success.

NOTES

* This chapter benefited from the advice and support of Brad Selway (1955–2005) and is dedicated to his memory.

1 Depending on the context, the term "Commonwealth" refers to the national (federal) government or (less frequently) to the federation as a whole.

2 See John A. La Nauze, *The Making of the Australian Constitution* (Carlton: Melbourne University Press, 1972).

3 Richard C. Baker, *A manual of reference to authorities for the use of the members of the National Australasian Convention, which will assemble at Sydney on March 2, 1891, for the purpose of drafting a constitution for the Dominion of Australia* (Adelaide: W.K. Thomas and Co., 1891); and T.C. Just, *Leading Facts connected with Federation. Compiled for the information of the Tasmanian Delegates to the Australasian Federal Convention 1891* (Hobart: The Mercury Office, 1891). See also, John S.F. Wright, "Anglicizing the United States Constitution: James Bryce's Contribution to Australian Federalism," *Publius: The Journal of Federalism* 31 (Fall 2001): 107–129.

4 Cheryl Saunders, "Australia," *Handbook of Federal Countries 2002*, ed. Ann Griffiths (Montreal: McGill University Press, 2002), citing *McGinty v. Western Australia* (1996) 186 C.L.R. 140.

5 Enid Campbell, "Southey Memorial Lecture: Changing the Constitution – Past and Future," *Melbourne University Law Review* 17 (1989): 1; and Cheryl Saunders, "Future Prospects for the Australian Constitution," *Reflections on the Australian Constitution*, eds., Robert French, Geoff Lindell, and Cheryl Saunders (Sydney: Federation Press, 2003), pp. 220–221.

6 Geoff Lindell, "Why Is Australia's Constitution Binding? The Reasons in 1900 and Now, and the Effect of Independence," *Federal Law Review* 16 (1986): 29; George Winterton, "The Acquisition of Independence," in French, Lindell, and Saunders, *Reflections on the Australian Constitution*, p. 31; and Geoff Lindell, "Further Reflections on the Date of the Acquisition of Australia's Independence," in

French, Lindell, and Saunders, *Reflections on the Australian Constitution*, p. 51. See also *Sue v. Hill* (1999) 199 C.L.R. 462.

7 Edmund Barton, Speech to Australasian Federation League, Ashfield, April 1898. See G.C. Bolton, *Edmund Barton* (Sydney: Allen and Unwin, 2000), pp. 172–173.

8 For the statistical details of Australia, see the Australian Bureau of Statistics, <http://www.abs.gov.au/> (accessed 1 October 2003).

9 Department of the Parliamentary Library, *Research Note*, 1 October 2003, <http://www.aph.gov.au/library/pubs/rn/2001–02/02rn21.pdf>; and OECD, GDP per capita, 2001 at current prices, in U.S. dollars, <http://www.oecd.org/dataoecd/48/5/2371372.pdf> (accessed 1 October 2003).

10 Alex C. Castles, *An Australian Legal History* (Sydney: Law Book Co., 1982), pp. 24–25.

11 Philippa Mein Smith, "New Zealand," *The Centenary Companion to Australian Federation*, ed., Helen Irving (Melbourne: Cambridge University Press, 1999), pp. 400–405.

12 Brian de Garis, "The Colonial Office and the Commonwealth Bill," *Essays in Australian Federation*, ed., Alan W Martin (Melbourne: Melbourne University Press, 1976), p. 94.

13 Gerard Brennan, "The Privy Council and the Constitution," *Australian Constitutional Landmarks*, eds., H.P. Lee and George Winterton (Melbourne: Cambridge University Press, 2003), pp. 328–329.

14 For an account of the legal issues, see Greg Craven, *Secession: The Ultimate State Right* (Melbourne: Melbourne University Press, 1986), chap. 3.

15 *Northern Territory Surrender Act 1908* (SA) and *Northern Territory Acceptance Act 1910* (Cth). (Here and throughout "Cth" stands for "Commonwealth.")

16 *Northern Territory (Self-Government) Act 1978* (Cth). For statehood, see Northern Territory Government, <http://www.nt.gov.au/ocm/media_releases/20030522_statehood.shtml> (accessed 1 October 2003).

17 All section numbers in the text refer to Australia, *Constitution* (1901).

18 Alfred Deakin, *Federated Australia: Selections from Letters to the Morning Post, 1900–1910*, ed., John A. La Nauze (Melbourne: Melbourne University Press, 1968), p. 97.

19 See Brian Galligan, *A Federal Republic: Australia's Constitutional System of Government* (Melbourne: Cambridge University Press, 1995), chap. 8.

20 Gordon Greenwood, *The Future of Australian Federalism* (Melbourne: Melbourne University Press, 1946); Bill Brugger and Dean Jaensch, *Australian Politics: Theory and Practice* (Sydney: George Allen and Unwin, 1985); and Graham Maddox, *Australian Democracy: In Theory and Practice* (Melbourne: Longman Australia, 1991).

21 Galligan, *A Federal Republic*, p. 59.

22 *Re Wakim; Ex Parte McNally* (1999) 198 C.L.R. 511, 556 (McHugh J).

23 *Re Australian Education Union; Ex parte Victoria* (1995) 184 C.L.R. 188.

24 For example, *Australian Citizenship Act 1948 (Cth)*, *Migration Act 1958 (Cth)*, and *Telecommunications Act 1991* (Cth).

25 *Constitutional Alteration (Social Services) Act* (1946) (Cth).

26 *Kartinyeri v. The Commonwealth* (1998) 195 C.L.R. 337.

27 *Constitutional Alteration (Referendums) Act* 1977 (Cth), *Constitutional Alteration (Retirement of Judges) Act* 1977 (Cth), *Constitutional Alteration (Senate Casual Vacancies) Act* 1977 (Cth), s. 15.

28 See generally, George Winterton, *Monarchy to Republic* (Melbourne: Oxford University Press, 1994).

29 *High Court of Australia Act* 1979 (Cth), s. 6.

30 *Kable v. Director of Public Prosecutions (NSW) (1996) 189 C.L.R. 51 and A-G (Qld) v. Fardon* [2003] QCA 416.

31 *Cole v. Whitefield* (1988) 165 C.L.R. 360.

32 *South Australia v. Commonwealth* (1942) 65 C.L.R. 373 (*First Uniform Tax Case*) and *Victoria v. Commonwealth* (1957) 99 C.L.R. 575 (*Second Uniform Tax Case*). See generally, Cheryl Saunders, "Uniform Income Tax Cases," in Lee and Winterton, *Australian Constitutional Landmarks*, chap. 3.

33 Cited in D. James, "Federal-State Financial Relations: The Deakin Prophesy," Research Paper 17, Department of the Parliamentary Library, 2000.

34 Galligan, *A Federal Republic*, chap. 9. See also Cheryl Saunders, "Government Borrowing in Australia," *Melbourne University Law Review* 70 (1989): 187.

35 *Succession and Gift Duties Abolition Act* 1976.

36 *Ha v. NSW* (1997) 189 C.L.R. 465.

37 Cheryl Saunders "Hardest Nut to Crack: The Financial Settlement in the Commonwealth Constitution," *The Convention Debates 1891–1898 Commentaries, Indices and Guide*, ed. Greg Craven (Sydney: Legal Books, 1986), p. 149.

38 Cheryl Saunders, "Budgetary Federalism: Balancing Federalism and Responsible Government," *Mensch und Staat: Festschrift for Thomas Fleiner*, ed. Peter Hanni (Universitatsverlag Freiburg Schweiz, 2003), pp. 175–199.

39 *New South Wales v. Commonwealth* (1908) 7 C.L.R. 179. See generally, Brad Selway, "The Federation: What Makes It Work and What Should We Be Thinking about for the Future?" *Australian Journal of Public Administration* 60, 4 (2001): 116–22.

40 *Victoria v. The Commonwealth and Hayden* (1975) 134 C.L.R. 338.

41 For instance, *University of Adelaide Act* 1971 (SA) and *Melbourne University Act* 1958 (Vic).

42 *Austin v. Commonwealth (2003)* 195 C.L.R. 321.

43 Section 51 (xxxvii). See *Re Wakim; Ex Parte McNally* (1999) 198 C.L.R. 511.

44 Section 120. See *Leeth v. Commonwealth* (1992) 174 C.L.R. 455.

45 Australia, *Constitution*, Section 51 (xxxix). See *Le Mesurier v. Connor* (1929) 42 C.L.R. 481.

46 Jeremy Kirk, "Constitutional Implications (I): Nature, Legitimacy, Classification, Examples," *Melbourne University Law Review* 24 (2000): 669–670.

47 *Victoria v. The Commonwealth and Hayden* (1975) 134 C.L.R. 338.

48 *King v. Barger* (1908) 6 C.L.R. 41.

49 *Amalgamated Society of Engineers v. Adelaide Steamship Co. Ltd.* (1920) 28 C.L.R. 129.

50 *Austin v. Commonwealth* (2003) 195 C.L.R. 321.

51 *Commonwealth v. Tasmania* (1983) 158 C.L.R. 1.

52 *Lange v. Australian Broadcasting Corporation* (1997).

53 *Review of the Law of Negligence*, [Ipp Report], <http://revofneg.treasury.gov.au/content/home.asp> (accessed 1 October 2003).

54 Report of the Advisory Committee to the Constitutional Commission, *Distribution of Power* (Canberra: AGPS, 1987), p. 2.

55 Henry B. Higgins being the most obvious.

56 Owen Dixon, *Jesting Pilate: And other Papers and Addresses* (Melbourne: The Law Book Co., 1965), pp. 101–102.

57 Australia, *Constitution*, Section 95.

58 *Austin v. Commonwealth* (2003) 195 C.L.R. 321.

59 *Mobil Oil Australia Pty Ltd. v. Victoria* [2002] HCA 27, *Re Residential Tenancies Tribunal (New South Wales); ex parte The Defence Housing Authority* (1997) 190 C.L.R. 410; and Brad Selway, "The Australian 'Single Law Area,'" *Monash University Law Review* 29 (2003): 30–48.

60 Quick and Garran, *The Annotated Constitution of the Commonwealth of Australia*, pp. 612–613.

61 For an account of the operations, see Henry B. Higgins, *A New Province for Law and Order* (Sydney: Constable and Co., 1922).

62 See, for example, *Children's Protection Act* 1993 (SA) and *Guardianship and Administration Act* 1986 (Vic).

63 *Kartinyeri v. Commonwealth* (1998) 195 C.L.R. 337. See Robert French, "The Race Power: A Constitutional Chimera," in Lee and Winterton, *Australian Constitutional Landmarks*, p. 180.

64 See above n. 5.

65 *Constitution Alteration (Local Government) Bill*, 1988 (Cth), *Constitution Alteration (Parliamentary Terms) Bill*, 1988 (Cth), *Constitution Alteration (Rights and Freedoms) Bill*, 1988 (Cth), *Constitution Alteration (Fair Elections) Bill*, 1988 (Cth) and *Constitution Alteration (Establishment of a Republic) Bill*, 1999 (Cth).

66 The Senate is a body of fixed existence, with half the members normally facing the voters every three years.

67 It should be noted that, oddly, the interpretation of the Australian Constitution is not part of the original jurisdiction. See Section 75.

68 *Privy Council (Limitation of Appeals) Act* 1968 (Cth), *Privy Council (Appeals from High Court) Act* 1975.

69 See references in Brad Selway, "Constitutional Interpretation in the High Court of Australia," *Queensland Judges on the High Court*, eds., Michael White and Aladin Rahemtula (Brisbane: Supreme Court of Queensland Library, 2003), pp. 1–20.

70 Leslie Zines, *The High Court and the Constitution* (Sydney: Butterworths, 1997), pp. 1–15.

71 *Re Australian Education Union; Ex parte Victoria* (1995) 184 C.L.R. 188.

72 *South Australia v. Commonwealth (First Uniform Tax Case)* (1942) 65 C.L.R. 373.

73 *Ha v. NSW* (1997) 189 C.L.R. 465.

74 *Koowarta v. Bjelke-Petersen* (1982) 153 C.L.R. 168, 192 (Gibbs CJ) and 241 (Murphy J).

75 *Victoria v. Commonwealth* (1971) 122 C.L.R. 353, 396.

76 *The Queen v. Public Vehicles Licensing Appeal Tribunal (Tas.); Ex parte Australian National Airways Pty. Ltd.* (1964) 113 C.L.R. 207 and *Port Macdonnell Professional Fishermen's Association Inc. v. South Australia* (1989) 168 C.L.R. 340.

77 *Commonwealth v. Tasmania* (1983) 158 C.L.R. 1.

78 *Victoria v. Commonwealth (Federal Roads Case)* (1926) 38 C.L.R. 399.

79 K. Wheelwright, "Commonwealth and State Powers in Health: A Constitutional Diagnosis," *Monash University Law Review* 21 (1995): 53–83.

80 *Queensland Electricity Commission v. Commonwealth* (1985) 159 C.L.R. 192 and *Re Australian Education Union; Ex parte Victoria* (1995) 184 C.L.R. 188.

81 *Australian Securities and Investments Commission Act* 2001 (Cth) and *Trade Practices Act* 1974 (Cth).

82 See (1 October 2003). See also Glyn Davis, "Carving Out Policy Space for State Government in a Federation: The Role of Coordination," *Publius: The Journal of Federalism* 28 (Fall 1998): 147–164.

83 *Re The Residential Tenancies Tribunal of New South Wales: ex parte The Defence Housing Authority* (1997) 190 C.L.R. 410; and *Victoria v. Commonwealth (Industrial Relations Case)* (1996) 187 C.L.R. 416.

84 *Mewett v. Commonwealth* (1997) 191 C.L.R. 471; and *British American Tobacco Australia Ltd. v. Western Australia* [2003] HCA 47.

85 *Wilson v. The Minister for Aboriginal and Torres Strait Islander Affairs* (1996) 198 C.L.R. 1.

86 Alan Peachment and Gordon S. Reid, *New Federalism in Australia: Rhetoric or Reality?* (Bedford Park: Australasian Political Studies Association, 1977); and Galligan, *A Federal Republic*, pp. 203–206.

87 *Racial Discrimination Act* 1975; and *Koowarta v. Bjelke-Petersen* (1982) 153 C.L.R. 168.

88 Cheryl Saunders, "Dividing Power in a Federation in an Age of Globalisation," *Beyond the Republic: Meeting the Global Challenges to Constitutionalism*, eds., Charles Sampford and Tom Round (Sydney: Federation Press, 2001), pp. 129–145; and Brian Opeskin, "Australian Constitutional Law in a Global Era," in French, Lindell, and Saunders, *Reflections on the Australian Constitution*, pp. 171–191.

Belgium

Capital: Bruxelles (Brussels)
Population: 10.3 million (2003 est.)

Kilometres

Sources: CIA World Factbook
ESRI Ltd. UН Cartography Department

UNITED
KINGDOM

NORTH
SEA

NETHERLANDS

GERMANY

BELGIUM

Bruxelles
(Brussels)

Flemish Region

German Community

Walloon Region

FRANCE

LUXEMBOURG

Kingdom of Belgium

HUGUES DUMONT, NICOLAS LAGASSE,
MARC VAN DER HULST,
AND SÉBASTIEN VAN DROOGHENBROECK

It is not easy to use simple language to describe something that is not simple, and Belgian federalism is far from simple. Built without preconceived ideas or an overarching doctrine, it accumulates original – sometimes labyrinthine – solutions as it goes along. In this chapter we attempt to describe the distribution of powers in Belgium as briefly as we can, without doing violence to its richness and complexity – concentrating on major characteristics rather than on an exhaustive inventory of rules. After reviewing the evolution of Belgian federalism along with its social and historical context, our chapter examines the principles that govern the distribution of powers in Belgium, paying special attention to the asymmetry of this distribution. The logic behind the development of the distribution of powers, particularly the political logic, is also discussed, as are the various problem-solving techniques used to prevent or solve conflicts stemming from the distribution of powers. The conclusion reviews how the Belgian system is functioning today and deals with the system's prospects for the future.

HISTORICAL AND CULTURAL CONTEXT OF THE FEDERAL CONSTITUTION

Belgium has some 10,309,795 inhabitants; its territory measures 32,500 square kilometres. Gross domestic product per capita is €23,690 (or roughly US$28,000). The kingdom's population is divided into three main groups: six million Dutch speakers (Flemish) in the north and the Brussels area; four million French speakers in the south (Walloons) and in the Brussels area as well; and 71,000 German speakers in a small territory in the east of the country, along the German border. French, Dutch, and German are the kingdom's three official languages (Articles 4 and 189 of the Constitution).

These data illustrate that the fundamental patterns of force in Belgian political life are bipolar: Belgian politics are propelled by a duality – often a conflict – between the Flemish and the francophones.

From a Unitary Belgium to a Federal Belgium

Rooted in the traditions of Roman and Germanic jurisprudence, Belgium's present Constitution is the product of successive revisions of the original Constitution of 7 February 1831, chiefly those of 1893, 1921, 1970, 1980, 1988, and 1993. Between 1831 and 1970 the Belgian state had every characteristic of a decentralized unitary state. Its territorially decentralized subentities, the provinces and municipalities, did not have the power to make statutory law but only regulations, and they were under the central state's control. The shift towards federalism dates to 1970, but only in 1993 was the state officially declared federal (Article 1 of the Constitution). The transformation of Belgium from a unitary to a federal state originated with the intersection of Flemish demands for cultural autonomy and Walloon demands for economic autonomy. The first explicit demands for cultural autonomy according to a federal scheme date to 1937. They came from the northern part of Belgium, home of the country's Dutch-speaking Flemish population. These demands were made in reaction to the cultural and social hegemony of the French language and the French-speaking bourgeoisie, who pervaded the organization of the state and, in particular, the relationship between the citizen and the administration throughout the nineteenth century and the beginning of the twentieth. These cultural demands were at the root of the 1970 creation of the three communities: the French-speaking, the Flemish-speaking, and the German-speaking. These comprised the first type of federated political entities in Belgium.

Demands for economic autonomy, originating in Wallonia in the 1960s, aimed to spur the south's aging and declining industrial base. These economic demands led to the 1980 creation of the first two regions (Wallonia and Flanders) and the 1988 creation of the region of Brussels. These regions constitute a second type of federated entity.

In truth, the restructuring of the state did not follow a coherent federal doctrine. During its emergence in the 1970s and 1980s Belgian federalism was never perceived as an authentic political process built on a founding consensus but only as a pragmatic response to disputes to be resolved. Each successive constitutional revision may be analyzed as a pragmatic response of the political elites to a specific crisis. No agreement was ever reached on a global and coherent design aiming to stabilize the new structures of the state.

One of the principal obstacles to a stable and coherent theoretical model for Belgian federalism is the persistent disagreement about the final status of the Brussels-Capital region. Starting in 1970 the most influential Flemish politicians have based their federal doctrine on the division of the state into two large parts, the Flemish- and French-speaking communities. For them, Brussels is merely an extension of Flanders and Wallonia, and it ought not to have any status but that of a capital region under the control of the central government. To the contrary, the most influential French-speaking political agents support the division of the country into three regions: Wallonia, Flanders, and Brussels. The status given to Brussels in 1988, then, was a compromise between these two points of view.

Why this disagreement on the fundamental political balance of the system, with some advocating a division into two and others a division into three? The answer lies in the geographic division of the linguistic groups. Although the Flemish are the majority in Belgium, they are a minority in the Brussels region.[1] For this reason, the Flemish have never accepted that Brussels should be a region like the others. They feared that they would be rendered a minority if the Belgian federation came to be simply composed of three regions, with two being primarily francophone. Therefore, they demanded that, unlike Flanders and Wallonia, the Brussels region be subordinate to the federal government in certain areas, at least in de jure terms.

Individual and Collective Rights

The division of Belgian political society between the Flemish- and French-speaking communities is by itself sufficient to explain why such a small country has become so complicated. But there is also a division described as "ideological and philosophical" that must be taken into account if the Belgian system of political decision making is to be grasped in all its complexity. The interaction of these two divisions, linguistic and philosophical, explains why political scientists classify the Belgian political system among "consociational democracies." Since 1831 the Constitution has guaranteed freedom of religion (Articles 19–21) at the same level as other individual liberties. It also provides for government salaries for the ministers of legally recognized religions (Article 181, Section 1). Currently, six religions are recognized by law: the Roman Catholic, Protestant, Orthodox, Anglican, Jewish, and Muslim faiths. It also recognizes the "secular" (non-denominational) philosophical community (Article 181, Section 2). The principle of equality forbids privileging any of these groups. However, the Roman Catholic Church profits from a number of advantages, owing to its long-standing preponderance in Belgian civil society, especially in the north.

In the 1970s, the era of the creation of the communities, this preponderance of Christian ideological and philosophical tendencies was centred in the new Flemish-speaking community. The opposite situation existed in the French-speaking community, which came to be dominated by secular ideological and philosophical tendencies. The secular minority in the Flemish-speaking community, then, found a natural ally in the secular majority in the French-speaking community, while the Catholic minority there became allied with the Catholic majority among the Flemings. This counterbalancing symmetry of minorities produced by the advent of the communities is the reason for the only collective rights recognized by the Belgian Constitution since 1970: Articles 11 and 131. The first guarantees non-discrimination on the basis of ideological and philosophical tendencies, while the second grants the federal Parliament responsibility for guaranteeing such non-discrimination. Based on these provisions, an act passed on 16 July 1973 guarantees the protection of the "ideological or philosophical tendencies" that have come to have a minority position within the communities. They are entitled to certain collective rights: non-discrimination on the basis of ideology or philosophy in the area of cultural policies, all of which are under the communities' jurisdiction, as well as various rights to participate in the development and implementation of these policies.

CONSTITUTIONAL SHARING OF RESPONSIBILITIES

Federated Entities

As already noted, the evolution described above led to the creation, by successive constitutional reforms, of two types of federated entities: the three communities (French-speaking, Flemish-speaking, and German-speaking) and the three regions (Wallonia, Flanders, and Brussels-Capital). The territories of these two levels of federated entities are superimposed on one another, which is why Belgian federalism is said to be in "superposition."

On a strictly legal level, autonomy and equality characterize, in principle, the relations among the federated entities and those they have with the federal government.[2] The federated entities thus have their own executive and legislative powers (governments and councils), in whose composition and operation the federal government as such has no right to interfere. This composition and operation are regulated exclusively by the Constitution, institutional reform laws, and, when appropriate, the "constitutive authority" granted to these federated entities (see discussion below under "asymmetry"). The Constitution gives each of the federated entities the power to enact legislation with the same hierarchic rank as federal law, with the partial exception of the Brussels region (see discussion below). The three communities and the Flemish and Walloon regions enact decrees, while the Brussels-Capital region enacts ordinances (explained below). Note that the Belgian federated entities do not have a judiciary of their own: the organization, operation, and responsibilities of the courts and tribunals derive in principle from the federal power.

The territorial jurisdictions of the three regions and three communities are defined according to four linguistic regions whose boundaries were demarcated in 1963, to wit: the Dutch language region in the north, the French language region in the south, the German language region in the southwest, and the bilingual Brussels-Capital region in the centre.[3] Accordingly, the Flemish region's territory is defined by the Dutch language area, the Walloon region by the French and German language areas, and the Brussels region by the bilingual area.

The communities' territorial jurisdiction is more remarkable: although their decrees apply to the institutions *and persons* in the Dutch and French language areas, the Flemish and French communities' territorial jurisdiction also extends into the bilingual Brussels region, *but only to institutions.* These two communities, then, act concomitantly in this region, each within its sphere of power, but independently of each other. In practice, inhabitants of Brussels are subject to the decrees of one or the other community according to which one runs the institution they are using. For example, in the field of education, parents are subject to the decrees of the Flemish-speaking community if they have chosen to send their children to a Flemish school. If they send another child to a French school, they will be bound, with regard to that child, by the laws of the French-speaking community. Thus, the community status of Brussels residents is neither direct, exclusive, nor definitive. The juxtaposition of the two communities' jurisdiction in the Brussels area is one of the most striking examples of personal federalism in Belgian institutional structure. As for the German-language community, its decrees apply only to the German language area.

Allocated Powers and Residual Powers

The Belgian federal system is the fruit of a decentralization movement acting on a formerly unitary state. It is thus logically and naturally inclined to allow the federated entities only those allocated powers specifically listed in the Constitution and in special majority legislation made by virtue of the Constitution. Residual powers are federal (central) jurisdiction.

However, the institutional reforms of 1993 added Article 35 to the Constitution, which reversed this division of power. The federal government would retain only those powers specifically given it by the Constitution and by special majority laws in virtue thereof, while the residual powers would go to the communities and regions. Nevertheless, this provision is not yet in force, and it is doubtful it ever will be. Two particularly delicate measures must take place first: a constitutional inventory of matters that will remain in federal jurisdiction; and the passing of a special majority law determining whether the regions or the communities will take on the residual powers. It can thus be said that, at this point in time, Article 35 is basically symbolic.

Matters Reserved "to the Law"

In some of its provisions, the Constitution reserves the power to deal with certain matters by or in the "law" alone.[4] One of the classic questions in Belgian constitutional law[5] is whether by "law" the Constitution means only "an act of the legislative branch as opposed to the executive branch," or whether it means "federal law as opposed to community and regional ordinances and decrees." In the first case, the rules concerned would not be regulating the distribution of powers and therefore would not necessarily have to be modified in order for the matters concerned to be transferred to the jurisdiction of the communities or regions. In the second case, however, they would be power-distribution rules: they would absolutely have to be changed in order to transfer the matters concerned towards the federated entities.

Nobody at present claims to have a sure and definitive answer to this question. The simplest answer would be to note that, when the Constitution reserved a matter to the "law" before 1970[6] (when the Belgian central government as such was the only legislator) it could not have been distributing powers; whereas when the Constitution mentioned the "law" after 1970 (when several different federal entities with legislatures existed) it produced a distribution of power in favour of the federal government. Decisions on the 2001 reforms, handed down in March 2003 by the Belgian constitutional court (*Cour d'arbitrage/Arbitragehof*), tended to support this view on first reading;[7] but when examined more deeply, it appears that they do not support all of it.[8]

Powers Allocated to the Federated Entities

The powers assigned to the communities and regions by the Constitution and the Special Majority Laws on Institutional Reform correspond to the demands – cultural and economic – that led to the creation of the two types of federated entity. Articles 127 to 130 of the Constitution give the communities responsibility for cultural matters in the broadest sense, including the arts, libraries, radio and television, continuing education, cultural activities, recreation, and tourism as well as sports, general education, language policy (in the administrative sector, education, and employee-employer relations) and so-called "person-related" matters (i.e., those involving "person-to-person relationships" such as health policy, social assistance, policy on disabled people, and youth protection).[9]

Unlike the communities' situation, the regions' legislative powers are only derived in small part from the Constitution; instead, Article 39 says that their powers shall be determined by special majority laws.[10] In particular, regions are broadly responsible for large sectors of economic policy, foreign trade, energy policy, labour policy, public works, transportation, agriculture, and ocean fisheries. Furthermore, regions also have authority over planning, the environment, water policy, rural renewal, and nature conservation, even though these matters are only tenuously related to the economy in its broader senses. Finally, the regions have jurisdiction over the organization and control of the pre-existing decentralized political entities – provinces and municipalities (*communes/gemeenten*) – although these powers must be exercised within the constitutional limits applicable to these decentralized local entities. These limits include guarantees of municipal and provincial autonomy, direct election of their councils, and the openness of their meetings (Articles 41 and 162 of the Constitution).

However, the various areas of responsibility accorded to the communities and regions are larded with exceptions, specifying many domains in which the federal government alone has jurisdiction. The main justification given for these exceptions is concern for the protection of minorities. Thus, for example, Article 129, Section 2, of the Constitution states that the decrees of the Flemish and French-speaking communities will not apply to the use of language in certain municipalities located along the linguistic border. These municipalities have a special status with regard to language policy owing to the presence of "linguistic minorities" there. Likewise, although in principle the regions have jurisdiction to pass organic legislation relative to the municipalities, multiple exceptions were added during the 2001 institutional reforms to guarantee the rights of "linguistic minorities" in municipalities both along the linguistic border and in Brussels.[11]

Furthermore, there are a large number of exceptions to the powers of the regions based on the principle that Belgium must remain, despite its federal status, an "economic and monetary union" where the free circulation of persons, goods, services, and capital is ensured.[12] Based on this principle, special majority laws reserve to the federal government matters such as monetary policy, price and revenue policy, and competition, intellectual property, commercial, and labour law.

The Principle of Exclusive Legislative Powers

Belgian federalism rests on the central principle of jurisdictional exclusivity: for any given matter, only one authority has jurisdiction – the federal government, the communities, or the regions – to the exclusion of all others. With very few exceptions, Belgian federalism is not a federalism of execution or administration, in which the federated entities are called upon to implement the rules promulgated by the federal authority.[13]

The principle of exclusiveness must, however, be applied in a reasonable way, respecting the proportionality principle.[14] No authority, whether federal, community, or regional, may exercise its powers in such a way as to make the exercise of another authority's powers impossible or excessively difficult.[15] Behind this principle, which the constitutional court has reaffirmed several times, one can see the traces of the principle of federal loyalty (known in German federalism as "Bundestreue"), enshrined in Article 143, Section 1, of the Constitution.[16]

Corollaries of the Exclusiveness Principle

Based on the principle of exclusiveness, Belgian federalism has no formally overlapping jurisdictions; that is, there are no cases where a matter falls under the authority of more than one level of government and must be resolved according to which level has priority or paramountcy (e.g., *Bundesrecht bricht Ländesrecht*). Nevertheless, this principle forbidding overlapping jurisdictions has some exceptions. Some are provided for in the texts. For example, Article 170, Section 2, of the Constitution, as well as an act passed on 23 January 1989, provides that the communities and regions may only impose taxes in matters that are not yet subject to a federal tax; if a federal tax is later imposed, it takes priority over an existing community or regional tax. Article 6*bis*, Section 3, of the special law of 8 August 1980 also establishes a type of overlapping jurisdiction with regard to scientific research: it authorizes the federal government and Parliament, under certain conditions, to take initiatives, create structures, and budget funds for scientific research in matters that fall under community or regional jurisdictions. Besides these overlaps established in the texts, there are some others in the margins. These "unofficial" overlapping jurisdictions spring from the complexity of Belgian power-distribution rules and the inevitable blurring of boundaries between community, regional, and federal jurisdiction. Thus, the constitutional court recently ruled that the federal legislature may create a detention centre for young offenders, even though under a strict reading of the Special Majority Law on Institutional Reform of 8 August 1980, the communities have jurisdiction over young offenders.[17] As justification, the court asserted that the federal intervention remained subsidiary and proportionate and was within the bounds of a co-operation agreement with the communities. A de facto form of overlapping jurisdiction was thus permitted.

Similar observations apply to the question of spending powers. Belgian federalism, under the exclusiveness principle, technically prohibits spending outside the sphere of legislative or executive powers, both by the federal government and by the federated entities: an entity may finance an activity only if that activity falls within one of its areas of responsibility. However, certain embryonic forms of spending powers exist on the fringes of this principle. In the absence of legal justification, this development is explained on the one hand by a certain tendency to blur some of the rules of distribution of powers (as seen in a number of cooperation agreements), and on the other hand by the non-trivial disparities of wealth between the different federated entities. Thus, for example, the French-speaking community and the Walloon region agreed to have the latter finance certain activities that officially fall under the jurisdiction of the former.

The Exception to Exclusiveness: Implied Powers

Together, Articles 10 and 19 of the special institutional reform law of 8 August 1980 are the basis for implied powers. On these grounds, the communities and regions are able to legislate in matters that, in principle, fall under federal jurisdiction – including matters "reserved" to it by the Constitution, such as the organization, jurisdiction, and operation of courts and tribunals.

Constitutional case law, however, has consistently subjected the use of implied powers to three conditions.[18] First, such an action must be necessary to the exercise of the powers allocated to the region or community concerned. Second, the matter in which the implied powers are to be used must lend itself to differing regulations. Finally, the concrete measures adopted by the federated entity on the basis of its implied powers must not have more than a "marginal impact" on the matter in question. It is an open question whether the federal government itself can claim implied powers to adopt measures within the jurisdictions of the federated entities.[19]

Softening of the Exclusiveness Principle: Cooperative Federalism

Cooperative federalism, and in particular the cooperation agreements that are its concrete form, is not intended to be an exception to the exclusiveness principle in Belgium but, rather, to complement it. The Council of State (the judicial body dealing mainly with administrative law) and the constitutional court agree that a cooperation agreement "cannot involve the exchange, abandonment, or resumption of powers" as determined by or by virtue of the Constitution.[20] Cooperation agreements are governed by Article 92*bis*, Section 1, of the Special Majority

Law on Institutional Reform of 8 August 1980, which provides that the federal government, the communities, and the regions "may conclude cooperation agreements calling in particular for the joint creation and management of common services or institutions, for the joint exercise of their powers, or for the development of joint initiatives."[21] It is left to the federal government and the federated entities to undertake to create and develop these agreements, under the rules establishing their respective areas of responsibility; they are in this sense "optional." Besides these agreements, the special majority law provides for a range of matters – such as so-called "mixed" international treaties – where a cooperation agreement *must* be signed ("obligatory" cooperation agreements).[22] In practice, a rather paradoxical tendency can be seen. Although the levels of government make heavy use of these "optional" agreements to resolve various matters, in some cases they neglect to conclude cooperation agreements that the special law describes as obligatory.

Disputes stemming from the interpretation or execution of an obligatory cooperation agreement are adjudicated by a cooperation tribunal (*juridiction de coopération/samenwerkingsgerecht*) whose members are named by the federal and/or federated entities involved (each naming one member). Such tribunals can also be set up, with the same purpose, in the case of optional cooperation agreements, if the parties to the agreement so decide. However, in practice, cooperation tribunals have never been used, with collaboration and compromise always having been preferred to date.

Instrumental Powers

The Constitution and the related laws give the federated entities a number of "instruments," in a broad sense of the term, which allow them to exercise their responsibilities. Here we will discuss penal, international, and fiscal powers.

Penal powers of the communities and regions   Article 11 of the Special Majority Law on Institutional Reform of 8 August 1980 authorizes the communities and regions to define certain acts, within the bounds of their jurisdictions, as penal infractions with corresponding penalties. However, the federated entities' penal autonomy is limited: the consent of the Council of Ministers (i.e., the Cabinet of the federal government) is necessary when a community or region wishes to establish a "new" penalty (i.e., one that is not already provided for by the federal government).

International powers of the communities and regions   Article 167 of the Constitution lays down the principle of parallelism between internal and external powers. Belgian federated entities have received treaty-making power in matters under their exclusive jurisdiction: the government of the community or region involved negotiates and signs the treaty, while that entity's council (legislative assembly) provides, through decree or ordinance, the necessary parliamentary assent for the treaty to come into force in the community or region.

The treaty-making power of the Belgian federated entities is, however, accompanied by a number of mechanisms for information, cooperation, and substitution in order to ensure the stability of Belgium's overall international relations and the coherence of its foreign policy. Therefore, upon engaging in negotiations for a treaty, the government of the federated entity involved must inform the federal Council of Ministers (Cabinet). The Council, in turn, may decide within thirty days to suspend the negotiations. In this case, the Interministerial Conference of Foreign Policy (*Conférence interministérielle de politique étrangère [CIPE]/Interministeriële Conferentie voor het Buitenlands Beleid [ICBB]*) – composed of representatives from the federal government and the governments of the federated entities – is informed; it then decides by consensus whether to let the process towards the signing of the disputed treaty continue. If the conference reaches no consensus, then the king may confirm the suspension of the negotiations, but only under four circumstances: (1) if the contracting party with whom the treaty is to be signed is not recognized by Belgium; (2) if Belgium has no diplomatic relations with the contracting party; (3) if a decision or act of state has ruled relations between Belgium and the contracting party to be broken, suspended, or badly compromised; or (4) if the treaty is contrary to Belgium's foreign obligations. In practice, this procedure has to date never been used.

There are special political and legal difficulties with so-called "mixed" treaties (i.e., treaties dealing with matters falling under the jurisdiction of several levels of government, such as European Union or human rights treaties). The consent of each entity involved would be necessary for such a treaty to enter into force in Belgium. This is why, in such cases, the special institutional reform law requires an obligatory cooperation agreement. This agreement, reached on 8 March 1994, set up a complex procedure of information, cooperation, and substitution, with the CIPE/ICBB in a central role.

Also, by application of the parallelism of powers principle, it is the responsibility of the federated entities to carry out Belgium's international obligations within their sphere of jurisdiction – including obligations stemming from primary or secondary European Union law. However, in order to guarantee the stability of Belgium's international relations, the Constitution (Article 169), supplemented by Article 16 of the Special Majority Law of 8 August 1980, allows the federal state to take over and carry out the obligations of a delinquent federated entity. This possibility of substitution is subject to several conditions, and under no circumstances can it be carried out unless the delinquency at issue has first been condemned by an international tribunal. It should be noted that this process has not yet been used.

Fiscal powers of the communities and regions Very broadly, the "fiscal resources" of the federated entities come from different sources, including non-fiscal revenues from the exercise by the federated entities of their powers,[23] federal tax revenues that are transferred to them, and whatever loans they may take out.

Under Article 170, Section 2, of the Constitution, the communities and regions also have the power to raise their own taxes within their areas of responsibility. However, the same disposition allows the federal legislature to impose exceptions to this fiscal power. On this basis, an act of 23 January 1989 provided that "the [community and regional] Councils are not authorized to raise taxes in matters that are already the subject of a federal tax." (See also the discussion above on corollaries of the exclusiveness principle.)

In practice, the regions have already put their fiscal powers to use. The communities, on the other hand – specifically, the French- and Flemish-speaking communities – face an unsurmounted though not insurmountable obstacle to the use of their fiscal powers. This relates to the application of their decrees in Brussels: community decrees may not directly impose obligations on individuals in Brussels. A solution in which Brussels residents would be exempt from taxation by the French- and Flemish-speaking communities conflicts with the principle of equality of taxation of citizens.[24] Another solution would be to impose only some of the taxes of each community on the citizens of Brussels. However, this would conflict with the principle of "no taxation without representation," inasmuch as Brussels citizens would have to pay taxes mandated by an assembly (for some the Council of the French-speaking community; for others, that of the Flemish-speaking community) in which they are not represented.[25] Some authors therefore consider the only practical solution to this question to be a cooperation agreement between the Flemish- and French-speaking communities. However, this does not appear to be on the political agenda at the moment. The upshot of the above is that, at least for the present, the taxing powers of the communities remain theoretical.

LOGIC OF THE DISTRIBUTION OF POWERS

Here we concentrate on two key aspects of the distribution of powers: first, the responsibilities for the welfare state; second, the fundamentally asymmetrical nature of the federal arrangements.

Primary Responsibilities of the Welfare State

Belgium has a long tradition of state intervention through the operation of a welfare state aiming to help the kingdom's inhabitants to deal with the vagaries of chance. To this end, after the Second World War the country put together a system of social security offering a high degree of coverage.

The progression from a unitary Belgium to a federal Belgium led to a division of powers over the welfare state, which we here describe very broadly. Communities are responsible for person-related matters pertaining to individuals (Article 128, Section 1 of the Constitution), including, in particular, under the heading of "assistance to individuals," family policy, social assistance, adaptation and integration of disabled people, general policy on disabled people, policy on the elderly, and so on. Nonetheless, in each of these community matters there are some responsibilities that are reserved to the federal government. This is the case, for example, with regard to rules and funding for disabled persons' benefits as well as with regard to the determination of the minimum amount, conditions, and funding for the legally guaranteed income supplements for elderly people. More generally, the Special Majority Law on Institutional Reform of 8 August 1980 reserves the otherwise undefined jurisdiction of "social security"[26] to the federal legislature, confirming the intention of Article 128 of the Constitution.

In the actual state of the law, the distinction between community "assistance to individuals" and federal "social security" is a delicate legal matter and has provoked controversy between French and Flemish legal authors.[27] The former promote a broad interpretation of federal powers, while the latter support an expansive interpretation of community powers. The controversy is all the more delicate for involving very important underlying financial stakes: having a great number of federal social programs would cause a redistribution of wealth from the economically flourishing north of the country to the weaker south.

The Belgian Council of State and the constitutional court have ruled on this delicate question; however, even though their decisions were more or less in agreement, they have not met with unanimous approval in the legal world on either side of the linguistic divide.[28] In a decision rendered on 13 March 2001 the constitutional court put forward a broad interpretation of community responsibilities with regard to assistance to individuals as well as a narrow interpretation of reserved federal powers pertaining to social security – specifically, that they apply only to those social benefits that are currently organized by federal legislation.[29] Any benefits not already provided for by such legislation could be introduced by community legislatures to deal with new needs.

Asymmetry

In Belgian constitutional law the concept of asymmetry relates to the lack of uniformity in the rules governing the *organization* and *powers* of federated entities of the same type (i.e., the regions and the communities). *Organizational asymmetry* can be seen, for example, in that the institutions of entities of the same type obey different rules. We will not expand on this here. *Asymmetry of powers,* however, means that there is a difference in the scope of competences among federated entities. One or more entities has more formal legal powers than do the others. In the Belgian case this arises, on the one hand, directly from the Constitution and Special Majority Law on Institutional Reform and, on the other hand, from the decision of certain federated entities to exercise or not to exercise certain options open to them under the Constitution. We examine these two cases in turn.

Asymmetries "imposed" on federal entities by the Constitution and Special Laws
The Walloon and Flemish regions have identical responsibilities and powers; from this point of view, their situation is symmetrical. However, the Brussels-Capital region is subject to an asymmetry: its legislative acts, called ordinances, are subject to a broader judicial control than is imposed on Flemish and Walloon decrees;[30] the Brussels ordinances are also subject (purely theoretically to date) to direct control by the federal government in certain matters.[31] Likewise, the powers and responsibilities of the French- and Flemish-speaking communities are a priori identical. However, the German-speaking community is largely deprived of a competence enjoyed by the other two: language policy.[32]

Note too that the Constitution (Article 118, Section 2) gives the Walloon region, the French-speaking community, and the Flemish-speaking community a "constitutive authority" of which the German-speaking community and the Brussels-Capital region are at present deprived. "Constitutive authority" is, in essence, the right of a federated entity to modify, to a limited extent and in matters that concern it alone, the organizational rules imposed on it by the special institutional reform laws.

Asymmetries "authorized" by the Constitution   The Constitution contains three mechanisms by which a region may come to exercise the powers of a community or vice versa. First, Article 137 allows special majority legislation to organize a sort of "merger" or "absorption" between communities and regions. In other words, the councils of the French or Flemish-speaking communities could come to exercise the powers of the Walloon and Flemish regions, respectively. Such a "merger" has in fact been carried out in the north between the Flemish region and the Flemish-speaking community but not in the south between the Walloon region and the French-speaking community: another source of asymmetry.

Second, Article 138 of the Constitution allows the French-speaking community to transfer the exercise of one or another of its powers to the Walloon region (with regard to its powers in the unilingual French language region) and to the French-speaking community commission (with regard to its powers in Brussels).[33] Such transfers, unlike the foregoing, do not require special majority law;[34] some have already taken place (e.g., in matters such as professional training, sports facilities, tourism, school transport, and several powers relating to social assistance). The Constitution does not provide for the equivalent among the federated entities in the north (Flemish region, Flemish-speaking community, and Flemish-speaking community commission for Brussels): another example of asymmetry of power.

Third, Article 139 of the Constitution allows the Walloon region to transfer certain regional responsibilities to the German-speaking community, which would then exercise them in the German-speaking region of the country. Such transfers have also taken place (e.g., in regards to tourism and protection of monuments and sites). These transfers also deepen the asymmetry between the regions, on the one hand, and the communities, on the other.

Logical basis for the asymmetries   The various asymmetries described above have, on the one hand, led to a refocusing of Belgian federalism around "community federalism" in the north and "regional federalism" in the south and, on the other hand, allowed the Brussels-Capital region's distinct status relative to the other regions to persist.

This dual phenomenon is largely explained by the demographic composition of Belgium. Although the Flemish are plainly in the majority in Belgium, they are a minority in Brussels, and Flemish speakers in Brussels make up no more than 2 percent of the total Flemish population of Belgium. This is why the Flemish movement does not want to see Brussels obtain the status of a full region. Conversely, the Flemish movement did not have any objection to the absorption by the Flemish-speaking community of the Flemish region as the community provides a link between Flemish speakers in Flanders and in Brussels. In contrast, the demographic and political weight of Brussels in the total French-speaking population of Belgium is much greater (more than 20 percent). This explains why the Walloons, protective of their identity, have avoided an absorption of the Walloon region by the French-speaking community (which links the francophones of Wallonia and Brussels) and why they have chosen instead to divide up the community's powers pursuant to Article 138 of the Constitution.

THE EVOLUTION OF THE CONSTITUTIONAL
DISTRIBUTION OF POWERS

The distribution of powers has undergone frequent revision. Since the first reform of the state in 1970 there have been no fewer than four reforms: in 1980, in 1988–89, in 1993, and in 2001. These reforms have not involved systematic changes to institutional structure; rather, each one has devolved federal powers to the communities or regions. There has been no movement in the other direction. These multiple transfers of power have not been without consequences for the relations among the different levels of government or for the operation of some of the powers concerned (such as in foreign policy).

The Centrifugal Dynamics of Reform

The constitutional or legislative changes that bring about new transfers of powers are often the result of extended negotiations between representatives of the two main cultural communities. It can also happen that some powers are given to the regions and communities outside these large institutional reform processes. For example, the power to grant licences for the import and export of weapons and ammunition was attributed to the regions by a special majority law of 12 August 2003. Nevertheless, these transfers have been the subject of debate between the country's two main communities. It also happens that certain levels of government attempt, alone or with others, to change the existing division of power by political agreements or unilateral legislation. Furthermore, the constitutional court and the legislative division of the Council of State also participate in the definition of this dynamic institutional structure. In general, these three elements have tended towards the progressive diminishment of federal powers.

Institutional Reform through Negotiation of the Two Main Communities

The motor of this centrifugal evolution is to be found in the conflict between the communities and the will, mainly on the part of Flemish political parties, to obtain more autonomy for the federated entities. Even though Flemish and francophone institutional points of view agree at certain points – for example, on the July 2001 regionalization of organic laws on local powers – this is not the usual state of affairs; most often, the topic of and approach to the negotiations vary according to the community.

In general, the Flemish political parties have pushed for continuing devolution towards the regions and communities, as has been going on since 1970. Now that their initial linguistic and cultural demands have led to the creation of communities with a large sphere of responsibilities, the Flemings are calling for further autonomy, this time in the economic domain. Thus, following a Flemish demand, the special majority law of 13 July 2001 gave the regions the power to levy and collect new taxes and to give tax reductions to their citizens. French-language political parties denounce these demands for the separate management of revenues, coming, as they do, now that the Flemish region enjoys a more favourable socioeconomic position than do the other two regions. They note also that Flanders has benefited in its turn from interpersonal and interregional solidarity (i.e., the merging of the community and regional administrations).

From a strictly legal point of view, the transfer of new powers is the work of the federal government; it alone can modify the Constitution and the laws establishing the institutional structure of the state. Neither the electorate nor the federated entities as such take part directly in this process. Constitutional revisions follow the three-step process outlined in Article 195 of the Constitution: the national Parliament identifies the parts of the Constitution that need to be altered; immediately thereafter, the two houses of Parliament (the House of Representatives and the Senate) are dissolved and an election is held; then, the new Parliament and the king (which means, in practice, the government) decide on the revision and its nature, subject to a two-thirds majority vote with at least two-thirds of the members in each chamber present. This procedure has not been altered since 1831 and does not involve the federated political entities created in 1970; its usefulness and legitimacy is therefore a current object of debate among constitutional scholars and in the political arena. Since 1970 most institutional reform laws have required not only a two-thirds majority in order to be passed but also a majority among both of the two linguistic groups in both Houses of Parliament.

In this process the Senate is not functioning as a truly federal chamber (i.e., a chamber in which all the federated entities are represented directly as governments [the German model] or where their people are represented on an equal footing for each constituent unit [the American model]). Therefore the regions and communities cannot be said to participate in the development of the federal structure via the upper house. The most that can be said is that the constitutionally required linguistic parity within the federal government as well as the "special majority" required for votes on institutional reform laws – in particular, the requirement for a majority within both linguistic groups in the federal assemblies – allow a partial and indirect expression of the two large linguistic communities in institutional reform.[35]

However, in practice, votes on constitutional or legislative reform simply confirm agreements negotiated between the representatives of political parties from the north and south of the country, each representing the interests of their own community and region. The institutional history of Belgium contains an impressive number of "round tables," "conferences," or "community-to-community dialogues" in which French-speaking and Flemish-speaking parties have squared off against each other. Owing to Belgium's essentially bipolar structure, negotiators tend to side with their linguistic or community affiliation rather than with the federal authority or the federated entities. At the last round of institutional negotiations in 2001 each party's delegation was composed of ministers from all three levels of government. Furthermore, before the negotiations, parliamentarians or ministers from federated governments, less constrained than their federal colleagues to reconcile their views with those of their coalition colleagues from the other community, can prod the negotiations by adopting very pointed resolutions. In Flanders, just before the federal and regional legislative elections of 13 June 1999, all the parties of the Flemish parliament adopted a common basis for negotiation, calling for broad transfers of power and a substantial modification of the structure of the state. Considering the absence of "national" parties, as well as the importance of political parties in Belgian political and institutional life as connectors between the various legislatures and levels of government in the federation, this stance on the part of all the political parties of the Flemish parliament could not help but influence the course of past and future institutional discussions. In sum, while it is plain that the federal Parliament has the legal right to oppose any new transfer of powers or modification of institutional structures, in practice this exclusive power does not prevent the continual "downsizing" of federal responsibilities.

Institutional Reform by Exceptional Cases

Institutional changes of a political nature also take place outside the negotiations described above. They are usually of controversial legitimacy vis-à-vis the existing legal framework. Some of them are the fruit of decisions negotiated between the federal authority and the regions with regard to an individual issue, whereas others are the work of regional legislatures or governments.

Among the negotiated decisions, we can take as an example the cooperation agreement signed by the federal state and the three regions with regard to the development and funding of railway infrastructure. The governments decided that the regions could, if they wished, accelerate investment beyond the agreed-upon pace by providing bridge financing without interest. The Council of State, however, concluded that, by allowing the regions to take on some of the cost of railway investment (even by absorbing the cost of interest that would not be reimbursed by the federal government), the agreement violated the Special Majority Law on

Institutional Reform of 8 August 1980, under which the federal state has exclusive jurisdiction over railways. From a legal perspective it would have been better to change the law, but this solution faced two political obstacles. Since the French speakers had traditionally opposed the regionalization of the railways, they could not agree to amend the law without giving the impression of going back on their previous stance. On top of this, the government did not have the majority in the federal parliament that would be necessary to amend the law.

To take another case, the Flemish government has adopted circulars (providing administrative guidance), and the Flemish parliament has passed decrees, which, without violating legal or constitutional norms, nevertheless interpret them in highly autonomist ways. This was the case with the Flemish government's circular on federal laws over the use of languages in administration. Although according to the Constitution the official language used in administration is a federal matter, the Flemish government advised its regional administration and subordinate authorities to restrictively interpret the linguistic laws guaranteeing the French-speaking minority certain rights in administrative matters. By a decision of 23 December 2004 the Council of State has decided that the circulars, whose legality had been disputed in French-speaking political and legal circles, are not illegal.

Similar initiatives have appeared in the Walloon region. In order to preserve the Formula 1 Grand Prix at Francorchamps, whose survival was threatened by a federal law forbidding all tobacco advertisement, the Walloon legislature used its economic powers to justify the adoption of a decree permitting dispensations from the federal law for international sporting events. However, when proceedings for annulment were referred to the constitutional court, it struck down the Walloon interpretation of the law.

Institutional Reform Imposed by the Courts

Through the reforms and the agreements between levels of government, the federal level of government has lost powers to the regions and the communities. However, political agents are not solely responsible for this phenomenon. The courts – both the constitutional court and the legislative division of the Council of State – have also tended to favour this trend.

In the last few years, the constitutional court has rendered several important judgments in disputes over areas of responsibility. On the other hand, and more generally, the court has exercised only a light control over the institutional reform laws that ratify political agreements between the two communities.

The constitutional court has played an important role in interpreting the areas of responsibility – both material and territorial – of the various levels of government. In particular, by applying the proportionality principle in disputes over areas of responsibilities, the court has given its tacit blessing to the principle of federal loyalty. Even so, the court also permitted certain transfers of powers, for example by recognizing a sort of joint responsibility in the very touchy area of social security (see above).

However, it is clear that, when the court is called upon to rule on challenges to new institutional reform laws that transfer powers to the regions and communities, it has kept constitutionality firmly in check, refusing to challenge political balances arrived at through negotiation. Since these laws aim at ratifying political agreements produced by give-and-take and delicate compromises between the two communities, the court's striking down part of the agreement for legal reasons would risk weakening one of the parties relative to the other. In practice, it can be seen that constitutional judges have acted with extreme prudence and have deliberately limited their range of action. They have made no secret of avoiding the disturbance of political compromises and, consequently, of favouring a light touch with the legislative text. Instead of forcing politics to respect constitutional principles, the constitutional court has borne in mind the political reasons for the adoption of the acts.

Consequences of the Federalization of the State for Relations
between Levels of Government

The centrifugal movement in the evolution of Belgian federalism is far from over. All indicators point to the various political movements at the root of the pressures for reform (for federalism, even for confederalism) continuing their activities in the years to come. It is therefore difficult to take stock definitively of the power relations between different levels of government or to identify the exact consequences of all of these developments. However, two main patterns of force can be identified.

First, although the federal government has been weakened after thirty years of continual "downsizing" of its powers, it is still an essential part of the structure of Belgian federalism. The federal level remains a meeting place between the two communities: even though the north and south regularly disagree over health care, justice, youth protection, or railway policy, the fact of their presently unavoidable cohabitation in the federal government forces coalition partners to compromise despite the tensions (even at the risk of costly or irrational solutions). In practice, the French- and Flemish-speaking partners in the federal government are induced to exchange peace offerings or "loyalty guarantees" when a federated entity attempts an institutional show of force or opposes federal decisions. The existence to date of nearly identical majorities in the different levels of government has probably contributed to this dynamic of appeasement.

However, the question could be raised whether there are still "federal interests" different from those of the two main communities. Both in government and in Parliament disagreements appear more and more often to be based on a community division rather than on an ideological one. It is reasonable to perceive that the necessary collaboration between French- and Flemish-speaking political parties leads to a common management of more and more divergent interests, no matter which parties are involved in the coalition. This is not enough to condemn Belgian federalism's current way of operating; but the question is raised whether the "federal" character of the state masks anything more than a simple conjunction of more or less contradictory interests.

Next, it appears that the necessary collaboration within the federal government (and in the Brussels government, which also includes French- and Flemish-speaking members) carries over to other levels of government. As is see in the next section, the airtight division of powers between different levels of government does not prevent continuing dialogue between them. On the contrary, the "shared" division of exclusive areas of responsibility naturally leads those in charge in the different levels of government to harmonize their policies, whether within the peak intergovernmental body called the Coordinating Committee (*Comité de concertation/Overlegcomité*) or within the various interministerial conferences under it.

This cooperation is even more apparent in international relations since the Belgian system is characterized by the parallelism between internal and external powers (see above). The federal government, therefore, does not take the place of the federated entities in the negotiation and ratification of treaties or in the adoption of positions within international organizations in matters that are within the areas of responsibility of the federated entities. It is thus not surprising that the federated entities participate in meetings of international bodies – including the European Union and the Council of Europe – when their areas of responsibility are concerned. (This issue of participation in European Union matters is discussed below.)[36]

MAINTENANCE AND MANAGEMENT OF POWER SHARING

The constant dynamic of the Belgian federal model is explained in part by the many conflicts over management of the division of power. These tensions, however, do not prevent cooperation between the different levels of government. These institutional advances have, however, led to a governmental landscape that is largely incomprehensible to most citizens.

There are many causes for conflict in the area of division of powers. First, these conflicts can result from lack of legal precision on the extent of the powers. The constitutional or legal criteria for the attribution of powers generally emerge from negotiations and political compromise, and in the process some imprecision can emerge in the definition of these criteria. As a result their interpretation can lead to controversy.

Conflicts may also stem from a desire on the part of a level of government – usually a region or community – to expand its area of responsibility or from its refusal to accept the consequences of a law passed by another level of government. It can also happen that the communities and regions agree on a way to put forward a common argument to representatives of the federal government. This type of informal agreement and negotiation, coming before discussion with the federal government, generally appears on particular, immediate topics where the federated entities have a common interest.

Resolution of the many conflicts over areas of responsibility are in principle under the jurisdiction of the constitutional court (*Cour d'arbitrage/ Arbitragehof*) if a law is under dispute. Such a dispute may arise through right of action (at the request of the government, of a parliament, or of a citizen who proves to have an interest) or by exception (an interlocutory question posed by a trial judge during a proceeding). A number of criteria for the attribution of powers have therefore been established by the Court's jurisprudence. When a legal controversy arises over administrative jurisdiction, the dispute comes before the Council of State.

In many cases, however, the tensions end in a compromise between levels of government. In practice, the number of disputes over areas of responsibility adjudicated by the constitutional court has dropped over the last few years. This can be explained by several factors. In particular, where there are politically symmetrical coalition governments on several levels, they are probably less inclined to initiate legal disputes, preferring to settle certain more legally delicate questions by agreements (such as cooperation agreements) as the process is simpler and there is less call for legal intervention. It is also more difficult for citizens to prove that they have an interest in disputes over areas of responsibility than in disputes over rights and freedoms.

Cooperation, Collaboration, and Compromise in the Management of Powers

It is clear that the conflicts over management of the division of powers has not prevented organic[37] cooperation (e.g., in the Coordinating Committee), procedural cooperation (by assent, consultation, information procedures, etc.), and conventional cooperation from increasing in significance over the last few years.

Thus the exclusiveness of jurisdictions has not ruled out dialogue and cooperation between the different levels of government. On the contrary, owing to the interdependence between the powers of the different levels of government, cooperation has been a necessary consequence. It can concern matters as diverse as employment, environmental protection, transportation, youth protection, or international relations. Furthermore, it has taken diverse forms, whether as informal contacts between members of government, protocols on the order of gentlemen's agreements, or full cooperation agreements. We saw above that, although many of these agreements have been reached voluntarily, special majority legislation has mandated the regions and communities to make agreements with each other or with the federal government in certain matters (e.g., management of roads, waterways, and public transit networks that pass through more than one region).

The Coordinating Committee, a veritable intergovernmental discussion forum, serves as a space for meeting and exchange between the representatives of the different levels of government. It has been the scene of the discussion and conclusion of many agreements both formal and informal. The specialized subgroups of this committee bring together the ministers involved with certain specific portfolios (interministerial committees on external relations, agriculture, etc.).

The matter of international relations deserves special attention. Despite the parallelism of internal and external responsibilities, the Belgian state has a single voice in the decision-making bodies of international organizations, such as the Council of Ministers of the European Union. Unless Belgium is no longer to have a single voice at the European Union, that voice cannot be multiplied and spread among various concerned internal levels of government. Therefore, collaboration is required, first to decide whether a regional, community, or federal minister will represent the Belgian position in the body concerned and, second, to decide together on the position to be put forward by the nominated representative.[38] Whatever the matter in question, this dual collaboration is required: when the European ministers of culture meet, the communities take turns representing Belgium, with the agreement that each of them will present the position agreed upon together with the two others. This collaboration on making a common decision may appear paradoxical to the extent that it partially goes against Belgian federalism's natural trend towards diversity.

Besides the rare exceptions examined above, which have remained largely theoretical up to now, the Constitution does not provide for any exceptions either to this cooperative logic or to the underlying principle of the equality of the federated entities. Since the Constitution cannot be "suspended either in whole or in part" (Article 187), it does not allow for any possibility of interference by the federal authority in regional or community powers – not even, for example, during war. There is therefore no doctrine of emergency powers. The only exceptional powers ever activated were used during the First World War (i.e., before the advent of the federal system) and concerned only public freedoms.

In some cases, cooperation is pushed to excess. For essentially political reasons, certain aspects falling under the sole purview of special majority legislation have been left to cooperation agreements. For instance, as just noted, an agreement between the federal state, the regions, and the communities defines how Belgium shall be represented before international and supranational organizations, and how the various levels of government will arrive at Belgium's positions within these organizations. Likewise, a cooperation agreement lays out how "mixed" treaties – that is, treaties that deal with matters under the responsibility of more than one level of government – shall be concluded.

RELEVANCE AND FUTURE OF THE DISTRIBUTION OF POWERS

To conclude, we offer a brief evaluation of the distribution of powers in the Belgian federal system by looking at it from four points of view: (1) that of effectiveness, (2) that of financial efficiency, (3) that of administration, and (4) that of its prospects for future stability, in light of the various political positions that are being expressed about it.

Clarity of the System

The Belgian system of division of powers is opaque to the vast majority of citizens – a state of affairs that seems to bother very few. However, it only adds to the confusion that elections for Belgium's federal parliament (every four years) are separate from those for the assemblies of the federated entities (every five years), especially since political parties sometimes campaign on issues that are not directly linked to the areas of responsibility of the assembly for which the election is being held.

Effectiveness of Rules for the Distribution of Power

The distribution of power as it is actually practised seems in general to conform to the legal rules that govern it. This may be due to the relatively recent adoption of the rules (i.e., through sets of reforms since 1970) compared with the more ancient federal constitutions elsewhere.

However, when comparing theory and practice in more detail, certain differences between law and practice can be observed. It is difficult to determine the breadth of these gaps owing to certain delicate controversies about the interpretation of the rules in effect, which hinders definitive measurement. As long as these controversies are not decided in court, the very existence of a gap between law and practice is debatable. Furthermore, certain legal decisions have not affected the doctrine, whereas other anticipated decisions have never occurred (due to the lack of a petitioner with an interest sufficient to make the case admissible).

Leaving aside these points of confusion, certain gaps are undeniable. Some are explained by the rigid procedure for revising the Constitution or by the large quorum required for votes on modifying special majority laws. Political actors thus sometimes lack the patience or the majority required to conform to these procedural requirements. They therefore outpace constitutional change by passing a law of dubious constitutional footing.

But most of the gaps between law and practice have other explanations. They usually stem from the extreme complexity of certain rules for the division of powers (to the point where they are widely unknown among practitioners), from the political impossibility of simplifying them due to lack of a consensus on doing so, and from the necessity of nevertheless agreeing on pragmatic solutions, especially for putting in place and financing certain policies. This is particularly the case with cooperation agreements, with matters in the jurisdiction of the federated entities but where the distinction between community and regional responsibilities is difficult to respect, and with Brussels (where the network of applicable rules and competent organizations forms a morass that is particularly hard to sort out).

Efficiency of the Distribution of Powers on the Financial Level

The extension of regional fiscal autonomy in 2001 partly pursued the laudable goal of making the distribution of powers more coherent and practicable than it had been before. Since then, the same fiscal autonomy applies to all regional taxes: the regions alone have the right to determine their tax base, rates, and exemptions. Further, the entire revenue from all these taxes now goes to the regions. This reform fortunately came with certain safeguards, in particular to avoid incentives for migration for fiscal reasons and to preserve budget neutrality. It is too early to say how much effect can be expected from these mechanisms; instead, we discuss the increasingly fragile revenue of the Brussels-Capital region.

The revenue situation for Brussels is unique for two reasons. First, owing to the density of its building wealth, regional property-based taxes make up more than twice as large a proportion of its total revenue as they do in the other two regions. The proportion made up by income tax on individuals is correspondingly less. However, Brussels has not been sufficiently buffered against the risk of decreasing revenues from the new regional taxes. Further, due to its geography, it is the region most exposed to fiscal competition.

Finally, and most important, it is discriminated against by the application of a common method of financing that does not take its unique characteristics into account.

Bearing in mind that structural underfunding of the French-speaking community was the political impetus for the last two reforms of the system (1993 and 2001), we may anticipate that yet more negotiations and give-and-take will begin when the Brussels-Capital region starts to complain vigorously that it is being fiscally strangled.

As for the reform of regional fiscal autonomy with regard to personal income taxes, it also began by having to clarify the previous system. And, as often happens, this necessary clarification provided the opportunity to go further by increasing regional autonomy. In and of itself, this increase is quite appropriate to the logic of the federal model. But it is first necessary to channel this autonomy with measures to reduce the damaging effects of fiscal competition. And there it becomes clear that the safeguards – the respect for certain margins, the ban on reducing the progressiveness of the tax system, the forbidding of all unfair fiscal competition – suffer from several gaps and deficiencies. It is inevitable that these will also lead to new demands for reform.

Finally, one should comment briefly on the 2001 refinancing of the communities. This was indispensable because of the excesses of the previous federal government, which had left a legacy of structural problems to the French-speaking community (and it alone, due to the merger of community and regional budgets in the north of the country). However, the means to put into practice the fiscal power of the communities, in theory provided by Article 170, Section 2, of the Constitution, has still not been found. Some believe that an act of institutional imagination must still be agreed upon in this area since a political entity without its own fiscal powers, such as the French-speaking community, is structurally weak. For others, this deficiency is quite incurable because the technical and political difficulties that would have to be resolved (given the communities' inability to impose direct obligations on individual citizens of Brussels) seem insurmountable.

Administrative Efficiency of the Distribution of Powers

Each regional and community government has its own administration, institutions, and personnel. It has the responsibility to decide on the organization of its administration and on the status of its personnel, although bound by some general rules established by federal law. It would seem broadly that the federated entities have the administrative means to exercise their powers. Due to a lack of systematic study of this question, however, it is difficult to verify this hypothesis. Yet there are a number of cases in which a federated entity, inheriting responsibilities from the federal government, has lacked the administrative know-how to deal with the newly transferred responsibilities. This was the case, for example, with the Brussels-Capital region's new powers in external commerce.

Politics and the Future of the Distribution of Powers

Has the Belgian federal system achieved a satisfactory equilibrium, or are new changes necessary to the rules on distribution of power between the federal government, the communities, and the regions? It is of course this subject that attracts the liveliest debate. It may be that federal structures are unstable by definition, subject to constant adjustments to resolve conflicts between its members. These conflicts may not be negative but, instead, feed the internal dynamism of all federal political systems. However, there are a great many reasons to suggest that Belgium's case might be different. Its instability runs much deeper and is of a more structural nature than that of other federal systems. This arises from the combination of current political movements and the state of the law.

First of all, it does not appear that the successive reforms of the Belgian federal structure have given certain of its federated entities the degree of autonomy they want. Even though the French-speaking side is essentially satisfied with the autonomy attained and does not want to get involved in a discussion that might put the present broad equilibrium into doubt, the Flemish side is calling for more autonomy. Though the Flemish political parties, on the whole, want more autonomy for their community, some are concentrating on more transfers of powers within the framework of a federal political system, whereas others go so far as to call for "confederalism." The latter term is used non-specifically: it could mean further transfers of power towards the federated entities or an agreement between separate, sovereign states. All these different demands have been the subject of great debates in the Flemish Parliament, ending with the adoption of certain resolutions on 3 March 1999. Since only part of these resolutions was implemented by the most recent reform in 2001, they are still a major issue. The as yet unfulfilled demands deal in particular with interregional financial transfers, which are judged too favourable to the south; further fiscal autonomy for the regions; and sharply increased decentralization of policy on the economy, employment, certain branches of social security, and the railways, among other policy fields.

Besides these demands regarding the distribution of powers, other arguments in the same set of Flemish resolutions depart from the current institutional layout. They favour not a federal Belgium with communities and regions as specified by the Constitution but, rather, a Belgium made up of two federated states, one Flemish and the other francophone, flanked by two entities (Brussels and the German-speaking community) that would be of a different nature. The French-speaking political parties, for their part, have a different vision: while they do call for adjustments and improvements to the system, they do not favour a complete reorganization. Further community tensions are thus certainly on the horizon.

The state of the law also favours instability. Born of difficult compromises, the legal texts that deal with the distribution of powers in Belgium have gaps and unclear parts, which will almost inevitably lead to further debate. Given the disagreement on the overall vision of the political system, the only political logic that can transcend the succession of reforms, crises, and negotiation is that of a steady erosion of federal powers: each partial transfer of responsibilities from the federal government to the communities and regions leads to demands for a larger transfer.

It is therefore particularly difficult to hazard guesses on what Belgium will come to look like in the long term. If one had to guess, current trends suggest that the most probable future for the Belgian state (though not necessarily the most desirable one) would be its transformation into a unique and very lightweight structure, resembling a confederal model more than a federal one. This structure would not be far from reducing the federal government to little more than a passport and a mask, with its own unique system of autonomies (but without cutting the Gordian knot of the status of Brussels) and occupying the single seat that each member state may have in the Council of Ministers of the European Union.

NOTES

1 Going by electoral results, Brussels contains about 85 percent French speakers and 15 percent Flemish speakers.
2 For a general discussion on these community competences see André Alen, "The Competences of the Communities in the Belgian Federal State: The Principle of Exclusivity Revisited," *European Public Law* 3, 2 (April 1997): 165–173.
3 See Article 4 of the Constitution. According to this rule, the boundaries of the linguistic regions cannot be modified except by a law adopted by special majority in the national Parliament (i.e., a majority vote within each linguistic group and an overall two-thirds majority of the total vote).
4 For example, Article 22 ("Everyone has the right to the respect of his or her private and family life, except in the cases and under the conditions established by the law"); Article 146 ("No tribunal or court may be established except by a law").
5 See, among many others, Wouter Pas, "De door de Grondwet aan de 'wet' voorbehouden aangelegenheden: Vroeger en nu," *De vijfde staatshervorming van*

2001, ed. André Alen (Bruges: Die Keure, 2002), pp. 27 to 63; Xavier Delgrange, "Les matières réservées: faut-il choisir entre rationalité et constitutionnalité?" *Les lois spéciales et ordinaires du 13 juillet 2001: La réforme de la Saint-Polycarpe* (Brussels: Bruylant, 2002), pp. 45 to 66. See also the contributions of Marc Uyttendaele and Jean-Claude Scholsem in *Administration Publique*, 2002/ 2–3–4, *Numéro spécial: Saint-Polycarpe, Lombard et Saint-Boniface – une réforme à plusieurs visages*, pp. 153–160 and 161–172, respectively.

6 According to Article 19§1 of the Special Majority Law of 8 August 1980 on Institutional Reform as amended by the Special Majority Law of 13 July 2001, by which the "distributive effect" of these constitutional provisions referring to "the law" is limited to constitutional provisions enacted after the coming into force of the Special Majority Law of 8 August 1980, (i.e., 1 October 1980). Most scholarship, however, holds that this date is not correct as the constitutional reform of 24 December 1970, in creating the communities, brought forth the first new political entities whose standards had the force of law. More fundamentally, there is currently a controversy over whether the theory of matters reserved to the law is based on the Constitution itself or on Article 19 of the special law.

7 Cour d'arbitrage, n°35/2003, 25 March 2003, *Moniteur belge*, 15 April 2003.

8 See Pascal Boucquey, Pierre-Olivier de Broux, Xavier Delgrange, Luc Detroux, Hugues Dumont, Isabelle Hachez, Bruno Lombaert, François Tulkens, and Sébastien Van Drooghenbroeck, "La Cour d'arbitrage et Saint-Polycarpe: Un brevet de constitutionnalité mal motivé," *Journal des Tribunaux* n.v. (2003): pp. 525–528.

9 Certain community responsibilities discussed by Articles 127 to 130 of the Constitution are detailed in Articles 4 and 5 of the Special Majority Law on Institutional Reform of 8 August 1980.

10 These attributions are listed in Articles 6 and 6*bis* of the Special Majority Law on Institutional Reform of 8 August 1980.

11 See Article 6, sect. 1, VIII, 1°, 4°, 5°, of the Special Institutional Reform Law of 8 August 1980. See also Articles 7*bis* and 16*bis* of the same law.

12 Article 6, sect. 1, VI, para. 2, 2°, 2nd para., of the Special Majority Law on Institutional Reform of 8 August 1980.

13 See Article 6, sect. 1, IX, 3° (application of rules concerning the occupation of foreign workers).

14 See Cour d'arbitrage, n°58/95, 12 July 1995, *Moniteur belge*, 31 August 1995, pt. B.8.5.

15 See Cour d'arbitrage, n°42/97, 14 July 1997, *Moniteur belge*, 3 September 1997, pt. B.10.2.

16 Also Cour d'arbitrage, n°49/ See 94, 22 July 1994, Moniteur belge, 6 July 1994. On the issue of federal loyalty in federal theory and practice, see Bertus deVillers, "Intergovernmental Relations: '*Bundestreue*' and the Duty to Cooperate from a German Perspective," SA *Public Law* n.v. (1994): 430–437.

17 Cour d'arbitrage, n°166/2003, 17 December 2003, not yet published in the
   Moniteur belge. Available on the Web at <http://www.arbitrage.be/> (accessed
   1 May 2004).

18 See, among many others, Cour d'arbitrage, n°58/2003, 14 May 2003, *Moniteur
   belge,* 8 October 2003, pt. B.5.3.

19 The Council of State decided in the affirmative on this question (Conseil de
   l'État, 4 April 1986, *Journal des Tribunaux,* 1987, note Yves Lejeune). For discussion of the doctrines related to this question, see among others Johan Vande
   Lanotte and Geert Goedertier, *Overzicht Publiek Recht* (Bruges: Die Keure,
   2001), p. 1031.

20 Cour d'arbitrage, n°17/94, 3 March 1994, *Moniteur belge,* 13 April 1994.

21 Under Article 92*bis,* sect. 1, para. 2, of the Special Majority Law on Institutional
   Reform of 8 August 1980, "cooperation agreements are negotiated and signed
   by the authority with jurisdiction. Agreements dealing with matters ruled by decree, as well as agreements that could burden the community or region or bind
   individual Belgians, come into effect only after being ratified by decree. Agreements dealing with matters governed by law, as well as agreements that could
   burden the State or bind individual Belgians, come into effect only after having
   been ratified by law."

22 See Article 92*bis,* sects. 2, 3, 4, 4*bis,* 4*ter,* 4*quater* of the Special Majority Law on
   Institutional Reform of 8 August 1980.

23 For example, for the regions, revenues from forestry exploitation or the sale of
   hunting permits.

24 See Elisabeth Willemart, *Les limites constitutionnelles du pouvoir fiscal* (Brussels:
   Bruylant, 1999), p. 35

25 In August 1991 the federal government submitted to the legislative section of
   the Council of State a draft bill for a special law modifying the special law of
   16 January 1989 regarding the financing of the communities and regions. The
   intent of the draft bill was to make the French- and Flemish-speaking communities fiscally autonomous. The draft provided for Brussels citizens to pay
   80 percent of French-speaking community taxes and 20 percent of Flemish-
   speaking community taxes, with the revenues from Brussels being divided in
   the same proportion between the two communities. In an opinion handed
   down on 28 August 1991 the Council of State ruled that this would have given
   the community legislatures the power to tax citizens they did not represent and
   was, therefore, incompatible with the principle of consent to taxation enshrined in Article 170 of the Constitution (Avis n° 21.104/2/V of 28 August
   1991, *Documents parlementaires* Chambre, 1990–1991, n° 1767/1).

26 Article 6, sect. 1, VI, para. 5, 12° of the Special Majority Law on Institutional Reform of 8 August 1980.

27 On this question and the various positions on it, see Xavier Delgrange and
   Hugues Dumont, "Bruxelles et l'Hypothèse de la défédéralisation de la sécurité
   sociale," *Autonomie, solidarité et coopération: Quelques enjeux du fédéralisme belge au*

XXIème siècle (Brussels: Larcier, 2002), pp. 235 et seq., and, from the same collection, Jan Velaers, "Brussel en de hypothese van de defederalisering van de sociale zekerheid," pp. 267 et seq.

28 See Xavier Delgrange, "La Cour d'arbitrage momifie la compétence fédérale en matière de sécurité sociale," *Revue belge de droit constitutionnel*, 2001: 216 et seq.

29 Cour d'arbitrage, n°33/2001, 13 March 2001, *Moniteur belge*, 27 March 2001.

30 Article 9 of the 12 January 1989 special law on Brussels institutions provides, in essence, that the judicial courts and tribunals and the Council of State may ensure the compliance of Brussels ordinances with the special law itself as well as with constitutional dispositions whose oversight would not yet have been handed over to the constitutional court.

31 See Article 45 of the 12 January 1989 special law on Brussels institutions, which puts the international role of Brussels and its function as capital under this kind of federal control. The federal government may intervene in public works, transportation, urban planning, and land use. In the case of a dispute between the region and the federal authority, the House of Representatives will decide by a majority of the two linguistic groups. This makes the use of this control rather improbable.

32 The German-speaking community has no powers in language policy except with regard to education.

33 This includes the members of the Council of the Brussels-Capital region who are from the French linguistic group.

34 Three decrees are all that is needed: one adopted by a two-thirds majority by the French-speaking community and two others adopted by a simple majority by the Walloon region and the French-speaking community commission.

35 See Article 99, Section 2, of the Constitution: "With the possible exception of the Prime Minister, the Council of Ministers includes as many French-speaking members as Dutch-speaking members."

36 See also Robert Senelle, "The Role of the Communities and the Regions in the Making of Belgian Foreign Policy," *European Public Law* 5, 4 (December 1999): 601–618.

37 Organic cooperation involves the presence of authorities representing different political entities (state, communities, or regions) within a single government body.

38 When the matter in question falls primarily under the responsibility of the regions and communities, the federal authority steps aside to allow one of the regions or communities to represent Belgium. A cooperation agreement sets out the procedures for this substitution as well as for information exchange, the creation of a permanent structure for collaboration, and rules for the composition of delegations.

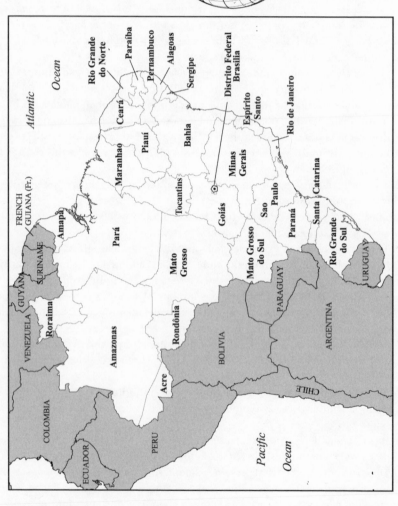

Brazil

Capital: Brasilia
Population: 178 Million
(2004 est.)

Brasilia, the Capital, is situated
within the Distrito Federal.

Boundaries and place names are
representative only and do not
imply official endorsement.

N

500

0

500

Kilometers

Sources: ESRI Ltd.; CIA World Factbook;
Times Atlas of the World

Atlantic

Ocean

Rio Grande
do Norte

Paraíba

Pernambuco

Alagoas

Sergipe

Distrito Federal
Brasilia

Espírito
Santo

Rio de Janeiro

Ceará

Piauí

Bahia

Minas
Gerais

Maranhão

Tocantins

São
Paulo

Santa Catarina

Goiás

Paraná

Rio Grande
do Sul

URUGUAY

Pará

Mato Grosso
do Sul

PARAGUAY

ARGENTINA

Amapá

FRENCH
GUIANA (Fr.)

SURINAME

GUYANA

VENEZUELA

Roraima

Mato
Grosso

Rondônia

BOLIVIA

CHILE

Amazonas

Acre

COLOMBIA

PERU

ECUADOR

Pacific

Ocean

The Federal Republic of Brazil

MARCELO PIANCASTELLI

This chapter provides an overview of the distribution of powers and responsibilities in Brazil's federal Constitution, tracing its historical development and describing how it works in practice. Brazil has a vast territory and a complex federal system. Its economy, in terms of gross domestic product (GDP) in U.S. dollars, is among the ten largest in the world. Attempts to implement a federal form of government can be traced back to 1831. It was in 1891 that the first republican federal constitution was promulgated. The present Constitution has been in operation since 1988, when democracy was re-established. It demonstrates a clear trend to decentralization, intended to bring power closer to the people. Moreover, the 1988 Constitution has been in constant evolution through legislation known as complementary laws. The objectives of the Constitution are to consolidate democracy, to implement decentralization, and to improve social conditions. Meanwhile, the country has been trying to achieve economic stability while struggling against social inequalities and regional disparities. Constitutional rules have been changing over time, to a great extent in order to adapt to the new economic context. Republican federalism as a form of government organization, however, has shown remarkable stability.

THE FEDERAL CONSTITUTION
IN HISTORICAL-CULTURAL CONTEXT

Territorial and Demographic Background

Brazil occupies 47.7 percent of the South American continent, covering a total of 8,511,965 square kilometres. It has the fifth largest territory in the world, after Russia, Canada, China, and the United States. According to the latest estimated demographic figures, Brazil's population totalled

174.7 million in 2002. Annual population growth has been falling steadily from 2.48 percent in 1970 to 1.32 percent in 2002. Its workforce stood at 83.2 million in 2001. The Brazilian federation consists of twenty-six states plus the federal district. The states are grouped into five major regions: North, North-East, Centre-West, South-East, and South.[1] The population is mainly concentrated in the southeast, northeast and south regions. The capital, Brasília, with a population of 2.05 million, is located in the central plateau. The largest cities are São Paulo (10.4 million), Rio de Janeiro (5.8 million), Salvador (2.4 million), and Belo Horizonte (2.2 million). The rural population, which in 1940 accounted for 69 percent of the total population, had fallen to 21 percent in 2000.

Economic and Social Context

The Brazilian economy (GDP) grew at an annual average rate of 9.32 percent in the 1970s. Job creation did not, however, keep pace and was insufficient to absorb the growing workforce. Economic growth was limited to capital-intensive sectors such as mining, heavy industry, and import-substitution industries. Employment expanded most in the services sector, however. In the mid-1970s public spending focused mainly on the basic industrial and energy sectors, with giant state-owned corporations being set up in key sectors. To finance this drive, the government relied on foreign capital. However, international market conditions towards the end of the decade led to the collapse of this growth pattern. This collapse triggered an external credit squeeze and debt crisis, with consequent difficulties in financing the public sector in the decades of the 1980s and the 1990s. As a result, annual inflation leapt to three-digit figures.

The 1980s marked the longest period of economic stagnation in Brazil's history. According to the Central Bank of Brazil, annual GDP growth averaged 2.3 percent whereas per capita GDP fell by 2.7 percent. By the end of the decade the fiscal deficit had soared to almost 7 percent of GDP. The government proved unable to perform its basic social responsibilities, failing to guarantee the investment required for maintenance of GDP growth rates. Growing concerns regarding political instability led to the election of a national constitutional assembly with the aim of writing a new constitution. The political scene began to change in the early 1990s, clearing the way for the implementation of a new pattern of distribution of powers, according to the new Constitution, and for monetary reform and an economic stabilization policy introduced in 1994, known as the "Real Plan."

There has been a great drive to promote growth and to improve the social conditions of the country. It should be noted, however, that improvement in certain social indicators (such as life expectancy, infant mortality rate, adult literacy rate, secondary school net enrolments, and public spending in education and health) do not reflect the often glaring differences encountered from one region to another in Brazil. The country's Human Development Index (HDI)[2] formulated by the United Nations Development Program (UNDP) in 2000, is 0.766 for the year 2000. If the same criteria are applied to Brazil's regions separately, the HDI for the South is 0.807, South-East 0.791, Centre-West 0.800, North 0.725, and North-East 0.675, which reveals wide interregional disparities.

Government Structure

Brazil has a presidential system of government. The president and vice-president are elected by direct ballot for a four-year term in office. They are presently assisted by thirty-six ministers of state, all directly appointed by the president. Together they make up the executive branch of the federal government. State governors and municipal mayors are also elected by direct vote.

The legislative branch consists of the bicameral National Congress, in which the lower house, the Federal Chamber of Deputies, represents the population as a whole, and the upper house, the Federal Senate, represents the states and has among its specific duties the supervision of federal financial matters. The eighty-one senators in the Federal Senate are elected by majority vote (three per state) and serve a term of eight years. Two-thirds of the members of the Federal Senate are renewed at the end of eight years and one-third four years later, at the end of their eight-year terms.

The Chamber of Deputies has 513 members elected for a four-year term by an open list proportional representation system for each state and the Federal District. The highest court in the judicial branch is the Federal Supreme Court, whose brief is to safeguard the federal Constitution. The Court is composed of eleven judges appointed by the President of the Republic and submitted to the Federal Senate for approval.

The states' government structure is similar to that of the federal government. It is comprised of an executive branch, a state assembly, and the judicial branch. The state legislature's size in terms of number of deputies is, in general, triple the state's representation in the Federal Chamber of Deputies. If this number exceeds thirty-six, then a state's local representation is increased by the number of the state's representation in the Federal Chamber of Deputies, minus twelve, as dictated by Article 27 of the federal Constitution. According to Article 11 of the federal Constitution, each state also has its own constitution. Municipal government structure differs from that of the federal and state governments insofar as it does not have its own judicial branch. The legislative branch of municipal government is in charge of writing so-called "organic municipal law" (OML), which embodies local administration government plans and passes annual budget laws.

A particular feature of Brazil's Constitution is the special role of municipalities as they have acquired full political autonomy, independent of the federal and state governments (discussed more fully below). Municipal citizens are able to elect their own mayors and vice-mayors as well as representatives in local municipal chambers.

Present Constitution

The process of federation started in 1831. The current Constitution, however, was promulgated in 1988 by a national constitutional assembly (drawn from both houses of Congress) elected for this particular task. It is based on a civil law tradition, as it explicitly grants the private rights of citizens. Common law (unwritten law developed from old customs) does not play a predominant role. The 1988 Constitution was approved by two rounds of roll-call voting in the National Congress.

The drafters of the federal Constitution aimed to achieve a decentralized organization, seeking to bring people closer to government in order to enhance the consolidation of the democratic process in the country. There is no indication that the Constitution was influenced by any kind of foreign interference or that any type of specific pressure moulded the distribution and sharing of powers. In fact, all orders of government are considered autonomous (Article 18), and any change to the original division of the country into states or municipalities is only possible if authorized by a public vote on the part of the populations who are directly affected. The creation, division, or merging of any state has to be approved by a complementary law (CL) passed by Congress, requiring a two-thirds majority vote in both houses. On the other hand, the creation, division, or merging of any municipality requires a state law and depends on a referendum of the population in areas directly involved.

It is difficult to assert that the drafters of the federal Constitution followed a particular political theory or a philosophical, cultural, or political economy outlook. Article 1 of the Constitution asserts that the federation is formed by a permanent linkage between the federal government, states, and municipalities, with the aim of preserving sovereignty, citizenship, the dignity of human beings, the social value of labour and of private business, and political plurality. Article 2 states that the fundamental objective of the federal republic is to build a free, just, and united society and to guarantee national development, eradicate poverty, and reduce social and regional inequalities. Nonetheless, it is apparent that, besides its main goal of legitimizing democracy, the present Constitution is guided towards achieving new goals such as improving the social conditions of the country and adjusting to a new economic reality, which means adapting to a new pattern of fiscal discipline.

The autonomy of the municipalities marks a major change in the political scene. Interventions by higher orders of government (the federal government on the states and municipalities, and the states on the municipalities) are only allowed under the strict conditions established by Articles 34 and 35 of the Constitution. In such cases interventions have to be required by the legislative branch of government or by a court. Most common is a request for intervention when a state or a municipal administration has not complied with provisions for the payment of the public debt. By the same token, removal of mayors or local officials, either by the federal or state governments, is also restricted to cases explicitly stated in the above mentioned Articles. Moreover, municipalities are now empowered to take decisions in most important areas, such as territorial management, land development, environment, local taxation issues, and industrialization.

Finally, Portuguese is the predominant language, despite Brazil's being a multiracial and multicultural society. Roman Catholicism is the most widely practised religion, although Article 5, items VI and VIII, of the Constitution assures the right of any individual to profess any other religion. In fact, there is a tendency for a decline in adherents to the major religious denominations in favour of smaller and local religious associations. Ultimately, all federal units (the union, states, municipalities, and the Federal District) are strictly forbidden from establishing any specific religious preference. Likewise, no distinction between races and racial groups among Brazilian citizens is permitted.

CONSTITUTIONAL DISTRIBUTION OF POWERS AND RESPONSIBILITIES

With the exception of the 1988 Constitution, the federal pattern laid down by previous constitutions makes it impossible to characterize Brazilian federalism by a single label with regard to the distribution of powers and responsibilities. Likewise, history reveals that the shape of Brazilian federalism has been neither one of consistent centralization nor one of consistent decentralization. It has always been adjusted according to political and economic circumstances. Since the first attempt to implement a federal organization in Brazil in 1831, there have been tensions between the different orders of government. Thus the constitutional process of the Brazilian federation has hardly been systematic. Under the terms of the 1988 Constitution, however, Brazilian federalism can best be described as "cooperative" or "collusive," depending upon the issue under discussion. Although decentralization as an issue has been the overriding imperative, controversies remain when fiscal and financial matters are considered. Recent measures, such as the restructuring of the financial debt of states and municipalities and consequential fiscal adjustment, have apparently given rise to a new trend towards centralization in the federal government. This is, however, a wide open issue in present federal relations in Brazil.

Nonetheless it is important to stress that the path of Brazilian history clearly reveals that centralization and decentralization trends have alternated over time. In the main, political and economic circumstances have determined the direction of events and, therefore, the profile of the distribution of responsibilities and powers.

Evolution of Power Shifts in the Federation

After the Emperor's abdication in 1831 the first Constitution was promulgated in 1834, with an emphasis on decentralization. Local assemblies were created, with new powers being assigned to the provinces (states were introduced after the 1891 Constitution). A revenue-sharing system was introduced as well as a local judicial system; local councils were established to rule on local issues; and a national guard was created. The dissatisfaction of the provinces with the provisions of the revenue-sharing system and local political ambitions gave rise, however, to a difficult period in which four regional rebellions emerged: Cabanada in the State of Pará (1835–40), Balaiada in the State of Maranhão (1838–41), Sabinada in the State of Bahia (1837–38), and the Farrapos War in the southern state of Rio Grande do Sul (1835–40). Thus, the first attempt at federalizing resulted in a fractured political system, and a new conservative constitution was promulgated in 1841, which tended towards centralization. The pattern of the distribution of powers was reversed, the role of local assemblies reduced, and a new federal judicial system and police force were introduced. The centre of power was brought back to Rio de Janeiro, the country's capital at the time.

The next attempt to implement federalism during the Imperial period (1841–89) took place in the 1870s. A budgetary dispute between the civilian chief of Cabinet and the army resulted in the fall of the Cabinet and in the publication of the 1870 *Republican Manifesto*. Later on, in 1885, a republican bill proposing new federal rules was submitted to the imperial Cabinet, but it was not approved. A few years later, in 1889, when a new dispute between the army and the National Assembly over military funding was not resolved satisfactorily, an internal crisis emerged within the imperial government. The outcome of this crisis was the abolition of the imperial system of government and the proclamation of Brazil as a federal republic on 15 November 1889.

The immediate challenge to the new republican federal government was to form a national congress when most of the representatives were still sympathetic to the monarchy. Republicans had little popular political appeal, and the National Assembly remained in the hands of the monarchists. The republicans adopted a strategy to curb the power of monarchists, and this involved the creation of the Federal Supreme Court by the Constitution of 1891. A constitutional amendment was introduced, and from then on the Federal Supreme Court has had the power to veto any law passed by the National Congress or by local assemblies – either from the states or by local councils – that contravene the federal Constitution. Thus, judicial control of the constitutionality of laws in Brazil was created by a republican need to eradicate political memories of the empire.

In the early years of the republican era, however, the strong presidential power was reinforced against the increasing influence of state "presidents," not yet known as governors. In this period Brazil witnessed a latent conflict between the federal government and the states and municipalities, and this remained the case until 1930. Interventions by the federal government and confrontations among states and among municipalities were common.

During the 1930s the rationale behind the political system and the distribution of responsibilities and power became clear: to reduce the power and responsibilities of the states. The 1934 Constitution introduced important new elements. The "presidents of the states" became simply "governors," and two fundamental elements of their power were removed. First, they lost control of their military police. They now had to submit the men and equipment they had to the control of the National Army. Second, the 1934 Constitution established a new degree of autonomy for the municipalities as a means of offsetting the power of the state governors. Governors also lost control over the mayors of local communities. Interference by the state governors in any municipal issue could now give rise to intervention in the state government by the federal government. Whenever the opposition won local elections, they could count on the protection of the president of the republic.

The development of federalism, therefore, suffered various setbacks. In the 1930s the tendency for centralization became clear and was confirmed by the dictatorial rule imposed in 1937. In 1945, after the Second World War, calls from the international community and from the Brazilian political establishment for a liberal democracy became frequent. Free elections, then, were held in 1946 and a new Constitution promulgated. The 1946 Constitution opened the door to some modest decentralization. First, a revenue-sharing scheme was again introduced in order to address the vertical imbalance. Second, specific steps towards decentralization were introduced by the new Constitution. The equilibrium between both houses in Congress, the upper house (the Federal Senate) and the lower house (the Federal Chamber of Deputies) was ruptured. According to the new rules, the Senate assumed added responsibilities, such as looking after the interests of the states, ratifying certain appointments to key positions in the executive branch of government, and deciding on financial matters (credit operations) relative to states and municipalities. This meant that the Senate could approve legislation related to financial issues of interest to states and municipalities without interference from the Federal Chamber of Deputies. On the other hand, due to changes in the internal rules of Congress, bills not related to financial issues of the states and municipalities could be approved by the Federal Chamber of Deputies and promulgated by the president without necessarily being approved by the Senate.

These new legislative procedures had clear repercussions for decentralization. First, because of the structure of the Federal Senate, with eighty-one members (three from each state), the upper chamber began taking a more cautious approach when dealing with federal government issues and started defending the interests of the states. Furthermore, whenever constitutional issues emerged relating to a federal law allegedly interfering in the states' and municipalities' jurisdiction, the Federal Supreme Court was called on to have the final say. As such, the Federal Supreme Court held the last word on constitutional interpretation.

Under the new dictatorial military rule following the 1964 military coup, no new constitution was immediately issued. However, there was a massive centralization of power and responsibilities in the hands of the federal government as tax reform and a new revenue-sharing system were introduced. The Constitution of 1967, with the amendments introduced in 1969, provided a legal structure to the new pattern and boosted the centralization of political power and responsibilities, including public finance. Complementary Act no. 40 of 1968 allocated 88 percent of personal and corporate income tax (IR) and the selective value-added tax on industrialized products (IPI) to the central government. At the same time, participation (i.e., revenue-sharing) funds were created: the Participation Fund for the States (FPE) and the Participation Fund for the Municipalities (FPM). Each received 5 percent of the total tax revenue from both IR and IPI taxes.

The budgetary rules and the tax reforms introduced by the 1967–69 Constitution were an attempt to implement a new pattern for distributing powers and responsibilities. Efforts to foster economic development were carried out by a kind of "cooperative federalism" and gave rise to fiscal "asymmetries" that characterize the Brazilian federal system today. Fiscal asymmetry is understood as the unbalanced redistribution of financial resources (through the revenue-sharing system) towards the least developed states (i.e., those from the North and North-East regions). On the other hand, "cooperative federalism" was implemented for all states through the investment programs established by the federal government. These were aimed at fostering investment in economic infrastructure such as transportation, telecommunications, and energy in order to support industrialization. Funding for such activities was raised by specifically linking contributions on fuel, electricity, and telecommunications, which were shared by federal agencies, states, and municipalities.

Thus, the "cooperative federalist model," as conceived by the 1967 Constitution, was based on three elements: participation (revenue-sharing) funds, budgetary allowances from the central government directed towards investment in infrastructure, and the cooperative efforts of states and municipal governments (which operated through fiscal incentives) geared towards implementing industrial investments. The system worked relatively well throughout the 1970s, and some degree of convergence of per capita income levels was achieved among the different regions of the country.[3]

As has been the case throughout Brazil's constitutional history, tensions between the different orders of government have persisted, and what occurred after the 1988 constitutional reform has been no exception. These tensions became more evident as the municipalities were granted full autonomy by the new Constitution. The drafters, mainly from opposition parties, emphasized a decentralization process with the major aim of bringing power closer to the people in the ultimate hope of enhancing democratic institutions.

Since the 1988 Constitution, federalism in Brazil has adopted a more visibly "cooperative" pattern, especially in areas such as health, education, social welfare, law and order, and social security. However, federalism in Brazil can now also be seen as "collusive" whenever there emerges an issue of national interest such as balanced development and national welfare. On such occasions the federal government usually exercises its clout in order to convince Congress of the need for emergency legislative approval. The drift of power towards the federal government in such cases has included issues of extreme importance to the economic stabilization programs. The various attempts to implement stabilization programs since 1986 are good examples of both cooperative and collusive federalism as, at some stage, all of them were approved by Congress.

Finally, one may note that Brazilian "competitive" federalism emerged in the early 1990s as a consequence of the vertical redistribution of resources – the new revenue-sharing system introduced by the 1988 Constitution.[4] States and municipalities benefited from the substantial increase in intergovernmental transfers. However, most of the new financial resources, which were supposedly aimed at improving social conditions and reducing regional inequalities, were now directed towards stimulating new investment so as to generate income and employment. Competition between states and municipalities developed with the aim of securing comparative advantage for new investment projects, especially in the industrial sector. The conspicuous face of competitive federalism, the so-called "fiscal war," was a complex bidding process for investments from abroad and/or from neighbouring states. Generally, states and municipalities offered to finance infrastructure costs and to provide tax holidays without proper cost-benefit appraisals.

Responsibilities and Powers in the 1988 Constitution

The 1988 Constitution, in Chapter II of Title III (Articles 20, 21, and 22), assigns the areas that are the exclusive property of the federal government (Article 20), areas of exclusive operational responsibilities and powers of the federal government (Article 21), and areas in which only the federal government is entitled to legislate (Article 22).

Properties of the federal government include all the existing physical assets, such as federal buildings, unexploited land, lakes, rivers in borders between states and foreign countries, islands in rivers and the territorial sea, potential hydroelectricity sites, mineral resources, and caves and land occupied by the Indian (Aboriginal) communities.

The federal government has exclusive power over, and operational responsibility for, declaring war, running foreign affairs, ensuring national defence, administering foreign monetary reserves, supervising financial operations and exchange rate policy, elaborating regional development plans, maintaining the postal service, exploiting natural resources (either directly or through concessions), telecommunications, radio services, electricity services, aviation, railways, and maritime and interstate highway services.

Areas in which only the federal government is entitled to legislate include civil rights, penal, electoral, agrarian, maritime, space and labour relations matters, water, energy, telecommunications, postal service, credit, foreign exchange policy, insurance, foreign trade, transportation policy, citizenship, emigration and immigration, judicial organization, federal police, social security, education guidelines, public notary, nuclear activities of any kind, and general rules for government procurement.

Article 23 defines the areas of operational joint responsibility of the federal, state, and municipal governments, such as preservation of the Constitution, laws, democratic institutions, and public assets; health and protection and guarantees of the handicapped; protection of historical documents and assets of historical, cultural, and artistic value; provision of access to education, culture, and science; environment and pollution control; preservation of fauna and forests; fostering agrarian production and organizing food supply; housing; sewage services; poverty reduction; exploitation of natural resources; and traffic control. The terms and conditions of these areas of concurrent jurisdiction must be set by complementary laws approved by Congress (Article 23, para. 1°).

Article 24 specifies the areas in which the federal government, the states, and the Federal District are entitled to legislate concurrently, such as taxation, finance, the penal system, the economy and urbanism, budgeting, costs of the judicial system, production and consumption, forestry, hunting, fishing, environment, education, social security, health and public health, the handicapped, protection of children, and civil police. However, the federal government is in charge of general (or framework) rules (Article 24, para. 1°). Whenever federal legislation does not yet exist, legislation of the states and municipalities prevails (Article 24, para. 2°), but federal legislation would prevail in the case of conflict with state or municipal laws (Article 24, para. 4°).

States and Municipalities

Chapter III, Articles 25 through 28, deals with the powers and responsibilities of the states. Article 25, para. 1°, explicitly says that states' powers and responsibilities are those not explicitly prohibited by the federal Constitution (i.e., a reserve of powers). However, as has been seen above, complementary laws passed by Congress can enable mechanisms for joint responsibilities between the federal government, states, and municipalities, especially in social policy areas. As well, Articles 26, 27, and 28 determine how the administration of the states should be organized, including electoral rules and mechanisms defining salary rules for governors, vice-governors, and elected representatives in local assemblies.

Chapters IV and V, Articles 29 through 32, define the powers and responsibilities of the municipalities. As for the states, rules for the administrative organization of the municipalities are explicitly expressed, and Article 30 establishes the following responsibilities of municipalities: to legislate on issues of local interest; to supplement federal and state legislation whenever necessary; to collect local taxes established by the Constitution (mainly property taxes, taxes on services, and duties on water, sewage, and waste collection); to rule on concessions for public services; to maintain technical and financial cooperation with the federal and state governments in programs of primary and secondary education; to maintain technical and financial cooperation with the federal and state governments in programs of health; and to regulate land use and the preservation of historical, artistic, and ecological sites.

Taxation: Responsibilities and Powers

Taxation autonomy is one of the key issues in the federal Constitution of Brazil. The National Taxation System (STN), defined in Title VI, Chapter I, Articles 145 through 156, details the powers and taxation responsibilities of each order of government. The federal government, the states, the municipalities, and the Federal District can use the following revenue instruments: (1) taxes; (2) fees, by virtue of the exercise of police power or for the effective or potential use of specific and divisible public services, rendered or made available to the taxpayer; and (3) benefit charges, resulting from public works. Benefit charges cannot use the same fiscal base as do taxes. A complementary law approved by two-thirds of Congress is required to resolve any tax conflict among the units of the federation. Such a law can impose compulsory loans under specific conditions, such as war or imminent danger to the nation.

The federal government may also apply special "Contribution" levies, usually on payroll or business turnovers. Originally temporary measures, these are now a permanent feature and are the main source of financing for the federally run social security system. Their main characteristic is that they are not shared with states and municipalities. They cannot be applied either to exports or to the commercialization of oil or its byproducts. However, an exception to that rule was approved by the latest attempt at tax reform, in 2003, when a contribution on liquid fuel began to be shared by the three orders of government (i.e., the Contribution for Intervention in the Economic Dominion, the so-called CIDE). The incidence of the special levy can be either in "ad valorem" terms or as a percentage of unit value.

More generally, the federal government has the power and the responsibility to impose the following taxes: (1) importation of foreign products (customs duties and tariffs) (II); (2) exportation to other countries of national or nationalized products (IE); (3) income and earnings of any nature (IR); (4) a selective value-added tax on industrialized products (IPI); (5) credit, foreign exchange, and insurance transactions, or transactions relating to bonds and securities (IOF); and (6) rural property (ITR), under the terms of a specific Complementary Law. Additional forms of taxation may occur. In the case of gold, when considered a financial asset, IOF is incurred. The proceeds of "IOF gold" are shared with the states (30 percent) and the municipalities (60 percent).

The states have only three types of taxes. The first is a tax on transactions relating to the circulation of goods and to the rendering of interstate and intermunicipal transportation services and services of communication, even when such transactions and rendering begin abroad (ICMS). The ICMS is the most productive tax and the most nationally lucrative. The second is transfer by death and/or donation of any property or rights (ITCD). The third is tax on the ownership of automotive vehicles (IPVA). As noted, the Federal Senate is responsible for supervising and representing the interests of the states on any taxation issue.

The municipalities have the power to impose three taxes: (1) on urban buildings and urban land property (IPTU); (2) on *inter vivos* transfer (ITBI), on any account, by onerous act, on real property, by nature or physical accession, and on real rights to property (except for real security) as well as on the assignment of rights to the purchase thereof; and (3) on services of any nature not included in Article 155, II (related to the ICMS, as explicated above), as defined in a complementary law (ISS).

Public Expenditure and Borrowing: Responsibilities and Powers

The borrowing, taxation, and spending powers of each order of government was regulated recently by Complementary Law (CL) 101/2000, entitled the Fiscal Responsibility Act (LRF). It has been a major breakthrough in Brazilian public finance because it establishes general rules for financial administration by each order of government. In fact, Complementary Law 101/2000 implemented the constitutional stipulation, expressed in Article 165, Paragraph 9°, that rules for the financial management of both direct and indirect administration (state-owned companies, foundations, and other government institutions) should be regulated by complementary laws. The LRF deals with public finances, internal and external financial debt, concession of guarantees by any government entity, issuance and payment of any government bond, control of government-owned financial institutions (especially government-owned banks), foreign exchange operations, and control of financial institutions devoted to regional development. The LRF has also imposed limits on government spending (particularly relating to payrolls) and on public debt, and it has set a number of control parameters for public finances. In a sense, the LRF could be understood as a movement towards centralization. However, such legislation has been passed as a major guideline for all orders of government and has been required by Article 165 of the Constitution. Since the objective of the new constitutional provisions was to enforce coherent fiscal behaviour and discipline and, thus, contribute to the harmonization of fiscal policy in the country as a whole, it would not be appropriate to see it as centralization as such.

Further Political Aspects of the Distribution of Responsibilities and Powers

Implementation of the present constitutional rules still requires, in certain important political areas, specific complementary laws. For instance, in terms of the federal structure of government, Article 23 explicitly states that complementary law will rule on cooperation between the federal government, states, and municipalities regarding balanced development and national welfare. Balanced development and national welfare must be understood as policy efforts and institutional mechanisms aiming to reduce regional and social inequalities. However, given the complexity of intergovernmental relations among the twenty-six states and the Federal District, existing regional disparities, and a fractured party system, it has not yet been possible to devise a project for a complementary law on this topic to be submitted to Congress. This would require a great deal of political and financial negotiation. In other words, implementation of the constitutional rules promulgated in 1988 is an ongoing process in areas such as health, education, social welfare, social security, and, more recently, law and order, but it has yet to begin in the more politically sensitive areas of balanced development.

As Celina Souza points out, "Brazil has had difficulties in maintaining a stable federal democracy able to prevent periods of authoritarian rule, reduce social and regional inequality and poverty, and reconcile social democracy with the constraints of the world economy."[5] The main problem is the difficulty that governments face in changing policy priorities when they encounter economic constraints that were unforeseen by the makers of the Constitution. There is, in fact, a gap between constitutional governance and political and economic circumstances, with the latter prevailing over constitutional mandates.

THE RATIONALE BEHIND THE CONSTITUTIONAL DISTRIBUTION OF POWERS AND RESPONSIBILITIES

As noted, the distribution of powers and responsibilities in Brazil's Constitution do not follow a particular philosophical, cultural, or economic theory. The Constitution's ultimate aims are to build a free society, guarantee national development, reduce poverty and regional inequalities, and promote well-being without discrimination on the basis of colour, race, sex, or religion. The historical context for establishing a new, free, democratic constitution after twenty-four years of military rule has determined the nature of this document: the implementation of a process of gradual change in Brazilian society within a stable democratic environment. Combining a decentralization process with political stability and economic progress has been politically complex and economically costly. In this context, the redistribution of responsibilities and powers reflects pragmatic responses to particular issues.

Many of the powers and responsibilities held by the federal government can be seen as the minimum requirement for overall governance. Some responsibilities aim to secure national sovereignty (e.g., national defence, declaration of war, issuance of money, control of foreign reserves, naturalization, and national and regional development plans). Governments must also have the right to use their power to establish law and order and to secure access of citizens to basic services (e.g., education, health, and housing).

In terms of the overall political and administrative structure of government, the Constitution introduced a symmetrical distribution of responsibilities and powers. Symmetry, in this context, is understood as the harmonious and balanced correspondence of the distribution of powers among the orders of government. Each order has its independent branches of government (executive, legislative, and judiciary), and one order of government can only intervene in the area of another in strict accordance with prescribed constitutional rules. However, from an economic and social viewpoint, in practice the Constitution does not produce symmetry. The federal Constitution embodies the explicit presumption that, as long as it is implemented, it will address endemic social and regional inequalities. The emphasis on social aspects is unequivocal; yet Brazil is far from being a modern welfare-state. The distribution of powers and responsibilities has limited the powers of the federal government to the provision of guidelines for the majority of social policies and services; the states and (mainly) the municipalities are responsible for their implementation. Primary and secondary education, health care, care of the elderly, and child-care are all state and municipal responsibilities. In a sense, however, they are shared responsibilities as the federal government remains a major provider of funds and dictates general rules. Nevertheless, there is an ongoing process of "trial and error." Financial constraints, the absence of previous successful experience, geography, and lack of managerial expertise all hamper the task.

The basic mechanism employed to redress economic asymmetry is the revenue-sharing system of the States Participation Fund (FPE) and the Municipalities Participation Fund (FPM). These funds are deliberately tilted to favour the poorest regions: the North and North-East. This bias reflects the principle that governments generally have a positive social welfare obligation regardless of whether they are federal, state, or municipal. Notwithstanding the social emphasis, the system exhibits a major flaw as it has not linked the transfer of funds to specific social or economic targets. Therefore, the welfare objective has not yet been fully implemented.

In addition to the revenue-sharing system, and as an attempt to remedy the growing concern with social conditions, constitutional rules relating to social sectors such as health, education, social welfare, social security, and law and order have received special priority. A substantial amount of complementary regulatory legislation has already been passed by Congress, but the implementation of the Constitution is not complete in this respect. Many areas (e.g., sanitation, water supply, environment, metropolis management, and land development) have yet to be subjected to complementary legislation. Undoubtedly, the evolutionary process has been positive; yet it remains affected by the constraints of the country's public finances and the complex multiparty political system. These are difficulties of a federal system in which substantial regional economic and social disparities still prevail.

EVOLUTION OF THE CONSTITUTIONAL DISTRIBUTION OF POWERS AND RESPONSIBILITIES

The Brazilian constitution has shown a remarkable degree of flexibility. The constitutional amendment process is regulated by Article 60. Proposals for amendments can be submitted by the president of the republic, by a minimum of one-third of the members of Congress (Federal Chamber of Deputies and Federal Senate), or by half of the state assemblies, each one having previously approved the proposal by a majority of its members. A constitutional amendment has to be twice voted on by both houses of Congress. Its approval requires three-fifths of the votes in each house. Proposals for constitutional amendments aimed at abolishing the federal organization of the state, the secret direct ballot, the separation of powers (executive, legislative, and judiciary), and individual rights and guarantees are prohibited.

There is also a provision for the direct role of the people in changing the Constitution. Article 61, para. 2°, states that any popular proposal can be submitted to the Chamber of Deputies when signed by a minimum of 1 percent of voters, distributed in a minimum of five states, and signed by a minimum of 0.3 percent of the voters in each.

The provision for a formal constitutional review was established when the Constitution was enacted in 1988. Article 3 of the transitory provisions stated that, after five years, a formal review procedure would be set up by Congress. As a result, six constitutional amendments were approved in 1994. The most important amendment was the creation of the Social Emergency Fund, which reduced the constitutionally mandated transfers to the states and municipalities in order to allocate additional financial resources in 1994 and 1995 to health, education, social welfare, social security, and other governmental programs considered to be of social relevance. Apart from this and according to the provision of Article 60 mentioned above, forty-two constitutional amendments were approved from 1992 to 2002. Of the forty-two amendments most were more important in terms of procedural or textual adjustments than in terms of substance. In some cases the amendments dealt with short-term economic and financial matters, but two important amendments were related to concessions for public services and to the installation of natural gas infrastructure.

With respect to the distribution of powers and responsibilities, Amendment 31/2000 has been the most important. It created the Fund for the Reduction of Poverty under which the states and municipalities are required to create a similar fund in order to receive federal funds destined for the same social welfare program. Otherwise, the most significant changes in the constitutional distribution of powers and responsibilities have come as a result of demands for improving the social conditions of the population. Constitutional provisions related to such areas as health, education, social welfare, social security, and (later) law and order have occurred mainly through complementary laws, which require a qualified majority (two-thirds) of votes in both houses of Congress. In the case of health care and primary education, it is not only complementary laws that have been issued but also constitutional amendments for each of these services, earmarking federal, state, and municipal revenues. However, complementary laws can be considered as essentially a constitutional mechanism for implementing the actual distribution of powers and responsibilities. The evolution of such a process has been of substantial significance and has started a gradual change in the country's social policies.

Following a general propensity in favour of decentralization, the 1988 Constitution introduced important provisions that added health services to the new responsibilities of the municipalities. As the municipalities have always been the major provider of health care, a concurrent responsibility emerged (Article 23, item II) under which the power of the federal government was limited to the issuing of general rules. As a result, a new system of revenue sharing was created for the health sector. This was clearly expressed, in terms of decentralization, in Article 198, I, and in terms of the participation of municipalities in Article 198, item III, forming the embryo of a Unified System of Health – the so-called SUS. After the passage of the Organic Law of Health (Law 8080, 1990), it took three years to spell out a clear strategy for the decentralization process. The Basic Operational Rule was issued by the Ministry of Health (NOB/SUS 01/93), and this defined the rules and procedural regulatory measures of decentralization for the health sector.

Given the diversity of economic conditions, populations, and administrative capacity of Brazil's municipalities, the redistribution of responsibilities for health care adopted, from its beginning, three patterns: incipient, partial, and semi-complete management authority. This system has recently evolved into only two categories: municipalities with "complete" health systems and those with "advanced" health systems. Municipalities classified as complete do not receive block grants for their health system; rather, they negotiate with the federal and state governments for specific funds for health care. An advanced system implies that the municipalities have full authority to distribute the funds according to their own priorities and are, thus, able to use the full amount of financial resources from the federal government for funding their hospitals and unit care centres. As for the education sector, Article 22, item XXIV, of the Constitution was implemented by Complementary Law 9394/1996, which defined general rules for the national education system. This legal instrument provided that the federal government, the states, and the municipalities are responsible for the administration of public education in Brazil. Each order of government is in charge of one category of public education within the current educational system. The states are mainly responsible for secondary education and the municipalities for primary and pre-school education. In this latter case the states and the federal government provide technical and financial assistance. A system of cooperation has thus been established in order to maintain and finance public education.

According to Complementary Law 9394/1996 the federal government, in cooperation with states and municipalities, is responsible for financing certain official teaching institutions (federal universities and technical schools located in each state) as well as for the elaboration of the National Plan for Education. According to the same 9394/1996 Law, each order of government is prohibited from acting in any category of education other than the one originally and legally allocated to it (unless the educational requirements of the population for which it is responsible are fully satisfied).

In 1996 the federal government went beyond its responsibilities for the general supervision of the educational system. The constitutional amendment 14/1996 created the National Fund for the Maintenance and Development of Education (FUNDEF), which introduced deep changes to primary and secondary education financing. New federal funds were made available to states and municipalities under Article 2 of Complementary Law 9424/1996, according to the number of enrolments at each local school. The implementation of FUNDEF has been extremely important for the municipalities as it has enabled them to increase their responsibilities with regard to basic education.

Articles 203 and 204 of the Constitution established the guidelines for the country's social welfare system. The major aim of this system, according to Article 203, is to provide protection to families, children, teenagers, elderly persons, and the handicapped; to integrate them into the labour market; and to maintain a minimum subsistence income. Government action in this area is to be carried out within a decentralized system in which the federal government is in charge of coordination and general rules (Article 204). States and municipalities are in charge of actual program implementation, with the cooperation of private and non-governmental institutions. The legal framework for implementing this aspect of the Constitution was established by Complementary Law 8724/1993 and by the Operational General Rules issued by the federal government on 16 April 1999. Social welfare benefits include medicines, food, transportation, school teaching materials and services (e.g., books, teaching equipment, school meals, and school buses), a minimum monthly income, family assistance, funeral assistance, and maternity assistance. The distribution of all these benefits is carried out by the municipalities.

The distribution of responsibilities regarding social security was implemented by Complementary Laws 8112/1990, 8212/1991, and 8213/1991, which established the rules for a new system (in line with the Constitution). The first two complementary laws concerned social security in the private sector (including rural areas), which is funded by the federal government. These reforms comprise one of the most contentious and, at the same time, one of the major social achievements of the present Brazilian Constitution. Social security payments to rural workers in impoverished areas of the North and North-East regions are considered to be a major income redistribution mechanism, at least for the time being.[6] The third complementary law relates to social security for public servants, which is funded by each order of government. On 31 December 2004 the constitutional amendment 41/2003 revamped the financial rules for the funding of the social security system; however, as far as responsibilities are concerned, each order of government remained in charge of the pensions of their respective civil servants.

In sum, the evolution of the distribution of powers and responsibilities in Brazil has been marked by a deliberate decentralization towards states and municipalities. Whether or not this constitutes genuine decentralization remains an issue. It has been argued that, as most of the 5,585 Brazilian municipalities are not able to finance their own social needs and remain dependent on federal transfers (the FPM), centralization persists. The federal government is still the major provider of funds and provides the main guidelines for receiving and spending them. However, the federal government has become weaker, particularly in fiscal terms. The added pressure for more financial resources and an increase in revenue-sharing schemes with the states and municipalities has been straining the fiscal capacity of the federal government since the adoption of the 1988 Constitution. A review of the fiscal performance of the public sector in Brazil reveals that the country's tax burden has reached the extremely high level of 36 percent of GDP. This has mainly been accomplished through the implementation of "contributions" that are not shared with other constituent governments. According to the taxation system ratified by the 1988 Constitution, direct and indirect taxation should be the main source of federal revenues. However, 47 percent of these revenues are redistributed to the states and municipalities. Throughout the 1990s the federal government became weaker in fiscal terms and gradually introduced special levies, or "contributions," for social security. The latest constitutional amendment (EC) (EC 42, 31 December 2003) has not adequately addressed this trend, largely due to latent fiscal conflict between the federal government and the states. The state governors have, in this context, re-emerged as key political actors in influencing Congress on taxation matters, through lobbying and representation to their state representatives in the two houses of Congress.

MAINTENANCE AND MANAGEMENT
OF THE DISTRIBUTION OF POWERS
AND RESPONSIBILITIES

The maintenance and management of the distribution of powers and responsibilities in Brazil's federal system is based on the assumption of cooperation. Collective responsibilities underlie the functioning of the whole system, but the role of each order of government, in many instances, is still indeterminate. The most conspicuous example of this is Article 23 of the Constitution. This article requires a complementary law to rule on cooperation schemes among the federal government, states, and municipalities with respect to balanced development and welfare conditions nationwide. So far, no bill has been submitted to Congress. The success of any such bill requires a favourable political context involving a major cooperative effort among the parties in Congress. In the meantime, the issue is not ready to be resolved, and legal deliberations generate many controversies. The governors are able, informally, to block its path in Congress. This commonly occurs with international matters, issues of taxation, allocation of major industrial and infrastructure investments, industrial relations, and the environment.

Notwithstanding the cooperative assumptions in the sharing of responsibilities and powers among the orders of government, latent conflicts of interest between the federal government and the states and municipalities emerge frequently. The federal government, in some instances, has to use its clout to offset specific initiatives by the states and municipalities. The most important tool at the federal government's disposal is its financial power, which enables it to fund investments in the deputies' and senators' constituencies and thus induce the compliance of the two subnational governments. This involves voluntary transfers of funds on the part of the federal government, which uses federal budget mechanisms to release funds for special projects proposed by members of Congress (obviously in favour of their respective constituencies). This financial power is, in practice, an important instrument for keeping the government coalition in Congress together whenever a crucial majority vote is needed.

Thus, in relative terms, the executives of the federal government, the Federal Senate, the Chamber of Deputies, and the political parties are the main actors with regard to the distribution of powers and responsibilities. Decision-making in Congress, which is regulated by its internal procedural rules, provides sufficient transparency for citizens to know who is voting for or against their wishes.

When states or municipalities are not adequately carrying out their responsibilities, there is no mechanism for providing direct orders to their executives or legislatures; instead, the federal government has to act cooperatively in order to assess operational difficulties or, as a last resort, to submit new legal rules to Congress in order to enforce actions that need to be taken. In exceptional cases of a threat to public security or damage to established law and order, the federal government can intervene in any state or municipality. Because such an intervention can only be implemented as a last resort, and because it departs from the normal autonomy of a constituent government, no new constitutional amendment can be undertaken while it lasts. On the other hand, whenever an incumbent administrator in the federal government or a state or municipal government is identified as not functioning in accordance with the constitutional distribution of powers and responsibilities, a legal impeachment process can be initiated. This procedure has been used frequently in cases of financial or electoral corruption, and, in the interest of better governance, removals from office have also been frequent.

ADEQUACY AND FUTURE OF THE DISTRIBUTION OF POWERS AND RESPONSIBILITIES

The present distribution of powers and responsibilities in the Brazilian federal system conforms to the original constitutional framework, although smooth relations between the federal government and the constituent state and municipal governments have yet to be achieved. The distribution of powers and responsibilities is compatible with the ability to democratically respond to citizens' demands. However, there are several reasons why Brazilian federalism faces considerable future challenges.

First, the design of the 1988 Constitution was the result of a wide consultation process, which aimed to introduce new democratic rules and to address social and regional inequalities. Second, the Constitution evinces a decentralizing tendency with regard to a number of public services, especially in the social sectors. Third, the substantial increase in transfers to the states has had a great impact on the public finances of the country. Interestingly, the social nature of these objectives was never in dispute; rather, the differences were over the exact source of funds to finance them. Fifteen years after the promulgation of the Constitution, public finances have not yet reached a balance between available resources and the required level of expenditures. The executive branch is still struggling to raise revenues and to reorganize public expenditure in order to achieve permanent and sustainable rates of growth.

As can be seen, the excessive emphasis on decentralization without a corresponding redistribution of responsibilities is a source of great difficulty. In Brazil, decentralization has always been seen as a way to guarantee the maintenance of democracy.[7] Furthermore, decentralization has been regarded as a good control mechanism with regard to the supply and quality of public goods and services as well as a means to achieving greater transparency. However, decentralization is costly. It makes difficult the achievement of a balance between public expenditures and tax revenues in the finances of the public sector as a whole. Moreover, the substantial increases in FPE and FPM (the constitutionally mandated transfers of shared revenues to the states and municipalities, respectively) has had a negative impact on the general health of the country's public finances. The structure of the constitutional revenue-sharing system is unbalanced and has thus far failed to address Brazil's regional and income disparities. Nonetheless, fiscal balance is an important prerequisite for lower inflation, greater economic stability, sustainable growth, and the reduction of regional and social inequalities.

In practice, the distortions now arising within the federal system may also have their roots in the inadequacies of the current electoral and political systems. Partisan politics poses a major challenge to Brazilian federalism. The process of building a "majority" in Congress is costly. The structure of Brazilian political parties remains fractured because political mandates belong largely to individuals. Election votes are generally for the candidate rather than for the party. The political parties concentrate on obtaining a high proportion of votes in order to obtain a high electoral quota (number of votes required to get a candidate elected). Candidates with the number of votes equal to or higher than this quota in each state are considered elected. Therefore, political parties always try to enroll as many candidates as possible, and, in turn, candidates are chosen by the number of votes that they can bring to a particular political party. It is very common, however, to see several candidates from the same party competing for votes in a particular constituency. Such an electoral system raises the costs of political campaigns to extremely high levels. Once Congress is elected, then, given the individual agendas of the representatives, building a majority becomes a major task. This weak party cohesion means that the president and the executive branch have to participate in difficult negotiations over each bill discussed in Congress.

As part of this executive-legislative interplay at the federal level, state governments use their political influence to obtain concessions from the federal government. This was the case in several bailing-out operations for state domestic and external debts in the 1990s. On such occasions, the federal government engaged in technical assistance and assisted the states in designing a medium-term fiscal adjustment program.

As for changes in the future, the "overrepresentation" issue is key, deserves more investigation, and is likely to be at the top of the political reform agenda. José Serra and José Roberto Afonso[8] have dealt with this issue in detail. They have demonstrated that overrepresentation causes a major redistribution of power within the federation. For example, representation in the Federal Chamber of Deputies requires representatives from the South-East and South regions to have sixteen times more votes than do representatives from the North and North-East regions. These peculiarities in the Brazilian representation system were, in fact, constructed deliberately in order to offset the economic preponderance and political influence of the more prosperous states of the South-East and South regions.

This being the case, "per capita" federal transfers in 1998 to states of the North region were us$360, while states of the South-East region received less than us$90 (at the current exchange rate). On the other hand, for each dollar collected as tax by the federal government in the South-East and South regions, only $0.18 returns to them as their share of the participation funds. With regard to social contributions (special levies), 70 percent are collected in the South-East region while returns from the federal government in the form of basic social programs are 23 percent for rural social security, 29 percent for social welfare programs, 37 percent for school lunches, and 40 percent for primary health care programs. The North-East region, which collects 10 percent of the overall social contributions, receives a share ranging from 45 percent to 30 percent of social security, education, and health care programs.

As in the rest of the world, in Brazil federalism is seen as the model of government best capable of reconciling the simultaneous pressures of small and large states with the requirements of the modern world. In Brazil in particular, the adoption of a form of federalism that emphasizes decentralization is seen as a practical way to enhance democratic rule for all orders of government. Centralization or decentralization trends have alternated through different periods of Brazil's history as, accordingly, have the distribution of powers and responsibilities.

Future modifications to the allocation of powers and responsibilities will have to address the reform of the political system, resolve the fiscal war among the states, design a new and sustainable mechanism for restructuring the financial debt of the states and of more than 100 municipalities, deal with the overrepresentation issue in the Chamber of Deputies, and, last, but not least, tackle the country's social and regional inequalities. Indeed, there is no better way to describe Brazilian federalism than to say that it is a system in constant evolution.

NOTES

1 The states and the regions in which they are located are: North region (Amazonas, Pará, Rondônia, Acre, Roraima, Amapá and Tocantins); North-East region (Maranhão, Piauí, Ceará, Rio Grande do Norte, Paraiba, Pernambuco, Alagoas,

Sergipe, Bahia); South-East region (Minas Gerais, Espírito Santo, Rio de Janeiro, São Paulo); South region (Paraná, Santa Catarina, Rio Grande do Sul); and Centre-West region (Goiás, Mato Grosso, Mato Grosso do Sul, Distrito Federal).

2 United Nations Program for Development (UNDP), *Human Development Report* (New York: Oxford University Press, 2000); and UNDP/IPEA/FJP/IBGE, *Atlas do Desenvolvimento Humano no Brasil* (Brasilia: UNDP/IPEA, 2000).

3 Afonso Ferreira, "Convergence in Brazil: Recent Trends and Long-Run Prospectus," *Applied Economics* 32 (2000): 479–489.

4 Marcelo Piancastelli and Fernando Perobelli, "ICMS: Evolução Recente e Guerra Fiscal," *Texto Para Discussão N° 402* (Brasilia: IPEA,1996), pp. 7–53.

5 Celina Souza, "Constitutional Aspects of Federalism in Brazil," in *A Global Dialogue on Federalism*. Vol. 1: *Constitutional Origins, Structure, and Change in Federal Democracies*, eds. John Kincaid and G. Alan Tarr (Montreal and Kingston: McGill-Queen's University Press for Forum of Federations, 2005).

6 Guilherme C. Delgodo, "Previdência Rural: Ralatório de Avaliação Socio-enconômico," *Texto de Discussão No. 477*, ed. IPEA (Brasilia: IPEA, 1997): pp. 1–55.

7 For discussion, see Bruno Frey, "Is Decentralization Really Bad? The Answer Is: No, It Is Good," *8th International Forum in Latin America Perspectives* (Paris: OECD, 1997), pp. 1–11; Eduardo Wiesner, "Fiscal Decentralization and Social Spending in Latin America: The Search for Efficiency and Equity," *Working Papers Series 199* (Washington: Inter-American Development Bank, 1994), pp. 1–34; Remy Prud'homme, "On the Dangers of Decentralization," *Policy Research Working Paper* (Washington: World Bank, 1994), pp. 1–36.

8 José Serra and José Roberto Afonso, "Federalismo Fiscal à la brasileira," *Revista do BNDES* 6, 12 (1999): 3–33.

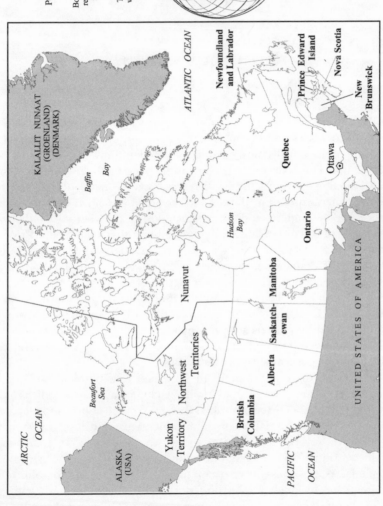

Canada

Capital: Ottawa
Population: 31.5 Million

Boundaries and place names are
representative only and do not
imply official endorsement.

The three northern territories,
while administrative divisions,
are not provinces.

Sources: ESRI Ltd.; National Atlas of Canada;
Times Atlas of the World

Canada

RICHARD SIMEON
AND MARTIN PAPILLON

The division of powers and responsibilities in Canada reflects the country's unique history, social and economic makeup, and institutional design. Canada is one of the world's most decentralized federations. This is a result both of the federal character of Canadian society and of the design of its institutions. "Functional" criteria for the division of powers are deeply affected by alternative criteria rooted in the tensions between Canadian nation-building, Quebec nation-building, and "province-building" elsewhere. Canada is also an example of "dual" (or "divided") federalism rather than "shared" (or "integrated") federalism.[1] The logic is based on separate lists of powers, but the reality is considerable de facto concurrency as well as a considerable degree of de facto asymmetry. The result is a high degree of autonomy for the provincial governments combined with a high degree of interdependence among them. Intergovernmental cooperation and coordination are necessary if the needs of citizens are to be met effectively. Canada combines high levels of cooperation in specific areas of public policy with considerable competition among governments in other areas.

The division of responsibilities in Canadian federalism has adapted to changing economic, social, and political circumstances as well as policy agendas. This has been accomplished through limited constitutional amendments, judicial interpretation, fiscal arrangements, and intergovernmental negotiations. Nevertheless, debates about "who does what" in areas such as social, environmental, and economic policy remain on the intergovernmental agenda. As we discuss, it is perhaps in its capacity to adapt to political and social changes in Quebec that the federation has been somewhat less successful. A common view of Canadian federalism in Quebec is that it is a rigid system, unable to adapt to the specific reality of the sole political community in North America with a francophone majority. Other fundamental issues on the current agenda concern the potential powers and responsibilities of Aboriginal authorities and local governments.

This chapter explores these issues. After a brief description of the main geographic and demographic characteristics of the country, we discuss the confederation settlement and the division of powers set out in the British North America Act, 1867.[2] We then trace the evolution of the division of powers through the major social and political changes in Canada over time before examining the contemporary division of roles and responsibilities. We conclude with a discussion of the continuing agenda and an assessment of Canada's capacity to adjust its division of powers to changing social and economic conditions.

THE CONSTITUTION
IN HISTORICAL-CULTURAL CONTEXT

The Canadian Context: Geography, Economy, and Society

The economic, social, cultural, and political environment in which Canadian federalism operates has changed enormously since 1867. At Confederation,[3] Canada consisted of just four provinces – Ontario, Quebec, Nova Scotia, and New Brunswick. Soon afterwards, Prince Edward Island (PEI) joined. Westward settlement led to the creation of Manitoba in 1870, the admission of British Columbia in 1871, and of the prairie provinces of Alberta and Saskatchewan in 1905. Newfoundland (now named Newfoundland and Labrador), on the Atlantic coast, was the last province to join, in 1949.

Canada now comprises ten provinces. In addition, there are three territories established under federal legislation, covering the vast, resource-rich, but thinly populated Canadian North. These territories – the Northwest Territories, Yukon, and the recently created Nunavut – have been moving closer to provincial status. Their administrations are now responsible to locally elected leaders, and they are today full partners in the machinery of Canadian intergovernmental relations. Nunavut, established in 1999, has a public government that is elected just like the governments of the other two territories; however, because its population (26,000) is overwhelmingly Inuit, it constitutes Canada's most advanced example of Aboriginal government.

In 1867 Canada had a population of just 3.5 million; today it numbers over 31 million.[4] Canada remains thinly populated, with its people heavily concentrated close to the southern border with the United States. The country's vast spaces remain a major part of Canadians' sense of place, but Canada is one of the world's most urbanized countries. Almost 80 percent of the population resides in cities of 10,000 or more, and 51 percent is concentrated in the four largest metropolitan regions of Montreal, Toronto, the Calgary-Edmonton corridor, and Vancouver. Canada's provinces vary enormously in their size, wealth, and economic and demographic bases. Their populations range from just over 135,000 in PEI to 11.4 and 7.2 million in the two largest provinces, Ontario and Quebec, respectively. Disparities in income are also large, though not as great as in some other federations. Per capita gross provincial product (GPP) in 2003 varied from US$22,170 in PEI to US$42,657 in Alberta. Ontario and Quebec had GPPs of US$31,825 and US$27,600, respectively.[5] More important, the structure of the provincial economies varies considerably. Manufacturing and finance are concentrated in Ontario and Quebec. Despite important recent progress towards economic diversification, the other provinces remain heavily dependent on natural resources – fishing and forestry in the Atlantic provinces and British Columbia, agriculture in the prairie provinces, and oil and gas mainly in Alberta but also in other provinces. These regional differences have important implications for the division of powers. Regional disparities place fiscal "equalization," or sharing, high on the agenda. Differences in the economic bases of the provinces mean that it is often difficult to articulate a single national economic policy. The differences also generate provincial ambitions to manage their own development.

The other central feature of the Canadian economy is its increasing integration into the global and North American economies.[6] Canada is the most export-dependent of the G-8 economies. More than 80 percent of all its exports go to the United States. In recent years, north-south trade has been increasing much faster than has east-west trade within Canada. These continental linkages have been cemented by the North American Free Trade Agreement (NAFTA). Continental integration has important implications for the division of powers, in that the provinces have been concerned that the provisions of international trade treaties would be imposed upon them without sufficient consultation or, indeed, provide a pretext for federal law to override provincial jurisdiction. Thus far these issues have been resolved cooperatively and without significant constitutional challenge, but if further integration requires deeper regulatory harmonization, issues of jurisdictional balance between the federal and provincial orders of government will continue to arise.

Canadian society has also changed fundamentally since Confederation. In the Canada of 1867 the fundamental divisions were language and religion, then seen in terms of Protestantism and Roman Catholicism.[7] Section 93 of the Constitution guarantees rights to denominational education for Roman Catholic and Protestant minorities in certain provinces. The vast proportion of Canadian residents, other than Aboriginal peoples, were of British or French descent. Nation-building and westward settlement were soon to add many others to the mix – Eastern Europeans to settle the Prairies, postwar immigrants from Europe to fuel Canada's rapid growth following the Second World War, and so on. As a result, Canadian social life now revolves around four axes: two are old but remain highly salient; two are new. They interact in complex ways, and all of them have important implications for the roles and responsibilities of Canadian governments.

The first, and most fundamental, axis is language. Canada is a binational[8] federation. Just under one-quarter of the Canadian population is francophone. They are highly concentrated in the Province of Quebec, where they constitute 85 percent of the population and share a deep sense of a Québécois national identity. This sense of nationhood has had a profound impact on the evolution of the division of powers in Canada. In 1867 it meant that the new country was to be federal. Later, it meant that Quebec vigorously opposed extension of the federal government's powers. This resistance was especially strong in the years following the Second World War, when Ottawa was taking the lead in constructing the Canadian welfare state. Following the "Quiet Revolution" of the 1960s,[9] Quebec governments sought to extend provincial jurisdiction in many areas in order to pursue a nation-building project, and it called for constitutional amendments that would recognize its "distinct status" within the federation.[10] The *Parti Québécois*, seeking an independent Quebec linked in an association or partnership with the rest of Canada, was formed in 1968 and first took office in 1976. Since then, it has alternated in Quebec government with the Liberal party and conducted two referenda on Quebec sovereignty (in 1980 and 1995). It lost both but, in 1995, only by a margin of a few thousand votes. Thus it is not surprising that "Quebec" and "national unity" have been at the heart of all Canadian debates about the division of powers and that pressure from Quebec has been the primary driver of a decentralized federation. For Quebec nationalists, the fundamental story of the division of powers is the struggle against domination by the federal government and the struggle for greater Quebec autonomy; for most scholars outside Quebec, it is a story of increasing provincial autonomy and decentralization.

The second axis is that of region. In the rest of Canada, provincial identities and distinctive regional interests remain strong. Residents of smaller provinces in the east and west often feel subordinate to the large provinces of Quebec and Ontario and the weight they have in the federal government.[11] Strong provincial loyalties, combined with competent, assertive provincial governments, have also worked to strengthen the decentralist character of Canada's federation.

Language and regional differences are the fundamental Canadian divisions that Canada's federal system was designed to manage. The third and fourth axes cut across this territorial conception of the country. The first is "multiculturalism." In recent decades, Canada has had the world's highest rates of legal immigration. Its diversity is especially evident in major cities – Toronto, Montreal, and Vancouver – where the majority of newcomers settle.[12] This too has implications for the division of powers, in terms of the sharing of responsibilities for immigration and for programs aimed at integrating new residents.

Finally, Canada's original inhabitants, the Aboriginal peoples, are now central to the policy agenda.[13] Their struggle for land claims and self-government, and their distressed economic and social conditions, raise two sets of issues for the division of powers. First, as Aboriginal governments have taken on more responsibilities, there is the question of what powers they will exercise and how these will relate to existing federal and provincial orders of government. Second, there is the question of how federal and provincial governments will divide the responsibility for services to Aboriginal peoples, a majority of whom now live "off-reserve," usually in large cities.[14]

The Institutional Context

The dynamics of Canadian federalism are greatly influenced by the political framework within which federalism is embedded. First, Canada is a parliamentary federation. Like Australia, both orders of government – federal and provincial – follow the British pattern of responsible parliamentary government. The legislative and executive branches are tightly bound together. Power is highly concentrated in the hands of the executive, especially the first ministers (the federal prime minister and the provincial premiers). This largely accounts for one of the primary features of intergovernmental relations; namely, "executive federalism," in which the primary contacts are among first ministers, cabinet members, and senior officials representing the executive rather than the legislative function as such.

Second, Canada has a weak Senate. It has formal authority that is almost co-equal with that of the elected House of Commons, and it provides for representation by region (though not by province). However, its role as a representative of provincial populations or governments within the federal legislature is fundamentally vitiated by the fact that senators are appointed by the prime minister. Canadians have discussed a number of reform proposals (using the German Bundesrat and the American and Australian Senates as possible models), but the present-day reality is that the Senate plays little role in working out the balance between federal and provincial governments.

Third, Canada is a constitutional federation. The division of powers is enforced by the courts, which can deem federal or provincial legislation ultra vires of the powers assigned to them. In Canada the courts (until 1949 the British Judicial Committee of the Privy Council; since then, the Supreme Court of Canada) have had a notable impact on the division powers. In the view of some,[15] they turned the centralist constitution of 1867 almost on its head, weakening federal powers and strengthening the provinces. Another aspect of constitutional federalism is the amending formula. Because the 1867 Constitution was an act of the British Parliament, only the United Kingdom could amend it. Soon the convention was established that Britain would do this only upon Canada's request. However, until 1982, Canadians could not agree on a domestic procedure. The 1982 amending formula sets a high bar for constitutional amendment: those relating to the division of powers require the assent of the federal Parliament together with the legislatures of at least seven provinces comprising at least 50 percent of Canada's population. The rigidity of these procedures, past and present, has meant that Canadian governments have generally sought non-constitutional ways to adapt the Constitution to new needs.

Some other features of the larger political system also underpin the image of Canada's model of federalism as "divided" in contrast to, for example, German integrated federalism. Federal and provincial parties, even those of the same name, are distinct from each other. The national party system is highly regionalized, with, in recent years, only one party able to claim "national" status, and the official Opposition consisting largely of regionally based parties.[16] Political leadership is also fragmented, with little mobility of ministers or officials between the two orders of government. This contributes to a pattern of intergovernmental relations that has been labelled "federal-provincial diplomacy."[17] The image of the division of powers that sometimes emerges is not so much one of eleven governments[18] that are collectively responsible for managing a single polity but, rather, of eleven governing bodies, each using the fulsome juridical and fiscal resources they have available in order to pursue rival state-building projects. This, as we now discuss, can be traced to the very origins of the Canadian federation.

THE CONSTITUTIONAL DISTRIBUTION OF POWERS

The Confederation Settlement

The federation created in 1867 was both a "coming together" and a "coming apart," a dynamic that has continued until the present.[19] The "coming apart" stemmed from the political crisis in the pre-1867 Province of "Canada," now the Provinces of Quebec and Ontario. After the British defeated the French in North America, the fundamental question remained: how would the two linguistic communities co-exist? A British commissioner, Lord Durham, reporting in 1838,[20] found in Canada "two nations warring in the bosom of a single state." His solution was a classic example of British colonialism: put the two linguistic groups together into a single political unit – Canada – and soon enough the French would assimilate to British values. As it turned out, the united province of Canada quickly took on the character of a consociational democracy with parallel French and English administrations. The rapid growth of anglophone "Canada West," and the resulting demand for "representation by population" generated deep conflict, the best solution to which appeared to be the reversion to a predominantly English-speaking Ontario and a predominantly French-speaking Quebec. Federation made this possible.[21]

The "coming together" focused on the other British colonies along the Atlantic coast (Nova Scotia, New Brunswick, PEI, and Newfoundland) and far away on the Pacific, British Columbia. They faced two sets of problems. With the British embrace of free trade, they were economically vulnerable, and with a self-confident United States to the south, fresh from its civil war, they were politically and militarily vulnerable as well. Coming together could address both these concerns.

These considerations had major implications for the design of the Canadian federation and its division of powers. First, it was not the product of a revolution. Unlike that of the United States, Canada's Constitution does not institutionalize a coherent theory of limited government, checks and balances, and the separation of powers; instead, it was a pragmatic response to a set of political, economic, and security challenges. Rather than repudiating the British model, it embraces it; Canada was to have a constitution "similar in principle" to that of the United Kingdom. Moreover, Canada was not to become fully independent in 1867; it would remain a "Dominion" of the United Kingdom and would not – until passage of the Statute of Westminster, 1931 – have a fully independent status as an international actor. Hence, the Constitution does not clearly delineate powers with respect to foreign affairs.

Second, two competing visions were in play in the debates preceding the creation of the federation. For the leading English-speaking advocate of Confederation, Sir John A. Macdonald, the goal was to create the institutional basis for a new British North American country that would eventually stretch from the Atlantic to the Pacific. His preferred model was unitary. The new national government should be endowed with all the instruments necessary to pursue this nation-building project. But Macdonald's chief ally in the Confederation debates was Sir Georges Etienne Cartier of Quebec, for whom the new system would be one in which, endowed with its own province, the French-speaking community would be able to preserve, protect, and advance its values. If Canada were to be a country, it would have to provide the political space for the francophone minority to exercise autonomy. He was supported by some leaders in Upper Canada, who also called for provincial sovereignty in local affairs, and by leaders of the other British North American colonies, especially in Nova Scotia, who feared that they might be submerged in the new union.[22]

The Division of Powers, 1867

The division of powers in the BNA Act reflects the tensions of the Confederation settlement. On one view, it establishes a system so centralized that K.C. Wheare could conceive of it as only "quasi-federal."[23] The colonial model of British relations with Canada was replicated in the design of the new federation. The Senate represented the regions, but its members were appointed by the prime minister. The governor general would appoint provincial lieutenant-governors, who would have the power to "reserve" provincial legislation for consideration by the central government.[24] Section 90 gives the federal government the unilateral power to "disallow" (invalidate) any provincial legislation; Section 92(10)(C) gives it the power to "declare" provincial works within exclusive federal jurisdiction. More generally, the opening words of Section 91, delineating federal legislative powers, states that the federal government has the power to "make laws for the Peace, Order and good Government of Canada" on any matter not exclusively assigned to the provinces – a powerful residuary clause in the hands of Ottawa.

Other sections of the Constitution Act, 1867, however, point in a more federalist direction. The "Peace, Order and good Government" clause is qualified by a list of specific powers set out in Section 91. This is followed by a list of subjects (Section 92) in which the provinces are empowered "exclusively" to make laws. This is the watertight-compartments model of Canadian federalism. In addition, the list of provincial powers includes two residual clauses – Section 92(13) "property and civil rights in the province," and Section 92(16) "Generally all matters of a merely local or private nature in the province."

However, the courts did not permit the "Peace, Order and good Government" clause to be a plenary allocation of power to the federal government; rather, it has been interpreted more narrowly, in two branches. First, it can justify federal action in a national emergency. Second, it can support federal action on issues of "national concern."[25] These include matters not contemplated at the time of Confederation (such as aviation and broadcasting) or that assumed national dimensions with the passage of time. The key criterion for justifying federal jurisdiction is provincial "inability"; that is, that the issue is beyond the ability of the provincial power to deal with it. Even then, "it must have a singleness, distinctiveness and indivisibility that clearly distinguishes it from matters of provincial concern and a scale of impact on provincial jurisdiction that is reconcilable with the fundamental distribution of legislative power under the constitution."[26]

In its enumerated powers, the federal government is given the basic powers necessary to pursue continental nation-building. These include the regulation of trade and commerce, defence, navigation and shipping,

banking, currency, and other such matters. The federal government is
given exclusive jurisdiction over "Indians and Land reserved for
Indians," and responsibility for criminal law. Provinces are allocated responsibilities that may have seemed unimportant at the time but that
were later to become of cardinal importance. These powers, set out in
Section 92, include management of public lands, establishment of hospitals and "eleemosynary" institutions, local government, the incorporation of companies, and the administration of justice. Section 93 gives
provinces exclusive control over education (subject to some rights for religious minorities).

Only two areas were originally designated explicitly as concurrent: immigration and agriculture, both of which were critical to the developmental
agenda of nineteenth-century Canada.[27] Implicit concurrency was found
in the combination of (1) federal responsibility for the criminal law and
for penitentiaries and (2) provincial responsibility for the administration
of justice and "public and reformatory prisons."

Four other elements of the initial architecture are important. First,
each order of government is to legislate, finance, and deliver the policies
and programs in its assigned areas of jurisdiction. Second, the Constitution allocates to both orders of government not only responsibilities for
specific policy areas but also policy instruments – taxation, spending,
and regulation – that can be applied across a wide variety of policy areas.
Both these characteristics had important implications for the evolution
of roles and responsibilities because, as new issues of public concern
(such as the environment) arose, both orders of government could find
the constitutional means to become involved. Third, there is no constitutional provision for the delegation of legislative powers between
governments, although the courts have permitted the delegation of administration and other devices, such as incorporation of other jurisdictions' law by reference or the passage of mirror legislation. Fourth, the
Constitution Act, 1867, did not include a bill of rights. While there
would be debate about which government had jurisdictional responsibility in any field, there was no sense of any limitation on government in
general until the Canadian Charter of Rights and Freedoms was enacted
in 1982.[28] In some ways, the Charter of Rights has transformed Canadian political culture, shifting the perspective from the Constitution as a
contract between governments to the Constitution as a contract between
people and their governments. It has dramatically increased the role of
the courts in Canadian policy making. However, on federalism issues,
the Supreme Court of Canada has in recent years emphasized a balance
between federal and provincial powers, and it has been careful to avoid
judgments that would swing the balance in one direction or the other.

EVOLUTION OF THE DIVISION OF POWERS

For Canada as for other countries, federalism is a process, not a fixed state. In its first few decades the federal government vigorously exercised its powers over the provinces, including the powers of reservation and disallowance. But a powerful set of factors began to gather that would substantially erode federal dominance.

First, a drawn out economic recession in the late nineteenth century eroded the new federal government's legitimacy. Second, strong provincial leaders emerged to challenge Ottawa. The first interprovincial conference, organized by the premiers of Quebec and Ontario, Honoré Mercier and Oliver Mowat, respectively, was convened in 1887 and mounted a strong attack on Ottawa. Mercier and Mowat articulated what came to be known as the "compact theory," which was based on a confederal image of Canada.[29] Third, over time matters clearly within provincial jurisdiction, such as hydroelectric power, mining, and the nascent welfare state, became more important on the national agenda. Fourth, judicial decisions began to chip away at federal powers. The federal government's powers over trade and commerce were interpreted narrowly. Its power in international affairs was reduced by a decision that stated that, while Ottawa has the power to negotiate treaties, their implementation must conform to the division of powers in Sections 91 and 92.[30] Canadian scholars debate the relative significance of these influences. Some focus on the role of the courts; others focus on the evolution of the society and the economy.[31] Both were important, but it is interesting to note that, while the draconian powers of disallowance and reservation remain in the Constitution, they have become constitutional dead letters.

By the 1920s Canadian federalism had come to look more like a classic dualist system. Then came the Great Depression of the 1930s. Only a strong federal government, many believed, could alleviate the crisis. The "dead hand" of the Constitution and the activism of distant courts came under increased criticism. The conclusions of Harold Laski concerning the "obsolescence of federalism" in the age of modern capitalism resonated strongly among many Canadians.[32]

After the Second World War, Canada, like all other Western democracies, embarked on the construction of the Keynesian welfare state, marrying a stronger government role in economic management with increased provision of income security and social services. Most responsibility for the building blocks of the welfare state lay in provincial hands; however, at the time, only the federal government had the resources and the pan-Canadian viewpoint to bring it about. One response to this dilemma was to transfer major new responsibilities to the federal government. Through constitutional amendment, this was done with respect to unemployment insurance and pensions. But provinces – led by Ontario, British Columbia, and Quebec – blocked any further transfer of responsibilities. Canada would develop the welfare state within its existing constitutional framework. The key instrument was a federal power that is only implicit in the Constitution – the "spending power."[33] This means that Ottawa can transfer funds to provinces for matters within provincial jurisdiction, such as health and welfare, and that it can attach conditions to these funds. Expansion of the spending power through a wide variety of "shared cost programs" was the vehicle through which de facto concurrency was greatly expanded as Ottawa became deeply involved in social policy. As a result, the "difficulties of divided jurisdiction" and the "complexities of federalism" affected the timing and means of delivering the modern welfare state rather than its basic substance.[34]

By the 1970s the world was changing again. The welfare state project was essentially complete; now debts, deficits, and economic volatility called into question the expanded role of all governments. Moreover, a new set of regionally divisive issues had come to dominate Canada's political agenda. Quebec's "Quiet Revolution" in the 1960s generated intense pressure for decentralization and a weakening of federal conditions on provincial programs. The "energy wars" of the 1970s precipitated by the global spike in oil prices generated severe interprovincial and federal-provincial conflict with respect to jurisdiction over pricing, taxing, management, and regulation of energy-related resources.[35]

By the turn of the century, two contradictory pressures were at work. On the one hand, the fiscal crisis of the state and the concomitant rise of neoliberal ideas about limiting the role of government were leading to "fiscally induced decentralization," best reflected in the dramatic reductions of federal transfers to the provinces following the 1995 federal budget. On the other hand, many Canadians worried about the implications of these developments for country-wide standards in social policy. The intergovernmental response was the 1999 Social Union Framework Agreement, which attempted to set out broad pan-Canadian objectives and an intergovernmental consensus that would enable them to be achieved collectively.[36]

This discussion underlines some important features of the Canadian division of powers. First, no reading of the Constitution Act, 1867, describes what different Canadian governments actually do. Some powers assigned in 1867 have disappeared as significant issues; others have assumed vastly greater importance. New areas of governmental concern, such as the environment, have arisen, about which the initial division of powers provides little guidance.

This suggests that a discussion of the contemporary division of powers should not begin with the words of the Constitution; instead, it should start with what governments do across the major areas of public policy, and it should ask what constitutional mandates, levers, instruments, and fiscal powers governments have at their disposal. This approach guides our analysis of who does what in the federal system today as well as our assessment of the adaptability of the existing division of powers in light of changing circumstances.

THE CONTEMPORARY DIVISION OF POWERS: DYNAMICS AND ISSUES

As we have shown, the evolution of the division of powers has resulted in two strong orders of government in Canada, each with broad authority to act. In few areas do they act independently. In most policy areas, federal and provincial governments have to coordinate their actions, if only because many contemporary policy issues cut across the jurisdictional boundaries originally defined in the Constitution.

Economic and Fiscal Policies

The federal government, through its exclusive responsibilities for currency, banking, trade, and tariffs, together with its spending power, controls most macroeconomic policy tools. Monetary policy is also in federal hands, through the arm's-length Bank of Canada. The federal government is also active in economic development by way of numerous programs supporting large and small businesses through tax incentives, regional development programs, research and development funds, trade promotion, and labour-market development and training programs. Provinces also play an important economic role through their tax powers, control over natural resources, ownership of public lands, and regulation of private economic activities, including financial markets. There is no federal equivalent of the U.S. Securities and Exchange Commission.[37] Provinces are active in promoting their own industrial development. Following a recent devolution (largely in an attempt to demonstrate federal flexibility following the close referendum result of 1995), provinces are now primarily responsible for labour market training.[38]

In fiscal terms, Canada is, together with Switzerland, perhaps the world's most decentralized federation. The federal share of total direct public spending is 37 percent, compared with 61 percent in the United States, 53 percent in Australia, and 41 percent in Germany. Canadian provinces are largely self-financing. Transfers from the federal government constitute only 13 percent of provincial revenues (though this varies greatly by province), compared with 30 percent in the United States and 41 percent in Australia. In Canada, the high-water mark in the federal share of taxing and spending occurred during the postwar period, with the construction of the welfare state. Since then provincial and local shares have increased steadily, a result not so much of declining federal spending as of rapid provincial growth.

Taxation

Ottawa has the power to raise revenues "by any mode or system of taxation," including customs and excise duties, which, in 1867, were the largest revenue source. Provinces may impose direct taxes as well as property taxes (which are delegated to local government), licence fees, and royalties from public ownership of resources. Today, both federal and provincial governments now rely on much the same revenue base. Both raise personal and corporate income taxes, and both levy sales taxes on the same taxpayers.

Such joint occupancy of the major tax fields could easily generate high levels of conflict, but there is considerable cooperation in this area, achieved largely through a set of tax collection agreements. Under these, the federal government, through the Canada Revenue Agency[39] (CRA), acts as the common income tax collector for all provinces except Quebec (and Ontario and Alberta, with regard to the corporate income tax). Federal conditions under the agreements have been steadily relaxed to allow provinces more freedom to design their own policies. Nonetheless, some provinces have recently debated the merits of departing from the arrangement in order to further enhance their autonomy. In general, however, these agreements have allowed a high degree of coordination within an otherwise highly decentralized revenue-raising regime, and they have greatly simplified the paper burden facing taxpayers.

Fiscal Transfers

Despite Canada's decentralized tax structure, an important gap remains between the expenditure responsibilities of the provinces and their revenues. As noted, Canadian provinces vary widely in their wealth and per capita income and, hence, in their capacity to raise the revenues necessary to fulfill their constitutional responsibilities. Intergovernmental fiscal transfers are thus an important part of the economic union and a key to understanding the dynamics of the division of powers in Canada today.

There are two major sources of fiscal transfers in Canada, both based on the federal spending power. Equalization payments were first introduced in 1957, and the principle was entrenched in Section 36 of the Constitution Act, 1982. They are designed to permit each province to provide "comparable levels of services, with comparable levels of taxation." Under this program, the ability of each province to raise revenues across all important revenue sources is assessed. Using a complex formula that has been renegotiated several times, the federal government then makes unconditional payments to the poorer provinces in order to narrow the disparities. The sum involved was estimated at Cdn$10.9 billion in 2005–06. In 2005–06 eight of the ten provinces were recipients of equalization payments, with only Alberta and Ontario not receiving such payments from the federal treasury.[40] Equalization is the fundamental instrument through which the Canadian federation reconciles equality and autonomy. Payments per capita ranged from $82 in Saskatchewan to $1,996 in Prince Edward Island.

The second mechanism for redistribution uses the spending power to make federal payments in policy areas under provincial jurisdiction. Conditional grants were a critical instrument through which Canada built its welfare state. Working, for the most part, cooperatively with the provinces and often building on provincial innovations,[41] the federal government used this power to create a wide variety of "shared cost programs." For example, in the 1960s universal, publicly provided health care was offered through the Medicare program, initially 50 percent funded by Ottawa. In the same period Ottawa assumed half the costs of provincially provided postsecondary education and welfare.[42]

In recent years, shared-cost programs have become much less prominent as instruments of public policy. This is partly due to provincial opposition to what were often considered federal intrusions into their areas of jurisdiction as well as to a perceived federal tendency to introduce and then modify such programs without sufficient consultation. It is also partly a result of the fiscal crisis of the early 1990s, which led Ottawa to substantially reduce its transfers to the provinces. The trend, in contrast to what has been happening in the United States, has been towards attaching fewer, rather than more, conditions to them. In 1995 several shared-cost programs were combined into the Canada Health and Social Transfer (CHST). With the CHST the federal government imposed a new blockfunding formula with fewer strings attached, but it also dramatically lowered the overall amount of transfers. There has been a partial recovery of funding levels since, especially for health care, and, in 2004, the CHST was replaced by two separate funds: the Canada Health Transfer and the Canada Social Transfer.

One result of these changes is that Canadian provinces are now much less dependent on federal transfers than are comparable units in other federations, and this trend is increasing.[43] There are big variations: Ottawa provides about 39 percent of revenue in Newfoundland but only 7 percent and 8 percent in Alberta and British Columbia, respectively. For the provinces and the territories as a whole, the downside of the overall reduction of the federal government's share in social expenditures is a constant struggle to cover the growing costs of social programs, most significantly the universal heath care system.

More generally, Canadians are debating whether there may be a basic mismatch between provincial responsibilities and their revenue-raising abilities. Is there a "fiscal imbalance?" The provinces, led by Quebec, argue that current pressures for greater spending fall largely on areas of provincial jurisdiction, that collectively provinces are running substantial deficits while Ottawa has a surplus, and that federal revenues are more elastic than the government lets on. Consequently, a readjustment of the allocation of resources is necessary.[44] The federal government replies that its fiscal position is also precarious, especially in light of new responsibilities related to security and other matters, that provincial fiscal difficulties are a result of their tax cutting as well as expenditure increases, and that, in any case, there is no constitutional restriction on provinces increasing their own taxes.[45] This is a highly politicized debate, and there exists no independent agency (such as the Finance and Fiscal Commission in South Africa) to make recommendations on these matters.

Trade

Another important dimension of economic policy involves the power to regulate trade and commerce. The federal Parliament has the power to make laws in relation to "the regulation of trade and commerce." Despite this broad language, Peter Hogg notes that, as a result of judicial interpretation, Canada's "trade and commerce clause turned out to be much more limited than its American cousin," despite almost identical wording.[46] This restrictive interpretation resulted from the overlap of trade and commerce with the power of provinces over "property and civil rights" (Section 92[13]) and the desire to avoid a broad interpretation that could open the door to sweeping federal powers. The courts thus made the economically dubious but politically important distinction between interprovincial and international trade (federal) and intraprovincial trade (provincial).

The limited coordination among provinces in regulating commercial activities created important non-tariff barriers to interprovincial trade. These became an issue in constitutional negotiations in the 1980s. Should Section 121, which guarantees free movement of "all articles of growth, produce or manufacture" across provinces, be strengthened? Should Ottawa gain greater powers to regulate the economy? or is strengthening the "Canadian economic union" an intergovernmental matter? The general trend towards trade liberalization, notably NAFTA, led to the 1995 intergovernmental Canadian Agreement on Internal Trade, the first concerted attempt by federal and provincial authorities to reduce internal trade barriers. Its purpose was to limit barriers in specific areas and to prevent the erection of new ones, and it was written in a language similar to that used in international trade agreements.[47] This is an important example of the achievement of "country-wide" policy through collaborative intergovernmental action.

Natural Resources

Section 109 of the Constitution and the 1930 Natural Resources Transfer Agreements (NRTA) give provinces ownership over the extraction and commercialization of natural resources, except for offshore resources and uranium mining. The latter was brought under federal jurisdiction through the federal declaratory power.[48] Otherwise, Sections 92 and 92A of the Constitution Act, 1867, give provinces exclusive legislative jurisdiction over resources and the production and distribution of energy. The federal government does regulate international and interprovincial movement of energy through the National Energy Board.

In the midst of the 1970s energy crisis the federal government sought to use its powers over interprovincial and international trade to strengthen the national dimension of energy polices and to protect the industrial core of the country from skyrocketing energy prices. It eventually led to the National Energy Program, which fostered Canadian ownership of extraction and distribution industries, established price controls to maintain a "made-in-Canada" oil price, increased federal taxation over extraction, imposed an export tax on natural gas, and created a national strategy for the development of Arctic and offshore energy resources, areas that lie under federal jurisdiction. The program, which was seen in central Canada as a national measure to respond to a national economic crisis, is still deeply resented in Alberta. It has been largely dismantled.[49]

The federal government is responsible for the management of seacoast fisheries. The dramatic decline in fish stocks on the Atlantic and Pacific coasts in recent years has spurred much criticism of federal management, and some provinces, notably British Columbia and Newfoundland and Labrador, seek more control over this essential part of their local economies. Conflicts over resource ownership have also pitted local residents and provincial governments against Aboriginal nations, which have made important judicial gains in recent years over the recognition of their title to the land and traditional use of resources such as fisheries and forests. The federal government often plays a dual role of arbitrator and interested party in such conflicts.

Agriculture

Along with immigration, agriculture was the only other domain defined as explicitly concurrent in 1867 (pensions were added in 1951). Both were key to Western expansion.[50] Concurrency remains the order of the day. National agricultural marketing boards that practise supply management are matters of both federal and provincial jurisdiction, the two orders effectively delegating their respective powers (over interprovincial and intraprovincial trade and commerce) to the marketing boards. Some provinces have sought greater control over export marketing of agricultural products, such as wheat, which is now managed through the federal Canadian Wheat Board.[51]

Social Policy

In 1867 governments had little role to play in social policy. Such matters were considered best left to local charitable organizations and churches. All of that changed with the advent of the modern welfare state. Provinces have exclusive jurisdiction for the provision and administration of primary, secondary, and postsecondary education; health and welfare; and workers' compensation. As a result, programs and credentials are defined provincially, although there is increasing coordination among provinces to seek greater harmonization of programs.

The federal government is, however, deeply involved in this. First, as a result of constitutional amendments in 1940, 1951, and 1964, it provides the basic income-security programs of insurance against unemployment and old age through Employment Insurance, Old Age Security, and the Canada Pension Plan (CPP). In the case of pensions, the amendments provided that, in any conflict between provincial and federal laws, the former would prevail. This made it possible for Quebec to establish its own pension plan, the *Régie des rentes*, an important element of asymmetry. The Canada and Quebec plans are closely coordinated and Ottawa may not amend the CPP without provincial consent.

The federal government plays an important role in other areas of social policy, mostly through fiscal transfers and the use of its spending power to fund health, postsecondary education, and social services. It also directly supports research and student aid in the postsecondary education sector as well as bilingual education at the elementary and secondary level. It plays a direct role in health care through, for example, the testing and licensing of food and drugs, and through support for research and infrastructure. It also plays a direct (though contested) role in training and employment.[52] Plus Ottawa provides some social benefits through the tax system.

There are two reasons for Ottawa's involvement in social policy. First is the financial story already discussed. At the end of the Second World War Ottawa had gained important fiscal leverage, while the provinces could not support the costs associated with the development of social programs. Second, the construction of a Canada-wide welfare system was closely associated with the development of a pan-Canadian citizenship regime.[53] The development of universal social programs equally accessible to all Canadians was as much a nation-building project (i.e., Canada as a nation) as it was a socioeconomic one, hence the term "social union." This has created a complex dynamic where many – especially in "progressive" social movements – see Ottawa as the "guardian" of the social union. This conception, however, has little resonance in Quebec, where social citizenship is focused on the province, and where there are competing ideas of nationality (i.e., Québécois and Canadian).

As noted above, major federal transfers in this area are now covered under the Canada Health Transfer, which provides block funding for health care, and the Canada Social Transfer, which supports postsecondary education and social services. Unlike previous transfer formulas, both allow provinces great flexibility in program design. The only substantial conditions that remain – apart from a requirement not to discriminate against citizens from other provinces – are the "national standards" defined in the Canada Health Act.[54]

The federal government's use of the spending power in areas of social policy remains controversial. Provinces have objected to Ottawa initiating programs without providing adequate consultation as well as changing funding formulae without providing sufficient notice. For its part, the federal government is concerned with ensuring relative uniformity across the country in terms of access to social programs as well as with political visibility and credit for programs that it helps fund.

The 1999 Social Union Framework Agreement (SUFA) was an attempt to address these problems. The federal government agreed not to start new, shared-cost programs in areas of provincial jurisdiction without the prior agreement of a majority of the provinces, and it also agreed to give notice before making any changes in financial arrangements. However, its power to spend in areas of provincial jurisdiction was confirmed. Quebec did not sign the agreement, arguing that it should have the right to "opt out" of shared programs without financial penalty. In recent years, ongoing federal-provincial tensions regarding funding for health care suggest that the agreement has had limited impact.[55]

Environmental Policies

Environmental concerns cut across a wide variety of policy areas; as a result, a de facto regime of concurrency has been established. The courts have confirmed that the environment is not a single matter falling entirely within either federal or provincial jurisdiction.[56] The provinces derive their authority over environmental matters mainly from their powers over property, natural resources, local government, and public lands. The federal government can act using its jurisdiction over criminal law, navigation, fisheries, interprovincial and international trade, and, more broadly, its general power to legislate for "Peace, Order and good Government."

Both federal and provincial governments established environmental departments in the late 1960s and early 1970s, creating a competitive dynamic in which both orders of government legislated and in which programs often overlapped, contradicted, or complemented each other. In the early 1990s talks of harmonization began under the auspices of an intergovernmental body, the Canadian Council of Ministers of the Environment (CCME). The Canada-Wide Accord on Environmental Harmonization was signed in 1998 by the federal government and all the provinces and territories, except Quebec. It emphasizes consensus-based decision making and single-window delivery of services together with a subsidiarity principle whereby the government closest to the problem is in charge of policy regulation and implementation. Many critics of the accord, especially environmental activists, suggest it amounts to an effective devolution of federal responsibilities to the provinces.[57]

Local Government

Local and municipal governments play increasingly important roles in the lives of Canadians. Policing, zoning and land-use planning, education, recreation, and many other services are designed and delivered locally. Municipal responsibilities with respect to welfare, housing, and the like have also increased in recent years as a result of "downloading" on the part of provincial governments. Yet municipalities have very limited independent powers. Indeed, it has been suggested that, if Canada is one of the most decentralized federations in terms of the relationship between the federal government and the provinces, it is also one of the most centralized in terms of the relationship between provinces and local governments. Under the Constitution, local governments are creatures of provincial governments, which define their boundaries, powers, method of election, and revenues. Direct relations between federal and local governments are limited, in contrast, for example, to the situation in the United States. Municipalities have a limited capacity to raise their own revenues, depending heavily on property taxes and licence fees.

In recent years, there has been discussion about whether municipalities should play a greater role in Canadian governance. The need for urban planning, transit, housing, and other services is growing rapidly, as are calls for a "new deal" for cities, giving them greater jurisdictional and fiscal autonomy, more financial support from senior governments, and a place at the intergovernmental bargaining table.[58]

Citizenship and Immigration

Citizenship and control over international boundaries falls under federal jurisdiction, while immigration is constitutionally defined as concurrent. Soon after Confederation, immigration law was essentially occupied by the federal government; provinces made no use of their authority in this area until recently. Quebec was the first province to negotiate agreements with the federal government, and this occurred in the 1970s.[59] The Canada-Quebec Accord of 1991 gives Quebec powers over the selection of immigrants and control of its own settlement services, while the federal government retains responsibility for defining immigrant categories, setting targeted levels of immigration, and enforcing immigration law.[60] Recently, more limited agreements have been signed with other provinces for funding and responsibility for settlement services as well as for a greater say in planning immigrant selection so as to attract business immigrants.

Municipal governments in the major urban centres, where most immigrants settle, are seeking support from Ottawa in order to respond to the growing needs of an ethnically, culturally, and linguistically diverse population. They need programs designed to help support settlement, language training, and labour-market orientation. In addition, a wide range of "multiculturalism" policies are now adopted by provinces and municipalities to facilitate the integration of newcomers to the host society.[61]

Aboriginal Peoples

Despite their presence for centuries before French and English settlers came to create what is now Canada, Aboriginal peoples were not part of the negotiations leading to Confederation. The federal government inherited the fiduciary obligation of the British Crown, maintaining jurisdiction over "Indians, and lands reserved for Indians" (Section 91[24]).[62] For most of the last century federal policy regarding Aboriginal peoples alternated between benign neglect and proactive attempts at assimilation. Provinces have generally been reluctant to take over any responsibilities for Aboriginal peoples or to deliver social programs on reserves and in other Aboriginal communities. Aboriginal treaties and titles to land were seen to potentially conflict with provincial jurisdiction over pubic lands and natural resources.[63]

The recognition of Aboriginal and treaty rights in the Constitution Act, 1982 (Section 35) represents an important historical shift in policy and legal structure, and it had a significant impact on Canadian federalism. While the extent and meaning of Aboriginal rights are not specified in this section, the Supreme Court has interpreted it broadly, giving a strong basis to Aboriginal claims to land and self-government. The main result has been to force the two orders of government to negotiate land claims and self-government agreements, especially in areas where no treaties had been signed previously (in British Columbia, northern Quebec and Labrador, and the northern territories) in order to avoid costly lawsuits and uncertainty about rights to resources.

While federalism was long been seen as a limit to the development of Aboriginal autonomy, given the federal-provincial "power grid" over the exercise of sovereignty, it is now increasingly seen as part of the solution for Aboriginal peoples.[64] The creation of an Aboriginal order of government with constitutionally entrenched powers was part of the failed Charlottetown Accord of 1992, and it was also a core recommendation of the Royal Commission on Aboriginal Peoples' final report, released in 1996. Self-government agreements, protected under Section 35, may be the first step towards a form of "treaty federalism" between Aboriginal peoples and the federal and provincial governments.[65]

International Affairs

International relations, defence, and security all fall within federal jurisdiction. The federal government has sole power to engage Canada in international treaties and agreements, to represent Canadian interest in international forums, and to define foreign policy. While the federal government has exclusive jurisdiction over negotiation and ratification of international agreements and treaties, this authority does not extend to the implementation of provisions falling into provincial jurisdictions.[66] In sharp contrast to federations such as those in force in Australia and the United States, where treaties, once ratified, bind all governments, a famous Canadian judgment held: "While the ship of state now sails on larger ventures and into foreign waters she still retains the watertight compartments which are an essential part of her original structure" (*A.-G. Can v. A.-G. Ont.* [1937] A.C. 326). This important limitation has forced the federal government to consult the provinces extensively during negotiation of international agreements in areas that affect them, especially trade and the environment.

However, Ottawa has stopped short of sharing its executive power to negotiate and to sign international treaties. This has created some tension between the provinces and the federal government. The former have called for a more formal role in defining Canada's position prior to international negotiations, while the latter is reticent to embark on a process that would limit its flexibility when negotiating with foreign states.[67] And Quebec has argued for more autonomy as an international actor in affairs linked to provincial jurisdiction.

Criminal Law and Administration of Justice

The criminal law is firmly within federal jurisdiction. The court system is also federally integrated, with federally appointed superior and appeal courts and the Supreme Court of Canada at the apex. This is perhaps the most important area in which, today, the United States and Australia may be considered to be more decentralized than Canada. The criminal law power also provides Ottawa with policy instruments (criminal sanctions) that strengthen its involvement in the environment and other regulatory arenas.

Again, however, the provinces are also involved in criminal law. They are responsible for the "administration of justice in the province," which includes prosecution services, management of the court system, and legal aid. Provinces establish and appoint the lowest level of courts and may establish penalties, including prison sentences, for violations of provincial law. Policing is also shared. Some provinces – Ontario, Quebec, Newfoundland – have their own provincial police forces, and larger cities have their own municipal forces that are regulated provincially. There is as well a national police force, the Royal Canadian Mounted Police (RCMP), which is responsible for enforcing federal law. In addition, most provinces have contracted with the RCMP to provide local policing in their provinces. In this role, the RCMP is accountable to the provincial government.

Language Policies

The Constitution Act, 1867, provides some important guarantees of minority language rights as well as denominational rights to religious education in Quebec and Ontario. Both Ottawa and the provinces have the power to legislate in this contentious area. The federal government passed the Official Languages Act, 1969, which was designed to provide for French-language services in federal institutions across the country and to ensure greater equality of French and English in the makeup and operation of the federal public service.[68] The first legislative enactment of the "indépendantiste" Parti Québécois government was Bill 101, which was designed to strengthen the francophone character of Quebec through regulations with respect to language use in the workplace, public signage, and access to education. Bill 101 has been subject to intense litigation, but its central provisions – such as requiring immigrant children to attend French-language schools – have remained intact. Canada's most bilingual province, New Brunswick, has also legislated to provide for equality of the two official languages, a commitment now enshrined in the Constitution.

Marriage and Divorce

Another historical anomaly in the original Constitution is that "marriage and divorce" are federal (Section 91[26]), while the "solemnization of marriage in the province" is provincial (Section 92[12]). This division of responsibility might have remained a historical artifact until the recent emergence of the issue of "same-sex marriage." Could Ottawa decide to permit such marriages but the provinces refuse to perform them, or vice versa? In the event, such conflict may be averted because the superior courts in the provinces and the Supreme Court of Canada, invoking the Charter of Rights, have ruled that both federal and provincial marriage law must allow same-sex unions.

EXPLANATION AND EVALUATION

No single factor or variable can explain the evolution or the current pattern of the Canadian division of powers. Institutional, cultural, and economic influences interact in complex ways. Several factors at the level of institutions have been critical. They include the basic structure of watertight compartments in the division of powers, despite the de facto concurrency; the Westminster pattern of parliamentary government, which places negotiation between strong executives at the centre of the process; the institutional design of the federal Parliament, which leads many regional interests to express themselves through strong provincial governments; and the role of the courts, which in the early years undercut federal power and later focused on balancing federal and provincial powers. But major shifts in the roles of federal and provincial governments have occurred with very little institutional change.

The second set of factors emphasizes the changing policy agenda, to which governing structures must adapt. In the early years the focus was on building a transcontinental Canada, with Ottawa in the lead; then the emphasis on resource-led development shifted the focus back to the provinces; the Great Depression, postwar reconstruction, and development of the postwar welfare state shifted the pendulum back to Ottawa; and today, the question of how to respond to globalization and North American integration as well as to a knowledge-based economy poses new challenges for how governments share responsibilities. Despite criticism from many quarters, the Canadian evidence seems to suggest that the division of powers provides enough flexibility to permit the country to respond to the changing policy agenda.

But how the institutions have worked and how the policy agendas have been addressed depends most fundamentally on the regionally and linguistically divided Canadian society. Quebec, with its francophone majority and sense of national identity, has from the start provided the strongest pressure for a decentralized Canada – in earlier periods resisting expansion of federal power and intrusion into provincial jurisdiction, in later periods arguing for greater provincial legislative and fiscal powers and for asymmetrical federalism. On many occasions, and on many issues, it has been joined by other self-confident provincial governments seeking the economic and social levers to develop their own societies. Relatively homogenous federations such as Germany and Australia have reacted to the contemporary policy agenda very differently from Canada, for the most part with an increase in central authority. As new issues have emerged, Canada's provinces have claimed both the legitimacy and the capacity to respond; there has been no easy assumption that a "country-wide" problem requires Ottawa-determined responses; rather, the dominant view is that effective responses require various combinations of provincial initiative, interprovincial cooperation, and federal leadership. This is a direct consequence of the strong sense of national identity in Quebec.

CONCLUSION

Despite its original rigidity, the division of powers in Canada turned out to be highly permissive. Each order of government is endowed with a wide range of substantive responsibilities and policy instruments that enables it to act in almost any situation it chooses. Canada thus has two powerful orders of government. Its original, highly centralized division of powers has evolved – through judicial interpretation and political developments – into a much more decentralized arrangement.[69] The limited asymmetry set out in the Constitution has also evolved into a high degree of functional asymmetry. The difficulty of finding consensus on constitutional amendment has meant that no fundamental reorganization of powers and responsibilities in light of changing circumstances has been possible; rather, adjustments have been the result of intergovernmental bargaining and informal agreements. The result is neither clear nor coherent, but it is workable.

A Continuing Agenda

Nevertheless, Canadian federalism does confront a number of issues that pose important questions about how the division of powers should operate in the future. These issues include:

- The roles, responsibilities, and financial resources of local governments and their place in the Canadian system of multilevel federal governance.
- The roles, responsibilities, and financial resources of Aboriginal governments and their place in the Canadian system.

- How to ensure that federal and provincial responsibilities are best suited to promote Canada's effective participation in the global and North American economies as well as in a knowledge-based economy. Does the implication that cities and provinces are best adapted to meeting these challenges suggest a diminution of federal powers or does adaptation require a more national response led by the federal government?
- How to ensure a proper fit between the roles and responsibilities of each order of government and the financial resources available to it.
- How to ensure the ability of the system to respond effectively when unexpected shocks occur. What is certain is that the system has been, and will be, assaulted by extraordinary events – security emergencies, natural catastrophes, health emergencies (such as the 2003 SARS outbreak), and others. A major challenge facing all governments in Canada is to devise institutions and processes to manage such events effectively.

Adapting the federation and its division of powers to the complex reality of a multinational state remains, as we have discussed throughout this chapter, a fundamental challenge facing Canadians. It means that purely "functional," efficiency-based arguments about who should do what have relatively little influence. Those are important questions, but they can be answered only through the filter of Canada's federal institutions and federal society.

In this interplay between federal society and federal state, public opinion plays complex roles. Survey evidence shows that Canadians identify strongly and positively both with their federal and with their provincial governments. Few want a fundamental transfer of powers either from Ottawa to the provinces or vice versa, though on balance and with important regional variations, pluralities trust provincial governments more than Ottawa to deliver services important to them, believe the federal government has too much power, and opt for more provincial powers.[70] Overwhelmingly, however, Canadians call for more intergovernmental cooperation to meet their needs, and reject the competitive, adversarial relationship that seems embedded in the institutional structure. Whatever the issue at hand, Canadians are telling their governments: we do not want to be hamstrung by the constitutional division of powers or by intergovernmental rivalries. They are saying, individually or collectively, get on with it. – nothing in the formal division of powers stands in the way of that.

NOTES

1 By dual (or divided) federalism we mean a federation in which powers are divided into separate federal and provincial lists, and in which each government

is responsible both for designing and implementing its own policy. Shared (or integrated) federations are characterized by high levels of concurrency, provincial implementation of national framework laws, and a close link between national and provincial politics. See Richard Simeon, "Considerations on the Design of Federations," *SA Public Law* 13, 2 (June 1998): 42–72.

2 It is now relabelled the Constitution Act, 1867.

3 This is the term that, since 1867, Canada has consistently used to label its system, even though it does not conform to modern usage, which defines a confederation as a system in which the central government is created by and responsible to the constituent units.

4 Statistics in this section are from Statistics Canada, *A Profile of Canadian Population: Where We Live*, March 2002, <www.statcan.ca:8096/bsolc/English/bsolc?catno=96F0030X2001003> (26 May 2005).

5 John R. Baldwin, Mark Brown, and Jean-Pierre Maynard, "Interprovincial Differences in GDP Per Capita, Labour Productivity, and Work Intensity, 1990–2003." Statistics Canada, 2005 <www.statscan.ca/english/research/11-624-MIE/11-624-MIE2005011.pdf> (accessed 26 May 2005).

6 For a discussion, see Richard Simeon, "Important? Yes. Transformative? No. North American Integration and Canadian Federalism," *The Impact of Global and Regional Integration on Federal Systems: A Comparative Analysis*, Harvey Lazar, Hamish Telford, and Ronald Watts, eds. (Kingston, ON: Institute of Intergovernmental Relations and McGill-Queen's University Press, 2003), pp. 125–171.

7 In the nineteenth century religion was at least as salient as was language in Canadian politics; it is much less so today.

8 If not tri-national, Aboriginal leaders would argue. While the multinational character of the Canadian federation remains politically ambiguous, as it is not clearly recognized in its institutional design, in the literature it is increasingly considered to be a sociological fact. See Michael Keating, *Plurinational Democracy: Stateless Nations in a Post-Sovereignty Era* (Oxford: Oxford University Press, 2001); and Alain-G. Gagnon and James Tully, eds., *Multinational Democracies* (Cambridge: Cambridge University Press, 2001).

9 Among the many works on the Quiet Revolution, perhaps the best is Kenneth McRoberts and Dale Posgate, *Quebec: Social Change and Political Crisis* (Toronto: McClelland and Stewart, 1980).

10 For a discussion of the evolution of Quebec's political relations with Canada, see Kenneth McRoberts, *Misconceiving Canada: The Struggle for National Unity* (Toronto: Oxford University Press, 1997).

11 Some prefer to use the term "national" government; however, this is inconsistent with the bi-national view of the country.

12 In 2001, 48 percent of immigrants settled in Toronto, 15 percent in Vancouver, and 12 percent in Montreal. Immigrants (people not born in Canada) constituted 44 percent of Toronto's Census Metropolitan Area population, making

it the most multicultural city in the OECD, before Miami and Sydney. See Statistics Canada, *Canada's Ethnocultural Portrait: The Changing Mosaic*, February 2003, <http://www.geodepot2.statscan.ca> (accessed 26 May 2005).

13 1.3 million persons reported Aboriginal ancestry in 2001, up 22 percent from the 1996 census. See Statistics Canada, *Aboriginal Peoples of Canada: A Demographic Profile*, March 2003, <www.statcan.ca:8096/bsolc/English/bolsc?catno=97F0011X> (accessed 26 May 2005).

14 See Frances Abele and Michael Prince, "Aboriginal Governance and Canadian Federalism: A To-Do List for Canada," *New Trends in Canadian Federalism*, eds. F. Rocher and M. Smith, 2nd ed. (Peterborough: Broadview Press, 2003), pp. 135–165.

15 This view was particularly prevalent among English-Canadian constitutional scholars in the 1930s, when the courts struck down federal legislation aimed at meeting the problems of the Great Depression. See F.R. Scott, *Essays on the Constitution: Aspects of Canadian Law and Politics* (Toronto: University of Toronto Press, 1977).

16 The 2003 unification of two such parties, the western-based Alliance Party of Canada and the historically powerful Progressive Conservative Party (now largely confined to Atlantic Canada) is designed to try to overcome this problem. The new party is called the Conservative Party of Canada.

17 Richard Simeon, *Federal-Provincial Diplomacy: The Making of Recent Policy in Canada* (Toronto: Toronto University Press, 1972).

18 Ottawa plus ten provinces, or fourteen when the three northern territories are included.

19 See Daniel J. Elazar, *Federalism: An Overview* (Pretoria, South Africa: Human Sciences Research Council, 1996); and Alfred Stepan, *Arguing Comparative Politics* (New York: Oxford University Press, 2001), pp. 320–323.

20 Gerald M. Craig, *Lord Durham's Report* (Toronto: McClelland and Stewart, 1963).

21 John Meisel, Guy Rocher, and Arthur Silver, *As I Recall, si je me souviens bien: Historical Perspectives* (Montreal: Institute for Research on Public Policy, 1999), pp. 45–53.

22 Ibid., 58–63.

23 K.C. Wheare, *Federal Government*, 4th ed. (London: Oxford University Press, 1963), p. 19.

24 True to its British constitutional roots, Canada is a constitutional monarchy. The Queen of Great Britain and the Commonwealth is the formal head of state. On the advice of the Government of Canada, she appoints the Canadian governor general and the lieutenant-governors of the provinces. The Crown in Canada is thus divided between a "federal" and a "provincial" Crown. The governor general and lieutenants-governors exercise all the prerogatives of the monarchy in Canada, but they do so only "by and with the advice" of the elected Cabinet.

25 Peter Hogg, *Constitutional Law of Canada* (Scarborough, ON: Carswell, 2000), p. 431.
26 *R. v. Crown Zellerbach* [1988] 1 S.C.R. 401.
27 Two other areas were added later. See below.
28 Without the support of the government and legislature of Quebec. However, the Charter remains the law in that province, and many parts of it have broad public support.
29 See E.R. Black, *Divided Loyalties: Canadian Concepts of Federalism* (Montreal and Kingston: McGill-Queen's University Press, 1975).
30 In a famous phrase, the British judge Lord Haldane ruled that, "while [Canada's] ship of state now sails on larger ventures and into foreign waters, she retains the watertight compartments which were an essential part of her original structure" (*A.-G. Can. v. A.-G. Ont.* [1937] A.C. 326).
31 For a review of these arguments, see Alan Cairns, "The Judicial Committee and its Critics," *Canadian Journal of Political Science* 4, 3 (September 1971): 301–345
32 Harold J. Laski, "The Obsolescence of Federalism," *New Republic* 3 (May 1939): 367–369
33 See Hogg, *Constitutional Law of Canada, pp.* 163–168; Douglas Brown, "Fiscal Federalism: The New Equilibrium between Equity and Efficiency," *Canadian Federalism: Performance, Effectiveness and Legitimacy,* Herman Bakvis and Grace Skogstad, eds. (Toronto: Oxford University Press, 2002), pp. 59–85.
34 See Keith G. Banting, *The Welfare State and Canadian Federalism,* 2nd ed. (Montreal and Kingston: McGill-Queen's University Press, 1987).
35 G. Bruce Doern and Glen Toner, *The Politics of Energy* (Toronto: Methuen: 1985)
36 The agreement is discussed in the following section under social policies.
37 Many believe that, in an age of globalization and stricter controls over corporate behaviour, Canada should create a single national regulator; however, several provinces, including Quebec and Alberta, are opposed. See William D. Coleman, "Federalism and Financial Services," in Bakvis and Skogstad, *Canadian Federalism,* pp. 178–196, at p. 191.
38 See Herman Bakvis, "Checkerboard Federalism? Labour Market Development Policy in Canada," in Bakvis and Skogstad, *Canadian Federalism,* pp. 197–219.
39 Until 2004, Canada Customs and Revenue Agency (CCRA).
40 The amounts per person ranged from Cdn$1,195 in Newfoundland, to Cdn$628 in Quebec to Cdn$118 in British Columbia, which only recently became eligible for equalization payments. See Department of Finance Canada, Equalization Program (Federal Transfers to Provinces and Territories, March 2005. <www.fin.gc.ca/FEDPROV/eqpe.html> (accessed 26 May 2005).
41 The most dramatic case is the introduction of universal Medicare, pioneered by Saskatchewan.
42 More than 100 shared-cost programs, most of them temporary in nature and designed for specific purposes, have been created since the Second World War. See Hogg, *Constitutional Law of Canada,* p. 157.

43 In 1970 more than 20 percent of provincial revenue came from Ottawa; by
   1999, it was 13 percent.

44 See the 2001 report of Quebec's *Commission sur le déséquilibre fiscal* (better
   known as the Séguin Commission) at <http://www.desequilibrefis-
   cal.gouv.qc.ca/en/document/publication.htm> (26 May 2004).

45 For a summary of Canada's recent debates on fiscal federalism, see Centre for
   Research and Information on Canada, *Sharing the Wealth: For the Federation*
   (Ottawa: CRIC, 2002). For equalization, see pp. 9–13.

46 See Hogg, *Constitutional Law of Canada*, p. 434. The main case in Canada creating this restrictive interpretation is *Citizens' Insurance Co. v. Parsons* [1881]
   7 App. Cas. 96.

47 Opinions vary about the impact of the agreement. For a discussion, see Mark R.
   MacDonald, "The Agreement on Internal Trade: Trade-Offs for Economic
   Union and Federalism," in Bakvis and Skogstad, *Canadian Federalism*, 138–158.

48 The federal "declaratory power" is another of the broad federal powers in the
   1867 Constitution, and it permits the federal government to declare any "works
   and undertakings" to be to the general advantage of Canada. This too has
   fallen into disuse.

49 One response was the addition of Section 92A to the Constitution in 1982 in
   order to strengthen and clarify provincial jurisdiction over natural resources.

50 Vernon Fowke, *Canadian Agricultural Policy: The Historical Pattern* (Toronto: University of Toronto Press, 1946), chap. 6.

51 Under the "declaratory power," grain elevators had been declared works for the
   general advantage of Canada.

52 The federal jurisdiction over training is contested by provinces, which claim it
   falls under their jurisdiction over education. In recent years the federal government has entered into a number of agreements with provinces to transfer responsibilities for training and employment programs to provincial
   governments.

53 For a discussion, see Keith Banting, *The Welfare State and Canadian Federalism*
   (Kingston: McGill-Queen's University Press, 1987); and Jane Jenson and Susan
   Philips, "Regime Shift: New Citizenship Practices in Canada," *International Jour-
   nal of Canadian Studies* 14, 2 (June 1996): 111–135.

54 In the United States 100 percent of federal transfers to the states have significant conditions attached; in Canada the figure is 43.6 percent, but even here,
   conditions are minimal. See Ronald L. Watts, *The Spending Power in Federal Systems: A Comparative Study* (Kingston: Institute of Intergovernmental Relations,
   1999), p. 56.

55 SUFA has generated a large literature, both pro and con. Two themes predominate. One is that SUFA has failed to strengthen the Canadian social union and
   national standards; the other is that, like previous federal initiatives, it under-
   cuts the aspirations of Quebec. For a discussion, see Alain-G. Gagnon and
   Hugh. Segal, eds., *The Canadian Social Union without Quebec* (Montreal: Institute
   for Research on Public Policy, 2000).

56 Although recent decisions have significantly increased the federal government's jurisdiction. See, especially, *R. v. Hydro-Quebec* [1997] 1 S.C.R. 213. For
a discussion, see Mark Winfield, "Environmental Policy and Federalism," in
Bakvis and Skogstad, *Canadian Federalism,* 124–137.

57 See Winfield, "Environmental Policy and Federalism," p. 133.

58 See, for example, Federation of Canadian Municipalities, *Early Warnings:
Will Canadian Cities Compete?* February 2002, <www.focal.ca/pdf/
Canada_local_governments.pdf> (accessed 26 May 2005). For a discussion,
see F. Leslie Seidle, ed., *The Federal Role in Canada's Cities: Four Policy Perspectives.*
CPRN Discussion Paper F-27 (Ottawa: Canadian Policy Research Networks,
2002).

59 The Meech Lake Accord of 1867 would have entrenched the Cullen-Couture
Agreement of 1979.

60 Under the Canada-Quebec Accord, 1991, Quebec has sole responsibility for selecting all independent immigrants and refugees abroad who wish to settle in
Quebec. People who are selected receive a "Certificat de sélection du Québec,"
and the province advises the visa office responsible. Canadian Immigration and
Citzenship (CIC) then issues immigrant visas to those who have met all other
requirements, such as medical, security, and criminality checks. For more
details on the agreement, see <http://www.cic.gc.ca/english/press/fed-
prov2004/bkgr-agreements.html>. (Accessed November 2004).

61 See Martin Papillon, "Immigration, Diversity and Social Inclusion in Canada's
Cities," *The Federal Role in Canada's Cities: Four Policy Perspectives,* F. Leslie Seidle,
ed., CPRN Discussion Paper No. F|27. (Ottawa: Canadian Policy Research Net-
work, 2002).

62 The term "Indian" applies to the majority of indigenous peoples in Canada but
not all (i.e., not to Inuit or to Métis). Also, while the term "Indian" still has
meaning in law, it is no longer the preferred collective term of the indigenous
peoples themselves, who use "Aboriginal," "indigenous," "First Nations," or indeed the names of their specific nations, such as Mohawk, Mi'kmaq, Nisga'a,
and so on.

63 J. Anthony Long, "Federalism and Ethnic Self-Determination: Native Indians in
Canada," *Journal of Commonwealth and Comparative Politics* 29, 2 (June 1989),
p. 193.

64 For the former point of view, see Radha Jhappan, "The Federal-Provincial
Power-Grid and Aboriginal Self-Government," *New Trends in Canadian Federalism,* F. Rocher and M. Smith, eds. (Peterborough: Broadview, 1995), pp. 11–85.

65 David Hawkes, "Indigenous Peoples: Self-Government and Intergovernmental
Relations," *International Social Science Journal* 167, 1 (January 2001): 153–161;
James (Sakej) Henderson, "Empowering Treaty Federalism," *Saskatchewan Law
Review* 58, 3 (September 1994), p. 242.

66 The Judicial Committee of the Privy Council made this crucial distinction in
1937 in the case of *Attorney General for Canada v. Attorney General for Ontario,* also
known as the Labour Conventions case.

67 See Grace Skogstad, "International Trade Policy and Canadian Federalism: A Constructive Tension?" in Bakvis and Skogstad, *Canadian Federalism*, p. 159.

68 For a discussion, see Louis Balthazar, "History and Language Policy," *Languages and the State: The Law of Politics and Identity*, ed. David Schneiderman (Cowansville: Editions Yvon Blais, 1991), p. 84; and McRoberts, *Misconceiving Canada*, chap. 2.

69 Many observers from Quebec would argue that the opposite is occurring, with increasing involvement of the federal government in provincial jurisdictions such as health care, postsecondary education, and childcare.

70 See John Kincaid, Andrew Parkin, Richard L. Cole, and Alejandro Rodriguez, "Public Opinion on Federalism in Canada, Mexico, and the United States in 2003," *Publius: The Journal of Federalism* 33, 3 (Summer 2003): 145–162. See also Fred Cutler and Matthew Mendelsohn, "What Kind of Federalism do Canadians (Outside Quebec) Want?" *Policy Options* 22, 8 (October 2001): 23–29.

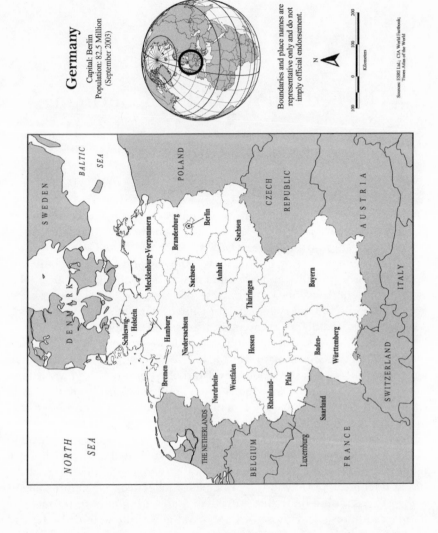

Germany

Capital: Berlin
Population: 82.5 Million
(September 2003)

Boundaries and place names are
representative only and do not
imply official endorsement.

N

Kilometers

100   0   100   200

Sources: ESRI Ltd.; CIA World Factbook;
Times Atlas of the World

SWEDEN

BALTIC
SEA

POLAND

CZECH
REPUBLIC

AUSTRIA

ITALY

SWITZERLAND

FRANCE

BELGIUM

THE NETHERLANDS

DENMARK

NORTH
SEA

Schleswig-
Holstein

Mecklenburg-Vorpommern

Brandenburg

Berlin

Sachsen

Sachsen-
Anhalt

Niedersachsen

Hamburg

Bremen

Nordrhein-
Westfalen

Hessen

Thüringen

Bayern

Rheinland-
Pfalz

Baden-
Württemberg

Saarland

Luxemburg

The Federal Republic of Germany

HANS-PETER SCHNEIDER

Like every federal order the German system is characterized by the principle of "strict separation" of powers and functions between the federal government (*Bund*) and the states (*Länder*). Both are vested with the three branches of public power: the legislative, the executive, and the judiciary. And each is responsible and accountable for its own acts and decisions, even if a federal law delegates legislative power to state parliaments. However, unlike the federal system in the United States, the German federal system is not based on two completely distinct and separate columns of federal and state powers with no connections between them; rather the German system is like an unbalanced scale or a seesaw, with a concentration of legislative functions at the federal level and of administrative powers at the state level. This is so because the Länder implement not only their own statutes but also a large part of federal law. The judiciary is also organized hierarchically: the lower and middle courts are the jurisdiction of the Länder, the higher courts of the federal government. Besides its detailed provisions dividing governmental authority between the federal government and the Länder, the German federal system also implies special duties of fidelity and loyalty to the principle of federalism.[1] What this means is that, in exercising their authority, the Länder are bound to respect one another's interests and those of the federal government, and the federal government is required to respect the interests of the Länder, including due process and good faith behaviour in bargaining situations.[2]

This chapter surveys the essentials of these basic features of the distribution of powers and responsibilities in the Federal Republic of Germany. In the process, several major themes emerge. These include: the increasing strength and influence of federal law as compared with Länder law making and, thus, the increasing trend towards what I refer to as "unitarization" of the federation; the increasing dissatisfaction in the federation as a whole regarding entangled federal-state programs and financial arrangements that blur proper accountability; the complex interaction of federal-Länder matters on European Union (EU) affairs; and, finally, the increasingly important role of the *Bundesrat*, the upper chamber of the federal Parliament, as both a house of review and as the focal point for intergovernmental negotiation not only over domestic matters but also over European and other international affairs.

THE FEDERAL CONSTITUTION IN HISTORICAL-CULTURAL CONTEXT

The Federal Republic of Germany consists of sixteen Länder, including three city states (Hamburg, Bremen, and Berlin). Its population numbers 82.1 million (with a declining trend). The total area of the Federal Republic covers 375,000 square kilometres. The national language is High German, but there are regional dialects and two separate languages (Frisian and Sorbian). The predominant ethnic group is German. In addition, there are some ethnic minorities (e.g., Frisians in the northwest, Sorbs in the east and – spread over the whole country – Turks and others with German citizenship). The Danes in the north also form a national minority. In the course of European integration there is now increasing migration of population from EU member states to Germany, just as Germans migrate to other EU member states. This is due to the freedom of movement of workers guaranteed in the EU treaty. Roughly 55 million Germans are Christians, of whom 28.2 million are Protestants and 27 million are Roman Catholics; in addition there are 1.7 million Muslims and only 54,000 of the Jewish faith (this represents a mere 10 percent of the Jewish population in Germany before the Holocaust). In 2003 the per capita GDP was approximately US$28,000.

HISTORICAL BACKGROUND

The Constitution of the Federal Republic of Germany was drawn up in 1948–49 and came into force as the Basic Law for the Federal Republic of Germany (hereafter referred to as BL) on 23 May 1949. It was based on a draft framed by a group of experts appointed by the prime ministers of the Länder (*Herrenchiemsee* Draft) and passed by the Parliamentary Council, which consisted of sixty-five members elected by the Länder (state) parliaments. Subsequently, it was confirmed by the state parliaments and finally approved by the Allied occupying powers. It was not subject to a referendum at that time since, because of the division of Germany, it was conceived as being only provisional. The decision in favour of a federal political system was, in fact, already predetermined by the Allies' demand for the drawing-up of a federal constitution (Frankfurt documents).[3]

However, it is based on a German federative constitutional tradition that dates back to the early Middle Ages.[4] The first German federal state with relatively weak central powers, the Bismarck Empire, came into existence in 1871, having gradually developed from the initially more strongly confederative structures.

After the First World War a federal order was again created simultaneously with the transition to democracy, but the Weimar Republic was more strongly unitary in outlook than was the Bismarck Empire. This federal order was destroyed by the Nazi regime, which began with the abolition of the Länder as early as 1933. Nevertheless, after the Second World War the new federal structure resulted from two forces. On the one hand, it was pre-shaped by the influence of the Allied powers, who built from the bottom up by re-establishing the Länder (which were distributed between the zones of occupation); on the other hand, and simultaneously, the clear and undisputed belief of the Parliamentary Council in the federal principle resulted in the building of a federal structure from the top down.

The main goals of the framers of the BL consisted, on the one hand, of distributing political power roughly equally to two levels of government (division of powers) in order to strengthen democracy (by "bringing power nearer to the people") and, on the other hand, of counteracting the dangers of too strong a central power in the middle of Europe, which would threaten peace and security. Different approaches with regard to educational and cultural policy were also to be supported by assigning the appropriate responsibilities to the Länder. In addition, in order to preserve national unity and to promote a free market economy throughout the whole of the Federal Republic, and as a kind of precaution against separatist tendencies, the objective of creating equal or equivalent living conditions throughout the federal territory was included in the Constitution (Article 72, para. 2, no. 3; Article 106, para. 3, sent. 3, no. 2 BL).[5]

As an additional unifying incentive the basic rights of citizens (i.e., the individual rights of freedom and equality of human beings) were placed in the very first section of the BL. This was to counteract the experience under National Socialism and to emphasize the outstanding importance of these rights. The BL, however, does not recognize the rights of interest or pressure groups or of other collective identities, beyond assuring their members of their individual rights as citizens[6] (although, as Germany becomes increasingly multicultural, more discussion is taking place). Nor does it recognize an official language or the preferential treatment of culture or religion. On the contrary, it expressly stipulates that the state is to behave with neutrality and indifference when it comes to cultural and religious points of view. Further, the BL does not provide for any basic duties of German citizens. Nevertheless, it does contain the unwritten principle of the loyalty of the Länder to the federation (and vice versa) as well as the loyalty of the Länder to each other (*Bundestreue*).

Cultural Influences

In their work, the authors of the BL were influenced neither by a particular political theory nor by any religious or ideological orientation but, above all, by certain demands made by the Allies and by the different political interests of the re-established Länder. However, there were differences among the political parties regarding the distribution of responsibilities between the Federation and the Länder. The Social Democrats aimed at a more strongly centralist system, while the Christian Democrats preferred a more decentralized federalism. As a result of the process of unification in 1990 five new Länder joined the federation, all of which were parts of the former German Democratic Republic (GDR) (Brandenburg, Mecklenburg-Vorpommern, Sachsen, Sachsen-Anhalt, and Thüringen).[7] In gaining access to the BL they confirmed the federal system but turned the German culture in a more Protestant and more Eastern direction. Finally, the transborder relationships of some Länder with such countries as France, Spain, Denmark, and the Netherlands functions as a component of European integration, promoting multiculturalism and the internationalization of Germany.

THE CONSTITUTIONAL DISTRIBUTION OF POWERS AND RESPONSIBILITIES

Cooperative Federalism

In general, the original federal structure laid down in the BL with regard to the distribution of functions and responsibilities between the federal government and the Länder can be described as a cooperative kind of federalism. After a strongly federative phase in the 1950s a creeping centralization has occurred as a result of the federal government's almost exclusive use of its concurrent legislative jurisdiction, to the point where Germany is now described as a unitary type of federalism. Two typical features marked this development. First, the Federal Constitutional Court treated the employment of concurrent legislative powers by the federation in accordance with Article 72, para. 2, BL as a "political question," thus declaring it to be non-justiciable.[8] Second, in practice, the Länder handed over much of their concurrent responsibilities in exchange for stronger participation in federal legislation through their role in the Bundesrat. In this way the proportion of those laws that require the consent of the Bundesrat has increased from the original figure of about 25 percent to more than 60 percent.

The Bundesrat is a key federal legislative organ. It is involved both in federal legislation and in the administration of federal laws, as well as in EU matters, and it participates in the appointment of justices to the Federal Constitutional Court. In addition, and at the same time, it serves to coordinate affairs among the Länder. Its members are not elected directly by the electorate of the Länder or their parliaments but, rather, are nominated by the governments of the Länder as delegates from their cabinets. It is therefore a focal institution for the processes of "executive federalism." The number of Bundesrat members that each state government can appoint is fixed by the BL, and this varies between three and six, depending on the Land population (discussed further below). The votes of each Land can only be cast unanimously as a block. Therefore, the political composition of the government of each Land plays a leading role in the decisions of the Bundesrat. Moreover, the Bundesrat has an absolute veto over lower house (*Bundestag*) laws requiring its approval and thus acts as a genuine second chamber in the federal Parliament. The same applies to ministerial orders requiring its consent (Article 80, para. 2, BL) and general administrative regulations, provided that they involve the implementation of federal laws by the Länder.

Although from a constitutional perspective the structure of the Bundesrat is based on Länder interests, the operation of political parties at the Länder level means that party differences have a strong influence on the decision-making process in the Bundesrat. In other words, if the parliamentary opposition in the federation has a majority among the governments of the Länder (and thus a majority of the votes in the Bundesrat), it can block federal legislation whenever the consent of the Bundesrat is required. Since this has been the case in more than thirty of the years since 1949, the country has, in all practical terms, been governed by a "Grand Coalition" of the major parties, thus producing a "negotiated federalism." In addition, each Land election has come to constitute a mini federal election. Under these circumstances the voters have been able to enforce political accountability by assigning credit to policies that they favour and disparagement to those that they do not. Consequently, in most Land elections the federal government is held accountable for its failures as well as for its successes.

Since the end of the 1960s, cooperative federalism has become even more significant in Germany because of the joint tasks[9] and joint taxes[10] provided by 1969 amendments to the BL. In the meantime, this excessive cooperation has produced many disadvantages, such as a lack of transparency, unclear responsibilities, and an erosion of the power of Land parliaments. An attempt at federal reform is now being made in order to disentangle concentrated and interrelated responsibilities, and to incorporate competitive elements into the federal system. However, essential change to the basic distribution of responsibilities is unlikely. This means that, for the most part, legislation will be centralized and that the implementation of federal laws will, to a great extent, remain decentralized.[11]

Vertical Division of Powers: The Two Levels of Government

As the federal order of the Constitution primarily deals with the relationship between the Bund (federal government) and the Länder, the BL only contains general regulations concerning the constitutional structure and responsibilities of the local level of government (i.e., municipalities and districts). Thus the communes are not regarded as a third order of government in addition to the federation and the Länder but, rather, as constituent parts of the Länder, which regulate their internal constitutions through legislation. Just like the federal government and the Länder, the communes must, however, provide for the democratic representation of the people through secret ballots at general, direct, free, and equal elections (Article 28, para. 1, BL). Within this legislative framework the communes have the right of self-administration: they have the right to govern themselves regarding all matters of the local community and to do this under their own responsibility (Article 28, para. 2, BL). Their right of self-administration also includes, to a certain extent, responsibility for their own finances and the right to their own constitutional source of tax revenues (local autonomy).[12]

The two orders of government, federal and Länder, are basically independent of each other. They have governmental autonomy, which is restricted only by their constitutions. Both also enjoy territorial autonomy. Their borders can be changed by federal law (i.e., with the consent of the federal Parliament) within the framework of the so-called new demarcation procedure (Article 29 BL) only with the consent of the people in the Land involved. The situation is different for the communes. Their boundaries are at the disposal of the Land legislature, but the affected communes must be heard by the responsible parliament before territorial reform takes place.

As far as taxation is concerned, the Länder are dependent on federal acts of Parliament. On the other hand, they are largely autonomous with regard to borrowing, provided that they remain within the framework of the limits set out in the constitutions regarding investment levels and those set out in the Stability Pact of the EU (which sets a limit of 3 percent of the GNP per year on governmental borrowing). The situation with the communes is slightly different: in each case, their right to raise taxes lies in the hands of the federal or Land legislature. And their right to borrow money is dependent on municipal supervision by the Land authorities.

In principle, not only the federal government and the Länder but also the communes have regulatory autonomy, and here the passing of formal laws is reserved to the federal and state parliaments, while the communal councils can only take decisions on by-laws and other regulations (i.e., legal norms of lesser importance, which must remain within the framework of federal and Land law). As long as each of these three levels of government has its own material and natural resources at its disposal, it can redistribute them independently of the others. In the field of executive responsibility, the federal government, the Länder, and the communes are completely autonomous only when carrying out their own laws or regulations. When the Länder administer federal laws, however, they are subject to legal supervision on the part of the federal government. When the communes implement federal or Land laws, they, in turn, are subject to the Land's supervision. In the field of judicial power, the courts of the Bund and the Länder do, in fact, decide matters independently (although not separately, in the sense that they are both equally bound by federal and Land law).

From the financial point of view both the federal government and the Länder can extend their influence to the lower tiers (subnational or local government) by means of special grants, thus restricting their power to shape their own affairs. First, the federal government can give the Länder general supplementary grants within the framework of the tax equalization scheme between the two (Article 107, para. 2, sent. 3). Second, the federal government can grant financial aid for particularly important investments (Article 104a, para. 4, BL). Similarly, a Land can provide its communes with so-called unconditional "key grants" as supplements to their general budgets or with specially appropriated (conditional) grants so that they can fulfill particular tasks. In addition, the federal government has concurrent legislative power with regard to the most important taxes, which it has already exercised fully. The result is that, as far as the type and productiveness of the tax sources are concerned, the Länder and communes have become largely dependent on the federal government.

Horizontal Division of Powers: The Three Branches of Government

In Germany all the responsibilities of the state, not only in the field of legislation but also in the fields of administration and the judiciary, are distributed between the federal government and the Länder. Here, the BL makes use of the subtraction model: all those responsibilities not expressly given to the federal government in the BL are automatically the tasks of the Länder. Article 30 BL states: "Except as otherwise provided or permitted by this Basic Law, the exercise of state powers and the discharge of state functions is a matter for the Länder." For legislation, a corresponding regulation is to be found in Article 70 BL; for general administration see Article 83 BL; and for the administration of justice see Article 92 BL. Consequently, no order of government has comprehensive powers from which responsibilities are delegated or transferred either to a higher level or to a lower level. Following the wording of the Constitution, one might assume that the focal point of responsibilities lies with the Länder as they are provided with the original residual power. However, in constitutional practice this is not the case. The BL distributes responsibilities to the federal government and the Länder completely, leaving no loopholes in the Constitution. Consequently, the political balance lies in favour of the federal government because its exclusive and/or concurrent responsibilities are more important and more powerful than are those of an individual Land or even of all the Länder together.

Legislative Powers

With regard to the allocation of legislative jurisdiction, the Constitution provides the federal government with three lists of areas. There is a distinction between the exclusive responsibilities of the federal government (Article 71 BL) in the first list (Article 73, nos. 1 to 11, BL) and its concurrent responsibilities (Article 72 BL) in the second list (Article 74, para. 1, nos. 1 to 26; and Article 74a, para. 1, BL). The latter are by nature "Janus-faced"; that is, they are the responsibilities of both the federal government and the Länder, but the former has a one-sided right of access to these with regard to issues concerning equal or equivalent living conditions or the needs of legal and economic unity in the federation as a whole (Article 72, para. 2, BL). The third list of so-called framework legislation (Article 75, para. 1, nos. 1 to 6, BL) represents a subdivision of exclusive federal responsibilities, which is distinguished from those of the first list by the fact that the federal government may only lay down a legal framework that leaves sufficient room for Land legislation. One can thus talk of the shared responsibilities of the federal government and the Länder. In practice, however, the federal government has often laid down such detailed regulations for the Länder that they could only implement federal regulations.

One finds no catalogue of the legislative responsibilities of the communes either in the BL or in the constitutions of the Länder. The relevant texts are restricted to a general clause through which the right to promulgate regulations is passed on to the communes regarding "all matters of the local community."

The lists of legislative responsibilities are, for the most part, concrete and detailed (above all with regard to the solution of postwar problems), but they also contain very broad descriptions of each field of responsibility (e.g., Article 74, para. 1, no. 6 [public welfare]; no. 11 [economic affairs]; no. 12 [social security]; nos. 11a, 24, and 26 [technology and environmental law]). This enables the federal government to find a suitable basis for almost all its legislation. These lists are by no means complete because, in the BL, one may always find additional exclusive federal responsibility, where a particular article enables the federal government to regulate "further details" by means of federal law. The legislative responsibilities of the federal Parliament in the field of taxes are not to be found in the lists but, rather, in Chapter 10 of the BL, which deals with "Finance" (Article 105 BL). There one also finds the only exclusive legislative responsibility of the Länder expressly formulated by the BL. This concerns local taxes on consumption and expenditures insofar as they are not substantially similar to taxes imposed by federal law. On the basis of this provision, for example, some towns and municipalities in much visited tourist areas have introduced a so-called secondary home tax, which covers the additional expenditure of the infrastructure for inhabitants who have a second home but do not live there permanently.

As far as the individual lists are concerned, the exclusive legislative competence of the federal government includes: citizenship, immigration, and naturalization; elections to the Bundestag, the European Parliament, and political parties; communications; transportation; cooperation between the Länder in the field of internal security; national defence; foreign affairs and international relations; and the diplomatic service. Concurrent legislative responsibility, which, as mentioned above, has, in practice, been fully handled by the federal Parliament, includes: economic policy making (economic union, monetary policy, fiscal policy, international trade and commerce, and interstate and domestic trade and commerce); production and provision of energy; agriculture; protection of the environment; social welfare, labour, unemployment, and workers' compensation; health care; civil and criminal law and the organization of the judiciary.

The exclusive responsibilities of the Länder extend to: elections to the Landtag (state parliaments) and to local councils, language policy and culture, religious matters (such as religious instruction in public schools), natural resources, education, internal security and policing, and foreign affairs (insofar as the Länder are responsible for legislation in, for example, the fields of culture and education [Article 32, para. 2, BL]). In practice, however, along with their limited jurisdiction in the fields of economic cooperation, development aid, and European integration, the Länder also conduct "sideline foreign affairs" (or transnational relations), which is a behaviour not always welcomed by the federal government (see below).

Executive Powers

The BL names only a few areas that are administered exclusively by the federal government (e.g., the foreign service, border police, customs, armed forces, and federal roads and waterways [see Articles 86, 87 and 87a BL]). Within all other policy fields the relevant federal laws are implemented by the Länder, either in their own right under the legal oversight of the federal government (referred to as "execution by the Länder in their own right" [see Articles 83 and 84 BL]) or on the instructions of, and in accordance with, the federal government (referred to as "execution by the Länder on federal commission" [Article 85 BL]). In addition, the Länder naturally have to implement their own laws (i.e., Land administration).[13]

Where the federal government has the right to establish its own administrative authorities, it also has the right to privatize its tasks and administrative duties. Provided that rights of sovereignty do not have to be exerted, this means that the federal government not only has the right to transfer administration to a private legal firm (organizational privatization) but that it also has the right to transfer the execution of state tasks by means of private law (functional privatization). Examples of this include the privatization of the postal service, telecommunications, the federal railways, and, in part the construction of roads and tunnels. In all these cases, of course, the federal government maintains certain rights of control (e.g., by retaining a decisive percentage of shares), which are exerted through planning and regulation authorities. In addition to the federal government and the Länder, the forerunners of administrative privatization are, above all, the communes, which have almost completely privatized service-provision facilities (e.g., power and water, waste disposal) and cultural facilities (e.g., theatres, museums, and sports facilities).[14]

Judicial Powers

Judicial powers are divided between the federal government and the Länder (Article 92 BL), but here the emphasis is on the Länder. The federal government is only responsible for the five supreme courts of appeal and the Federal Constitutional Court. The five appeal courts are the Federal Court of Justice, the Federal Administrative Court, the Federal Labour Court, the Federal Social Security Court, and the Federal Finance Court. All other courts are in the jurisdiction of the Länder, including the courts of appeal, which become active when the special conditions for access to a federal court are not fulfilled. In addition, almost all the Länder (apart from Schleswig-Holstein) now have their own state constitutional courts, which make decisions regarding the compatibility between state constitutions and acts taken by Land authorities. These courts are constitutional watchdogs, as is the Federal Constitutional Court, whose sole standard is the BL.

Intergovernmental Relations

The BL provides for a close interrelationship between the orders of government within the Federation in the area of executive responsibilities. It expressly obliges the Länder to implement federal laws to the extent that the federal government has not created its own authorities for this purpose. As a rule, the Länder implement these federal laws at their own discretion (i.e., "administration by the Länder in their own right"). In these cases the federal government retains an oversight concerning the legality of the implementation of these laws, and it issues general administrative regulations guaranteeing the uniformity of this implementation throughout the federal territory (see Articles 83, 84 BL). However, the Länder are even more closely bound to the federal government whenever they "execute federal laws on federal commission" (e.g., in the field of nuclear energy). Here, the federal government can issue individual instructions and even examine the effectiveness of the concrete measures of the Land involved (referred to as "expert control").

The Constitution itself provides a special procedure for executing federal laws "on federal commission," in which the federal government retains all the responsibility for their content as well as for their substance. This leaves the Länder with responsibility for carrying out the law but with very little flexibility in doing so. In other words, when the respective law comes into force, the federal government is the master and the Länder are the servants, and possibly even the slaves. This is because they have to follow even unconstitutional instructions that issue from the federal government (Article 85 BL), at least until these have been challenged in court. The only remaining – and of course often substantial – influence wielded by the Länder is their involvement, through the Bundesrat, in the formulation of those laws.

The BL does not prevent the transfer of state tasks from one level to the other (i.e., from the federal government to the Länder or vice versa). This can be done through a law or through an agreement between the Länder, provided that the responsibilities laid down in the Constitution and the limits of constitutional change are adhered to (Article 79, para. 3, BL). In addition to the written responsibilities of the federal government, however, unwritten responsibilities are recognized in three different ways. First, responsibilities in the form of "implied powers" may arise from the "nature of the matter" (e.g., in relation to the design of the federal flag Article 22 BL only states that it should be black, red, and gold). Second, responsibilities can follow from an insoluble "subject connection" (e.g., when a written responsibility cannot be carried out adequately without including a related matter). Third, an unwritten responsibility can be derived from the need to regulate an inessential "annex," which derives from a written responsibility and which is required in the interest of completeness.

In some areas the federal government has, in fact, renounced its right of regulation or its power for political structuring, either voluntarily or under pressure from certain interest groups. Thus, for example, Article 15 BL provides that property, natural resources, and the means of production can be "socialized" (i.e., transferred to public ownership) by federal law. However, in the interests of maintaining the free market economy, this has so far not occurred.[15] The same applies to so-called "compulsive intervention" (*Bundeszwang*, Article 37 BL), with which the federal government – if necessary, even with the help of the army – could force the Länder to fulfill their duties in accordance with the Constitution.

Some taxes foreseen in the BL have not in fact been raised, although they are permitted by the Constitution (e.g., entertainment tax, alcohol tax, capital tax – at least to a certain degree). Based on a decision of the Federal Constitutional Court,[16] Article 74, no. 25, BL provides for concurrent legislative powers with respect to state liability. The federal government has not yet made use of this provision, however, because it is the Länder, which have to bear the main burden of the administration, that would primarily be affected by it. Finally, under pressure from the trade unions, the federal government, despite its concurrent responsibility for the field of labour law (Article 74, para. 12, BL), has declined to regulate labour disputes through legislation on strikes and lockouts, continuing to leave these matters to the courts.

Since all federal responsibilities must be directly provided for in the BL, whenever there is no constitutional provision for federal regulation, or whenever federal regulation is restricted outright, the field of state responsibilities is a matter for the Länder (Article 30 BL; for legislation see Article 70 BL; for executive power see Article 83 BL). Thus the Länder have a kind of residual power. The communes, which have the exclusive task of dealing with all matters pertaining to local affairs (see Article 28, para. 2, BL), can to this extent also claim some residual power. However, in practice these residual powers are not of great importance because all orders of government tend to make full use of the responsibilities with which they are charged by the Constitution (save only the few exceptions mentioned above).

Finally, in Germany, whenever anybody has the right to competency, as a rule they do not renounce it voluntarily. Thus the clauses that permit the federal government to ignore areas of concurrent jurisdiction or even to return assumed responsibilities to the Länder (see Arts. 72 Para. 3, 125 a Para. 2 BL) have so far not had any practical importance. On the contrary, the BL contains a "regulation of vested rights" that favours the federal government and that means that no federal law can be questioned or challenged subsequent to its implementation (Article 125a, para. 1, BL). The criteria pertaining to the use of concurrent responsibility were considerably tightened by the federal government some time ago (Article 72, para. 2, BL).

THE LOGIC OF THE CONSTITUTIONAL DISTRIBUTION
OF POWERS AND RESPONSIBILITIES

The federal order in the BL follows neither a fundamental logic nor – apart from its liberal democratic structure – a particular philosophical, cultural, political, or economic theory. In particular, German federalism is not based on the principle of "subsidiarity," as is the Roman Catholic social doctrine. According to that doctrine the responsibilities within the state ought to be distributed in such a way that the lower unit, within the framework of its capacity, is given precedence over the superior unit in each case. In other words, tasks that local governments can fulfill ought to be situated with the local governments rather than with the Land or the federal government. Resting on hierarchic assumptions rather than on the principle of federal equality of (subnational) states, the principle of subsidiarity may have been the model for some members of the Parliamentary Council. Essentially, however, the restoration of the federal system in 1948–49 was based both on German constitutional traditions dating back to the Middle Ages and on the desires of the Allies. Thus, in spite of some centralist tendencies among the Social Democrats, there was no real alternative to a federal structure either from a practical or a theoretical point of view.

Theoretical Aspects of German Federalism

Nevertheless, even in Germany there has been no lack of attempts to theoretically justify the federal system. Above all, the federal system vertically distributes powers between different orders of government and, thus, serves to limit state power. In addition, it strengthens democracy because it brings power closer to the people and gives them the opportunity to express their political will through elections and votes on various issues. In this way federalism simultaneously promotes both the multiparty system and competition between political parties. It permits political innovation and social experiments through competition among the Länder. As individual constitutional laboratories, the Länder can gain experience with new concepts and policies before these are adopted by other Länder or by the federal government and then applied to the republic as a whole. Last but not least, German federalism constitutes and supports political opposition within the federation because the political parties constituting the opposition in the federal Parliament always rule in some, if not in a majority, of the Länder. Thus Germany's political leaders receive training before they enter federal politics. With only a few exceptions, since 1949 all federal chancellors in Germany had first been prime ministers of Land governments.

The BL has created a symmetrical type of federalism. The Bund and the Länder are on an equal level: both have state or sovereign qualities within their spheres and thus also have the same constitutional status. Above all, the BL charges all the Länder with the same tasks, independent of the size of territory, size of population, economic performance, and financial strength. Thus the BL distinguishes only between responsibilities of the federal government and those of the Länder, but not, as in Spain or Russia, between functionally different federated units. This means that there is only one type of constituent or subnational unit: the Länder. The only differentiation that the BL makes between the Länder concerns the number of their votes in the Bundesrat: Länder with more than seven million inhabitants have six votes, those with more than six million have five votes, those with more than two million have four votes, and all those beneath this figure have three votes (the current total of Länder votes in the Bundesrat being sixty-nine). Thus, after reunification, the territorially large Länder in the west (i.e., Bavaria, Baden-Württemberg, Lower Saxony, and North Rhine-Westphalia), with their twenty-four votes, have achieved the status of a blocking minority in the Bundesrat.

Although the BL assumes, in principle, that the tasks and responsibilities divided between the federal government and the Länder are to be exercised independently ("principle of separation," Article 104a, para. 1, BL), the framers of the 1969 Constitution nevertheless added other areas of activity. As noted above, these were (1) the joint tasks of the Bund and the Länder and (2) the joint taxes to which both were entitled. The joint tasks include construction and enlargement of institutions of higher education, improvement of the agrarian structure and coastal preservation (Article 91a BL), and educational planning and the promotion of research (Article 91b BL). The preparation and implementation of individual projects to fulfill the joint tasks is a matter for Bund-Länder commissions, in which the federal government, with its sixteen votes together with the six votes from some "poor" Länder (the city states, Mecklenburg-Western Pomerania, Saxony-Anhalt, and, Saarland), has a two-thirds majority and therefore can realize its own interests. This has often met with the resistance of the large and "rich" Länder. For this reason the present federal reform movement, which is pursuing the goal of "disentanglement," is considering abolishing these joint tasks. The same pressure is being applied to the joint taxes (i.e., the income and corporation tax and the turnover tax, which are split roughly equally between the federal government and the Länder, with a small share going to the local governments).

However, Germany's most far-reaching deviation from the dual model of federalism lies in the fact that the federal government does not execute its own laws but, as a rule, relies upon the Länder to do so (Article 83, seq. BL). Thus the BL, by giving the federal government legal control over how the Länder executes its laws as well as the authority to issue directives in the administration of its tasks, has given cooperative federalism a hierarchical component. In constitutional practice, however, this hierarchical component is moderated by cooperative patterns of action arising from the approximately 900 working groups and ministerial forums common to the federal government and the Länder. These have developed in order to debate, coordinate, and even (sometimes) solve problems pertaining to the implementation of laws.

Special Features of German Federalism

Among the special features that characterize the German system of federalism, which is neither dual nor purely vertical, and that emphasize its cooperative structure are bodies in which the federal government and the Länder function jointly. Foremost among these is the Federal Convention (*Bundesversammlung*), which has the task of electing the federal president and which comprises all the members of the German Bundestag, along with an equal number of representatives nominated by the parliaments of the Länder (Article 54 BL). Another is the Mediation Committee (*Vermittlungsausschuss*), which is composed of one Bundesrat representative from each Land and the same number of representatives from the Bundestag. This committee seeks compromises when the legislative process is bogged down by ongoing disagreement between the Bundestag and the Bundesrat (Article 77, para. 2, BL).

As far as the distribution of state functions and responsibilities in the BL is concerned, the premise that the Federal Republic of Germany sees itself as a "social federal state" (Article 20, para. 1, BL), or as a "social state under the rule of law," has played a decisive role. If one adds the constitutional goal of "the establishment of equivalent [until 1994, equal] living conditions" (see Article 72, para. 2; Aricle 106, para. 3, sent. 4, no. 2, BL) to this orientation towards the welfare state, then one sees why the corresponding legislative powers in the fields of public welfare, social security, and the guaranteed living conditions must lie with the federal government. Nevertheless, the Länder and communes also participate in realizing welfare state objectives. Not only do they implement the social laws of the federal Parliament but they also complement them. For example, they may help to fund places in kindergartens and establishments providing childcare, or they may make payments towards supporting blind people. They are also frequently responsible for funding federal social programs. For example, social aid (guaranteeing the subsistence level) is paid by the municipalities but regulated by the federal government. In addition – unlike the BL – the constitutions of the Länder also contain basic social rights (e.g., the right to work, education, housing, and social security), which oblige a Land to gear its policies and finances towards realizing these rights.

EVOLUTION OF THE CONSTITUTIONAL DISTRIBUTION OF POWERS AND RESPONSIBILITIES

Spheres of Constitutional Powers

Germany has, in effect, two spheres of constitutional law, each separate from the other: the federal Constitution (i.e., the BL) and the constitutions of the Länder. In the interest of uniform constitutional structure, however, the BL specifies that the constitutional order in the Länder must correspond to the principles of the democratic and social state (the so-called homogeneity clause; Article 28, para. 1, sent. 1, BL). Thus the basic structures of the Constitution of the federation (i.e., those pertaining to the republic, rule of law, democracy, social welfare, and federal order) cannot be altered by any amendments to the Constitution. The same applies to the division of the federation into Länder and to the participation of the Länder in federal legislation (Article 79, para. 3, BL). Outside this inviolable core, the wording and content of the BL can be changed at any time by a two-thirds majority of the Bundestag and the Bundesrat. However, such an amendment must take the form of a change to the existing text of the Constitution itself (Article, 79, paras. 1 and 2, BL). This also applies to the distribution of legislative powers and responsibilities, whose shift in favour of the federal government during the past fifty-five years has been the overwhelming reason for the fifty-one amendments to the Constitution made so far. The transfer of Länder responsibilities to the federal government, or of exclusive federal responsibilities to the Länder, thus always require a formal change to the wording of the Constitution. In contrast, the federal government can, by means of a simple federal law, (re-)transfer to the Länder, at any time, the concurrent responsibilities assumed by it (see Articles 72, para. 3; Article 125a, para. 2, sent. 2, BL).

If the Länder want to shift or concentrate their own – mostly administrative – responsibilities among each other, then this can be done by means of interstate treaties. These merely require the consent of the Land parliaments. There is no provision for ratification or other forms of popular participation in the constitutional amendment process. Thus, the people in the federation as a whole have, as a rule, no direct influence on changes in the distribution of powers and responsibilities, either between the federal government and the Länder or among the Länder themselves.

Nor do the federal or Länder constitutional courts have a direct influence on the distribution of powers and responsibilities.[17] However, where there is a disagreement these constitutional courts can pronounce judgment on the content and limits of a certain power, and they can also have a decisive influence on the way in which that power is exerted. Thus, for example, the Federal Constitutional Court has to decide on disagreements between the federal government and the Länder concerning their responsibilities, particularly with regard to the exercise of federal supervision (Article 93, para. 1, nos. 3 and 4, BL). In the same way, the increasing proportion of laws requiring the consent of the Bundesrat[18] is based on the relevant decisions of the Federal Constitutional Court.[19] This has occurred largely because, whenever a single provision in a law (e.g., concerning administrative procedure) justifies Bundesrat consent, the court has declared that the entire law requires Bundesrat consent.

With regard to interpreting the federal features of the BL to the advantage or disadvantage of the federal government or the Länder, the Federal Constitutional Court has not pursued a uniform course. When the matter concerns a federal claim to powers, the court has usually favoured the Länder, but when the matter concerns the control and directive rights of the federal government vis-à-vis the Länder's execution of federal laws, the court has favoured the federal government.

"Unitarization" of Powers and Attempted Reforms

Since 1949 state tasks have been increasingly concentrated in the hands of the federal government and, in particular, there has been an increasing shift towards federal legislation. The federal government has not only made full use of its existing responsibilities in the field of concurrent legislation, but, through numerous changes to the Constitution, it has also obtained even more responsibilities. Examples of this may be seen in environmental protection, state liability, transplantation and reproductive medicine, and gene technology.

However, this trend has by no means occurred contrary to the will of the Länder; rather, it has had their express consent in the Bundesrat. Thus the autonomous legislative power of the Länder has, in effect, been exchanged for a co-determination of federal laws.[20] The winners in these processes have been the federal government (with its greater regulative power) and the Länder governments (with their veto power in the Bundesrat); the losers were obviously the Länder parliaments as they had to give up the option of exercising concurrent legislation. Interest groups, trade unions, and professional associations also benefited from this development as they were able to achieve their demands more easily and more effectively at the federal level than through decentralized negotiations with a large number of Land governments.

In order to stop the trend towards "unitarization," in 1994 the Joint Constitutional Commission of the Bundestag and the Bundesrat tried to make it more difficult for the federal government to employ its concurrent legislative responsibilities. It did so by replacing the non-justiciable "need clause" for uniform federal regulation with a new criterion of "indispensability" for equivalent living conditions or the maintenance of legal or economic unity

(Article 72, para. 2, BL). The Land parliaments were consequently given the right to take legal action in the Federal Constitutional Court against the federal legislature's abuse of these criteria (Article 93, para. 1, no. 2a, BL). Nevertheless, these approaches have so far had little effect. To date, the Federal Constitutional Court has ruled against the federal Parliament in only one such case: it declared the federal law concerning the care of the elderly to be unconstitutional.[21] Again, the losers in this ongoing development towards a "unitary federal state" are not the Länder but the Land parliaments. This is also why these parliaments are currently the most vocal in demanding the reform of federalism in Germany; above all, they are calling for a revision of the distribution of legislative responsibilities.

Corresponding to increasing legislative unitarization has been a trend towards the federalization of executive power. Here, the federal government often acts as the "paymaster," and the Länder have to implement the jointly developed programs.[22] Despite the intentions of the 1969 reform of financial responsibilities, the basis in constitutional law for this "entanglement of policy" was the introduction of the right of the federal government to grant financial aid to the Länder and communes. This aid was supposed to avert the disturbance of the overall economic equilibrium, to equalize differing economic capacities within the federal territory, and/or to promote economic growth (Article 104a BL). With the help of special federal grants Land governments have undertaken urban planning and the renovation of the historical quarters of towns, supported local transport, built and maintained hospitals, subsidized the coal mining industry and the shipbuilding industry, and undertaken other projects determined to be in the national interest. In accordance with the principle of "whoever pays for the music also calls the tune," however, the Länder have retained only a small window for decision-making and policy-shaping in such fields. The Länder fall into a "policy entanglement trap" that makes it almost impossible for them to make a clear distinction between their responsibilities and those of the federal government. This entanglement also reduces transparency in administrative and decision-making processes. So far there have not been any other decentralization processes in the Federal Republic of Germany, although, since around 1994, there have been many calls for reform. However, a decentralization effort could have a real chance of coming to the fore during the course of the reform work currently being addressed by the Commission of the Bundestag and the Bundesrat for the Modernization of the Federal Order.[23]

Influence of the European Constitution

During the past three decades the whole federal system in Germany has been affected and modified by the process of European integration. Right from the beginning the BL has provided by law for the transfer of sovereign powers to international organizations (Article 24, para. 1, BL). As a member of the EU, the Federal Republic of Germany has been taking part in establishing a united Europe. This was constitutionally recognized in Germany in 1993 through the creation of a special constitutional provision for the European integration process (Article 23, para. 1, BL). Consequently, an enormous transfer of responsibilities to the EU has already taken place, largely in the fields of industry and commerce, currency, and international trade. In these areas the EU already has almost exclusive responsibility. The European law created by the EU in these cases takes precedence over all national law (including national constitutions). Due to its sovereignty over external relations, the federal government is not prevented by the BL from transferring the exclusive powers of the Länder to the EU (e.g., in the field of culture, education, and/or internal security). For this reason, Article 23, paras. 2 to 5, BL provide for massive participation rights of the Länder in policy making in relation to the EU. If the transfer of Länder responsibilities to the EU affects essential Länder interests, then the federal government is required to pay strict and detailed attention to the opinions of the Länder regarding these decisions. In cases of transfer of exclusive Länder powers the Länder can, if necessary, send their own representatives to the bodies of the EU. In such cases they speak on behalf of the Federal Republic of Germany as a whole. However, this external power of the Länder is now being questioned because it is seen as impeding the effective enforcement of German political interests in Europe.

The current draft of a new constitution for the EU leaves the existing system of responsibilities between the EU and its member states largely untouched. However, it strengthens the possibilities of control on the part of the member states with regard to observing the subsidiarity principle through the creation of an early-warning system. This would place the national parliaments in a position to examine whether they could formulate a particular regulation better and more effectively than could the EU. In this case, the member-state parliaments could make a complaint against such European institutions as the European Council and, if necessary, could take legal action at the European Court of Justice. Since the Bundesrat is considered to be part of the national parliament (i.e., its second chamber), a majority among the Länder will, thus, for the first time be given the right of direct access to the European Court of Justice.

MAINTENANCE AND MANAGEMENT OF THE DISTRIBUTION OF POWERS AND RESPONSIBILITIES

Cooperation between the Governments

In practice, the handling of the distribution of governmental powers and responsibilities is almost entirely of a cooperative nature, with the struggle for agreement and the search for compromises a dominant feature. From the point of view of the federal government, however, the relationship between it and the Länder can involve conflicts if the respective party majorities in the Bundesrat and the Bundestag drift apart. Elements of collusion may occur when the federal government tries to "buy" majorities in the Bundesrat by means of providing financial help for the poorer Länder. Alternatively, individual Länder may, for party reasons, support the policy of the federal government in the Bundesrat contrary to, or in spite of, their regional interests. In recent years German federalism has assumed certain competitive traits as a result of the lack of economic growth, leading to empty coffers and declining economic resources. This has made it considerably more difficult for the financially weaker Länder (in particular in the eastern part of Germany) to make the necessary investments or to obtain highly qualified personnel.

The main fields in which the senior governments cooperate are: (1) the fulfilment of joint tasks; (2) the horizontal and vertical redistribution of income among federal government, the Länder, and the communes; and (3) the preparation for decisions in the EU. The federal government regularly displays collusive behaviour when it seeks agreement for its policies from individual Länder by means of financial privileges. The federal-Länder relationship also involves conflict whenever the parliamentary opposition in the Bundestag can compensate for its inferiority by a majority in the Bundesrat. This is particularly so in the case of laws requiring Bundesrat consent, thus enabling the majority there to block government policy. In particular, competition occurs over decisions about financial resources – especially the content of fiscal legislation and the right to raise taxes – but also concerning the shape of intergovernmental revenue redistribution. This has been the case since the establishment of the Federal Republic. Taken as a whole, where the regional interests of the Länder are primarily involved, conflict has been mainly among the Länder, whereas in the case of party or ideological interests, the line of conflict tends to run between the federal government and politically allied Länder on the one hand, and the opposition Länder on the other hand.

In the extensive field of concurrent responsibilities, which comprises more than 90 percent of all federal legislation, conflicts between the federal government and the Länder are, in fact, rare. This is because the BL itself standardizes the preconditions under which the federal government can avail itself of concurrent responsibility and because these preconditions have become justiciable with the new criteria of "indispensability" in Article 72, para. 2, BL. Apart from this, Article 31 BL also determines, clearly and unmistakably, that "Federal law takes precedence over Land law." As a result of this constitutional provision no further regulations are required to solve a possible conflict of laws in favour of one or the other level. Thus the Federal Constitutional Court has rarely had a role in judging conflicts about responsibilities between the federal government and the Länder.[24] This means that, in practice, the responsible actors at both levels have been forced to gain sufficient clarity among themselves (concerning the distribution of powers and joint responsibilities) to govern their actions.

So far, only the transfer of international agreements previously made by the highly centralized "Third Empire" (under the Nazis) to the new federal order of the BL has caused uncertainty. In this case, the Federal Constitutional Court has decided, for example, that the provisions on education in the 1934 "Reich Concordat" with the Vatican is now the responsibility of the Länder.[25] In the case of state liability law, it is unclear whether this is part of civil law (with concurrent jurisdiction available to the federal government) or not (with the result that it would come under the jurisdiction of the Länder).[26] Where doubts arise in practice, or where particularly important matters are involved, the solution has been found in federal-Länder agreements. Thus, for example, the question of preconditions and procedures for the granting of federal approval for the Länder to sign an international treaty that falls within their legislative jurisdiction (Article 32, para. 3, BL) is regulated in a formal agreement between the federal government and the entirety of the Länder. This is known as the Lindau Agreement.

Again, despite the relatively clear distribution of responsibilities laid out in the BL, it is the "cooperatively" exercised responsibilities that frequently provide citizens with reasons for doubt and confusion. If, for example, the Länder become active on the instructions of the federal government and are given a federal directive to establish a permanent disposal site for nuclear waste or to approve the transportation of spent fuel rods through their territory, the population assumes that this decision has been taken by the individual Land. In fact, it had been taken by the federal government. Or, if a Land has to cancel or postpone the building of a planned institution of higher education because the federal government will no longer provide the funding, this is generally believed to be the failure of the Land government responsible for educational matters rather than of the federal government. Individual citizens cannot attach decisions to the correct level and, therefore, cannot realize accountability. For this reason, the disentanglement of joint responsibilities is a key area and was under review by the Commission of the Bundestag and the Bundesrat for the Modernization of the Federal Order.

Conflicts among the Governments

Since so few conflicts or controversies have arisen over the distribution of state powers and responsibilities in the German federation, little change has resulted from legal jurisprudence. In a few cases, however, decisions of the Federal Constitutional Court have had an impact on the way in which responsibilities are exercised. Thus, for example, the judgment on the authority of the federal government to issue administrative directives has meant that, in cases of administration on federal commission, the Länder have had to obey even unconstitutional directives.[27] Länder administration in these cases has, therefore, been reduced to a masked federal administration, with the Länder merely performing what amounts to a service function. On the other hand, the increase in the number of laws requiring the consent of the Bundesrat has allowed this part of the parliament, contrary to the intentions of the drafters of the Constitution, to become a genuine and active federal second chamber. At the same time, as noted above, the Federal Constitutional Court no longer exercises control by ruling on the need for unified federal regulation in the field of concurrent jurisdiction, with the result that the federal government has assumed virtually exclusive legislative responsibilities.

Finally, in Germany, with regard to resolving conflicts there is not a major distinction between formal institutions and informal political mechanisms. In comparing the role of the Bundesrat (as the only formal organ of mediation) with that of the informal conflict management role of intergovernmental executive forums and institutions, the only difference is that the former deals mainly with conflicts of a political nature (mostly involving party policies) while the latter deal with disagreements concerning particular policy topics. As the formal and independent guardian of the distribution of federal responsibilities, the Bundesrat occupies a hybrid position between the federal government and the Länder. This means that, in principle, it is subject to the influences of both levels. The Bundesrat is made up of members of the Land governments who, of course, not only influence it but essentially pre-form and co-determine its decisions. However, whenever the political majorities in the Bundesrat and the Bundestag correspond, the federal government has a strong influence on the former, particularly since it has the right to speak in that house and must keep it informed about how its business is being carried out at the federal level (Article 53 BL). Nevertheless, the Bundesrat is independent of the Bundestag to the extent that its legislative decisions can be taken autonomously and without regard to the decisions taken in the Bundestag. It is also worth noting that the membership in the Bundesrat and the membership in the Bundestag are derived from different sources.

Executive Federalism

The maintenance and administration of the distribution of powers and responsibilities lie primarily in the hands of the executives.[28] Here, with regard to the duty to implement federal laws, the Länder executives have had most of the practical experience, and they have therefore assumed a particularly significant role. In contrast, the main interest of the federal executives has been in being informed about this experience and in coordinating the Länder executives in order to make them apply federal laws uniformly. This is done primarily with the assistance of the Bundesrat. As noted above, coordination is also achieved with the support of numerous intergovernmental institutions, ranging from joint discussions between experts and heads of federal and Länder departments right up to ministers' conferences and the Forum of Prime Ministers (with the participation of the federal chancellor). As in other federations, this predominance of the executive power in making use of and handling federal distribution of responsibility is referred to in Germany as "executive federalism." In comparison with executive federalism, the importance of the legislatures is, in fact, slight. This is because the federal government has always made full use of its exclusive and concurrent responsibilities, and the Länder, as legislative authorities, have consequently been forced into the background.

Federal Supervision of Länder Administration

As noted above, since the BL distinguishes clearly and unambiguously between federal legislation on the one hand, and Land legislation on the other hand, the federal government has the right to observe and to control Länder when the latter execute (federal) laws in their own right (Articles 83 and 84 BL) or when they are federally commissioned to do so (Article 85 BL). In these cases the federal authorities can send commissioners to the Länder to obtain information on whether federal laws are being executed legally. If federal laws have been infringed the federal government can issue the Länder with a reprimand and require remedial action. Finally, in the case of a dispute both the federal government and the affected Land government can address the Bundesrat and then the Federal Constitutional Court. If the federal law is executed on federal commission, its supervision extends to the appropriateness of the execution. In individual cases this includes the authority to issue directives. However, the federal government has no influence on the Land legislature and the Land authorities' execution of federal laws provided that the Länder fulfill their constitutional duties towards the federation.

The constitutional duty of the Länder includes the precept of friendly behaviour to the federal government based on the principle of federal loyalty. Only if a Land has been shown to offend against its duties to the federation can the federal government, with the agreement of the Bundesrat, take the necessary measures to force the Land to fulfill its duties. In such a case the federal government or its commissioner has the authority to issue directives to all the Länder and their authorities (Article 37 BL). All disputes that arise from measures of federal supervision or federal compulsion can also be dealt with by the Federal Constitutional Court. In such a federal-Länder dispute the Court decides on the constitutionality of these measures (Article 93, para. 1, nos. 3 and 4, BL). The federal supervision of the legitimacy of the execution of federal laws may also involve the Bundesrat, whose decision about whether a Land has violated federal law has to be obtained before the Federal Constitutional Court can be appealed to. Any federal or Länder influence on the decisions of the Court is excluded because Article 97 of the BL establishes the independence of the judiciary. Nevertheless, the Länder have some influence through the election of the justices via the Bundesrat.

In the case of an exceptional situation or a state of emergency with regard to internal security the federal government can become active if the Land in which the danger threatens is not able to combat it. The federal government then has the right to place the police forces of the Land under its direction and to employ units of the Federal Border Police (Article 91, para. 2, BL). If the emergency concerns a natural disaster or a particularly serious accident that can endanger the territory of more than one Land, the federal government can even employ its own forces to support the police forces of the Länder involved (Article 35, para. 3, BL). In all other cases the initiative has to be taken by the Land affected. It can call upon police forces from other Länder, the Federal Border Police, or even armed units of the federal army. In these cases it is only the Land that is responsible for the necessary emergency measures.

All supporting actions on the part of the federal government in exceptional situations and states of emergency rest on the mutual duty of both orders of government to provide each other with legal and administrative assistance (Article 35, para. 1, BL). For this reason it is not possible for the federal government to suspend or remove regional or local office bearers from their positions or even to take over the government of the Land involved. Under the BL this is forbidden by the principle pertaining to the mutual recognition of the independence and sovereignty of each order of government within the federal system. Therefore, in such cases the federal authorities are always limited to issuing directives. However, these directives enable the federal government to subordinate Land authorities to such a degree that the formal assumption of governmental and managerial power or the removal of officials is not necessary. It is only at the level of local government that the supervisory authorities of the respective Lands have the right to take over the decision-making power of the communes or to install a commissioner to directly manage their self-administrative organs. In the reverse situation, if the Länder are of the opinion that the federal government is not fulfilling its constitutional duties or is violating the distribution of powers laid down in the

BL, then they can claim a federal-Länder dispute and appeal to the Federal Constitutional Court (Article 93, para. 1, nos. 3 and 4, BL).

ADEQUACY AND FUTURE OF THE DISTRIBUTION OF POWERS AND RESPONSIBILITIES

Para-Constitutional Tendencies and Shifts in Federal Practice

If one looks at the actual distribution of the powers and responsibilities within the federal system and compares it with the demands of the Constitution, then one will see that, in this respect, political reality more or less corresponds to constitutional law. The practice of exercising responsibility through the constitutional organs of the federal government and the Länder certainly falls well within the framework of the BL. Of course, there have been some shifts in the system of responsibilities in the form of transfers of constitutional responsibilities to the federal government or the transformation of what were originally Länder tasks into joint tasks. In addition, the relationship between the rules and exceptions in Article 30 BL, according to which, in principle, the Länder are primarily responsible for fulfilling state tasks and exercising state powers, have, in practice, now been reversed. Furthermore, another level of government, involving the so-called self-coordination of the Länder – a kind of grey area within constitutional law – has become increasingly important without being formally recognized. Apart from these largely marginal changes, however, in Germany it is hardly possible to find serious deviations from the written Constitution with regard to the distribution of powers and responsibilities. The reason for this may lie in the fact that, if the federal or a Land government were to make unconstitutional use of its powers, then the Federal Constitutional Court, drawn in by the adversely affected party, would take action very quickly.

The question of whether the constitutional and actual distribution of power produces an adequate and politically acceptable balance between effective government at the federal level and equally effective government at the Land level depends upon what one understands by balance. If one judges it from an objective point of view, one will hardly be able to deny that a balance of this kind does indeed exist. An equilibrium is always formed in every system of power, and this remains effective as long as state decisions have public acceptance. Nevertheless, in Germany one increasingly hears complaints from the Länder as well as from parts of the federal government that this equilibrium is becoming more and more disturbed. This is mostly due to one side or the other being accused of exceeding or misusing its constitutionally guaranteed powers. Thus, for example, the Bundesrat is accused of blocking the policies of the federal government for reasons of party tactics. The parliaments of the Länder insist that the federal legislature has assumed too much legislative power and/or that it has even gone so far as to transfer this power to the EU. Both levels of government regularly complain about the supposed inadequacy of their funds.

On the face of it, one could conclude that, when all sides complain about the lack of balance, it is precisely this that indicates that a balance exists. In fact, it is true that the political scope within which a Land can take action has been considerably reduced in the past fifty years and that the high degree of intertwining of policy making has reduced the transparency and public control of the decision-making process. In recent decades these developments have actually led to a concentration of powers at both levels of government, with power and finances approximately equally distributed. However, these power blocks, which have a deleterious effect on political accountability, are so closely linked with each other that the political process has become bogged down.[29] The federal government and the Länder agree on the diagnosis of immobility, but they do not agree about the therapy for treating it. While the federal government insists on a perceptible reduction of legislation requiring Bundesrat consent, the Länder often misuse their veto power to reject unfunded federal mandates.

Deficiencies of the German Federal System

Even if the practice of exercising the responsibilities of the federal government and the Länder still conforms to the BL framework, the present situation of the federal system in Germany is regarded by many as not very satisfactory and as requiring fundamental reform. Financially, the Länder are practically, and the local governments almost completely, dependent on decisions taken by the federal government. In the fiscal field they have an almost entire lack of legislative responsibility (apart from Article 105, para. 2a, BL). Nor do they have the right to introduce new taxes or to raise taxes themselves. In this situation the federal government tends to raise only those taxes that provide additional income for itself (such as the tobacco tax and petroleum-based fuels tax), without taking note of the needs of the Länder and communes. The current financial situation of the communes is especially threatening. On the one hand they are instructed to take over more and more new tasks, but on the other hand their main source of income, the commercial tax, has almost dried up due to the weak economy. For these reasons, as noted above, the Bundestag and the Bundesrat recently decided to establish the joint Commission of the Bundestag and the Bundesrat for the Modernization of the Federal Order,which is comprised of an equal number of Land and federal representatives, one from each Land and sixteen from the federal government (for thirty-two in total). Its mandate includes dealing with the financial resources of the Bund, the Länder, and the communes.[30]

If, in accordance with the recommendations made by this commission, the financial provisions for the Länder and the communes should be improved, then both would no doubt have the capacity to collect, administer, and spend these additional funds. However, the question of whether the political will exists for such reform is frequently raised. The prevailing public impression is that governments already place such a burden on their citizens in the form of taxes, contributions, and levies that there is no room to increase them. And, indeed, the public is no longer prepared to accept tax raises of any kind. In addition, in recent years the efficiency of all governments is perceived to have greatly declined, with people receiving less and less service for more and more money. This widely held public opinion has had a negative effect on the willingness of the political leadership at all levels to make decisions since all fear that this would result in their being punished at the next elections. The parties now outbid each other with suggestions whose half-life is becoming shorter and shorter. Thus the arguments for and against the reintroduction of the capital tax, for and against raising the estate duties, for and against the hazardous waste charges of the communes, and for and against the packaging tax fill entire archives. In this debate, so far there have been no signs of a generally rational, long-term solution that would alleviate the financial problems of the federation and that would receive general consent.

The seemingly permanent financial crisis of the federation has to be considered within the context of the transfer of significant economic powers to the EU, including those pertaining to the restrictive monetary policies pursued by the European Central Bank. In Germany the planned net credit borrowing for the fiscal year 2004 grew to more than two times the originally planned figure (i.e., from €18.9 billion [or about US$22 billion] to approximately €42.5 billion [or about US$51 billion]). Consequently, it exceeded the convergence criteria of the European Stability Pact (which limits the annual net credit borrowing to no more than 3 percent of GDP) by almost one whole percentage point.

Despite this financial weakness, the federal government continues to finance the expenditures of the Länder and the communes to a considerable extent. To enable it to do this, the BL essentially provides it with four instruments: (1) the co-financing of joint tasks (Articles 91a and 91b BL); (2) grants for particularly important investments on the part of the Länder and communes (Article 104a, para. 4, BL);[31] (3) the authority to relinquish parts of the sales tax jointly due to the federal government, the Länder, and the communes; and (4) the federal government's participation in balancing Länder budgets (Article 107 BL). Above all, general, unconditional federal funding is particularly important for the ability of the Länder and communes to shape their own policies based on income from their general budgets (rather than on funding granted for specific projects). In addition to financial support in accordance with Article 104a BL, the general unconditional financial transfers include federal payments to the poorer Länder in order to cover their general financial needs (i.e., fiscal equalization [Article 107, para. 2, sent. 3, BL]). The purpose of this equalization is, on the one hand, to balance out the shortage of funds in the budgets of these Länder (*Fehlbedarfszuweisungen*) and, on the other hand, to cover special needs in the new Länder in the Eastern part of Germany (*Sonderbedarfszuweisungen*). Total equalization payments by the federal government to the Länder and communes in 2003 was about €30 billion (or about US$36 billion).

So long as there is adequate financial provision for the Länder and communes, these levels of government will have the necessary constitutional powers to fulfill their functions as well as to attract sufficiently qualified and trained personnel. With the increasing privatization of governmental services, the Länder and communes are active in the labour market and are able to recruit suitable personnel without being bound by the strict conditions of the regulations that govern the civil service. There is the general political will to improve the provision of public services and to fulfill all the tasks and functions for which the three levels of government (the federal government, the Länder, and the communes) are responsible in a way that is as efficient and as competent as possible. In particular, the local governments could take over more tasks if they had the necessary funds and were not prevented from doing so by the Länder. The local authorities could also further privatize administrative tasks in order to save money and to free themselves from the rigid guidelines of public budgetary law.

Additional Requirements for Reforms

During the 1980s and 1990s the political decision-making process in Germany became increasingly cumbersome. In fact, there was growing social awareness of the need for fundamental reforms. This awareness, however, met with little response in political practice. The legislative process was blocked as a result of different majorities in the Bundestag and the Bundesrat. Moreover, the experience of the last five decades indicates that different party majorities in the Bundestag and Bundesrat, respectively, represent Germany's constitutional reality. Such a constellation can lead, in the most favourable instances, to grand coalitions based on the lowest common denominator. But the potential for blockage due to different Bundestag and Bundesrat majorities is built into the "marble-cake" federalism of Germany's Constitution. Federal legislative authority has grown continuously while Länder authority has decreased to the point where Länder are now only responsible for the administration and implementation of legislation. In the meantime, the framework for this distribution of responsibilities has been fundamentally altered by German unification and by the process of European integration. Thus, in the long term the current arrangement threatens to weaken the political capacity for action.

The processes of European integration and economic globalization have fundamentally altered the basic conditions for political management in virtually all federal countries. These processes point to the need to strengthen the legislative authority of the state (i.e., the subnational) order of government. The integration of international markets demands ever-greater business specialization in countries with high production costs. As a consequence, sectoral and regional differentiation is becoming increasingly important in the competition between locations. In countries like Germany this is leading to the growing importance of the Länder as economic policy actors. These changing conditions of German federalism are already sufficient to make a review of the German Constitution a pressing political issue. At the core of this issue lies the question of the distribution and disentangling of federal and Länder responsibilities as well as financial reform. The "fossilized" federal structures of the Constitution hardly allow for flexible reactions to modern societal changes. Market forces and their systems of distribution demand a more adaptable political system. However, the constitutional reality in Germany – as a result of joint tasks, the integrated system of tax revenue redistribution, and the continual extension of legislation requiring Bundesrat consent – have left the political system even less flexible than it was before.

Today it is a question of optimizing the ability of Germany's political system to act under new circumstances. It is not a matter of reform at any price, and certainly not of change shaped by ideology or even by party politics. In addition to a basic consensus on common assumptions, reform also requires scope for a greater variety of solutions. Such a variety can only be obtained, however, through more autonomy and a willingness to take risks at both an individual and an institutional level (particularly at state levels). The federal state, as understood in the Constitution, needs reforms that will restore the federal balance. There must be less emphasis on establishing uniformity and on the principle of equality, and more emphasis on equality of opportunity and autonomy.

NOTES

1 For more on the "Bundestreue," or principle of federal loyalty, see Bertus DeVillers, "Intergovernmental Relations: *Bundestreue* and the Duty to Cooperate from a German Perspective," *SA Public Law* 13 (1994): 430–437.

2 See David Currie, *The Constitution of the Federal Republic of Germany* (Chicago: Chicago University Press, 1994), chaps. 2 and 3.

3 See Johannes Wagner, *Der Parlamentarische Rat 1948–1949: Akten und Protokolle*, vol. 1 (München: Vorgeschichte, 1975), p. 31.

4 The so-called "Goldene Bulle" of 1356, well known as the first constitution of the "Holy Roman Empire of the German Nation," established a quasi-federal system consisting of seven electorates, fourteen imperial districts, and some free imperial cities. See Hans-Peter Schneider, "Federalism in Continental Thought during the 17th and 18th Centuries," *Federalism and Civil Societies*, eds. Hans-Peter Schneider and Jutta Kramer (Baden-Baden: Nomos, 1999), pp. 43–52.

5 All articles of the Basic Law quoted in this chapter can be examined in an English version of the German Constitution available in the "German Law Archive," <http://www.iuscomp.org/gla/index.html> (accessed in 2005).

6 The only exception in Article 21 BL refers to the status, the functions, and the rights of political parties. In Article 9, para. 3, BL the existence of trade unions and employers' associations is guaranteed.

7 See Hans-Peter Schneider, "Der Föderalismus im Prozeß der deutsch-deutschen Vereinigung," *Chancen des Föderalismus in Deutschland und Europa*, ed. Tilman Evers (Baden-Baden: Nomos, 1994), pp. 79–93.

8 See the following cases of the Federal Constitutional Court: 2 BVerfGE 213, 224 (1953); 4 BVerfGE 115, 127 pp. (1954); 10 BVerfGE 234, 245 (1959); 13 BVerfGE 230, 233 pp. (1961); 26 BVerfGE 338, 382 pp. (1969); 33 BVerfGE 224, 229 (1972); 65 BVerfGE 1, 63 (1983); 65 BVerfGE 283, 289 (1983); 67 BVerfGE 299, 327 (1984); 78 BVerfGE 249, 270 (1988).

9 "Joint tasks" are tasks of the Länder, co-financed by the federal government according to decisions of "Joint Planning Commissions" composed of sixteen delegates of the federal government and sixteen representatives of the Länder (e.g., construction of universities, improvement of regional economic and agrarian structures, coastal preservation, educational planning, promotion of research institutions, etc.). For further details, see Articles 91 a and 91 b BL.

10 "Joint taxes" are taxes that accrue jointly to the federal government, the Länder, and the municipalities (communes) (e.g., the income and corporation tax, the turnover tax). All three orders of government share these taxes, with a specific percentage share being regulated by the Constitution.

11 See Nevil Johnson, *Federalism and Decentralisation in the Federal Republic of Germany* (London: HMSO, 1973).

12 See Renate Mayntz, "Intergovernmental Relations and Local Autonomy in Germany," *Rivista Trimestrale di Diritto Pubblico* 32 (1982): 608–624.

13 See Hans-Peter Schneider, "L'execution des lois fédérales par les Länder: Aspects juridiques et financiers," *Les cinquante ans de la République Fédérale d'Alemange*, ed. Michel Fromont (Paris: Publications de la Sorbonne, 2000), pp. 65–78.

14 See Peter Katzenstein, ed., *Industry and Politics in West Germany: Toward the Third Republic* (Ithaca, NY: Cornell University Press, 1989).

15 Notwithstanding the fact that, traditionally, some big companies are owned or co-owned by public authorities (Volkswagen, Lufthansa, Deutsche Bahn, Telekom).

16 61 BVerfGE 149, 173 pp. (1982).

17 See R. Davis and D.J. Burnham, "The Role of the Federal Judiciary in the Development of Federalism in West Germany and the United States," *Boston College International and Comparative Law Review* 12 (1989): 63–88.

18 An increase from approximately 25 percent in 1949 to more than 60 percent today, thus functionally and institutionally strengthening the Bundesrat.

19 See 8 BVerfGE 274, 294 pp. (1958); 24 BVerfGE 184, 195 (1968); 55 BVerfGE 274, 319, 326 pp. (1980).

20 See Konrad Hesse, *Der unitarische Bundesstaat* (Karlsruhe: C.F. Müller, 1962).

21 106 BVerfGE 62, 135 pp. (2002).

22 The inverse situation of unfunded federal mandates that are imposed upon the states (as in the United States of America) could often be avoided by the Länder thanks to their veto power in the Bundesrat. This always provides a window for bargaining.

23 The commission was established in October 2003. The organization, the procedures, and all the material produced by the commission (documents, minutes, motions, submissions, legal opinions, etc.) are published on the Internet (<http://www.bundestag.de/parlament/kommissionen/modern>) with a link to *Bundesstaatskommission.*

24 See Prodromos Dagtoglu, "The Change in Federal Conflicts: Some Remarks in Modern West German Federalism," *Devolution: Essais,* ed. H. Calvert (London: Professional Books Ltd., 1975), pp. 155–173.

25 6 BVerfGE 309, 340 pp. (1957).

26 61 BVerfGE 149, 173 pp. (1982).

27 81 BVerfGE 310, 332 pp. (1990); 84 BVerfGE 25, 31 pp. (1991).

28 See Nevil Johnson, *Government in the Federal Republic of Germany: The Executive at Work* (Oxford: Pergamon Press, 1973).

29 See Fritz Scharpf, "The Joint Decision Trap: Lessons from German Federalism and European Integration," *Wissenschaftszentrum Berlin* (Berlin: Wissenschaftszentrum Berlin, 1985), p. 62. This article is also available in *Public Administration* 66, 2 (1998): 239–278.

30 See note 23.

31 Both the joint tasks as well as grants for important investments are being reviewed by the "Commission on Federalism." There is a tendency in the commission to abolish the joint tasks; but the Länder are still looking for adequate compensation.

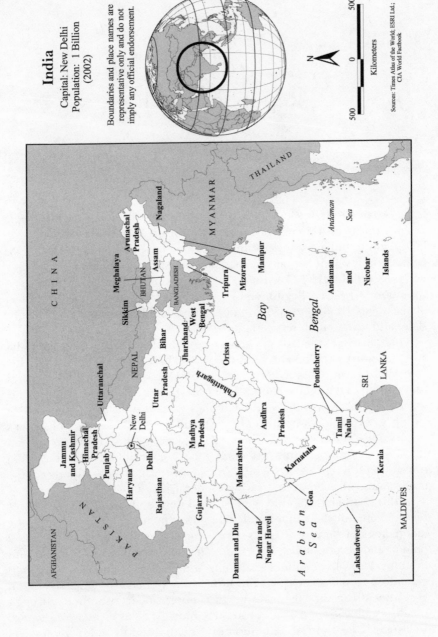

India

Capital: New Delhi
Population: 1 Billion
(2002)

Boundaries and place names are
representative only and do not
imply any official endorsement.

N

500   0   500
Kilometers

Sources: Times Atlas of the World; ESRI Ltd.;
CIA World Factbook

CHINA

AFGHANISTAN

PAKISTAN

Jammu
and Kashmir

Himachal
Pradesh

Punjab

Haryana

Uttaranchal

NEPAL

Sikkim

BHUTAN

Arunachal
Pradesh

Nagaland

Assam

Meghalaya

BANGLADESH

Manipur

Mizoram

Tripura

MYANMAR

THAILAND

New Delhi

Delhi

Rajasthan

Uttar
Pradesh

Bihar

Jharkhand

West
Bengal

Madhya
Pradesh

Chhattisgarh

Orissa

Gujarat

Daman and Diu

Dadra and
Nagar Haveli

Maharashtra

Goa

Andhra
Pradesh

Karnataka

Pondicherry

Tamil
Nadu

Kerala

SRI
LANKA

Bay

of

Bengal

Andaman
Sea

Andaman

and

Nicobar

Islands

Arabian
Sea

Lakshadweep

MALDIVES

Republic of India

GEORGE MATHEW

India became independent from British colonial rule on 15 August 1947. Besides the British-Indian provinces, 562 princely states became part of independent India. The Constitution of India was adopted by the Constituent Assembly on 26 November 1949, and it came into force on 26 January 1950. At the time the Constitution was adopted, India had 14 states and six union territories. Beginning in 1956, and after several reorganizations of the states (the latest in November 2000), India now has twenty-eight states and seven union territories.

When, in 1858, the British Crown took over the administration of India after a century of colonial rule by the British East India Company, a highly centralized form of government was established with the governor general functioning as the agent of the British government. This centralizing trend was evident even in independent India's Constitution as it envisaged "a strong Centre."[1] However, in the last half century or more of India's history, several developments have taken place, leading India towards an evolving federalism within a federal-unitary continuum. With the 1989 transformation of the party system from a one-party to a multiparty configuration, India has grown increasingly federal.

In this chapter I examine the historical development of the division of powers between the union[2] and state governments as well as the recommendations of various official reviews concerning the devolution of state powers and responsibility. I also look at constitutional amendments and examine the role of subnational units and local governments, which has generated considerable debate in India. I then look at whether the union government can directly deal with local government institutions through the direct allocation of funds to substate units (such as district *panchayats*). In closing, I deal with the question of decentralization and division of responsibilities, which is still a hot subject between the union and the states, and between the states and the local governments.

SOCIOCULTURAL CONTEXT AND THE EVOLUTION
OF THE FEDERAL POLITY

India covers an area of 32,87,263 square kilometres. Its population, according to the latest Census (2001), is 1,027 million.[3] The per capita GDP is US$2,900, and the literacy rate is 65.38 percent. India's uneven development is evident in the disparities between states – some (Kerala, Goa, Mizoram) are fully literate, while others are not (the literacy rate in Bihar, for example, is below 50 percent).

On the basis of interactive patterns between caste, tribe, ethnicity, religion, ecology, language, history, and administration, India has 91 macro regions (eco-cultural zones), 4,635 communities, and as many as 325 languages or dialects. The Constitution lists twenty-two "scheduled languages." The national official language is Hindi and it is spoken by about 30 percent of the population. English is the associate official language. The Constitution enjoins states to take special care of linguistic minorities by providing them educational instruction in their mother tongue at the primary stage.

All major world religions, including indigenous faiths, are present in India. Hindus constitute 82.8 percent (including 8.08 percent indigenous people), Muslims 11.7 percent, and Christians 2.3 percent. Indigenous reformist religions in India include Sikhism (2 percent), Buddhism (0.8 percent) and Jainism (0.4 percent). The Directive Principles of State Policy (Article 44) have set a common civil code as a desirable constitutional goal for the federation. According to Article 25 of the Constitution, the personal laws of Sikhs, Jains, and Buddhists are part of Hindu personal law.

The Constituent Assembly, which drafted and approved the Constitution, was indirectly elected by the provincial legislatures in 1946. These legislatures had been elected in 1936 through a franchise granted on the basis of property ownership and educational qualifications under the Government of India Act, 1935. No one was excluded on ethnic grounds. Suffrage was made universal by the Constitution in 1950.

The Indian Constitution is first and foremost a social document. It seeks to build a multicultural federal nation through the harmonious construction of the principles of social, economic, and political justice; liberty of thought, expression, belief, faith, and worship; equality of status and opportunity; and the promotion of fraternity among all, thus assuring the dignity of the individual and the unity and integrity of the nation. As the Constitution provides, such a federal nation must be founded on parliamentary democracy, secularism, federalism, and a market-driven but government-regulated economy. The principles of secularism are applied to ensure the subjective neutrality of government as well as the non-discriminatory, free growth of a civic-political nation. Individual or citizenship rights are duly mediated through minority community rights. Discrimination in any form is prohibited. However, for the purpose of attempting to integrate deprived and marginalized groups into the mainstream, the government, in keeping with the principle of social justice, practises affirmative action.

The Constitution defines India as a "Union of States" and has created a federal structure. Although the term "federal" does not appear in the Constitution, it often arose in Constituent Assembly debates. The Constitution makers wanted the Constitution to be federal if necessary but not necessarily federal. In several judgments the Supreme Court of India has used the epithet "federal" to characterize the "basic structure" of the Constitution. This "basic structure" has been declared unamendable since the 1973 *Keshavananda Bharati* case.[4]

The union is a composite whole, the integrity and sovereignty of which must be maintained by each structure of government. The Constitution of India includes some special integrated features, for example, a single constitution (excepting Jammu and Kashmir), single citizenship, a single integrated judicial system, a detailed outlining of structures and processes at the union and state levels, as well as *panchayats* (village councils) and municipalities and a unique set of All-India Services. As of now, there are three All-India Services: the Indian Administrative Service, the Indian Police Service, and the Indian Forest Service. The union recruits members of the All India Services, but they are placed under various state cadres whose responsibility is to serve both the state and the union.[5] This provides administrative synergy to the federal union of India.

Current federal provisions are in many ways a culmination of the devolution process developed under the act that laid down, in a limited manner, a system of responsible government in the provinces. However, it was the Government of India Act, 1935, that prescribed a federal structure. The act made a threefold division of the federal powers – a legislative list of exclusive federal powers (List I), a legislative list of exclusive provincial powers (List II), and a list of concurrent legislative powers (List III). However, the concurrent list was not applicable to the "federated states" (i.e., the provinces of British India, which had exclusive legislative power with respect to all subjects not included in the instrument of accession as federal subjects). It retained the element of centralization by allowing the federal government to encroach upon List II in times of emergency and, when requested to do so by two or more states. In cases of conflict between List I and List II, the former was given precedence over the latter. In a dispute between "entries [i.e., subarticles] in List III and entries in List II the former would prevail as far as the federal legislature was concerned."[6] The residuary (or residual) powers of legislation in the act were vested in the governor general. The act also provided for the creation of an inter-provincial council to resolve inter-procedural conflict. Judicial review was permissible by the Federal Court of India and the Judicial Committee of the Privy Council in London.

Since the 1949–50 Constitution of India came into being, several amendments have been effected to bring about changes in the original distribution of powers and responsibilities.[7] Broadly, these amendments cover four areas: (1) enlarging the ambit of the federal government's powers; (2) bringing items from the state list within the fold of the concurrent list (specifically, items that had produced excessive diversity of laws or had became too technical to be effectively handled by the states); (3) introducing a new part into the Constitution – one that devolves functions at the substate level, and (4) making cosmetic changes to the phrases and explanations of constitutional provisions, thus avoiding ambiguities in the judicial construction and interpretation of specific provisions. Some important amendments affecting federal distribution of powers include the Constitution (Sixth Amendment) Act, 1956, which affected the states' competence to levy taxes on items related to interstate trade and commerce. Parliament was assigned regulatory powers in this regard. Further amendments were introduced in Articles 269 and 286 in order to empower Parliament to formulate principles and to impose restrictions on the sale or purchase of goods of special importance (public and national). This amendment severely crippled the volume of states' revenues earned through sales tax levies.

The Constitution (Seventh Amendment) Act, 1956, inserted a new article, 258A, which gave state governors the power to entrust to the union government (or its officers) functions related to the "exclusive power of the state." The Seventh Schedule deleted Entry 33 of List I and Entry 36 of List II, related to the acquisition and requisitioning of property. These were reinserted in the concurrent list as Entry 42. Minor modifications regarding historical monuments were introduced in Entry 67 of the union list, Entry 12 of the state list, Entry 40 of the concurrent list, and Article 49 of the Constitution.

The Constitution (Forty-Second Amendment) Act, 1976, effected many crucial changes in the Constitution of India, relating to almost every aspect of governance. However, from the perspective of the distribution of powers and responsibilities, the most important was the insertion of a new article, 257A, by which the union Parliament assumed powers to deploy armed forces to any state. Although subsequently deleted by the Constitution (Forty-Fourth Amendment) Act, 1978, it is now inserted in List I. It should be reiterated that law and order is a state subject. Nevertheless, it is no longer deemed necessary for the federal government to seek a state's consent for the deployment of forces in that state. The rationale is to restore civil authority in the state, thereby protecting the integrity of the federation.

The Constitution Act, 1978, further transferred Entries 11 (education), 19 (forests), 20 (protection of wild animals and birds), and 29 (weights and measures) from the state list to the concurrent list. In addition, Entry 25 was rephrased as "Education, including technical education, medical education and universities subject to the provisions of entries 63, 64, 65 and 66 of List 1; vocational and technical training of labour."

The Constitution (Seventy-Third Amendment) Act, 1992, and the Constitution (Seventy-Fourth Amendment) Act, 1992, defining *panchayats* (village councils) and municipalities as "institutions of self-government" became Part IX of the Constitution in 1993. The Eleventh and Twelfth Schedules, which were added to the Constitution along with these amendments, have a suggested list of twenty-nine subjects to be transferred by the states to the *panchayats* and eighteen subjects to be transferred to the municipalities. These changes are not mandatory, but all the state conformity acts have more or less incorporated them. By an act of Parliament on 12 December 1996 the provisions of the 73rd Amendment were also extended to the tribal areas (Fifth Schedule).

FEDERALISM UNDER THE INDIAN CONSTITUTION

The founding fathers of the Indian Constitution drew from Euro-American federal traditions and from their own intellectual exposure to the theories of dual federalism and cooperative federalism. This was critically tempered by the then continuing federal administrative arrangements under the Government of India Act, 1935, and by concern for the future requirements of Indian nation building.

From this emerged the Indian model of federalism, unique in many respects, particularly with regard to its in-built mechanisms of centralization and regionalization. The union is a framework of federal nation building wherein the autonomy of the constituent units is moderated circumstantially and in accordance with the changing imperatives of the "national"[8] and larger "public interests."

In order to resolve the question of distribution of powers, the Constituent Assembly, through several expert committees, devised the notion of "domain specification," whereby the extent of powers and authority of each unit was determined on the basis of territoriality and functional manageability of an item (besides its co-relationship to the maintenance of national unity and integrity). We find both a hierarchical and non-hierarchical, non-centralized distribution of powers within the federal Constitution of India. The purpose was to provide union by an organic linkage to ensure unity of purpose and commonality of interests and destiny. The proposed union had to be indestructible.[9]

But a strong federal government cannot assume an authoritarian outlook, and therefore great faith was reposed in parliamentary democracy, particularly its central point that power must be exercised responsibly and under legislative sanction and scrutiny. This brings us to the notion of "consultation," or "consent," within the Indian Constitution, which acts as a check to the arbitrary use of certain exclusive powers of the union. This has three forms: (1) express consultation with the state (Article 3); (2) indirect or designated consent of the upper house of Parliament (i.e., the Council of States, known as the Rajya Sabha) (Article 249); and (3) majoritarian consent, appertaining to many constitutional provisions, the amendment of which cannot be effected unless approved by not less than half the total states of India (Article 368).

THE DISTRIBUTION OF POWERS AND RESPONSIBILITIES

Indian federalism is known for the "differential loadings" and varied arrangements of power distribution. The Seventh Schedule of the Constitution broadly divides and distributes competences, treating states on an equal basis. Articles 370, 371, 371A-G further modify this generality in order to provide for special arrangements of power distribution between the federal government and a particular class of states. The purpose of this is to accommodate features of regional and ethnic governance. In many respects these articles restrict the applicability of federal laws in a "special class" of states. The powers of these governors are different from those of their counterparts in the other Indian states. In many such cases, federal law is subject to the legislative sanction and approval of the concerned legislatures. The Fifth and Sixth Schedules of the Constitution provide for the creation of autonomous councils for tribal-ethnic people. Regional or autonomous councils cut into the legislative, administrative, and financial domains of the concerned state.

As one moves down the administrative institutional arrangements of Indian federalism, the locus of power distribution also changes. At the federal and state levels, legislative authority emanates from the Constitution itself, and the legislative distribution of competences is generally based on the recognition of the principle of sovereignty of some exclusive jurisdiction. The executive authority of each government (federal government and states) has been made co-extensive with its legislative competence. Legislative and executive authorities are complemented by the constitutionally ordained financial capacity of each unit. As the capacities are constitutionally protected, the power relationships between the federal government and the states are difficult to change by other organs of government, including the judiciary. The judiciary is expected to provide the interpretation of the boundary and domain of powers but not to reallocate competences either by way of interscheduling legislative entries or constricting the functional field of each entry in the schedule. Nonetheless, the Supreme Court has ruled that the Parliament was competent to levy wealth tax on agriculture, even though the latter is, as such, a state subject.[10] The apex court's interpretation in another case was that entries in the State List must be given a "broad and plentiful interpretation" and should not be limited by invocation of residuary powers because that would "whittle down the power of the State and might jeopardize the federal principles."[11]

However, at the intrastate level, the legislative competence of the autonomous regional councils is only minimally defined and protected by the Constitution. The councils' rule-making powers usually emanate from legislative and other validating acts of the respective state legislatures. And, at the lowest level of governance (district and below), the local government institutions are to prepare plans and implement schemes for economic development and social justice.

Another notable feature of the distribution of powers is that, while the legislative powers are horizontally distributed on the basis of territoriality, functional manageability, and financial viability between the federal government and the states (and, to a limited extent, between the states and autonomous councils), the administrative and financial competences are functionally arranged. Administrative devolution includes the delegation of executive power in accordance with the administrative and functional imperatives of the subject in question. This devolution varies from subject to subject, on a case-to-case basis. Examples include national highway-building responsibility and disaster management. However, this devolution is in addition to the constitutionally assigned executive powers of the units.

Financial distribution is made either on the basis of a tax division formula, as prescribed in the Constitution, or on the basis of recommendations of the statutory body (the Finance Commission). Discretionary grants are made to the units on the recommendations of the non-statutory body (the Planning Commission), which was created by an executive order of the union government.

General Distribution of Legislative Competence

The federal government and the states derive their respective legislative authority mainly from Articles 245 and 246. Article 245 provides for the territorial extent and limit to the laws made by the federal government and the states. Besides the federation-wide application, the federal laws also have extraterritorial jurisdiction. The same is not the case with state laws. State laws are applicable only within the territorial boundary of the state. Similarly, in no circumstances, except as per constitutional provision, can the legislative competence of a state be circumscribed by the federal Parliament. Encroachment on each other's competences is permissible, but it must be incidental, and it must qualify the judicial doctrine of "pith and substance." It is "true intent" that validates or invalidates an act made by the federal or state legislature.[12] Moreover, the Indian judiciary has made an interesting concession with regard to the question of state occupancy of the federal government's space in a concurrent list subject. The state occupancy is valid until the federal government itself occupies that field.[13]

Article 246 empowers the Parliament of India to make laws with respect to any of the matters enumerated in List i of the Seventh Schedule. But it shares its power with the states on the entries of List iii of the schedule (which lists matters subject to concurrent jurisdiction) and retains exclusive control over residuary items not covered in any of the lists. And the states exercise their plenary exclusive authority over the matters of List ii, known as "the state list." The judiciary has given the residuary powers the widest possible construction in order to validate the federal government's imposition of taxes that are not mentioned in any of the taxing heads of the three lists.

Judicial stress has recently been on first defining the ambit of the states' powers, as found under Lists ii and iii and in other parts of the Constitution.[14] Those found to be outside the constructed ambit of the states' powers belong to the federal government. Entry 97 of List i ("any other matter not enumerated in List ii or List iii, including any tax not mentioned in either of those lists") and Article 248 elasticized the power domain of the federal government. Thus, the court has upheld the legislative competence of the federal government to impose an expenditure tax (distinguished from the state power to impose a luxury tax). The Terrorist and Disruptive Activities (Prevention) Act, 1987 (since repealed), which allows the deployment of armed forces for the purpose of maintaining public order (either upon state request or federal initiative), has also expanded the scope of List i, enabling the federal government to encroach upon what was formerly state jurisdiction.

The Powers of the Union

So far as the constitutional allocation of union (federal) legislative fields is concerned, List i has ninety-seven entries. A careful examination of these entries reveals that the list has been so arranged that, in each entry, a principal function is laid down and then followed by a detailed description of the enabling capacities that will result in its effective performance.

A major field is national protection, referring to the maintenance of the country's internal and external security and defence. For the federal government to effectively perform this function, its enabling capacities must include raising and maintaining national armed forces (naval, air, and army) and central police reserves; prosecution of war; deployment of armed forces in aid of the civil power to maintain public order; preventive detention; Central Bureaus of Intelligence and Investigation; and the manufacture, purchase, and procurement of arms and ammunition.

As an aspect of the exercise and execution of sovereignty, the union has exclusive control of foreign affairs and treaty making. The ambit of this power includes subjects such as diplomatic, consular, and trade representation, as well as membership and participation in multilateral forums such as the United Nations. Above all, the federal government has exclusive power to implement international treaties, agreements, and conventions. Implementation confers upon the federal government the power to modify domestic laws, including state laws, and to make changes in the existing pattern of federal power distribution. On the other hand, the states' competences in this regard are extremely limited. States can, within the overall regulatory and supervisory control of the federal government, negotiate with foreign countries to attract foreign direct investment. Foreign trade and commerce, import and export across the custom frontiers, and the definition of custom frontiers falls under federal, not state, jurisdiction. These federal powers and functions extend to foreign jurisdiction, citizenship, naturalization and aliens, and extradition and immigration.

The federal power to establish national networks and national communication includes growth, development, and management of federally designated railways, airways, highways, and waterways, including regulatory control over shipping and navigation, maritime shipping and navigation, lighthouses, and ports (concurrent jurisdiction). Over these the states do not have any regulatory authority, except the constitutional obligation to maintain state railways and highways. The carefully worded Entry 31 places practically everything relating to telecommunications within the domain of the federal government. This includes post and telegraphs, telephones, wireless, broadcasting, and other like forms of communication. So far as Entry 31 is concerned, states have absolutely no function, not even an auxiliary one.

A large number of national economic functions fall within the purview of the federal government. It exercises exclusive power over national currency and coinage, banking and insurance, public bonds issued by public-sector undertakings, stock exchanges, foreign loans and central debt, interstate trade and commerce, industries, mines and minerals, and natural resources such as oil fields (among others).

The functions of the federal government in relation to the organization, constitution, and maintenance of federal agencies include: elections to Parliament, elections to state legislatures and to the offices of president and vice-president; the election commission; the constitution, organization, jurisdiction, and powers of the Supreme Court and other high courts; and the extension or inclusion of the jurisdiction of a high court from any union territory.

The power of the federal government with regard to education and educational institutions relates to coordination and determination of standards in institutions for higher learning and technical institutions. The determination of standards extends the government's power, enabling it to exercise control over institutions of higher learning that were established exclusively by the states.

In order to ensure the performance of the above functions, the Constitution empowers the federal government with taxing heads, such as, inter alia, non-agricultural income tax, custom and export duties, excise duties, corporation tax, taxes on capital assets, estate duty, stamp duties, taxes on the movement of goods, and consignment tax. However, the proceeds of many of these taxes are shared with the states. In this context it is important to note that federal taxes have been so allocated as to avoid double taxation and to ensure a single system of collection and appropriation. The federal union of India is also an economic union. Therefore, as far as possible, exclusive federal boundaries between the federal government and the states have been avoided. For example, taxes on transaction of goods and on consignment of goods are levied and collected by the Government of India and, subsequently, assigned to the states (Article 269).

The Exclusive Legislative Powers of the States

While List 1 contains ninety-seven entries, the list of exclusive state legislative powers contains sixty-six. Some important entries include public order; police administration; state civil services; public health and sanitation; local communications; local government functions (such as relief for the disabled and unemployed); agricultural development, including aquaculture and fisheries development; horticulture, sericulture, and so on; regulation of mines and minerals development (subject to List 1 provisions); and regulation and development of industries other than those that fall within federal government competence. The states' tax base includes items such as land revenue, agricultural income, succession and estate duties, tax on land and buildings, sales tax and consumption taxes, select excise duties, and other nominal toll taxes.

Concurrent Jurisdiction of the Union and States

In order to promote the diversity of laws, social traditions, and federal experimentation, the Constitution of India provides for areas of concurrent jurisdiction with equal competence for the federal government and the states. But where laws conflict, it is federal law that prevails. The concurrent field contains important subjects, such as: criminal law and procedure; civil law, property, and contracts; preventive detention vis-à-vis state security; maintenance of public order; maintenance of essential supplies and services; marriage and divorce; forest and wildlife protection; economic and social planning, including population control and family planning; social security and social insurance; labour welfare; education, including technical education, medical education, and universities (subject to the provisions of Entries 63, 64, 65, and 66 of List 1); and trade and commerce in, and the production, supply, and distribution of, any product declared by the federal government to be of national and public interest (e.g., oil seeds and oils, raw cotton, raw jute, coal, steel, iron ore, petroleum, etc.). The concurrent list contains forty-seven entries in all.

Revenue Sharing and Distribution

The Constitution of India provides for a variegated system of revenue distribution. All taxes and residual heads under the federal exclusive list are levied by the federal government, but such taxes are not necessarily collected and appropriated by the federal government. Taxes exclusively assigned to the federal government include custom duties, corporation tax, taxes on the capital value of assets, and surcharges on income tax and fees (as mentioned in List 1). The rest of the tax heads are subjected to differential modes of collection and appropriation. Stamp duties on bills of exchange, cheques, promissory notes, and so on, along with excise duties (as mentioned in the union list), are levied by the federal government but are collected and appropriated by the states within their territories. Taxes levied and collected by the federal government but whose proceeds are assigned to the states in which they are levied include succession duties, estate duties, terminal taxes, taxes on railway fares and freights, taxes on the stock exchange, and a central sales tax on newspapers. Taxes on the interstate consignment of goods are levied and collected by the federal government, with the proceeds going to the states. The federal government does not receive any revenue from these taxes.

Income tax and excise duties are levied and collected by the federal government, but the proceeds are divided (or rather redistributed) among states on the basis of a combination of specific criteria for fiscal equalization laid down by the Finance Commission. This combination generally includes population size, volume of industrial labour, per capita income, relative status of the state's economy and development, poverty index, and other such indices of development and underdevelopment. The states' percentage share in the allocation pool varies from case to case. In practice, the overwhelming concern has been distribution on the basis of relative population, poverty, and level of development.

Besides this sharing of revenues among the states, Article 275 provides for grants-in-aid to such states as Parliament may deem in need of assistance (particularly regarding the promotion of welfare of tribal areas). Grants are also sanctioned to meet the cost of such development schemes as may be undertaken by the state with the federal government's prior approval.

The Tenth Finance Commission of India (1995–2000) has provided for the sharing of 26 percent of the gross proceeds from federal taxes and duties (excluding stamp duty, excise duty on medical/toilet preparations, central sales tax, consignment tax, and cesses levied for specific purposes) in lieu of their current share in income tax, basic excise duties, special excise duties, and grants in lieu of tax on railway passenger fares. The states continue to receive 3 percent of all federal taxes and duties over and above this 26 percent. The objectives of federal grants are to compensate for the states' residuary fiscal needs in order to correct regional disparities, to promote social welfare schemes, and, above all, to seek a fine balance between the states' resources and their developmental needs.

LOGIC OF THE DISTRIBUTION OF POWERS AND RESPONSIBILITIES

Exclusive Powers of the Union

The Constitution of India generates a highly complex notion of a strong federal union. It assigns certain exclusive powers (in terms of legislative initiative and executive control) to the federal government, the exercise of which has a transforming impact on the polity. But interestingly, these powers are subject to varying degrees of federal concurrence, an in-built constitutional mechanism of checks and balances, and parliamentary accountability. In the arena of distribution of powers and responsibility, the notion of a strong union government can hardly be termed unfederal. Moreover, any perceptive analysis of Indian federalism must also take into consideration the important historical fact that the Indian federation is not the result of a compact between two or more pre-existing sovereign entities but, rather, has evolved from the sovereign will of the people to live together as one organic political union. Therefore, one Constitution, single citizenship, and one common and closely integrated framework of administration and justice are the hallmarks of Indian federalism.

Parliament has, by virtue of Article 3 of the Constitution, the exclusive power to form federal units. Any legislative proposal in this regard cannot be introduced, however, without obtaining prior presidential sanction (i.e., federal government sanction), which, in turn, must ascertain the views of the affected states before approving the introduction of such a bill in Parliament. In practice it is rarely possible for the federal Parliament to ignore the views of the states. The federal government, in effect, cannot concede to the demands of regional groups/communities for a separate state unless such a proposal is received from the state(s) in which these groups are currently located.

At the time the Constitution was adopted, India's fourteen states and six union territories were defined by the historical context of their governance and administration. However, after about five years the State Reorganization Commission was established and the states were reorganized on the basis of linguistic and cultural homogeneity; financial, economic, and administrative considerations; and, of course, preservation and strengthening of the unity and security of the nation. Since 1956 several reorganizations of the states have taken place, the latest in November 2000.

Constitutional Amending Powers

The Constitution of India empowers the union Parliament (and not the states) to initiate and effect changes in the Constitution. However, many constitutional provisions cannot be amended unless they are ratified by no less than half the states of the union. These include: the election of the president; the extent of the federal government's executive powers; presidential power to promulgate ordinances during a parliamentary recess; matters pertaining to the Constitution, organizational powers, and the authority of the Supreme Court and other high courts; distribution of legislative powers among the federal government and the states; the representation of the states in Parliament; and Article 368 (relating to the amendment procedure). Another significant aspect of the Constitution is the judicially innovated and constructed "doctrine of basic features of the Constitution" – features that are solely determined, defined, and interpreted by the judiciary and cannot be amended.

Centralizing Powers under Emergency Powers

The emphasis upon the union in India's federal polity constitutionally validates the centralization of powers in the federal government under certain special circumstances, thus temporarily allowing it to assume the competences of the states. These emergency situations include "war or external aggression or armed rebellion" (Article 352); "internal disturbance"; emergence of a situation in which the current state government cannot function or discharge its constitutional duties "in accordance with the provision of this constitution" (Article 356); and instances in which the "financial stability or credit of India or of any part of the territory thereof is threatened." During financial emergencies the federal government may reserve for further consideration all the state's money and finance bills as well as "reduction of salaries and allowances of all or any class of persons serving in connection with the affairs of a state."

Emergency powers also have a crucial impact on the legislative competence of the states. Article 356 of the Constitution vests powers in the president to assume all or any of the functions of the state government. Similarly, Article 353(b) widens the ambit of the legislative competence of

Parliament. The federal balance can be thereby transformed, with the federal government assuming authority not only for its own defined areas but also for areas not defined by the Constitution in the first instance. However, there are indirect measures to protect the interests and authority of the states through such procedures as legislative scrutiny of the application and implementation of emergency powers; judicial review of the federal government's decision to proclaim an emergency; limitation of the period of each emergency proclamation; and the provision that every proclamation must declare its intent (thereby allowing scope for judicial review), based on and supported by objective and verifiable documents and evidence. Such a declaration must clearly state what powers it seeks to reallocate and resituate. If it does not do this, then the legislative competence and executive authority of the state may remain intact.

The chapter in the Constitution dealing with emergency provisions has generated considerable argument. States perceive it as an encroachment on their autonomy and as a convenient tool enabling the federal government to impose its own political design upon them. Criticism has focused mainly on the federal government's misuse of Article 356. It is often argued that such a provision goes against the spirit of federalism as states do not possess any relevant legal role in decision making regarding the use of the emergency provision and the dislocation of federal balance. When this situation is analyzed, it becomes clear that what the states question is not the spirit of the emergency provision but, rather, the unquestioning acceptance of the power of the federal government. In this regard, it may be safely argued that the intended logic and rationale of the emergency provision was not the dislocation of the federal balance but, rather, the strengthening of the union as an integral whole and the protection of its internal and external sovereignty. Thus the emergency provisions have, as the founding fathers had hoped, a safety-valve function by which territorial integrity is kept intact, constitutional political order is maintained across the units, and electors (citizens) are protected from the arbitrariness of elected state representatives.

Since the Constitution has not provided any in-built mechanism to prevent the misuse of emergency powers, the Supreme Court has time and again set out certain requirements. These include procedural transparency, such as the governor's report – a "speaking document" substantiated by objectively ascertainable facts; the convention of issuing a warning to erring states before implementing emergency powers; consulting as much as possible with concerned state governments before resorting to Article 356; and other such measures. However, above all, the emergency provision of the Constitution functions as a federal aid mechanism, the purpose of which is to help the states in times of fiscal, natural, and political crises. Once this is realized, it can hardly be argued that the emergency provision is an unfederal feature of the Indian Constitution.

The Union's Legislative Power in the "National Interest"

Another interesting aspect of Indian federalism is the federal government's capacity to assume, through an act of authorization and consent, the responsibility for legislative construction and policy planning in relation to the state list. Thus, under the authorization of the Council of States, Parliament is competent to legislate on subjects enumerated in the state list. Such legislation must serve the "national interest"; however, what constitutes national interest is the definitional prerogative of the federal government. Over the years various judicial verdicts have attempted to lay down certain objective criteria for establishing substantive linkages between the subject and larger "national" imperatives. Usually the federal government's encroachment upon the state's jurisdiction is permitted with regard to: (1) those items that have a consequential bearing on India's defence and security; (2) maintenance and growth of national communications grids; (3) implementation of international obligations and treaties entered upon by India; and (4) those items that have grown to such a size and taken on such a degree of specialization that they require increased managerial skills and finances to regulate their development (e.g., heavy industry, petroleum, and subjects relevant to the execution of certain special directives found in the various parts of the Constitution – public order in terms of crimes that cut across states is a case in point).

In this context it is also important to bear in mind the basic constitutional fact that the federal government has been assigned certain regulatory powers to standardize norms and to harmonize rules pertaining to those items with translocal effects. Thus it is quite feasible for the federal government to issue guidelines concerning the use and exploitation of natural resources, including oil fields; protection and preservation of the environment; and the conservation of soils, rare species, and other such entities that require regulated behaviour. Federal guidelines may also relate to those issues having interstate ramifications. These include issues such as labour migration, cross-border movement of crime and criminals, human trafficking, drug trafficking, and the sharing of river waters. The federal government may also issue guidelines to states on those subjects that broadly relate to and affect the growth of a national human development index. Federal guidelines may be either in the form of directives or in the form of ministerial/departmental advice. If a directive is issued, state compliance is necessary. Non-compliance may attract some constitutionally corrective legal action, such as that available under the emergency provisions and in other articles of the Constitution.

This brings us to the question of the obligatory duties and functions of the states. The states' obligatory functions emanate from the nature and content of the administrative relationship between the federal government and the states. Thus, Article 256 enjoins the states to exercise their executive power in such a manner "as to ensure compliance with the laws made by Parliament and any existing laws which apply to that state." To ensure compliance, the federal government may issue necessary directions, which a state must follow in its executive and administrative conduct of its constitutional affairs.

Consensual Centralization and Mutual Delegation of Powers

Another facet of Indian federalism is that it allows for the consensual centralization and mutual transfer of functions between the federal government and the states. In other words, the distribution of powers and responsibilities may, by mutual consent, be either centralized or decentralized. Thus, under Article 252 Parliament may, on the resolutions of two or more states, assume the legislative competence of framing rules and regulations on those matters within the competence of the states referred to in those resolutions. Usually such transfers relate to matters with transboundary implications and that require uniformity of outlook and common legal treatment. This is legislation by delegation. States embark upon such authorizations in order to use the greater expertise, resources, and machinery of the federal government. Such delegation is made freely and voluntarily by the governments involved and lasts so long as the delegated authority is not withdrawn. However, parliamentary law enacted under delegation cannot be amended by any of the concerned states: it can only be amended or repealed by Parliament.

Mutual delegation also takes place substantially in relation to federal executive power. Consequently, with the consent of the state, the federal government can entrust to a state government, either conditionally or unconditionally, the performance of functions in areas that fall within its exclusive executive and administrative competence.

This delegation from the federal government to the states has two important features. First, conferment of powers on states has, in actual practice, led to states exercising a large measure of executive authority in domains originally allotted to the federal government. The federal government on its own administers only a few matters, such as defence, foreign affairs, taxes assigned to it under List 1 of the Seventh Schedule, imports and exports, and foreign exchange. Second, it is usually the federal government that bears the administrative costs incurred by the state in its execution of delegated authority. In other words, delegation under Article 258 is generally a remunerated delegation. Also, as stated above, the cooperative structure of the federal-state relationship makes delegation a two-way process. Thus Article 258A, inserted by the Seventh Amendment Act, 1956, provides that the "Governor of a state may, with the consent of the Government of India, entrust either conditionally or unconditionally to that Government or to its officers functions in relation to any matter to which the executive power of the state extends."

Asymmetrical Distribution of Competence

Articles 370, 371, and 371A-I make special provisions with regard to the exercise of regional autonomy and legislative competence to meet the regional problems and demands of some states (e.g., Jammu and Kashmir, Mizoram, Nagaland, Sikkim, Assam, Manipur, Andhra Pradesh, Maharashtra, Gujarat, etc.). These provisions also restrict the application of many federal laws in these states. Articles 371A and 371G, among others, make it abundantly clear that no act of Parliament can affect the religious and social practices of Nagas, Mizos, and other such ethnic communities; their customary law and procedure; the administration of civil and criminal justice in accordance with their respective customary laws; and the ownership and transfer of land and its resources unless so decided by a resolution of the concerned legislative assembly.

Similarly, Article 370, referring to the State of Jammu and Kashmir, renders inoperative many provisions of parliamentary acts and the general distribution of competence found under the Indian Constitution. In other words, many constitutional requirements and laws made thereunder would not apply to that state unless so resolved by the state assembly. The federal Parliament's jurisdiction is restricted to the matters enumerated in the union list (List I) and certain matters in the concurrent list (List III). Parliament's exercise of powers is, under Article 3 (relating to the formation of states and their boundaries) and Article 253 (relating to international treaty or agreement affecting the disposition of any part of the state's territory), inapplicable without the express consent of Jammu and Kashmir State.

Concurrence of the state is further required for application of Articles 352 (national emergency) and 365 (failure to comply with a union directive). Though Articles 356 and 357 are applicable to the State of Jammu and Kashmir, the meaning of the phrase "failure of constitution machinery" is construed as flowing not from the language of the Indian Constitution but, rather, from that of the state Constitution: "In Jammu and Kashmir two types of Proclamations are made: (a) the 'Governor's Rule' under section 92 of the Constitution of Jammu and Kashmir, and (b) the 'President's Rule' under Article 356 as in the case of the other states."[15] Constitutional amendments made under Article 368 cannot be extended to Jammu and Kashmir, except under a Presidential Order issued under Article 370(1). These examples make it clear that the Constitution of India does allow for a variety of arrangements pertaining to autonomy.

Distribution of Competence at the Intrastate Level

The Sixth Schedule of the Indian Constitution institutionalizes the notion of regional autonomy by making provisions for the creation of regional councils, constituted for the purpose of promoting community autonomy and governance, especially for those ethnic communities that are territorially concentrated. Interestingly, this schedule introduces the notion of autonomous regional and district councils as substate units of administration and governance. These councils, constituted largely on the basis of adult suffrage, have developmental and regulatory functions, which include the allotment and use of non-reserved land; dairy development; agriculture promotion; fisheries; communications; primary and secondary education; primary health and sanitation; hospitals and dispensaries; industry, trade, and commerce; and money lending. Other functions include identity-specific rights such as the regulation of the tribal practice of *jhum* (shifting agriculture), appointment or succession of chiefs or headmen, property inheritance, marriage and divorce, social customs, and the administration of justice in accordance with customary law by a specially created village council.

In order to partially compensate for their administration costs, the autonomous councils are empowered to assess and collect land revenue and to impose taxes on: (1) professions, trades, callings and employment; (2) animals, vehicles, and boats; (3) the entry of goods into a market for sale therein as well as tolls on passengers and goods carried in ferries; and (4) the maintenance of schools, dispensaries, or roads. Another source of revenue for the councils is royalties on the prospecting for or extracting of minerals in that region. Provisions have also been made to restrict the application of federal and state laws on the areas in which a council possesses the competence of framing and executing rules.

Local Governments

If the provisions in Article 243–243 ZG (as added by constitutional amendment in 1993) are made fully operational, the institutions of local self-government (i.e., local bodies at the district level and below) will become the third tier of governance. This will make India a multilevel federation, even if these bodies do not have law enforcement (police) or judicial powers. Some policy makers and intellectuals are of the view that *panchayats* must hold police and judicial powers, thus creating district governments.

While the Constitution suggests that states must transfer forty-seven subjects to the domain of local self-government institutions, the union government has taken no measures to institute greater power sharing. This has created an unhappy situation for the states. Moreover, in the absence of a

clear demarcation of powers and responsibilities in states where autonomous area councils exist, conflicts do occur between these councils and local government bodies.

The rural and urban division of districts by the seventy-third and seventy-
fourth amendments to the Constitution Act, 1992, has created serious
problems in administration and governance. Management and administration of institutions in a district, maintenance of services, transfer of administrative staff, and several other related issues are creating unfavourable
situations for the *panchayats* and municipalities. It is a matter of concern
that the states in general are not devolving functions, functionaries, and finances to local governments.

The National Commission to Review the Working of the Constitution
(2003) recommended further amendments to the Constitution in order to
make *panchayats* effective "institutions of self-government."[16] Its thrust was
to devolve to *panchayats* exclusive functions and the financial resources
(separate tax domains) that would enable them not only to become viable
local government institutions but also to prepare plans and to implement
schemes for economic development and social justice.

Resolution of Federal Conflicts

One of the underlying features of cooperative federalism is the mediation
and resolution of interstate conflicts. The Constitution of India grants a
mediation function to the federal government. Article 262 states: "Parliament may by law provide for the adjudication of any dispute or complaint
with respect to the use, distribution or control of the waters of, or in, any
inter-state river or river valley." The mediation may follow either course: it
may be informally negotiated through the federal departments or through
the Prime Minister's Office. But when the administrative-political negotiation fails, the federal government may constitute a tribunal (a semi-judicial
body) to resolve the issue legally and technically after a thorough examination of mutually competing claims by the states. While the scope of Article
262 is restricted to a specific issue, the federal government's creation of an
interstate council is significant. This council's scope covers anything related to federal-state and interstate relations. Article 263 provides that, if at
any time it appears to the president (i.e., in effect, the federal government) that the public interest would be served by the establishment of a
council, then it shall be lawful for the president, by order, to establish such
a council and to define the nature of its duties as well as its organization
and procedure. This council would be charged with the duty of: (1) inquir-
ing into and advising upon disputes which may have arisen between states;
(2) investigating and discussing subjects in which some or all of the states,
or the union and one or more of the states, have a common interest; and/

or (3) making recommendations on any such subject, particularly regarding the better coordination of policy and action with respect to that subject. The first council was constituted as recently as 1990, and its first meeting was held in 1996.

CONTEMPORARY DEBATES ON THE DISTRIBUTION OF POWERS AND RESPONSIBILITIES

The federal debate in India has largely centred around whether the federal system should be made up of a "strong centre versus weak states" or a "strong centre with strong states." The "strong centre versus weak states" proposition has two dimensions. The first is that the centre is already strong, to the cost of the states. Therefore, the federal government must devolve a large measure of autonomy – pertaining to legislative competence and fiscal capacity – to the states. This argument takes an absolutist position on federalism, viewing the role of the federal government as restricted to the discharge of certain limited functions. It prefers a minimalist federal government with maximalist states. The fallacy inherent in this type of argument is the belief that one level of government can be made strong at the cost of the other. The second dimension of the "strong centre versus weak states" proposition is integrationist and holds that a strong union is imperative in order to assert national strength and to keep the nation intact. Ingtegrationists believe that the states should be the subservient partners of a strong federal government. In this view, federalism as a theory embracing both autonomy and integration is lost.

The second proposition, "strong union with strong states," seeks to balance the power equation in such a way that neither the union nor the state is weak but, rather, that both gain equally from each other. How to fairly balance the power equation between the federal government and the states has led to the establishment of several review bodies concerned with federal-state relations. The first such body was the Administrative Reform Commission (ARC, 1968), which was appointed by the Government of India. The foremost concern of this commission was to depoliticize the structure of federal relations, particularly its administrative and financial aspects. It took up the issue of planning and development, listing three main reasons for the poor economic position of the states: (1) the own-source financial resources of the states are comparatively inelastic; (2) functions allocated to the states are such as to lead compulsively to expanding responsibilities, particularly in the context of ambitious development plans; and (3) foreign aid and deficit financing both tend to strengthen union rather than state resources.[17]

ARC recommended a new approach to union-state financial relationships based on the following principles: (1) arrangements for devolution should be such as to allow the states' resources to correspond more closely to their obligations; (2) devolution should be in a manner that enables an integrated view of the plan as well as non-plan[18] needs of both the union and the states; and (3) advancement of loans should be related to what the team referred to as "the productive principle."[19]

ARC also recommended unifying the Finance Commission and the Planning Commission into a single central institution, which would handle plan and non-plan grants to the states. It also suggested that the system of attaching patterns of assistance to plan schemes should be discontinued: "re-appropriation should normally be permitted freely at the discretion of the states from one scheme to another and from one head of development to another;" the states should be free to use block amounts or block federal grants at their discretion, and "for programmes of crucial importance the concept of tied assistance should be systematically introduced and rigorously implemented."[20]

In sum, ARC hardly questioned the notion of a strong union, but it did attempt to federalize the notion through fine tuning functional decentralization, recognizing the autonomy and the competence of states in select areas, and introducing transparency into the federal administrative organization.

It was the report of the centre (union)-state relations inquiry committee (the Rajamannar Committee), set up in 1971 by the State of Tamil Nadu, that, for the first time, critically questioned the notion of a strong union. The committee strongly favoured autonomy for the states and sought to unburden the union of many of its responsibilities as well as its occupancy of many fields that, in other federations, ordinarily belong to constituent units. It sought to adjust legislative relations through the redefinition and redistribution of entries in the Seventh Schedule. Other legislative recommendations included vesting the residuary powers of legislation and taxation in the states, granting the state legislature the power to amend acts of the federal Parliament, and instituting mandatory consultation with the states with respect to any federal government decision affecting state interests. On financial matters it favoured widening sharable taxes by placing corporation tax, custom and export duties, tax on the capital value of assets, and excise duties under state jurisdiction. It also recommended merging the surcharge on income tax with the basic rate of income tax. All grants (plan and non-plan) were to be made only on the recommendation of the Finance Commission. The Planning Commission was to be placed on an independent basis. Article 365 (one of the emergency powers) was to be deleted, and non-compliance with a union directive was not to be treated as a "failure of constitutional machinery."

The most exhaustive, insightful, and balanced treatment of the entire gamut of federal power sharing and distribution is found in the report of the Commission on Centre-State Relations, chaired by Justice R.S. Sarkaria

(1988). Unlike the ARC and Rajamannar Committee reports, the report of the Sarkaria Commission strove to situate the union framework of the Indian polity within the grand design of federalism as a "living theory." In other words, it tried to strike a fair balance between autonomy and integration on a case-to-case basis. It attempted to resolve the conflicted domain of the federal government's prerogatives and states' rights within the overall framework of the Indian Constitution. Another interesting aspect of the report was that it made the exercise of authority under various federal provisions of the Constitution as transparent and as objective as possible. Instead of effecting too many amendments to the Constitution, it favoured the growth of norms and conventions, a kind of federal political culture in which conflict would be resolved through negotiation. In the commission's opinion, "it is neither advisable nor necessary to make any drastic changes in the basic character of the Constitution."[21] This is because "the working of the Constitution ... has demonstrated that its fundamental scheme and provisions have withstood reasonably well the inevitable stresses and strains of the movement of a heterogeneous society towards its development goals."[22]

Major recommendations of the Sarkaria Commission included: (1) "residuary powers of legislation in regard to taxation matters should continue to remain exclusively within the competence of Parliament, while the residuary field other than that of taxation, should be placed in the concurrent list. The Constitution may be suitably amended to give effect to this recommendation";[23] (2) "ordinarily, the centre should occupy only that much field of a concurrent subject on which uniformity of policy and action is essential in the larger interest of the nation, leaving the rest and the details for state action within the broader framework of the policy laid down in the Union law";[24] "(3) on overlapping and concurrent jurisdictions, prior consultation with states must be a matter of regular practice" (however, it ruled out making consultations with states a matter of constitutional obligation); (4) parliamentary legislation with respect to the matters on the state list under the authority of Article 252 must be limited to a specific term; (5) Article 356 should be used very sparingly, as a matter of last resort, and then only after issuing a warning (a governor's report on this subject should be a "speaking document," which means that it must contain adequate reasoning); (6) reconstitution of the Inter-State Council (which is referred to as the Inter-Governmental Council) and the zonal councils to promote the spirit of cooperation between the federal government and the states; (7) that, "[b]y an appropriate amendment of the Constitution, the net proceeds of corporation tax may be made permissibly sharable with the states";[25] and (8) the creation of a body known as the National Economic and Development Council.

The Sarkaria Commission made several other significant recommendations pertaining to, among other things, different constitutional heads and federal functionaries, socioeconomic planning, language, and interstate disputes. Its significance lies in the fact that its report has become the standard official reference for resolving federal conflicts. It has also laid down a norm of federal conduct, especially in the arena of federal-state relations. The commission report has been exhaustively discussed by the Inter-State Council, and its recommendations (minus fifty-three out of a total of 247) are currently at various stages of implementation and execution.

Finally, given a liberalizing and globalizing economy, an assertive and participatory society, and the completion of over fifty years of a working Constitution, in the year 2000 the Government of India appointed another commission to review its functioning and to suggest measures for improvement. This commission submitted its report on 31 March 2003. Many of its recommendations with regard to the distribution of powers and responsibilities are in agreement with the Sarkaria Commission report. Some important recommendations include: (1) inclusion of a new subject, "Management of Disasters and Emergencies, Natural or Manmade," in the concurrent list of the Seventh Schedule; (2) listing of the services to be taxed by the states; and (3) the establishment of an authority known as the Inter-State Trade and Commerce Commission to carry out the objectives of Articles 301–304 (i.e., the provisions dealing with trade, commerce, and intercourse within the territory of India).[26]

CONCLUDING OBSERVATIONS

The "union model" of Indian federalism, following the initial reluctance of the Government of India during the pre-1989 period, is showing signs of resilience and flexibility. The federal government is strong, but attempts are under way to strengthen the states through various federal mechanisms for the transfer and sharing of powers. Since the 1990s federalism in India has moved from a situation of conflict to a reliance upon consensus, working through federal forums such as the Inter-State Council. In this context it must be emphasized that the coalition party system of governance at the federal level, by giving direct representation to powerful regional parties in the Union Cabinet of the Government of India, has also eased tensions between the federal government and the states. Regionalism and the regionalization process have carved out their own space, which has facilitated regional participation in decision making on federation-wide issues. Moreover, the federal government seems to have become receptive to accommodating the states' viewpoints when it comes to the federal dispensation of national power and resources. Imperatives of good governance and fiscal discipline on the part of the union and the states are also increasingly underlined.

One sees a perceptible change in the official understanding of federal unity and integrity. Regionalism or provincialism within the permissible limits of autonomy and integration is no longer treated as a threat to federal unity. Despite several shortcomings, the third tier of local government has de facto been successfully added to the federal structure in order to generate a perspective from below. This will surely have a positive impact on the refederalization of the power distribution within India. However, the constitutional provision of "autonomous regional councils" is yet to be realized in its full potential as one of the federal modes of substate governance. Such is also the case with the power distribution at the intrastate level. States, in contrast to their claims for autonomy in their federal-state relations, seem to be reluctant to devolve powers and functions to their intrastate institutions. As a result of the growing frustrations of the union and local government institutions in this regard, there has even been a move to get the union government to directly fund the district *panchayats*.[27] On the one hand, the union cannot bypass the state in order to deal with the local governments; on the other hand, people perceive federalism as one of the instruments of their empowerment, and, as a result of the current democratic upsurge, the nondevolution of powers and finances to the local governments is unlikely to last much longer. In short, decentralizing the "eminent domain" of the federal government in order to ensure federal unity through regional accommodation is a critical issue in India today.

NOTES

1 D.D. Basu, *Introduction to the Constitution of India* (New Delhi: Wadhwa and Co., 1997), p. 59.

2 "Union" and "federal" are used interchangeably in this chapter. The term "centre" is also commonly used in India to denote "union" or "federal."

3 Government of India, *India 2003: A Reference Annual* (New Delhi: Publications Division, Ministry of Information and Broadcasting, 2003).

4 *Keshavananda Bharati v. State of Kerala*, AIR 1973 SC 1461; *S.R. Bommai and others v. Union of India*, AIR 1994 SC 1918:(1994) 3SCC1. The basic features of the Constitution as spelled out by the Supreme Court include supremacy of the Constitution, democracy, rule of law, republican structure, separation of powers, federalism, secularism, judicial review, independence of the judiciary, free and fair elections, emergency provisions, the essence of fundamental rights, directive principles of state policy, freedom of the press, the concept of justice, and the limited amending power of Parliament.

5 Government of India, *India 2003*, p. 38.

6 Sangh Mittra, *Indian Constitutional Acts: East India Company to Independence* (New Delhi: Commonwealth Publishing, 2003), p. 298.

7 For details of each amendment act, see M.V. Pyle, *Constitutional Amendments in India* (Delhi: Universal Law Publishing Company, 2003). As of today there have been 102 amendments to the Indian Constitution.

8 Like the word "community" the term "nation" has also acquired a meaning in Indian parlance that does not entirely conform to Western usages (e.g., "civic-nation," or "cultural" nation). When the reigning ideological discourse uses the term "nation" in India, it always means composite multicultural secular nationalism. See R.S. Dinkar, *Sanskriti ke char adhyaya*, Foreword by Jawaharlal Nehru (Patna: Udayachal, 1956). Dinkar uses the term *samasik rashtrawad*, which, in Hindi, means "composite nationalism."

9 B. Shiva Rao, ed., *The Framing of India's Constitution: Select Documents* (New Delhi: The Indian Institute of Public Administration, 1998).

10 *Union of India v. H.S. Dhillon*, AIR 1972 SC 1061.

11 *International Tourism Corporation v. State of Haryana*, AIR 1981 SC 774.

12 *D.C. Wadhwa v. State of Bihar*, AIR 1987 SC 579.

13 *Western Coalfields v. Special Area Development*, AIR 1982 SC 697.

14 P.M. Bakshi, *The Constitution of India* (Delhi: Universal Law Publishing Company, 2004).

15 D.D. Basu, *Introduction to the Constitution of India*, 19th ed. (New Delhi: Wadhwa and Company, 2002), p. 256.

16 *Report of the National Commission to Review the Working of the Constitution*, vol. 1 (New Delhi: Universal Law Publishing Company, 2003), pp. 238–242.

17 Administrative Reforms Commission, *Report of the Study Team on Centre-State Relationships*, vol. 1 (New Delhi: Government of India, Ministry of Home Affairs, 1967), p. 17.

18 Ibid., 21–22. "Plan needs" are the needs of development-related programs and projects; "non-plan needs" are those of public establishment, including salaries.

19 Ibid. The "Productive Principle," as applied to loans, would mean that a loan should be used only for those activities that would increase output (say, goods and services).

20 Ibid., 15–44.

21 *Report of the Commission on Centre-State Relations*, part 1 (Nasik: Government of India Press, 1987), p. 544.

22 Ibid.

23 Ibid., 31.

24 Ibid., 66.

25 Ibid., 315.

26 *Report of the National Commission to Review the Working of the Constitution*, vol. 1, pp. 234–235.

27 United Progressive Alliance, *Common Minimum Programme* (New Delhi: 27 May 2004), p. 9; see also "Power to Panchayats" (editorial), *Times of India* (New Delhi), 1 July 2004, 14; "States Oppose Direct Funding of Panchayats," *The Hindu* (New Delhi), 1 July 2004, 1.

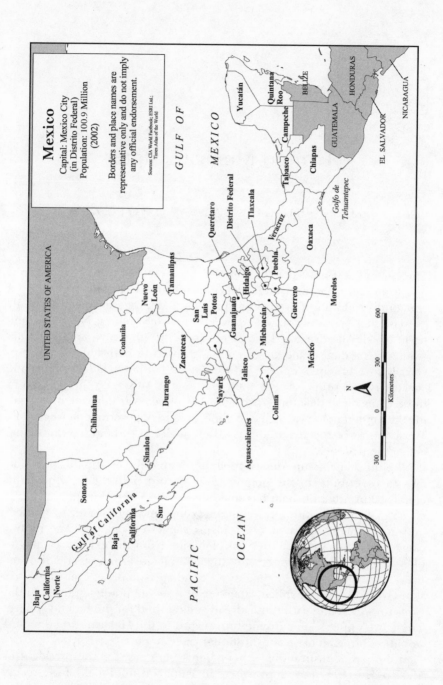

Mexico

Capital: Mexico City
(in Distrito Federal)
Population: 100.9 Million
(2002)

Borders and place names are
representative only and do not imply
any official endorsement.

Source: CIA World Factbook; ESRI Ltd.;
Times Atlas of the World

UNITED STATES OF AMERICA

GULF OF

MEXICO

PACIFIC

OCEAN

Gulf of California

Baja
California
Norte

Baja
California
Sur

Sonora

Chihuahua

Sinaloa

Durango

Coahuila

Nuevo
León

Tamaulipas

Zacatecas

Nayarit

Aguascalientes

Jalisco

San
Luis
Potosí

Guanajuato

Colima

Michoacán

Querétaro

Hidalgo

México

Distrito Federal

Tlaxcala

Morelos

Puebla

Veracruz

Guerrero

Oaxaca

Golfo de
Tehuantepec

Tabasco

Chiapas

Campeche

Yucatán

Quintana
Roo

BELIZE

GUATEMALA

HONDURAS

EL SALVADOR

NICARAGUA

N

0   300   600

Kilometers

300

United Mexican States

MANUEL GONZÁLEZ OROPEZA

The current and most pressing problem in the Mexican federal system is how to organize the distribution of powers. Since 1847 Mexico has had a type of distribution of powers in which the federal government may only exercise those powers granted *expressly* in the Constitution; no other country in North America has this type of rigid distribution. Not even Canada (which has a dual catalogue of powers granted to both federal and provincial governments) or the United States (with the all-encompassing "necessary and proper clause") are the same as Mexico in this respect. In those countries judicial interpretation has played a major role in extending the limited powers assigned to either sphere of government, whereas in Mexico most of this extension has been achieved through constitutional amendment alone.

All political actors in Mexico today agree that the existing distribution fails to contribute to the democratization and political growth of the country, but none of them has suggested realistic reforms. Because Article 124 of the Constitution forces an explicit grant of power to the federal government, most of the reforms suggested fall into one of two categories. They would either (1) eliminate from the explicit catalogue of Article 73 crucial powers for the federal government and transfer them to the states or (2) suggest a Canadian type of system, where the states would have an explicit catalogue of reserved powers granted in the Constitution, along with those already established for the federal sphere. These two options are extreme with regard to the Mexican situation and would require extensive constitutional amendments.

In the past, constitutional amendments were easy for the president of Mexico. However, since 2001, when the latest constitutional reform recognizing indigenous rights was ratified, the amending process for any constitutional change has become very difficult as political control is now divided among three major political parties and at least four other minor parties at the federal level.

Reform is particularly difficult to achieve because, in Mexico, all matters concerning the distribution of powers become a constitutional issue. These issues have not traditionally been subject to judicial interpretation (as they are in Canada and the United States) or to statutory regulation. The only source of legal authority is the written Constitution, and it leaves little space for judicial interpretation. In fact, Article 72, Section f, of the Constitution reads that in the *interpretation*, repeal, or change of any law, the amendment procedure must follow the same process as was followed when the provision was originally adopted. Thus, even though the judicial branch is authorized to exercise a *juridical* interpretation under Article 14 of the Constitution, this interpretation is submitted to the final authority of the legislature. Some are of the view that the Supreme Court is the final interpreter of the Constitution under Article 94, Paragraph 8, but again, this power is to be exercised in deference to the legislature. So judicial interpretation is not free spirited and independent but, rather, highly scrutinized and limited. Therefore the judicial interpretation process, being different from the legislative process, cannot effectively change any constitutional provision regarding distribution of powers.

This chapter discusses this dilemma and provides a glimpse of a possible solution. But first, we must review some general information on Mexico.

THE FEDERAL CONSTITUTION IN HISTORICAL CONTEXT

General Background

Mexico's population in the 2000 census was 100,349,800 inhabitants, making the country the eleventh most populated in the world and, after the United States, the second most populated in North America. The big increase in population came during the twentieth century: a population of 14.5 million in 1917 expanded to a projected population of around 107 million in 2005.[1] The annual population growth rate is considered to be 1.5 percent.[2] Mexico's continental territory is 1,964,381.7 square kilometres, or more than 756,066 square miles, and the islands constitute an additional 5,133.4 square kilometres. Its border with the United States in the north is 3,152 kilometres long, and that with Guatemala and Belize in the south is 1,149 kilometres long.

The predominant language, although not legally official, is Spanish. From 8 percent to 10 percent of the population are monolingual in one of the Aboriginal languages. Among the fifty-eight Aboriginal languages the largest are Nahuatl,[3] Mayan, and Zapotec.[4] The official statistics of Mexico do not classify population distribution according to race because such classifications were abolished at Independence. Nevertheless, it is possible to assert that the majority of the Mexican population consists of the product of *mestizaje* between the Spaniards and the indigenous people, accounting for roughly 90 percent of the population.[5]

Of the total population 96 percent is Roman Catholic while 1.2 percent is Protestant, 0.1 percent is Jewish, and 2.1 percent is other. Freedom of religion was first established through a constitutional amendment in 1873. By law, all churches are named as "Religious Associations" and must be registered with the federal government. States neither regulate nor enforce federal religion-related laws.

Mexico's GDP is US$6,030 per capita, the second largest Latin American GDP per capita after Argentina. Mexico has achieved the largest growing economy in Latin America and, since 2001, it has risen to US$617.8 billion per year.[6]

Constitutional Evolution

The current Constitution originated from a revision of the previous 1857 Constitution, which had reestablished the federal system. The first federal Constitution was actually enacted before that, in 1824, but internal crisis produced its replacement in 1836. The current Constitution was enacted on 5 February 1917 by a special constitutional convention called the year before and assembled in the City of Queretaro in central Mexico amid the struggles among the different supporting groups of the Mexican Revolution. The Constitution was a self-implementing document because most of the state legislatures had been dissolved by internal divisions during the more than six years of the revolutionary war. Consequently, the federal Constitution was not ratified by the states forming the union and no requirement for this was ever advanced.

The adoption of the republican form of government led to the federal system. The constitutional convention that approved the 1917 Constitution, led by a few lawyers and other professionals, consisted of a popular body of representatives who changed the constitutional draft of the then incumbent head of the executive branch, Venustiano Carranza. With complete freedom these representatives debated the main institutions to be included in the resulting constitution, including social rights and land reform. The very first debate considered the official name of the country. During most of the nineteenth century, during federalist times, its official name had been the United Mexican States; however, in the twentieth century it was deemed appropriate to consider changing the name to the Republic of Mexico. This issue aroused extensive debate as to whether the title of "Republic" was sufficient to show that the country was inspired by the federalist spirit. In the end, the opposing view prevailed and the official name of the country remains the United Mexican States.

The current Constitution followed the Reformation Act, 1874, in establishing judicial review, but the main institutions (including judicial review) are embedded within civil law. At first, the writ of *amparo* (shelter) was the remedy to protect human rights established in the Constitution and was the only judicial review procedure foreseen and intended for individuals. However, judicial review on the basis of amparo was very severely restricted by legislation. Impeachment was the procedure by which the legislatures were empowered to protect the Constitution from general violations.

Limitations on judicial discretion and the prevalence of legislative processes are major features of the Mexican system. Neither judicial precedents nor broad judicial interpretations are permitted – indeed they are constitutionally prohibited by Articles 14 and 92 of the Constitution. Thus the precedent value in judicial review for today's court resolutions are relative only to the courts from which they originate. In other words, Mexico does not have a stare decisis doctrine, and the judicial resolutions issued by the highest federal courts are binding upon other state and federal courts only when they are approved with a special majority of judges and their holdings are constant in five consecutive resolutions. No other authority is compelled to follow their rationale. Where judicial resolutions occur as a last resort, their binding force is embedded in the concept of "jurisprudencia" (i.e., they are binding only upon the judges, not upon all authorities). And so, in the area of the federal distribution of powers, judicial interpretation has made no major discoveries relating to the stipulated powers granted by the Constitution to the federal government. Every new subject is dealt with through the constitutional amending process so as to be in accordance with Article 124, which establishes that all federal powers have to be expressed exclusively in the text of the Constitution.

Concerning the other branches of government, the executive is the only branch to be vested in a single authority (as in the United States). Mexico had the chance to vest this authority in the hands of a "collective" executive, as in the French Constitutions of 1795 and 1799, respectively. However, the decision to adopt a single executive was finally made in the 1824 Constitution on the basis that the federal system, along with the separation of powers, would be effective enough to constrain any abuse of power. However – and significantly – the Constitution does limit many executive positions, including that of the president, to a single term in office.

In the same fashion, the federal legislative branch was originally deposited in two houses, the first devoted to popular representation and the second devoted to counterbalancing the overrepresentation of big states in the first. The Senate was created in order to achieve a balanced and equitable representation of the states rather than of the people. Some state legislatures established a second chamber, but these were all abolished by the end of the nineteenth century. Since 1977 Mexico has adopted proportional representation for election to all representative bodies (federal Congress, state legislatures, and municipal bodies). There are 500 federal representatives in the lower house, 300 as the result of direct election (since 1917) and 200 as representatives of five multiple-member constituencies. There are 128 members of the Senate, and they are elected through a combination of direct suffrage (three seats per state for a total of ninety-six) and proportional representation on a national basis (for thirty-two additional seats). So we can see that the federal system was fundamental to the structure of the various branches of government.

A long process of decentralization was involved in the creation of the federal system in Mexico. During colonial times, whenever it was feasible throughout the immense territory of New Spain (as Mexico was then called) centralization was a key tendency in government. The last part of that period coincided with the enactment of the 1812 Cádiz Constitution in Spain. This first Spanish Constitution allowed the existence of "Provincial Deputations" as autonomous governing bodies for each of the provinces. These deputations were politically active in the formation of the federal system in Mexico in 1824, once independence was achieved. However, since its creation, many politically influential sectors of the population have argued that the federal system does not fit Mexico's geographical and societal conditions. The prevailing system of centralized rule in Spanish America and the lack of definition in existing federations, mainly the United States, made it very difficult to change 300 years of tradition.

The 1917 Constitution involved a reform of the 1857 Constitution. However, the basic system of the distribution of powers dates back even earlier, to the Reformation Act, 1874. In the 1824 Constitution the allocation of powers was considered to involve a partnership between the "general" government and the state governments, who were expected to work with the same powers in a coordinated manner. However, when there were clashes between federal and state laws, the states would not agree to the nullification of their laws as decreed by the general Congress. The Reformation Act sought to solve this conflict by clearly stating the federal powers and excluding any state legislation from affecting any matters expressly granted to the federal government. In its way this was similar to the pre-1787 United States Articles of Confederation (Article 2), based on the principle that federal authorities shall perform only those powers granted expressly by the states in the Constitution.[7] In the same fashion, the undesignated reserved powers of the states are exclusive to them, are coordinate (or equal) to federal powers, and cannot be trampled by the federal government.

Article 124 of the current (1917) Constitution thus sets out the distribution of powers, resembling the original U.S. Articles of Confederation. As noted above, Article 124 sets out that every time a "new" competence is advised for the federal government, a constitutional amendment is required, notwithstanding the fact that Mexico does have a "necessary" clause in Article 73, Section xxx, of the Constitution. However, in order to have effect, this clause requires judicial interpretation which, as noted, is not in principle a prerogative of the judiciary. Exercising self-restraint, the Supreme Court has only interpreted the necessary clause once, in 1932. At that time it found that archeological monuments are a federal concern and therefore exclusive to federal legislation. This ruling struck down the state legislation in Oaxaca, despite the fact that the Constitution gave the federal government no power to do so. However, the value of this precedent is relative because, after the ruling, a constitutional amendment was approved to have the subject of archeological monuments explicitly written into the Constitution.

One may now move on to other significant trends in the evolution of the distribution of powers. During the administration of Porfirio Diaz, which began in 1910, a set of reforms was proposed (similar to an earlier reform proposal in 1883 dealing with commerce) to increase the limited and stipulated powers of the federal government. The 1917 Constitution followed the trend of the previous Constitution and the never-ending addition to new powers for the federal government grew in a disproportionate manner.

However, the main concern of the new Constitution focused, for the first time, on "social rights," the rights of communities and "minorities" who had been traditionally exploited (particularly peasants and workers). In this respect, the federal Constitution established the framework for all authorities, both federal and state, to act on behalf of these social groups and to guarantee their constitutional rights. The original intent of the new Constitution was to involve both levels of government in the administration of the "new justice" – an administrative justice that would not depend on the courts, who had been the allies of the Diaz administration. The new "administrative" justice would be integrated with the social sector. For instance, labour courts were established at both the federal and state levels, and they enforced both federal and state statutes until 1929. These were implemented by a "panel" of three judges, one appointed by the executive, one by the labour unions, and one by the corporations. In land reform, adjudication went in the first instance to state commissions and then, for final resolution, to the Federal Commission on Land Reform. Notwithstanding this initial arrangement, later reforms tended to centralize procedures and regulations so that federal agencies superseded state agencies.

This model for administrative justice had been reversed in some ways at the end of the twentieth century in view of the general lack of public confidence in the independence of the courts, which were seen as being controlled by the executive. Particularly important has been the transfer of electoral courts from the executive realm to the judicial realm. Labour and land reform courts are still under the influence and control of executives at both federal and state levels.

Intellectual and International Influences on the Federal Constitution

The core of the 1917 Constitution remains the same as that of the 1857 Constitution, which was influenced by the U.S. Constitution (and commentaries on the latter from such mid-nineteenth-century French writers as Alexis de Tocqueville and, later, Edouard Laboulaye). In the 1870s commentaries on the U.S. Constitution by writers such as Joseph Story, James Kent, George Paschal, and Thomas Cooley were also available in Mexico. However, during the constitutional convention that enacted the 1917 Constitution, the most influential author was Mexican jurist Emilio Rabasa, who had expounded on the U.S. Constitution.

The founding fathers were all inspired by the social issues that inspired the Mexican Revolution; that is, in the main, their inspiration was Mexican. The separation of church and state had been formally achieved, but shortly after the enactment of the Constitution, Mexico became involved in a religious civil war that began in 1925 and lasted several years. The civil war had no obvious impact on the Constitution. Indeed, the Mexican Constitution, being the first to set out social rights, served as a model for the Weimer Constitution (1919) and the Russian Constitution (1918) for social rights.[8]

The Constitution was formed with the idea that the federal government must assume a role as the driving force behind all the social changes needed after the revolution. However, even though the states were subordinate partners, they played a more significant role during the first years of the 1917 Constitution than they do today. Indeed, ever since the inception of the distribution of powers rule in 1847, the growing accumulation of federal powers at the expense of the states has cut deeply into the original distribution of powers. This trend has operated as a zero-sum game in which the powers granted to one level of government prohibit the other level from exercising the same powers. As a result, the states are now overwhelmingly subordinated to the federal government.

As noted above, the 1917 Constitution was the third federal Constitution, the first being enacted in 1824 and the second in 1857. Between the first two constitutions Mexico had several centralist constitutions: one in 1836, one in 1843, and the last in 1853. The main differences and similarities are that the 1824 Constitution established a cooperative model of federalism in which the powers exercised by the federal government and the states were not separate but, rather, were exercised in conjunction with one another (much like the U.S. model after *McCulloch v. Maryland*).[9] In 1847, however, the Reformation Act reestablished the 1824 Constitution (with several reforms) and changed the distribution of powers. It separated both spheres of government by granting expressed powers to the federal government and reserved powers to the states. The reason behind this change, given by the drafter of the Reformation Act, Mariano Otero, was that, when conflicts of laws had arisen between the federal and the state governments, Congress's practice of "disallowing" state laws was considered an intrusion (resulting in problems similar to those that arose in the first stage of the implementation of Canada's British North America Act, 1867). In 1847 in Mexico judicial review was not an available remedy to these conflicts; rather, resolution depended on political action in Congress. Not until 1917, under Article 105, was there a judicial remedy for constitutional disputes – a remedy that the Supreme Court still enjoys.

In sum, Article 124 of the Constitution sets out the current distribution of powers, which resembles that set out in the original U.S. Articles of Confederation. However, there is no record of any direct U.S. influence leading to Mexico adopting this form of power distribution in 1847, which is odd, given that this was the year the United States invaded.

Aboriginal Peoples, Languages, Religion, and Human Rights

Since 1992 an alternate legal system for indigenous communities has been given a constitutional basis, meaning that the customs and traditions of Aboriginal peoples, who represent at least 10 percent of the overall population in Mexico, prevail over state and federal law. Many of these customs and traditions are communal. On 14 August 2001 a constitutional amendment was approved for the first time within a multiparty environment, with the ratification of nineteen state legislatures, the abstention of four, and the opposition of eight. This is an exceptional case because the amendment dealt with indigenous rights, which had already been recognized by Mexico when it signed on to the International Labour Organization's Convention No. 169 Concerning Indigenous and Tribal Peoples in Independent Countries in 1990.

Human rights have been traditionally protected through the writ of amparo, but there has been very little advancement since the time that this remedy was first created. Judicial review is not invoked from class actions: it is rooted in personal injuries rather than in a collective and public interest under the law.

As noted, the Constitution does not declare any official language, nor, under Article 4, can any Aboriginal language be discriminated against. Since 1994 a notable effort has been made by all authorities to translate some fundamental laws into Aboriginal languages. This, unfortunately, is often a futile effort since the linguistic signs used to transcribe the Aboriginal languages are not commonly recognized by the native speakers.

Roman Catholicism was Mexico's official religion during most of the nineteenth century. The debate that divided Mexico was precisely the issue of the separation between church and state. A civil war was fought over this issue. The separation of church and state had implications not only for freedom of religion but also for the control of immense tracts of land; registration of births, deaths, and marriages; control of cemeteries; and even official holidays. The first big debate on the formation of the 1857 Constitution concerned the freedom of religion, but it was cancelled. From 1859 to 1862, during the reformation period, President Benito Juarez had to face an enemy inside the country; but from 1863 to 1867 the enemy was outside: the conservative forces allied with the Roman Catholic Church to allow the intervention of France in Mexico's internal politics. The constitutional provision that enabled freedom of religion was approved in 1873. Since then, under Article 24 of the Constitution, freedom of religion was established, complemented by the separation of church and state prescribed in Article 130. In recent years, in the southern part of the country, the expulsion of Protestant groups from indigenous communities has produced some bloody confrontations (e.g., Acteal, Chiapas in 1997).

Federal Loyalty and Unity

The *Bundestreue* principle embodied in the German federation is nonexistent in Mexico. The federal comity is not entrusted to the states; rather, the Mexican Constitution establishes several measures enabling federal intervention whenever a state encroaches upon federal jurisdiction. Such intervention is especially enforced by the Senate, which is considered to represent the states. Moreover, the supremacy clause, complemented by other constitutional provisions, obliges the states to function as a supplementary power whenever the federal government so requires.

Secession is not permitted and no judicial rulings have ever been issued on this topic. This stands in contrast to the United States, where the southern states attempted to secede and, later, Texas tried to separate.[10] There have been some threats of secession in Mexico, however, Chiapas being a case in point. In Mexico a constitutional amendment would be required to enable secession because all the states are cited in the text of the Constitution; thus, to eliminate one would require a virtual reform of the Constitution. This is parallel to the reasoning of the Supreme Court of Canada in its consultative judgment in *Reference Re Secession of Quebec*.[11]

CONSTITUTIONAL DISTRIBUTION OF POWERS AND RESPONSIBILITIES

Citizenship and Rights

Citizenship in Mexico is dual: each state recognizes a particular citizenship for electoral purposes as well as the fact that each of its citizens is a

Mexican national. At the beginning of the federal system colonization was also part of the states' powers, which were concurrent with those of the federal government. This was the case when the colonization of Texas was authorized by the State of Coahuila in the 1830s, making it easier for American colonists to settle in the Mexican province than would have been the case under the stricter measures applied by the federal government. Now immigration is exclusively federal.

Since 1970 Mexican citizenship has been granted to Mexican nationals older than eighteen years of age, in accordance with Article 34 of the Constitution. The rights entrusted to citizens are political in nature and differ from the rights of other nationals and foreigners resident in the country. Article 73, Section XVI,[12] enables Congress to legislate with regard to nationality, foreigners, citizens, naturalization, colonization, immigration, and the general health of the population. This means that state citizenship is dependent upon Mexican citizenship being recognized by federal authorities. At first, immigration was also concurrent, but it was federalized in the amending process leading to the 1857 Constitution, and since the 1917 Constitution came into effect it has been exclusive to the federal government.

The history of suffrage is quite interesting because it shows the contributions of the states and local governments to the advancement of political rights. The last level of government to recognize women's suffrage was the federal. The municipalities from the states of San Luis Potosi, a northern province of Mexico, were the first to recognize women's rights (in 1923), and the State of Baja California (in 1953) was the first to allow women to vote in state elections. After this, the federal government finally recognized women's suffrage at the end of 1953.

All elections occur within the jurisdiction of either the states or the federal government, according to the nature of the election being organized. However, the election registrar is federal and the election card is issued by the federal government, and the states must sign agreements with the Federal Election Commission to organize state elections. At the moment only one state, Baja California, has its own electoral registry. However, state elections are legally conducted by state election commissions, which also organize municipal elections. Each state has its own election courts so that elections can be scrutinized within the proper jurisdiction. Article 99 of the Constitution, however, enables judicial remedies to reach a final resolution in the Federal Election Courts, making elections, state or municipal, a federal issue under the guarantee of a republican form of government. Political parties may be registered at state and municipal levels by state election legislation; the current trend, however, has the prevalent and majoritarian political parties being registered at the federal level.

As already mentioned, Spanish is the most common language, but federal law has not declared it to be the official language of Mexico; indigenous

languages are respected under Article 4 of the Constitution, which establishes that all federal, state, and municipal authorities shall respect and enforce the customs and traditions of Indian communities. The Mexican
Branch of the Spanish Academy of Language attempts to correct the mistakes of colloquial language as well as of those taught at the universities, but
this is not an issue on the public agenda. The Constitution defines Mexican
society as "multicultural" rather than as "multiethnic" because, as is the case
in most Latin American countries, differences among ethnic and linguistic
groups are considered to be a matter of culture rather than a matter of race.

The separation between church and state, which was critical in the nineteenth century, has been relaxed by the 1992 constitutional amendments.
This has been especially beneficial for priests, who have acquired the right
to vote in elections. Their political rights are still incomplete, though, because they cannot be candidates for election nor can they use their ser-
mons to endorse or attack candidates or parties. Some problems involving
politics and religion are still under study, such as the tensions between
communities where clashes between Roman Catholics and other religious
groups have provoked bloody confrontations (in Juan Chamula and Acteal, Chiapas). However grave these problem, though, they are not as bad
as they are in many other countries.

Aboriginal and indigenous peoples are regulated under Articles 2 and 4,
which were incorporated by the recent amendment process approved in
2002. This new disposition applies to both federal and state jurisdictions in
relation to indigenous peoples. This reform was made in accordance with
Convention 169 of the International Labour Organization regarding the
rights of indigenous peoples and was signed by Mexico at the outset. Here,
one can appreciate the influence of international law upon domestic law.

The first regulation under the new constitutional provisions was instituted in 1990–92 in the State of Oaxaca, the state with the largest proportion of indigenous peoples. It established the possibility of enforcing an
alternate legal system based on indigenous customs and traditions rather
than on state law. Indian courts have also been established in the States of
Oaxaca and Quintana Roo (Mayan population), and they have proven to
be successful. There is still no federal statute regarding indigenous rights,
but many state laws have been enacted. An example is the Oaxaca Election
Code, in which the exercise of political rights falls within the scope of indigenous customs and traditions, and no political parties are involved in
the elections of 418 out of 570 municipalities.

Economy, Resources, Environment

Economic policy making is under the control of the federal government.
Since 1883 commerce has been an exclusive competence of the federal

government. The central bank was created without serious questioning in 1925, after the monetary crisis brought on by the Mexican Revolution. In addition, under the current Constitution, Article 131, the executive branch has full powers over international commerce.

Article 73, Section XVII, establishes the power of the Congress to enact legislation on general communications and transportation, but without excluding state regulation with regard to state communications and transportation (whether on roads or water).

Most natural resources are regulated by the federal government. Article 27 prescribes federal ownership of natural resources such as minerals and oil. The Continental Shelf and seabed also belong to the nation. Moreover, federal courts have ruled that, whenever the Constitution refers to "Nation," it should be understood that the federal government is its legal representative. Regulation of forests and hunting is concurrent, but federal legislation may preempt state legislation in these matters.

Since the 1960s energy policy has been controlled by the federal government and is not subject to private exploitation. Thus electricity and nuclear power have been exclusively under the authority of federal organizations, and no participation from the states has been allowed. Even taxation related to electric energy is exclusively federal, under Article 73, Section XXIX, Subsection 5a.

Agriculture is a concurrent subject that the states have neglected to develop, and their role has declined relative to that of the federal government's. This is because the federal budget has been the most important source of income for agricultural programs. Environment is also a concurrent subject, and both the states and the federal government regulate and enforce it. The overwhelming regulatory action of the federal government, however, overshadows that of the states. The right to a clean environment is established in the all-encompassing Article 4, and environmental protection is entrusted to federal courts as well as to federal regulatory agencies. Environmental legislation is extensively complemented through regulations – called "official rules" – approved by the secretary of the environment. These constitute a codification of rules regulating very specific issues. It is therefore possible to say that the subject is not only in the hands of the federal government but, primarily, in those of the president.

Labour and Social

There is no public unemployment insurance or compensation and, perhaps for this reason, the unemployment rate is not as high as those in Canada and the United States.[13] This also means that the duration of unemployment is generally shorter in Mexico than in Canada or the United States. The official unemployment rates are lower in Mexico than in the other countries of the region; however, some critics say that the official numbers are understated because of differences in the statistical definition of unemployment. Labour policies are shared by federal and state governments, but regulation has been exclusively federal since 1929. Courts dealing with labour conflicts are concurrent, but the enforcement of labour policies is under federal jurisdiction. Since 1942 social welfare has been a federal program directed towards public health, insurance, and pensions, but the agency in charge of it is more of a bureaucratic machine than an efficient agency. For that reason it always appears ineffective. There has been some discussion of privatizing this system, but such propositions encounter great opposition.

Since 1917 public health has been considered one of the fundamental responsibilities of the federal government. At that time a general health council was established under the authority of the president, but in 1940 a secretary of public health was created. Responsibility in the area is both federal and state, but the former tends to prevail. Many efforts have been made to give the states more responsibility in this field, however, and the federal government has tried to assume more of a regulatory than an enforcer role with regard to public health policies.

Education was a state power until 1934, when an amendment to Article 3 of the Constitution made it concurrent. Education in public schools is required to be non-religious, and all members of the population have the right to attend these schools until Grade 9 (which corresponds to primary and secondary education in North America). Public education is free. Colleges and universities may be established by federal and/or state governments, and they are also free (or they charge such insignificant tuitions that they are practically free). Since 1980 the characteristic of "autonomy" for certain public universities has been recognized in the Constitution, meaning that the executive branch has no authority over such institutions. They are subject only to general legislative and judicial controls. This constitutional provision applies not only to the federal chartered universities but also to the state universities.

Beginning in 1995 the federal government undertook educational reform as an exercise in "new federalism," and the states were given control of public primary and secondary schools. Many states claimed that this was merely a move to undermine the powerful teachers union by scattering the school system over thirty-one states and one federal district. Others confessed that they could not administer all these schools. In the end, this measure worked out, but it continues to show centralist features.

Security

Mexico took from the United States the general framework for internal security, but practice has tended to alter it. The so-called permanent armed forces – the army, navy, and air force – are under federal authority and the direct command of the president. These are primarily concerned with external security, but since the 1994 Chiapas turmoil, as well as increased concern about drug trafficking, they have increasingly been involved in internal issues. Although formally the states are part of the larger system through the militias under their control, since 1940 a federal statute has made state militias a reserve of the permanent armed forces subject to the federal government, thus excluding state intervention in civil protection. There was an attempt to reverse this trend in the 1999 constitutional amendment to Article 73, Section XXIX-1, by which "civil protection" was to be a common power of the three levels of government. In any case, since Mexico has not been involved in any foreign hostilities since the Second World War, the issue of security and even terrorism has ranked below other emergencies (such as earthquakes, hurricanes, and poverty).

National defence is an exclusive federal power in Mexico, just as it is in the United States; but the powers of the Mexican president are linked to congressional approval. Therefore, there is no Mexican equivalent to the American War Powers Resolution, which gives the American president the power to fight a war without the consent of the U.S. Congress.

Civil Law

Civil law is under the jurisdiction of both state and federal governments. In this realm there is no clear constitutional demarcation. Criminal law is also under state jurisdiction, although a uniform criminal code was published in 1963, with no binding effect upon the states. Article 73, Section XXI, allows Congress to define crimes as federal. As noted above, courts in Mexico are organized in accordance with federal and state powers. Scrutiny over criminal procedure under Article 14 is, however, a federal issue and, as a result, federal courts may deal with conflicts or violations of procedure and the wrongful enforcement of state criminal codes. In the end, all cases, civil or criminal, may go to federal courts for judicial review through the writ of amparo.

Foreign Affairs

Foreign affairs are conducted by the president with the consent of the Senate. Mexicans are beginning to debate whether the Senate should participate in treaty negotiations, but since there is no constitutional provision referring to "advice" by the Senate, the executive branch has been reluctant to let it intervene in the process of negotiation. Presidential powers over the making of treaties were increased by the Federal Act on Treaties, 1992, by which executive agreements signed by departments of executive and public agencies have the same authority as treaties. On the other hand, in accord

with Article 117, Section I, states have no power to sign international agreements despite the common practice of states along the U.S. border reaching agreements on various issues with their American counterparts. In
November 1999 the Mexican Supreme Court delivered a standard, or "thesis," by which international treaties were ranked below the Constitution,
with domestic law being lowered to third place (Thesis LXXVII/99).[14]
Following, in part, the opinion of U.S. Justice George Sutherland in *U.S. v.
Curtiss-Wright Export Corp. et al.*,[15] the Mexican Supreme Court ranked international treaties higher than federal and state laws. This was due to the
status given to the president as head of the Mexican State (and thus encom-
passing all levels of government) as well as the fact that the Senate represents all of the states. This doctrine has been highly criticized because of its
damaging impact upon federal and state laws. In the first place, federal laws
cannot be amended, repealed, or modified except according to the same
legislative procedure that led to their creation (Article 72, Section f),[16] and
treaties in Mexico are not necessarily implemented by legislative enact-
ments, being considered self-implementing (to use the language of common law countries).

Treaties and federal acts are made in accordance with different constitutional procedures and, therefore, the former cannot change the latter.
Similarly, as far as state laws are concerned, according to Article 133 treaties cannot be considered the supreme law of the land unless they follow
the distribution of powers given in the Constitution. At this point, the
court has not made it clear why treaties are not limited by this distribution
of powers, nor has it made it clear why the executive and the Senate are
considered to be beyond state powers. It should be noted, however, that
this last thesis has no binding force comparable to that of the *stare decisis*
doctrine of the common law countries, but it is the most recent dictum on
the subject.

DISTRIBUTION OF OPERATIONAL POWERS

Outside the regular control exercised by political parties, especially when
they are federation-wide, each level of government has its own elected authorities and its own heads of powers established in accordance with the
Constitution. Exceptions to this rule have been made for the growth of explicit federal powers by constitutional amendments and by judicial review
through the writ of amparo, a procedure sustained before federal courts.[17]
During the nineteenth century Mexican state constitutions were more assertive then they are now as they clearly stated that no final resolution by
the branches of state governments could be revised by any other power or
level; however, these dispositions have lost their meaning and have been
openly repealed.

The same is true for the intervention of state governments in the federal domain. With regard to the enforcement of Mexico's historic constitutions, state legislatures played a very important role in the formation and approval (or disapproval) of federal laws as well as in the designation of federal authorities. For example, the states initiated most of the constitutional amendments that were considered in 1847 for the reestablishment of the federal system after a period of centralist rule. Even today state assemblies have the right to initiate federal laws (Article 71, Section III), and amendments to the federal Constitution require approval by a majority of the states (Article 135). There has been significant state influence, as witnessed during the 2002 amendment to the Constitution concerning indigenous rights, when, for the first time during the twentieth century, a presidential bill to reform the Constitution was challenged by the states at the point of final passage.[18]

Since 1983 state assemblies have also been empowered to suspend municipal authorities whenever they deem it appropriate as well as to designate new municipal councils. The same process may apply when the federal Senate considers there to be an absence of legal authority in a state. In such circumstances the Senate is empowered to declare the absence of effective authority and to appoint a provisional governor in order to call for an election to renew law and order in that state (Article 76, Section V).[19] This was a common practice from 1879 to 1975, and although no declaration has been issued since then, the Senate's constitutional power remains.

Territories and Boundaries

After neglecting its borders at the beginning of the nineteenth century, Mexico learned about their importance during the U.S. invasion in 1847. The lack of definition of its Texas borders gave the United States a pretext to claim more western territory. Eleven treaties have since been made to precisely define these borders. In 1857 the internal borders among the thirty-one Mexican states and the federal district began to be drawn. The constitutional provision refers to the states as the primarily interested parties, with responsibility to determine their own borders by agreement. If this is not possible, then Congress can intervene as an arbitrator in order to define such borders (Article 73, Section IV). If the state parties do not agree, or if only one is reluctant to follow the congressional decision, then the Supreme Court takes the case (Articles 104 and 105). Congress has intervened many times to arrange borders, but some recent cases are now under consideration by the Supreme Court. Examples include the borders between the Colima and Jalisco, and between Quintana Roo and Campeche. These cases will probably be the first ones to be decided on judicial grounds as, in the past, whatever conflict these states might have had were solved by negotiation under the supervision of the federal government.

As mentioned above, state boundaries and territories are considered inviolate and can only be changed through constitutional amendment. One exception is Quintana Roo, where major tourism resorts are now established (i.e., Cancun). It suffered the alienation of its territory during the difficult years of the Mayan revolts, which occurred in Yucatan Peninsula between 1847 and 1911. In 1902 Quintana Roo was first created as a territory, then suppressed, and then reinstalled. In 1975 it was again recognized as a state, the youngest of the Mexican federation.

The most controversial territorial issue that Mexico has encountered – besides the secession of Texas and the cession of its territory in 1848 through the Treaty of Guadalupe Hidalgo – has been the formation of new states within the territory of other states. The procedure now contained in the Constitution (Article 73, Section III) derives from the creation of the State of Guerrero in 1849, when it separated from three other states: Mexico,[20] Michoacan, and Puebla. The procedure followed was not precisely that prescribed by the Constitutional Reformation Act, 1847, but one that was used in its creation. This exception subsequently became the rule, involving the state legislatures affected by the separation, then the opinion of the rest of the state legislatures, the federal government, and the people affected. This cumbersome procedure is harder to follow than is the simpler constitutional amending process, but it is now the current rule regarding the creation of new states within the territory of existing states.

A final territorial debate concerns the status of the federal district, Mexico City, which aspires to become a state, despite the doubts expressed by a number of politicians. Looking to Ottawa and Washington does not help Mexico City because its history and population are so different from theirs. Many Mexico City natives look, instead, to the examples of Buenos Aires, Vienna, and Berlin, all of which are city-states within their respective federations.

Fiscal Relations

There is no tax autonomy in Mexico. Virtually all revenues are controlled by the federal government. This has been the outcome of a process that occurred during the twentieth century and that involved centralizing taxation in the name of "fiscal coordination." If we apply the distribution of powers established in Article 124 of the Constitution, we might conclude that the taxation powers of the federal government would be those granted expressly by the Constitution and that the states would have power over "reserved taxes." This is not the case, however, because, under Article 73, Section VII, the federal government may levy taxes on all kinds of subjects – even those considered to be reserved powers of the states – for the purpose of covering the federal budget. Under Article 115 municipal governments have their own-source revenues, but the conditions are established by state law.

In 1980 the federal government began to sign fiscal agreements with all the states in order to consolidate centralization. The states would not be concerned with the administration of taxes, allowing the federal government to collect tax revenues and give the appropriate income back to the states (on condition that the states would not levy the reserved taxes that the federal government would be charging taxpayers). In this way double taxation could be avoided. This system is now under fire, however, and there is talk about reform.

States are prohibited from borrowing money from international sources or foreign corporations, and from contracting debt in foreign currency (Article 117, section VIII). Many states are in debt to such federal agencies as the Social Security Administration (health services) and the Federal Electric Commission (lighting and energy), but the payment of these debts involves many political nuances and negotiations. In the end, the federal government may subtract the indebted amount from federal grants to the states, but this is usually prevented by political pressure. The administration of federal revenues is approved by Congress, and the president can (and is supposed to) arrange flexible grants-in-aid to the states, taking account of the asymmetry in the development of the various Mexican states and channeling grants to meet actual needs and/or the payment of public debts.[21] There is no fixed rule though, and the management of federal money is up to the federal government.

Regulatory Agencies

The first regulatory autonomy formally recognized by law related to the governance of public universities, beginning with the National University of Mexico, which was declared autonomous in 1929. The debate around this new autonomy turned on the regime of subsidies from the federal government because, at the time, it was believed that all public agencies whose budget came primarily from the federal government had to be part of the centralized structure of the federal or state governments. In 1935 a national debate resolved the issue in favour of the subsidized but autonomous public universities. In 1980 this matter was taken to the constitutional level by the amendment of Article 3. The U.S. Tennessee Valley Authority served as a model for Mexico with regard to developing rural and severely impoverished areas in 1925 and 1934, when the Irrigation Commission and the Federal Electric Commission and other regulatory agencies were created. This trend has been augmented ever since in such strategic areas as central banking (Article 28), elections (Article 41), the environment, and oil and energy.

Article 90 is the constitutional basis for the establishment of regulatory agencies under the head of decentralized public administration. Until a few years ago judicial review of the acts and resolutions of these agencies was limited and was based on formalities of the Amparo Act, 1936; now, however, it is a remedy available for challenging whatever rule or act is issued by these agencies.

Municipal Relations

The centralized scheme of the federal budget and the distribution of grants to states and municipalities is repeated in the relations between states and municipalities, in which all local budgets are approved by the state legislatures and in which the state governments allocate grants to the municipalities. Land for agricultural purposes and the formation of *ejidos* (communal property) for *pueblos* (villages) is mainly the product of federal and state commissions on land reform. Federal and state property, as well as municipal property, can be severed from its original ownership by a formal resolution or decree and then granted to another level of government for a specific purpose (e.g., building a school, creating an ejido, or promoting other public interest projects). Since 1917 all laws in Mexico have been oriented towards the fulfillment of social goals, especially those that benefit peasants and workers. Consequently, programs to spend federal funds or to transfer property to these social groups receive special legitimacy. The main source for helping these groups is the federal budget, under Item 33 of the annual federal budget, which is aimed at fighting poverty.

Since 1917, when it was first devised, a specific judicial remedy concerning "constitutional controversies" (or litigation), as filed before the Supreme Court in its original jurisdiction, has been used to solve disputes over powers between federal and state jurisdictions. In the amending process of 1994, this remedy was widened to include municipalities as parties. Ever since, municipal governments have been the most active in filing constitutional controversies against state and federal legislation that they consider to be encroaching upon their autonomy. Since the constitutional reform approved for the State of Veracruz in 2000, the same remedy has been adopted by other states to protect the internal distribution of powers of state constitutions.

Constitutionally each level of government is autonomous and, therefore, no executive/administrative decision or appointment has to be reviewed by another level of government. Some grants-in-aid, however, do impose conditions on the state administrations to create agencies and to make appointments to their staff in accordance with federal guidelines or with the approval of the federal government, but such cases are exceptional. In the same fashion, states can replace the *Ayuntamientos* (city officials) when the legislatures suspend them on grounds of accountability (Article 115, Section 1). Municipalities are also generally responsible for the management of their resources (Article 115, Section IV), but, in many cases, there is the requirement of final approval from the state legislature. Consequently, hiring and the actual appropriation of municipal funds is a process in which municipalities are dependent upon final approval from the legislatures. For example, in the case of Garza Garcia City near the Monterrey state capital of Nuevo Leon, the Supreme Court revoked the Ayuntamiento resolution on wage increases for the members of the city council (1992) based on the fact that state legislation had established conditions for this increase and that no authorization from the legislature had been previously given.

EVOLUTION OF THE CONSTITUTIONAL DISTRIBUTION OF POWERS AND RESPONSIBILITIES

The distribution of powers is strictly a constitutional issue, and statutes to modify it are not permitted. Amending the Constitution involves the participation of the president, the Congress (by a two-thirds vote of a quorum of its members), and the state legislatures (with approval by a majority). More than 300 amendments have been made, largely on the initiative of the president. The first amendment was made in 1934, and the most recent in 2002.

As noted, the distribution of powers as established in Article 124 stipulates that the slightest doubt about a federal power should be solved expressly by a constitutional amendment and not by judicial interpretation or simple legislative resolution. This is the reason for the large number of amendments made during the twentieth century. However, during that period the predominance of one party (the Partido Revolucionario Institucional) at both levels made it easy for an incumbent president to modify the Constitution at the outset of his administration. This reality has vanished, and the amending process is much more difficult now because Mexico is no longer subject to single-party dominance.

Citizens are not authorized to play a direct role in the federal constitutional amendment process. In some states (Coahuila, Guerrero, Chihuahua, Veracruz, Tlaxcala, etc.) referendum and popular initiative processes have been incorporated in order to modify legislation, but that has not been the case for the constitutions of the states.

Again, it is important to emphasize that there is no broad judicial interpretation in the Mexican federal system. Mexico has few examples of this, and these are exceptional – such as the Supreme Court interpretation of the last part of the Mexican Supremacy Clause, which is a translation of the U.S. Constitution with respect to the role of state judges. The federal judiciary exercises a monopoly on judicial review, and state judges are not allowed, despite the constitutional provision in Article 133, to pronounce on the constitutionality of laws. The ancillary power established in Article 73, Section XXX, has only been interpreted once, in the Oaxaca controversy, but this was changed afterwards by a specific amendment to the Constitution (as noted above).

The first constitutional amendment to increase the power of the federal government was approved in 1883, and it dealt with commerce. Subsequently, over the course of the twentieth century, virtually all social matters (such as labour and social welfare) were absorbed by the federal government. In accordance with Article 124 every new power exercised by the federal government has been derived from a specific provision of the Constitution, and this has required a never-ending amending process. The original rule, crafted in 1847, called for allocating expressed powers to the federal government, the pretence being that this was limited to few powers and that the remainder was to be assigned to the states. Since 1883, however, more and more powers have ended up in the hands of the federal government, and fewer and fewer have been left to the states. This is because areas of jurisdiction are regarded as exclusive and, therefore, assignment to one level excludes assignment to the other. To complement this panorama the federal government has an ancillary power – not widely exercised but still there – that provides a further tool for the federal judiciary to favour federal over state jurisdiction.

THE ADEQUACY AND THE FUTURE OF THE DISTRIBUTION OF POWERS

Use of the Constitution's amending process to add new powers to the federal government was the main trend during the twentieth century. With the move towards pluralities of political parties rather than majorities, the amending process has been made more difficult and it has become harder for the federal government to reform the Constitution (and, therefore, the distribution of powers) at will. Consequently, the problem for Mexico is what to do about a highly centralized system that has proven to be inefficient and that even the federal government does not want because it adds to the number of policies for which it must be accountable. The issue has been under consideration by the Senate and the House for some time now, but there has been no final resolution.

The ideal solution would be to transfer some of the federal powers to the states. Many of these powers, however, cannot be taken from federal hands easily because, even though they might refer primarily to a state responsibility, they require some element of federal intervention. Furthermore, in some cases states are reluctant to receive additional powers because they do not consider themselves to be capable of performing them. An example of this is the episode of education reform (described above). Another choice would be to follow the dual system set down in the Canadian Constitution.

A broad agenda of reform proposals is now before Congress, with the following options: (1) keeping the federal powers more or less as they are today, without eliminating important functions; (2) striking from the Constitution the ancillary power established in Article 73, Section xxx, in order to avoid future interpretations in favour of the federal government; (3) listing the main state powers so that further federal encroachment is prevented; (4) allowing for delegation of powers from the federal to the state level, as occurs in the German federation, so that, on a case by case basis, many of the subjects now under federal jurisdiction may be shared with the states; and (5) spelling out the concurrent powers, shared constitutionally by both the federal and state governments. The solution probably lies somewhere within these five paths or in a combination thereof.

Since the presidency of Ernesto Zedillo (1 December 1994 – 30 November 2000) a "new federalism," American style, has inspired many programs of federal devolution to the states, beginning with reform on education. After Vicente Fox took office, the Mazatlan Declaration was signed in 2001 and the formation of the National Conference of Governors has put pressure on the federal government to undertake a major devolution of federal powers to the states, beginning with fiscal devolution. Despite this pressure and the agreement of the majority of political parties to embark upon this "reverse" federalism, no other actions have as yet taken place. Many bills have been introduced in Congress by representatives of all parties, and they are waiting to be approved. Nevertheless, there is an evident trend favouring a deliberate process of decentralization occurring throughout the country.

Mexico has yet to achieve a regional counterbalance to federal powers, despite the fact that roughly half of the states are governed by opposition parties. This situation is explained by the internal divisions within the three predominant parties, the lack of leadership from the incumbent president with regard to the party that supported him in the 2000 election, as well as the lack of leadership on the part of various governors. Above all, the legacy of the 300 constitutional amendments that strengthened the presidency during the more than eighty years when the Partido Revolucionario Institucional was in power made that office the most powerful in the country.

The development of the presidential system is the driving force behind all the changes that have pervaded the amending process of the Mexican Constitution not only with regard to the distribution of powers but also with regard to the separation of powers. Before 2000, centralization was an expression of the powers exercised by the president through the Partido Revolucionario Institucional. Now that Mexico has a truly pluralistic government, there are proposals for a new constitution that would eliminate the presidentially oriented provisions that have plagued Mexican constitutional reforms for more than eighty years.

Finally, to take another very recent development, the North American Free Trade Agreement (NAFTA) dispute resolution panels and the procedures of international committees have produced some changes in statutory rules but not in the constitutional distribution of powers. Academics take a negative view of the panel system within NAFTA, which they see as becoming an alternate means for adjudicating issues outside the national courts and applying different rules.[22] This has been true in labour cases, where the hierarchy of international treaties, signed between Mexico and the International Labour Organization, has changed the interpretation of the Mexican Supreme Court with respect to the supremacy clause and the role of domestic law and state courts (as discussed above). Thus, it would appear that, in the near future, common law concepts could influence some aspects of the Mexican legal system, just as happened in reverse with the influence of the European Union upon Britain. Some standing requirements within the environmental commissions of NAFTA have already been accepted by Mexico, altering the civil procedure rules that govern the national law.

NOTES

1 Some historical figures on Mexico's demographic growth are:

Year	Significance of the year	Population
1917	Current Constitution promulgated	14,630,000
2000	Last census	100,349,800
2005	Projected	106,719,000

2 The distribution of population within each of the thirty-one states and the federal district is located at the following Web site: <http://www.e-mexico.gob.mx/wb2/eMex/eMex_INEGI_Estadisticas_sociodemograficas> (accessed 20 February 2004).

3 This is the language spoken by the ancient Aztecs and is now the most widely spoken Aboriginal language. According to the Statistical Bureau of Mexico, almost 1,197,328 people speak Nahuatl, 713,520 speak Mayan, and 380,690 speak Zapotec. See Jorge de Buen on the Web site mentioned in note 2 (look under the descriptor "población hablante de lengua indígena. Diversidad lingüística y monolinguismo").

4 A complete analysis of the languages spoken in Mexico is found on the Web site mentioned in note 2.

5 This category may be equivalent to the Métis in Canada.

6 The GDP is 1.3 percent for the year 2003.

7 This article reads as follows: "Each state retains its sovereignty, freedom, and independence, and every power, jurisdiction, and right, which is not by this Confederation *expressly delegated* to the United States, in Congress assembled" (emphasis added).

8 Albert P. Blaustein, "The U.S. Constitution: America's Most Important Export," <www.usinfo.state.gov/journals/itdhn0304/ijde/ijde0304.htm> (accessed 19 July 2004).

9 *McCulloch v. Maryland* 17 U.S. 316 (1819).

10 See U.S. Supreme Court judgment in *Texas v. White* 74 U.S. 700, 1869.

11 *Reference Re Secession of Quebec* (1998) 161 D.L.R. (4th) 385.

12 Unless otherwise indicated, all articles cited refer to the 1917 Constitution, as amended.

13 <Bloomberg.com>, "Mexico Jobless Rate Has Biggest Rise in Almost a Decade (Update 2)." According to this source, at the end of 2003 the unemployment rate in Mexico was 2.96 percent (accessed 8 July 2004).

14 Suprema Corte de Justicia de la Nación, "Tratado internacionales: Se ubican jerárquicamente por encima de las leyes federales y en un segundo plano respecto de la Constitución Federal," (Tesis LXXVII/99) *Semanario Judicial de la Federación y su Gaceta*, 9a. época (November 1999), p. 46.

15 *U.S. v. Curtiss-Wright Export Corp. et al.* 299 U.S. 304, 1936

16 The Spanish version of the sentence just mentioned reads as follows in the Constitution: "Artículo 72, inciso f): En la interpretación, reforma o derogación de las leyes o decretos, se observarán los mismos trámites establecidos para su formación." This disposition goes back to the 1812 Cádiz Constitution.

17 Since its creation the writ of amparo has encompassed different procedures: habeas corpus as well as judicial review of laws and constitutional control measures combined in one action of law. Habeas corpus is mostly referred to as "indirect amparo." It is filed before a district court and is intended to protect the "individual guarantees" (human rights) established in the Constitution. The purpose of "direct amparo" is to review the final decisions of state courts, based on Articles 14 and 16 of the Constitution, which establish the due process of law, and it is filed before the circuit courts of the federal judiciary.

18 As mentioned, in that amendment nineteen states voted in favor, eight voted against, and four abstained.

19 This article enlists the exclusive powers of the federal Senate. Under Section 5 of the Constitution, the Senate may declare a provisional governor as appointed once the legitimate authorities of any state are absent or become illegitimate.

20 The name "Mexico" is given to three entities: the country as a whole, the capital city, and a state. In the past, Mexico City was the capital of the province as well as the entire country, but in 1824 the Constitution created a federal district separate from the province or state.

21 In 2001 the total amount of grants-in-aid to the states, taken from the federal budget, shows the degree of dependence: $158,756,733, 267 (equivalent to US$16 billion). From this, the State of Mexico ($2 billion), Mexico City ($1.08 billion), and Veracruz ($1 billion) received the lion's share. INDETEC, "Diagnostico sobre el sistema hacendario Mexicano" (unpublished document, 2003).

22 In August 2000 the British Columbia Supreme Court ruled in the case of *Metalclad Co. v. Mexico* under the Chapter 11 dispute resolution procedure of NAFTA, by which Mexico was ordered to pay damages for the expropriation of an American investor, making the interpretation of "regulatory expropriation" applicable, despite the fact that there is no such practice in Mexican law.

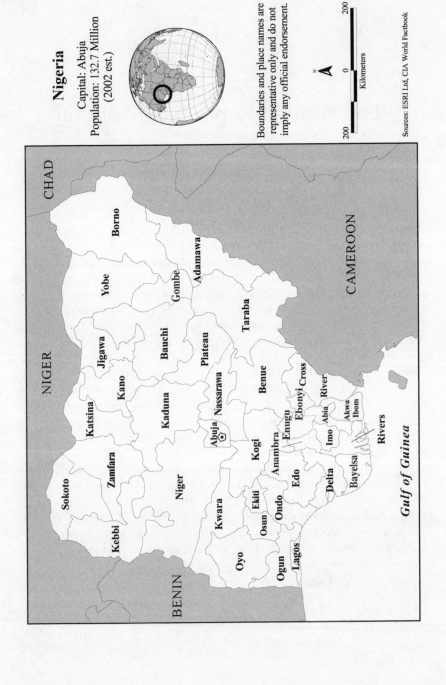

Nigeria

Capital: Abuja
Population: 132.7 Million
(2002 est.)

Boundaries and place names are
representative only and do not
imply any official endorsement.

N

200   0   200

Kilometers

Sources: ESRI Ltd, CIA World Factbook

CHAD

NIGER

BENIN

CAMEROON

Borno

Yobe

Gombe

Adamawa

Jigawa

Bauchi

Taraba

Katsina

Kano

Plateau

Kaduna

Nassarawa

Benue

Sokoto

Zamfara

Abuja

Kogi

Enugu

Ebonyi Cross

River

Kebbi

Niger

Kwara

Ekiti

Ondo

Edo

Anambra

Imo Abia

Akwa
Ibom

Oyo

Osun

Delta

Bayelsa

Rivers

Ogun

Lagos

Gulf of Guinea

The Federal Republic of Nigeria

J. ISAWA ELAIGWU

Nigeria became independent of British colonial rule on 1 October 1960. Except for a brief period (May-September, 1966) it has practised one form or another of federalism, even under military rule. The geographic and demographic size of the country and its communal heterogeneity and complexity have made federal compromise both attractive and a political imperative for Nigeria. Even within the context of authoritarian military rule, with its hierarchical structure, a decentralized administration based on relatively autonomous subnational states and local governments has operated.

Successive military regimes amended the Constitution to suit their modes of governance and often referred to themselves as "the Federal Military Government." When an attempt to establish a unitary government was made in 1966, it led to violent reaction. The fact that Nigerians have been so concerned about their form of government – unitary, federal, or confederal – raises a number of questions. What has been the nature of the actual distribution of power and responsibilities among the component units of the federation? What has been the logic for this distribution? How has it evolved over time? How has it been managed? And have there been any gaps between constitutional provisions for the distribution of powers and responsibilities and the operation of the federation? What does the future hold in terms of how these powers and responsibilities are shared among component governments? Are these powers adequate for each government?

In this chapter, I suggest that:

1 the federal constitution in Nigeria is a product of its sociopolitical history;
2 the constitutional distribution of powers is a reflection of Nigeria's experiences;

3 the logic of the constitutional distribution of powers and responsibilities is essentially to build a strong federation, which does not suffocate component units, while being able to keep the complex nation together;

4 the evolution of the constitutional distribution of powers and responsibilities indicates strong centripetal (if not unitarist) traits since Nigeria's experiences of civil war;

5 the maintenance and management of the distribution of powers and responsibilities have been problematic, often demonstrating gaps between constitutional provisions and constitutional practice; and

6 the future distribution of powers and responsibilities among the component units of the federation is likely to tilt in favour of subnational units (in response to their demands for a greater devolution of powers) without necessarily making the federal government weak.

THE FEDERAL CONSTITUTION IN HISTORICAL-CULTURAL CONTEXT

Nigeria is a multi-ethnic and multicultural society. It is composed of nationalities, subnationalities, and various conglomerations of people with differing population size and potentials, with particular cultural identities, social structures, traditions, values, hopes, and aspirations. Indeed, it is the pluralistic nature of Nigerian society, among other factors, that necessitated the country's original formal adoption of federalism within the colonial framework. Nigeria has a total area of 932,768 square kilometres, of which 910,768 is landmass and 13,000 is water. With a population of about 130 million people, as well as a population growth rate of 2.6 percent, Nigeria is one of the largest nation-states and the oldest surviving federation in Africa.

The people of Nigeria have well over 300 identifiable ethnic groups and over 400 lingo-cultural groups. This has made the country one of the world's most ethnically diverse societies. There are three large ethnolinguistic groups – the Hausa in the north, the Yoruba in the west, and the Igbo in the east. Consequently, the major languages of the Nigerian people are Hausa, Yoruba, and Ibo. English is used as the official language. The religious landscape of Nigeria is dominated by three major religions: African Traditional Religion (ATR), Christianity, and Islam. ATR is the oldest of all religions in Nigeria and has suffered the greatest impact from external religious onslaughts. Nigeria's GDP per head is US$850, with a real growth rate of 2.7 percent.[1]

The legal system is based on English common law, Islamic Sharia law (in some northern states), and customary law. Section 10 of the 1999 Constitution prohibits federal, state, and local governments from adopting any religion as the official or state religion. The implication is that no religion should be accorded primacy over the others. Section 35 of the same Constitution entitles all Nigerians to "freedom of thought, conscience and freedom of religion, including freedom to change his or her religious belief." Section 10 of the 1999 Constitution has been a subject of controversy. Some Muslims have questioned the secular nature of the Nigerian state by insisting that colonial rule, under the tutelage of both the Church of England and the State of England, created a more Christian than secular Nigerian state. Many of these Muslims feel that they are not being accorded their freedom of religion as enshrined in Section 35 of the 1999 Constitution.

As a compromise solution, the Constitution prohibits any tier of government from adopting an official religion; it also provides that states may elect to use Islamic (Sharia) customary law and courts. The establishment of the state Sharia Court and Sharia Court of Appeal as well as their constitution, practices, and procedure are governed by Sections 240–244 and 260–264 of the 1999 Constitution. In addition, the Constitution provides for Customary Courts and Customary Courts of Appeal in Sections 265–269. Mutual suspicions among religious groups (especially between Christians and Muslims) have on occasion raised the political temperature of the polity.[2]

Nigeria has had a number of constitutions since 1914 – about nine, not all of which were promulgated or implemented. Under colonial rule Nigeria had, in effect, six constitutions: the 1922, 1932, 1946, 1951, and 1954 Constitutions, along with the Independence Constitution of 1960. After independence, Nigerian governments authorized the writing of five constitutions: the 1963, 1979, 1989, and 1995 draft Constitutions, along with the 1999 Constitution of the current Fourth Republic.

Nigeria officially became a federation in 1954, after a series of stages of constitutional engineering, and it remains the oldest surviving federation in Africa. The federation neither emerged through a contract between states nor as a voluntary union of a number of originally independent states; rather, the modern history of Nigeria, as a political state, dates from the middle of the nineteenth century, when parts of what later became known as Nigeria came under the British colonial sphere of influence through charters granted to British companies and the eventual completion of the British conquest in 1903.

Initially, there were three separate territories that were treated as separate entities: the Lagos colony, the Oil Rivers Protectorate (from 1893 known as the Niger Coast Protectorate), and the Royal Nigeria Protectorate. In 1900 Britain revoked the company charters so that it could administer each of these territories more directly. The territories then became known as the Lagos Protectorate, the Protectorate of Southern Nigeria, and the Protectorate of Northern Nigeria. These territories were brought under unified administrative control with the amalgamation of the Colony of Lagos Protectorate and the Protectorate of Southern Nigeria in 1906, and then with the amalgamation of the Protectorates of Northern and Southern Nigeria with the Colony of Lagos in 1914 to form the Protectorate of Nigeria, with its capital in Lagos. With this development, Nigeria's identity took its final geographic form.[4]

The British Colonial authority did nothing further to integrate these territories until 1946, when it promulgated the Richards Constitution (named after the British governor who proposed it). The dissatisfaction of Nigerian nationalists with the unitary nature of this Constitution and with the level of Nigerian participation led to a number of constitutional reforms. The MacPherson Constitution, 1951 (after another British governor), created a quasi-federal Nigeria, and this was followed by the Lyttleton Constitution, 1954 (after the then British secretary of state for the colonies), which confirmed the Nigerian colonial state as a federation. The constitutional reforms that led to Nigeria's independence in 1960 saw further federalization. As the prospects for independence approached, Nigerian politicians mobilized for competitive politics largely on ethnic and geo-ethnic lines. Mutual fears and suspicions of domination among these different ethnic and geo-ethnic groups generated intense pressures on the colonial administration for a more federal Nigeria. This was a factor in the nature of the distribution of powers and responsibilities in the 1960 and 1963 Constitutions.

After the Nigerian Civil War in 1970–72, Nigerians reacted negatively to the earlier dualistic federalism of the 1960s and its weak federal government, which they felt had encouraged secessionist bids from subnational groups. As one of Nigeria's former military heads of state put it: "Under the old Constitution, the regions were so large and powerful as to consider themselves self-sufficient and almost entirely independent. The Federal Government which ought to give lead to the whole country was relegated to the background."[5]

Thus, under the inspiration of successive military governments, the objective of subsequent Nigerian constitutions has been to strengthen the central government. As a matter of fact, a number of factors led to the centralization of political power under military rule, making it easy for subsequent constitutions to be designed in favour of the central government. These factors include: (1) the nature of military legislation, which made it easier to issue decrees taking over the functions of the subnational units; (2) the civil war, which gave emergency powers to the federal government to take over the functions of the subnational units – powers that were not reversed after the war; (3) the creation of more subnational states (now thirty-six), which weakened the resource base of the states; (4) the increase in petro-naira,[6] especially through profit taxes that accrued to the central government; and (5) globalization, which has resulted in the strengthening of centralization, at least in the Nigerian case.

Given this background, it is easy to understand why the ostensibly civilian Constitution of 1979 tilted in favour of the federal government in its distribution of powers and responsibilities. The 1979 Constitution drew its inspiration from the previous military regimes, which umpired the transition to democratic rule. The military authorities had set up a constitution drafting committee consisting of forty-nine "wisemen," whose draft was debated and subsequently ratified with amendments by a 230–member constituent assembly. In the process, the outgoing military regime considered certain sections to be in the interest of the nation and entrenched them. As an illustration, the Land Use Decree – vesting ownership of land in government on behalf of the people – was entrenched in the Constitution in spite of opposition to it.[7] Similarly, the National Youth Service Corps[8] was also entrenched in the Constitution, again in "the national interest," as perceived by the military regime.

In 1987 the next military government, that of General Ibrahim Babangida, set up a constitution review committee to review the 1979 Constitution. A constituent assembly was then inaugurated to debate the draft. General Babangida identified seven areas not open to debate in the Constituent Assembly (CA). These included: (1) federalism as a form of government; (2) the injunction against the adoption of a state religion; (3) the creation of states and the alteration of boundaries of state and local governments; (4) presidentialism, respect, and observance of fundamental human rights; (5) a two-party-system; (6) the continuance of "the ban or disqualification placed on certain persons from participation in politics", and (7) belief in basic freedoms, including freedom of the press. The CA was precluded from deliberating on these issues, with regard to which the military regime felt that Nigeria had already arrived at a consensus. In his address to the CA, General Babangida stated categorically that "we need a strong federal government, we also need development-oriented state and local governments."[9] The resulting 1989 Constitution was modelled on the 1979 Constitution but with some amendments, and it remained in operation at local and state levels from 1992 to 1993.

The 1995 Draft Constitution, although the result of a national constitutional conference, was inspired by the military regime of General Sani Abacha. This draft constitution, unlike those of 1979 and 1989, tried to revisit the issue of the distribution of powers and responsibilities within the federation. It revised the legislative list and clearly established a state legislative list under which agriculture and education (which used to be in the concurrent list) were included. This draft was never promulgated into law, however, because General Abacha's death marked the end of his transition program.

His successor, General Abdulsalami Abubakar, set up the twenty-five-member Constitution Debate Collating Committee in November 1998 to review the 1979 and other constitutions and to come up with a new draft constitution. Without adequate consultations, the 1979 Constitution was "renovated" and dusted off to create the 1999 Constitution; however, elected officials and Nigerians did not see this document until after the elections, during the hand-over process. The Constitution of 1999 was promulgated on 29 May 1999. Many Nigerians believe that this Constitution suffers a crisis of ownership because, when it was created, there was not even a pretence of general public participation. It is this Constitution that I use as the basis of my discussion.

DISTRIBUTION OF POWERS AND RESPONSIBILITIES

Nigeria has a three-tier federal structure consisting of the federal, state, and local governments. Each level of government has constitutionally guaranteed autonomy in the area in which it operates. Local government is a guaranteed third-tier of government, even though the 1999 Constitution, Section 7(1) provides that state governments shall "ensure their existence under a law which provides for the establishment, structure, composition, finance and functions of such councils."

The legislative lists in the Constitution provide for the distribution of powers: the exclusive legislative list is assigned to the federal government; the concurrent legislative list is assigned to both federal and state governments and defines areas in which both can legislate; and the residual legislative list is assigned to the states. The exclusive legislative list has sixty-eight items, while the concurrent legislative list has twelve.

The exclusive legislative list includes: accounts of the government of the federation; arms, ammunition, and explosives; aviation (including airports); awards of honours and decoration; bankruptcy and insolvency; banks, banking, bills of exchange, and promissory notes; borrowing money inside and outside Nigeria for the purposes of the federation or any state; census; citizenship, naturalization, and aliens; commercial and industrial monopolies; construction and maintenance of federal trunk roads; control of capital issues; copyrights; creation of states; currency, coinage, and legal tender; customs and excise duties; defence; diplomatic, consular, and trade representation; drugs and poisons; election to offices of president and vice-president, governor, or deputy governor; evidence; exchange control; export duties; external affairs; extradition; immigration and emigration; implementation of treaties; insurance; incorporation, regulation, and winding up of corporate bodies other than those established by a law enacted by the state Houses of Assembly; labour; maritime shipping and navigation; meteorology; military (army, navy, and air force); mines and minerals; national parks;

nuclear energy; passports and visas; patents; trade marks, trade, or business names; pensions and gratuities payable out of the public funds of the federation; police and other government security services established by law; posts, telegraphs and telephones; powers of the federal National Assembly and the privileges and immunities of its members; prisons; public debts; public holidays; public service of the federation; quarantine; railways; regulation of political parties; service and execution in civil and criminal processes, judgments, decrees, and other decisions of any court of law inside or outside Nigeria, except for laws made by the states; stamp duties; taxation of incomes; profits and capital gains, as provided by the Constitution; trade and commerce; traffic on federal trunk roads; water from sources declared by the National Assembly to affect more than one state; weights and measures; wireless, broadcasting, and television other than those owned by states; any matter with respect to which the National Assembly has power to make laws under this Constitution; and any "matter incidental or supplementary to any matter mentioned elsewhere in this list."[10]

The concurrent legislative list includes: allocation of revenue; antiquities and monuments; archives; collection of taxes; electoral law; electric power; exhibition of cinematography films; industrial, commercial, or agricultural development; scientific and technological research; statistics; trigonometrical, cadastral, and topographical surveys; universities; technological and postprimary education. Section 4(5) of the Constitution provides that, "if any law enacted by the House of Assembly of a State is inconsistent with law validly made by the National Assembly, the law made by the National Assembly shall prevail, and that other law shall to the extent of inconsistency be void."

Unlike the 1995 Draft Constitution, which specified a state legislative list, the 1999 Constitution has no such list. However, all matters not identified in the exclusive federal, concurrent, and the local government lists come under the jurisdiction of the states. These residual powers are in fact extensive. They include, among others, health services, rural development, and social welfare. Nevertheless, states complain that the federal government has too much power and that the legislative lists should be revised in their favour. I return to this issue below.

The functions of the Local Government Councils are also clearly stated in the Fourth Schedule. These include: (1) participation in the economic development of the state (such as Section 1[a-k]); establishment and maintenance of cemeteries, burial grounds, and homes for the destitute and infirm; licensing of bicycles, trucks, and others; establishment, maintenance, and regulation of slaughterhouses, market, motor parks, and so on; construction and maintenance of roads, streets, drains, parks, and gardens; provision of public conveniences, sewage, and refuse disposal; registration of all births, deaths, marriages, and so on; (2) provision and maintenance of primary, adult, and vocational education; (3) development of agriculture, other than exploitation of minerals; (4) provision and maintenance of health services; and (5) any other functions conferred on the councils by the state House of Assembly.

The fiscal and monetary powers of each tier of government have also been delineated, especially by Decree No. 21, 1998, which has since become the Act of the National Assembly. The federal government's tax powers include: a profit tax on petroleum and personal income tax (with respect to members of the Armed Forces of Nigeria and the Nigerian Police Force as well as residents of Federal Capital Territory [FCT] Abuja, staff of the Ministry of Foreign Affairs, and non-resident individuals); import and export duties; a company income tax; a withholding tax on companies, residents of FCT Abuja, and non-resident individuals; a value-added tax (VAT) shared with other tiers of government; an education tax; a capital gains tax on Abuja residents, corporate bodies, and non-resident individuals; and stamp duties on "bodies corporate" and residents of Abuja.

State taxing powers cover personal income taxes (pay-as-you-earn or direct taxation or assessment); withholding tax (individuals only); capital gains tax (individuals only); stamp duties as instruments executed by individuals; entertainment tax (pools, betting, and lotteries as well as gaming and casino taxes); property tax, market taxes, and levies (where state finances are involved), along with naming of street registration fees at state capitals.

The Constitution expects local government councils to generate their revenues, in part, from: entertainment tax, motor park duties, property tax, trading and marketing licences; radio and television licences and rates; shop and kiosk rates as well as tenement rates; on-and-off liquor licences; slaughter slab fees; marriage, birth, and death registration fees; cattle tax payable by cattle owners only; signboard and advertisement permit fees; and customary burial ground permit fees.

In Section 162(1) the Constitution provides that all revenues of the federation shall go into the Federation Account (FA), except for salaries of the personnel of the Armed Forces of the Federation, the Nigeria Police Force, the staff of the Ministry of Foreign Affairs, and the FCT Abuja. Section 162(2) provides that the Revenue Mobilization, Allocation and Fiscal Commission (RMAFC) shall present a revenue formula to the president to be placed before the National Assembly for the purposes of distributing the resources in the FA. The distribution is both vertical (in terms of federal-state-local) and horizontal (in terms of allocation among the states). Account is to be taken of the revenue-sharing principles of "population, equality of states, internal revenue generation, land mass, [and] terrain as well as population density." The Constitution also provides that this formula should allow for 13 percent of the FA to be paid to the state that is home to the natural resources in question.

The revenue formula inherited by the civilian administration in May 1999 for sharing the FA vertically among tiers of government breaks down as follows: federal government 48.5 percent, states 24 percent, local governments 20 percent, and special funds 7.5 percent. When the Supreme Court declared the 7.5 percent special funds illegal, however, President O. Obasanjo signed a presidential order in May 2002 adding this fund to the federal government's allocation, thus bringing the federal government's share of the FA to 56 percent. State and local governments rejected the amendments contained in the presidential order. This led to another presidential order in July 2002, stipulating a new revenue formula: federal government 54.68 percent, states 24.72 percent, and local governments 20.60 percent.[11]

In 2003 the RMAFC presented a fourth proposed revenue formula to President Obasanjo, which he placed before the National Assembly as a revenue bill. The formula recommended by the RMAFC was: federal government 46.63 percent, state government 33 percent, and local governments 20.37 precent.[12] When it was clear to President Obasanjo that the wave of opinion in the assembly was in favour of downsizing the federal government's share of the FA, he cleverly withdrew the bill on the pretext that there was more than one version of the bill before the National Assembly. The National Assembly denied the allegation, but the president withdrew the bill, only to ask the RMAFC to consider increasing the federal government's share of the FA. Apart from the lingering controversies over the share of revenue accruing to the FA, the state and local governments also disputed the maintenance of the State Joint Local Government Account (SJLA). The local governments, and later the RMAFC, accused the state governments of misinterpreting and misusing the constitutional powers given to them in Section 162(5–8) of the 1999 Constitution, which provides for the redistribution of funds to the local government councils in each state. The state governments were alleged to have been illegally deducting funds meant for the local governments.[13] This has been a crucial area of conflict at the lower level of intergovernmental relations.

An interesting aspect of Nigerian federation is its approach to the management of the economy. In the first and second republics the civilian leaders believed in development planning as a technique of managing economic development. The government of the late prime minister, Sir Abubakar Tafawa Balewa, introduced the First Development Plan, 1962–68. General Yakubu Gowon introduced the Second Development Plan, 1970–75. The Third Development Plan, 1975–80, was initiated by Gowon but streamlined and executed by General Murtala/Obasanjo's government. Alhaji Shehu Shagari introduced the Fourth Development Plan, 1980–85. Since then, succeeding military regimes have abandoned development planning and have opted for three-year rolling plans. Even under the Obasanjo civilian government (i.e., since 1999), development planning has not been used as a technique of managing economic growth.

Similarly, the 1999 Constitution provides that borrowing of "moneys within or outside Nigeria for the purpose of the federation or any part" (Second Schedule, Part 1, Item 7) is an exclusive matter of the federal government. This means that states must get the approval of the federal government in order to borrow money to execute their programs, whether from within Nigeria or from external sources. This issue has become contentious given the mounting internal and external debt profiles of states and local governments. Recall that all revenues in the federation first go into the FA, from where they are shared. The president felt that many state and local governments were heavily in debt as a result of internal and external loans. He then proceeded to deduct these debts at source, thus leaving some states and local governments with zero statutory allocation from the FA. A Supreme Court judgment declared this illegal: thus the controversy over debts and debt-servicing continues. The RMAFC has suggested that, for the next twenty years, no tier of government should borrow money; but this call is unlikely to be heeded.[14]

In the Nigerian federation each tier of government has its own executive branch (including its own bureaucracy), legislature, and judiciary. Each level operates relatively autonomously. However, years of military rule, with its hierarchical character, seem to have robbed the current federation of its pyramidal structure.[15] The federal government carries out functions that many Nigerians do not consider to belong to it. Some Nigerians have argued that the excessive centralization of political and financial powers under military regimes has encouraged the federal government to take adventurous excursions into areas such as rural development (e.g., bore holes) and culture.

While operators of the Nigerian federation have described it as "cooperative federalism" (and it does demonstrate such traits), it is politically and financially dominated by the federal government. Under the distribution of powers in the 1999 Constitution Nigeria is a centralized federation with strong unitary elements. Currently, there are complaints about the overcentralization of power in the federal government (the product of long periods of military rule). This school of thought has argued that, if Nigeria wants to practise "true federalism," then it should go back to its 1963 Constitution. Yet there are centrists who continue to support a very strong federal government in order to counter Nigeria's history of political instability and civil war.[16]

There are areas of overlapping responsibility, such as education (primary and secondary school levels), housing, agriculture, and water, which many observers and practitioners of federalism believe should be transferred to the residual state jurisdiction. Their argument is one of subsidiarity: that state governments, being closer to the people, could handle these matters more appropriately, effectively, and sensitively than could the central government.[17] A persistent area of controversy is the Nigeria Police Force. While Governor Tinubu of Lagos has argued for a state police force, Governor Dariye of Plateau State cannot imagine spending his meagre resources on maintaining a large force. Important as state police forces are to the autonomy of the subnational states and to the dynamics of Nigeria's federation, the leaders at the state level are split over this matter. Given Nigeria's history, it is not clear that the current constitutional review exercise will result in the establishment of state police forces.

Similarly, there is a general outcry from subnational units over the current revenue allocation formula. State governors have lobbied the RMAFC and members of the National Assembly to increase the states' share of the FA to 40 percent. However, there is a general view among Nigerians that there is a high level of complacency among the three tiers of government over revenue generation. By 1999 statutory allocation from the FA accounted for 46 to 95 percent of the annual budget of states. Only the states of Lagos and Kano generated up to 40 percent of annual budget revenues from internal sources. The situation has gotten worse, even though a few states are making some positive efforts to generate funds from internal sources. This is because each government is heavily dependent on the statutory allocation from the FA, which is predominantly petroleum-based. Furthermore, many Nigerians are unhappy about the pattern of imprudent expenditure at all levels of government.

Also relevant is the gap between constitutional provisions and the operation of the federation. An illustration of this is the election to local government councils, which was due to be held in December 2002. No elections were held until the expiry of the term of these councils in May 2003, partly because state governors and the ruling political parties did not want new elections at this level. As an interim measure, and contrary to the constitutional provisions, state governors and the president met and decided on interim local government administrations under caretaker committees. This action was taken in spite of the advice of the federal attorney-general regarding the unconstitutionality of such an action. Shortly afterwards, the president announced a panel to review the local government system, yet another action regarded by many legal experts as unconstitutional. Since there was a need to review governance in the three tiers of government, many observers and practitioners felt that the matter should have been handed over to the National Assembly's Constitution Review Committee.

Eventually, elections to local government councils were held in April 2004, dogged by complaints of electoral malpractice. Unfortunately, the absence of elected local government councils gave some state governors the opportunity to appoint their political minions in a caretaker capacity. More disturbing still are the allegations that many state governors have diverted statutory FA allocations from local government councils to state coffers. This has hindered the level of development at the local, or grassroots, level, where most Nigerians live.

THE LOGIC OF THE CONSTITUTIONAL DISTRIBUTION OF POWERS AND RESPONSIBILITIES

It may be argued that there are three distinguishable periods in Nigeria's history with regard to the distribution of powers and responsibilities among the various tiers of government. The first period is 1960–65; the second is 1966–93; and the third is 1994–2004.

While the federal system in Nigeria was introduced in 1954, the country did not become independent until 1960. The period between 1960 and 1965 can be described as a time when Nigeria operated a "dualistic" federation. The impact of mutual suspicions and fears among ethnic and geo-ethnic groups in the terminal colonial period affected the distribution of powers among the three tiers of government. The regions were more autonomous than they were at the terminal colonial period; that is to say, the autonomy of the regions increased after independence. Agriculture and education (except postsecondary) were on the residual list. Local governments (or "native authorities" in the North) had their own police forces, except for the Eastern Region, which maintained the services of the Nigeria Police. On the concurrent jurisdiction list was the maintenance of law and order. The 1960 and 1963 Constitutions had regional constitutions appended to them.

In the operation of the federation, the regions often displayed their autonomy in various ways. Each region had a deputy high commissioner or regional agent in London who operated as though he represented a different country. In addition, the regions often interfered in areas that were the specific preserve of the federal government (such as foreign affairs). In 1963, for example, Israel gave scholarships to some Nigerian students to study in Israel. While the Eastern and Western Regions accepted these scholarships, the Northern Region rejected them because it did not recognize the State of Israel.[18] This was in spite of the Constitution, which did not provide for recognition of foreign countries by regional governments on the grounds that foreign affairs was an exclusively federal matter.

Interregional squabbles over the revenue allocation formula, and the allocation and location of industries such as the iron and steel complex under the National Economic Council, were reflections of the intensely centrifugal nature of the Nigerian federation. In fact, on a number of occasions in Nigeria's history, certain regions had threatened secession. The North had threatened to secede from the federation in 1950 if it did not receive 50 percent of the membership of the Legislative Council in Lagos.[19] In 1953 the Western Region threatened to secede if the colony of Lagos were not merged with it.[20] In 1964 the Eastern Region threatened to secede from the federation over that year's federal elections.[21]

After 1965 such movements became even more serious. In 1966 Adaka Boro, Nothinghan Dick, and Owonaro declared a Delta Peoples Republic, which the army had to put down.[22] In 1966 the North threatened to secede from Nigeria after General Ironsi declared the country a unitary state.[23] These centrifugal forces climaxed in the secession of the Eastern Region – as Biafra – in 1967. This was followed by two and a half years of civil war, which cost Nigeria an estimated one million lives.

After the civil war, General Gowon and his military government embarked on an aggressive centralization of power in order to enable the federal government to keep the country together and to give Nigeria a sense of direction. Thus from 1970 through to 1993 the emphasis of successive leaders was on how to strengthen the central government in order to avoid the aggressive centrifugal tendencies of the federation under the First Republic. By 1999 the central government had become so strong under military rule that emerging politicians began to complain of federal suffocation of the states.

This centralization became more manifest in 1994 when General Sani Abacha, following the incarceration of Chief M.K.O. Abiola, the alleged winner of the June 1993 presidential election (which was annulled). Opposition groups (especially Yorubas) began to push for a sovereign national conference to discuss the future of the Nigerian federation. They opted for a loose federation, like the one that had existed under the 1960 and 1963 Constitutions. In fact, Chief Anthony Enahoro, Nigeria's minister of information during the civil war, advocated the merging of existing states within a new federation. Similarly, Chief Alex Ekwueme, Nigeria's vice-president under the Second Republic, advocated eight new regions.

It was in this context that General Abacha convened a national constitutional conference in 1994–95. The result of this conference was a two-volume publication: the first volume contained a draft constitution, while the second volume set out the logic for the distribution of powers. The 1995 draft Constitution, which was never promulgated, revised the legislative lists, giving states functions that they had not had in the 1979 and 1989 Constitutions. The logic for this was provided by the report that came out of the Conference, which recommended in favour of "true federalism" and "the equitable distribution of political and economic powers between the federal government and the component units."[24]

When General Abdulsalami succeeded General Abacha, he realized that the centrifugal forces in the federation had again become very strong. The 1999 Constitution was promulgated on 29 May 1999, the day the military handed over power to the new civilian rulers. As noted above, even the new rulers had not been able to read in advance the Constitution they were expected to operate and defend. Nor had Nigerians.

In sum, the logic of the distribution of powers and responsibilities in the Nigerian federation has involved the desire to strengthen the federal government sufficiently to provide an overarching umbrella under which all groups can be accommodated. Like all federations, Nigeria has had to make adjustments. Often the federal pendulum has tended to alternate between two extremes, depending on whether the pressure was coming from centrifugal or centripetal forces.

The greatest inspiration for a centripetal federal constitution has been the military, which is always a major contestant in the Nigerian power equation. Successive military leaders have clearly pointed out that, if Nigeria is not to experience a repetition of its fratricidal war of the late 1960s, then it must have a strong federal government – strong enough to be interventionist and to keep the country together. This was partly why General Gowon[25] opted for a federation with a strong federal government, and why General Murtala Mohammed and his team preferred a presidential rather than a parliamentary system of government. They wanted to avoid a politically split executive (which they felt was a danger in a parliamentary system), and they believed that a presidential system would be more likely to provide effective leadership.

Since the civil war the objective in the distribution of powers has been to strengthen the federal government politically and economically in order to enable it to intervene in essential policy areas and to keep the country together. Again, the inspiration for this has been the military and its leaders, who, in spite of centrifugal forces in the polity, have had a centrist perception of Nigerian federation because, for them, survival/security is the first law of the state. At the same time, behind the distribution of powers and responsibilities lies the principle that each tier of government has political, social, and economic obligations. While the federal government has the cardinal responsibility for the security of the state and of lives and property, each tier of government has social welfare and developmental functions. Revenue allocation is a concurrent matter shared by both federal and state governments. Unfortunately, in many essential areas, there have, in practice, been few intergovernmental relations over the past four years. It should be noted that Nigeria operates as a symmetrical federation. Thus, even with regard to the sharing of FA resources among the states, the federal equality of states has been a cardinal principle.

EVOLUTION OF THE CONSTITUTIONAL DISTRIBUTION
OF POWERS AND RESPONSIBILITIES

Evolutionary Process

The evolution of the constitutional distribution of powers in Nigeria has
occurred neither through constitutional amendments nor through collective action by the states. All the major changes in the distribution of powers
and responsibilities in Nigeria have been through "megaconstitutional"
changes. Since colonial times all changes in the legislative lists have occurred as the result of a new constitution or traumatic changes (such as
military coups). These have usually had an adverse impact on the polity.

However, Section 9(2) of the 1999 Constitution does provide avenues
for altering or amending the Constitution. Except for the creation of additional states provided for in Section 8, the National Assembly may alter the
provisions of the Constitution if an amendment is "passed in either House
of the National Assembly" by not less than a two-thirds majority and is approved by a resolution of the Houses of Assembly consisting of not less
than two-thirds of all the states. In order to amend the provisions governing the mode of altering the Constitution, an act of the National Assembly
may be passed by either House and must be "approved by the votes not less
than four-fifths majority of all the members of each House, and also approved by resolution of the Houses of Assembly of not less than two-thirds
of all the States" (Section 9[3]).

So far, 1999 Constitution has not been amended, even though there
have been loud demands for its review and the National Assembly has
struck a committee for this purpose.

While the Supreme Court has interpreted constitutional provisions and,
in some cases, has given landmark judgments, the major changes to the
distribution of constitutional responsibilities have occurred after a military
coup, at which point a new constitution is usually written or the old one
amended. This always constitutes an attempt to bring the Constitution in
line with a military mode of governance.

Thus, the 1963 Constitution was amended only after the January 1966
military coup. The Federal Military Government (FMG) issued Decree
No. 1, 1966, giving it the "powers to make laws for the peace, order and
good government of Nigeria or any part thereof, with respect to any matter whatsoever."[26] The powers of the military governor of a region were
declared to be to make "laws for the peace, order and good government"
of that region. The governor could "not make laws with respect to any
federal matter included in the Executive Legislative List," nor could he
"make laws in matters included in the Concurrent Legislative List,"

except "with prior consent of the Federal Military Government."[27] These provisions were retained by successive military regimes.

The 1963 Constitution was replaced by the 1979 Constitution, which made drastic changes to the distribution of powers and responsibilities among tiers of government. The 1979 Constitution was replaced by the 1989 Constitution in 1992, but it was only operational at local and state levels during the military government's transition program. The 1989 Constitution was replaced by the current Constitution on 29 May 1999. Currently, the National Assembly has a constitutional review committee mandated to review the 1999 Constitution. Given that the political process is regularly punctuated by military coups, a legislative culture of making non-military amendments to the Constitution is yet to be adequately established. The political strains and stresses of "megaconstitutional" changes on the polity can be readily imagined. Indeed, while the National Assembly Constitution Review Committee is currently working on possible amendments to the 1999 Constitution, there have been demands from some sectors of the society for a national conference leading to a new constitution – one that would be owned by the people.

Specific Constitutional Changes: An Overview

The year 1954 marked the definitive federalization of Nigeria. In that year the Nigerian Marketing Board was regionalized and regional executives and legislatures began to operate. The 1954 Constitution was different from the 1951 Constitution, especially as it provided for a federal arrangement with two legislative lists: one that was exclusively federal and one that allowed for concurrent jurisdiction. All subject areas not covered by the two lists were residual and were reserved for the regions. In the event that federal law conflicted with regional laws, the former was to take precedence. The Constitution presented sweeping concessions to regionalism. It provided for a weak federal government as it reserved for the regions an extensive range of matters not included in the exclusive federal and concurrent lists. Regions became semi-independent entities, each with an independent judiciary, a civil service, and other organs of government.

As mentioned above, the Independence Constitution of 1960 gave the federal government exclusive legislative powers over forty-four items, including defence, external affairs, aviation, currency, Lagos affairs, customs, mines, external borrowing, and shipping. Twenty-eight items were placed on the concurrent list, and these included the judiciary, police, health, the civil service, and higher education. However, the regions were granted a large measure of autonomy in all matters outside the exclusive and concurrent lists, and were empowered to maintain good government and law and order.

The Republican Constitution of 1963 did not really make changes regarding distribution of powers between the federal government and the regions. As in 1954, Section 64(4) stipulated that, when a regional law conflicted with a federal law, it was the federal law that was to take precedence. But there were other provisions relating to emergency powers and the creation of states. Under Section 65 of the 1963 Constitution, the federal legislature had the power, at any time, to make laws for Nigeria or any part of it on all matter whatsoever for the purpose of maintaining or securing peace, order, and good government during any period of emergency. This meant that, in spite of the constitutional distribution of powers, the federal government could usurp the powers of the regions in order to make laws during emergencies. In 1962 the federal government declared a state of emergency in the Western Region and appointed an administrator for that region.[28] Similarly, the federal government was also empowered to legislate on residual subjects with the consent of the regional governor.[29] On balance, what existed between 1960 and 1966 is described by scholars and practitioners as a weak federal government – one in which the "regional tails" were "wagging" the federal dog.[30]

There was a gradual transition from the model of coordinate authority within the federation to an inclusive authority, or a model of collusion, especially from 1966 on as, under military rule, when the central government began to gradually usurp the powers of the regions. This process actually started in 1963 with the fragmentation of the regions from three into four. This was augmented from 4 into 12 in 1967, from 12 into 19 in 1976, from 19 into 21 in 1987, from 21 into 30 in 1991, and from 30 into 36 in 1996.

As noted, since 1966 all the military regimes in Nigeria have pursued the idea of a federation with a strong central government organized hierarchically to coincide with the command structure of the military. The military took a number of actions that led to the centralization of political authority in the Nigerian federation.[31] The nature of military legislation contributed to the increase of the federal government's authority at the expense of the states. In particular, with the military's overthrow of constitutional democracy, new states were created simply by decree. Decree No. 14, 1967, which created states, provided that these should inherit the powers of the former regions. Subsequently, however, Decree No. 27, 1967, announced that the "legislative and executive powers of the twelve newly created states in Nigeria are limited for the time being to residual matters."[32] With regard to the exercise of matters in the concurrent legislative list, "specific consent of the Federal Military government is required," whereas this used to be the prerogative of both regional and federal governments. The above decree, no doubt, placed limitations on the powers of the new states.

The 1979 Constitution simply consolidated this process of centralization. The powers of the federal government were extended to matters that had previously been exclusive to the regional governments. Let me provide an illustration. In the exclusive legislative list the 1979 Constitution listed sixteen items that had been within the concurrent competences of both federal and regional governments under the 1960 and 1963 Constitutions. These items included arms, ammunitions, and explosives; prisons; bankruptcy and insolvency; commercial and industrial monopolies; combines and trusts; registration of business names; registration of tourist industry; labour as well as professional occupations; regulation of political parties; census; and public holidays. The 1979 Constitution nevertheless recognized the autonomy of states. Still, the federal government was allowed to take over the executive functions of the state during emergencies, while the procedure for declaring a state of emergency made for minimal interference.

The 1999 Constitution, a document designed under the tutelage of the military, also enabled the pursuit of a centralist agenda through distributing powers in a way that reinforced the centrist tendencies of the 1979 Constitution. As mentioned earlier, the exclusive legislative list not only gives the central government exclusive legislative powers (Second Schedule, Part 1) over sixty-eight items, but it also provides it with concurrent powers over the remaining twelve items. And, as noted above, federal law is constitutionally paramount to state law (by virtue of Section 4[5]).

Also as noted above, the revenue allocation formula is skewed in favour of the federal government (the continued constitutional hegemony of the federal government has made it impossible to reduce the disproportionate amount of the FA currently retained by it). The police force is centrally controlled as it is exclusive to the federal government. The judiciary and its funding are now to be centrally controlled through the National Judicial Council. All high court judges in the states are paid by the federation, while such lower courts as the Customary Courts, the Magistrate Courts, and the Sharia Courts are paid for by the states. The federal government also continues to enjoy wide powers to legislate on matters incidental or supplementary to the exclusive legislative list and to establish and regulate authorities to promote the very comprehensive list of "Fundamental Objectives and Directive Principles of States Policy" enumerated in Chapter 2 of the 1999 Constitution.

In contradiction to the centripetal trend in the federal-state distribution of powers, the 1999 Constitution, like the 1979 and 1989 Constitutions, defined local government in Nigeria as a third tier of government. Section 7(1) of the 1999 Constitution specifies that "the system of local government councils is under this constitution guaranteed." It further states "the Government of every State shall ensure their existence under a Law which provides for the establishment, structure, composition, finance and functions of such councils." The Constitution provides that local governments will participate in the economic planning and development of their local

government area. Local government councils are expected to play important roles in the election of governors, in the creation of states, and in
boundary adjustments between states.

The Constitution now promotes a partnership model that involves the
devolution of substantial functions and powers to local governments, together with the financial resources to exercise these powers. The overall
aim is to institutionalize a culture of participatory democracy, cooperative federalism, and development in Nigeria through local governments,
which constitute the level of government nearest to the people and,
therefore, a level that may serve as a catalyst to development. The federal
government's blueprint for reform, contained in the Guidelines for Local Government Reform, involves: (1) making appropriate services and
development activities responsive to local initiatives by developing or delegating them to local representative bodies; (2) facilitating the exercise
of democratic self-government close to the local levels of society and en-
couraging initiative and leadership potentials; (3) mobilizing human and
material resources through the involvement of members of the public in
their local development; and (4) providing a two-way channel of communication between local communities and government.[33] Ironically, it took
a military regime, that of General Obasanjo, to bring in these 1976 reforms and thus make local government councils a guaranteed third-tier
of government. Local governments were no longer, as they were in 1966,
mere administrative units or agents to which powers could be granted
and withdrawn at the whim of the state government.

On balance, since the Nigerian civil war, the evolution of the distribution
of powers and responsibilities indicates a strong adjustment in favour of
centripetal forces. The greatest inspiration for the unitarist tendencies in
Nigeria's distribution of powers and responsibilities has come from military regimes. This has been so in spite of the loud, and at times rowdy, centrifugal forces in the federation.

MAINTENANCE AND MANAGEMENT
OF THE DISTRIBUTION OF POWERS
AND RESPONSIBILITIES

With regard to the maintenance and management of the distribution of powers and responsibilities, it is important to note that the current Constitution
only came into effect on 29 May 1999. Given the military rule that has peri-
odically punctuated democratic governance in Nigeria, there has been no
chance to establish a culture of constitutionalism that would, in turn, enable
an appropriate current evaluation of the gaps between the Constitution as
written and the Constitution as applied. The period since 1999 simply does
not provide us with enough time to adequately assess the situation.

However, we may identify a few issues that point towards the likely direction of future development. Designed as a cooperative federation, there has, in practice, been a cooperative–competitive relationship among tiers of government. Moreover, the residual militarism in the actions of the federal government tends to generate conflicts rather than to dampen them.

Overall Structure of Intergovernmental Relations

Unlike Germany, with its Basic Law, Nigeria has no provision enabling states to carry out federal laws. It is therefore necessary for the federal government to consult other tiers of government and to establish a framework for cordial intergovernmental relations. Unfortunately, President Obasanjo, as a former military head of state, lacks the skills necessary for consultation and compromise. At times he mistakes the pyramidal structure of the federation for the military command structure to which he is more accustomed. Consequently, intergovernmental relations in Nigeria have been characterized by reluctant cooperation and competition among the levels and arms of government. Areas that have generated intense competition between the federal and state governments are revenue allocation and the allocation of jurisdictional powers between federal and state governments (notably in the areas of primary education, agriculture and housing, control of local governments, inter- and intrastate boundary disputes, and the siting and execution of federal projects).

There are constitutional provisions in the third schedule (Part 1) of the 1999 Constitution that establish some institutions for dealing with intergovernmental relations. These include the Code of Conduct Bureau, the Council of States, the Federal Character Commission, the Federal Civil Service Commission, the National Judicial Council, the Federal Judicial Commission, the Independent National Electoral Commission, the National Defence Council, the National Economic Council, the National Population Commission, the National Security Council, the Nigeria Police Council, the Police Service Commission, the Revenue Mobilization Allocation and Fiscal Commission, the Independent Corrupt Practices and Related Offences Commission, the Economic and Financial Crimes Commission, and the Niger Delta Development Commission. Attempts have been made over the years to build national unity by ensuring that no unit within the federation feels that it can go it alone.[34]

Most of the Constitution's provisions promote the formation of national political parties and inculcation of a federal character into political (and other) appointments to the public service of the federal, state, and local governments. In fact, the Federal Character Commission is expected to monitor the implementation of the Federal Character Clause in Section 14(3) of the 1999 Constitution. The Federal Character Clause,[35] which first appeared in the 1979 Constitution, was designed to promote national unity and loyalty by ensuring various ethnic and sectional groups were adequately represented in both public service and government agencies at all three levels of government. This was expected to reduce the fear of domination by one group or section. The 1995 draft adopted a zoning system for the federation (North-Central, North-East, North-West, South-East, South-South, and South-West)[36] to aid in this endeavour. While this system remains non-constitutional and informal, political actors have been sensitive to it. However, the performance of the Federal Character Commission, especially at the federal level, has come under criticism from some sections of the Nigerian public.[37]

The 1999 Constitution also provides for exceptional or emergency situations that allow the federal government to intervene in the governance of states. Section 305 provides that the president can declare a state of emergency only when (1) "the federation is at war," (2) "the federation is in imminent danger of invasion or war," or (3) "there is actual breakdown of law and order and safety in the federation or any part thereof." Section 305(3–6) provides an elaborate process pertaining to the declaration of emergency.

Given the intensity of communal violence in four local government areas in Plateau State, on 18 May 2004 the President Obasanjo declared a state of emergency throughout the entire state and suspended the elected governor, Chief Joshua Dariye, and the State House of Assembly. He then appointed a state administrator. Since then there have been controversies over the presidential powers of emergency. Many legal luminaries in Nigeria, including Chief Rotimi Williams and Professor Nwabueze, expressed the opinion that the president had exceeded his powers and that his action was "a contradiction of all known principles of federalism."[38] The National Assembly has, however, passed resolutions supporting Obasanjo's actions.

General Federal-State Relations

The relations between the federal and state governments have run hot and cold. The state governors complain about Obasanjo using the Constitution as though he were a military president. They accuse the federal government of taking actions in flagrant disregard of the constitutionally guaranteed autonomy of state governments. A few illustrations give us an insight into the gap between constitutional provisions and their practice. On 1 May 2000 President Obasanjo announced a federal minimum wage of 7,500 naira (or US$56.8) per month and a minimum wage for state government as 5,500 naira (or US$41.7) per month.[39] State governors were furious. While minimum wage falls under the exclusive federal list, it was not an executive matter. The National Assembly was not even involved in the process, nor had it received any bill from the president. Obasanjo had not consulted state governments, which were already having problems paying the monthly wages of their staff. This led to crises all over the country, until the Nigerian Labour Congress finally engaged each state government in wage negotiations.

Similarly, primary education is a residual matter. However, President Obasanjo introduced the Universal Basic Education program in 2000. Again, state governments protested. After all, they were expected to implement this program, yet they had not been consulted. Nor was there a bill before the National Assembly. The federal government had the same sort of problems getting the cooperation of state governments with regard to the implementation of the Poverty Alleviation Program, now replaced by the National Poverty Eradication Program. State governments had to remind the federal government that they had their own poverty alleviation programs. They pointed out that, as state governments, they were not agents of the federal government. Where areas of mutual interests were involved they wanted, at the very least, to be consulted.

In the same vein, there were problems in federal–state relations with regard to the Nigeria Police Force and the maintenance of law and order. Given the ineptitude and inefficiency of the Nigeria Police Force, governors of states with large cities and high rates of crime found themselves unable to deal with crime. Policing is a federal matter, even though the governor of each state holds the title of chief security officer. State governors complained that state commissioners of police ignored their orders but took those from the inspector-general of police. In frustration, some governors demanded a constitutional amendment that would enable the states to establish their own police force. However, some governors were opposed to establishing state police forces because of the cost involved. These governors opted for decentralizing the Nigeria Police Force to enable it to respond more effectively and promptly to problems on the ground. In some states, governments officially resorted to using vigilante groups to maintain law and order.[40]

Revenue Sharing Issues

Distribution of resources is another major area of conflict between the states and the federation. While the 1999 Constitution provides for 13 percent of the FA to be paid to the states from which natural resources are exploited, the Niger-Delta States (Rivers, Delta, Akwa-Ibom, and Bayelsa) – that is, the states adjacent to offshore petroleum areas – are very dissatisfied. They are angry with the federal government for going to the Supreme Court to get a judgment distinguishing between onshore oil (13 percent of which was to go to the states in the form of mineral rents and royalties) and offshore oil (which was to go to the federation as a whole). The Supreme Court had judged in favour of the distinction, which meant that the littoral states (such as Akwa-Ibom) lost quite a substantial amount of funds from the FA.

Governor D. Alameseigha of Bayelsa State captured the feelings of many states:

for Nigeria to survive, the federal government should give up some of its powers to the federating units. At the moment, the federal government represents injustice to millions of minorities in Nigeria especially the Niger-Delta ... a federal government that does not produce but consumes is an unsustainable federal government and such federal government can only protect its unfair privileges through the force of arms.[41]

A new law listing the distinction between onshore and offshore oil has now come into operation, and this is a big relief for some littoral states. Many Nigerians feel that the federal government has so many resources at its disposal that this encourages its forays into areas in which it has no business, such as primary education. The calls for a review of constitutional legislative powers and the tax powers of each tier of government have, therefore, not abated.

Federal-State-Local Issues

The relations between the national and state assemblies have not been smooth. In view of the confusion over the actual tenure of chairs of local governments, state Houses of Assembly made laws limiting the term of office of these chairs to two years in some states and three years in others. In an attempt to sort out the problem, the (federal) Senate set up a committee to make recommendations to the National Assembly. The state Houses of Assembly decided that this was a usurpation of the powers given to them under Section 7 of the Constitution, which states that the "Government of every state shall ... ensure their existence under a Law which provides for the establishment, structure, composition, finance and functions of such [local] councils." They went to the Supreme Court,[42] which ruled in their favour.

Some state governments created, or tried to create, additional local governments. Bayelsa State, for example, created new local government councils and transferred the chairs of the old local governments to new local governments. The Senate of the Federal Republic declared this action to be null because it violated Section 8(3) of the Constitution, which provided elaborate processes for the creation of new local governments (including a referendum). In addition, the Senate argued that, unless the list of local governments as contained in the First Schedule, Section 3, Part 1, was duly amended, no new local government was legal. In May 2004 President Obasanjo withheld statutory allocations to local governments in the States of Niger, Nassarawa, Ebonyi, Lagos, and Katsina, which had created new local governments and conducted elections. At the Supreme Court

level, the affected states challenged the authority of the president to with-
hold statutory allocations. They argued that they were not asking for statutory allocations to the new local governments but, rather, to the old ones,
until such time as the National Assembly could make amendments to Section 8(3) of the Constitution.

In state-local government relations there have been what amount to cold
wars. Local governments complain about undue interference from state
governments. For example, the Sokoto State government was taken to
court by fifteen local government councils, and the court prohibited it
from deducting 3 percent of its statutory allocation to fund the Sokoto
Emirate Council, as passed by the State House of Assembly.[43]

In addition, local government chairs have argued that state governors
(especially where the chair comes from a party different from the governor's) plot to remove them by using the audit powers of the state. State
governors have also been accused of plotting with the state Houses of Assembly to shorten the tenure of three years of elected local government officials in order to put their supporters in office. In some states there have
been protests by elected local government officials against attempts by
state Houses of Assembly to reduce their term to two years. Thus, in Imo
State, the police arrested eleven local government councillors along with
300 others who had gone to the state House of Assembly to protest the reduction of their tenure from three to two years.[44] In the case of Bayelsa
State, where new local governments were created, some councillors have
taken the governor and chairs of the local government councils to court
because they believe that it is illegal to share FA funds with new and illegal
local governments. These chairs also went to court to protest that their deployment to new local governments is illegal and, in fact, a way for state
governments to disenfranchise the people.[45]

However, many governors claim that a majority of chairs and councillors
of local governments only sit down to share money drawn from the FA and
rarely embark on development projects. President Obasanjo has publicly
chided the chairs over this issue. The governors have been at pains to point
out that the chairs of local governments do not have the powers they had
under the 1989 Constitution and that they should be more enlightened on
this matter. In addition, the governors are angry that the federal government deals directly with local government councils. They argue that the
1999 Constitution, Section 162(6), provides for a state joint local government account into which the statutory allocation from the federal and state
governments accruing to the local governments should be deposited.

The states are therefore opposed to what they perceive as attempts by
the federal government to relate directly to local governments. They cite,
as evidence of federal interference in their area, the fact that, without their
knowledge and involvement, the federal government gave money to local

government chairs to buy security vehicles and gadgets for the maintenance of law and order at the local level. The state governors are the chief
security officers of the state and should, they argue, be involved in this
kind of arrangement.

ADEQUACY AND FUTURE OF THE DISTRIBUTION
OF POWERS AND RESPONSIBILITIES

Perhaps it is too early to assess the adequacy of powers and responsibilities with regard to the component units of the Nigerian federation. However, when one considers how the 1999 Constitution was promulgated
and the reactions to it since May 1999, it may be argued that there is a
need to revisit the legislative lists pertaining to the distribution of powers
and responsibilities.

The 1995 Draft Constitution was the result of a national constitutional
conference. If that conference captured the mood of Nigerian political
elites at all, it was to point out that the federation was too centralized. The
result was the transfer of functions such as agriculture, education, and
housing from the concurrent legislative list to the residual legislative list.

Yet in 1999 the document presented as the Constitution did not reflect
some of the conclusions of the 1994–95 constitutional conference. Why
was this so? The military rulers were wary of the centrifugal forces in the
polity, which gave the impression that the politicians had taken civil war for
granted or had forgotten the bloodbath of the late 1960s. Quite a number
of the young politicians on the scene had either been children or young
adults at that time. For the military rulers, what Nigeria needed was still a
strong and interventionist central government to keep the country together and to provide leadership in development.

The operation of the Constitution so far indicates widespread dissatisfaction with the distribution of powers and responsibilities among the three
tiers of government. There are also loud complaints about the inadequacy
of the tax powers allocated to the states and local governments in relation
to their functions. There are widespread pressures for a constitutional review or a national conference that would deal with the apparently preda-
tory and overwhelming federal government. That a former military ruler is
the president does not help matters. Obasanjo's style of governance is certainly not sensitive to the delicate compromises required in a federal polity.
The result is that a reaction against the president's style tends to get identified as a reaction against the federal government.

With regard to the adequacy of fiscal or tax powers, it is clear that all tiers
of government have been complacent about generating needed revenues.
The overdependence on the FA is not conducive to the fiscal autonomy and
accountability of the component governments of the Nigerian federation.

One may wonder if revising the tax powers would make any difference if the appropriate authorities do not collect these taxes. Internally generated revenue and accountability is an essential part of federal autonomy.

The future of the distribution of powers and responsibilities among the three tiers of government in Nigeria seems to indicate a coming period of exciting debate. As the Constitution review exercise continues, the pressures for a review of the legislative lists that would find in favour of states and local governments may be expected to increase. Centripetal forces do justify the need for a very strong federal government; however, it does seem as though a tilt in favour of states and local governments with regard to both the distribution of powers and responsibilities and taxation will not seriously weaken that government. In their relations with state governments, it does seem that local government councils will continue to have problems protecting their autonomy from the manipulation of state governments. The current trend of state interference in local government matters may not change significantly in the near future.

CONCLUSION

In this chapter I argue that Nigeria's federal Constitution of 1999 is a product of its sociopolitical and cultural history. Thus, the constitutional distribution of powers and responsibilities is a reflection of Nigeria's experience over time.

I also point out that the inspiration for a strong federal government in Nigeria has been dominantly derived from a long period of military rule (almost thirty out of Nigeria's forty-four years since Independence). The logic behind the constitutional distribution of powers and responsibilities is to build a federation with a strong federal government – one that is able to keep the country together. This is clearly evident in the evolution of the constitutional distribution of powers, which indicates strong centripetal (if not unitarist) traits since Nigeria's civil war (between 1967 and 1970). However, the maintenance and management of the distribution of powers and responsibilities have been problematic, often demonstrating gaps between constitutional provisions and constitutional practice. Ironically, while the 1999 Constitution opts for a strong federal government, in practice centrifugal forces have been pressing for greater powers and responsibilities for state and local governments.

As Nigeria revisits its Constitution, it seem as though, in response to popular demands, the distribution of powers and responsibilities among component governments of the federation may tilt in favour of subnational units without necessarily creating a weak central government. After all, given Nigeria's past, many Nigerians still believe that there is a need for a reasonably strong federal government.

NOTES

1 United Nations Development Programme, *Human Development Report 2003*
   (New York: Oxford University Press, 2003); and *The Economist, Pocket World in
   Figures* (London: Profile Books Limited, 2003), pp. 176–177.

2 Jonah I. Elaigwu, *The Shadow of Religion in Nigerian Federalism: 1960–1993*,
   (Abuja: National Council on Intergovernmental Relations, 1993). See also C.S.
   Momoh, C.O. Onikepe, and V. Chukwulozie, eds. *Religion and Nation-Building*
   (Lagos: CBAAC/NARETO, 1988).

3 See Sam E. Oyovbaire, *Federalism in Nigeria* (Hong Kong: Macmillan Press,
   1985); Wale Ademoyega, *The Federation of Nigeria* (London: Harvap, 1962);
   Uma Eleazu, *Federalism and Nation-Building: The Nigerian Experiences, 1954–1964*
   (Iltracorde: Arthur Stockwell, 1977); Kalu Ezra, *Constitutional Development in
   Nigeria* (London: Cambridge University Press, 1964).

4 James Coleman, *Nigeria: A Background to Nationalism*, (Berkeley: University of
   California Press, 1958) p. 30; J.P. Mackintosh, *Nigerian Government and Politics*
   (London: Allen and Unwin, 1966).

5 General Yakubu Gowon's Broadcast on 26 May 1968; see Federal Republic
   of Nigeria, *Faith in Unity* (Lagos: Federal Ministry of Information, 1970),
   p. 108.

6 "Petro-naira" refers to the revenue accruing from the sales of petroleum in
   Naira, Nigeria's currency.

7 Federal Republic of Nigeria, *Constitution of the Federal Republic of Nigeria, 1979*,
   Section 274 (5d).

8 The National Youth Service Corps was designed by the Gowon regime in 1973
   to promote national unity by deploying young graduates of higher educational
   institutions to states other than their own for one year of national service.

9 Federal Republic of Nigeria, *Portrait of a New Nigeria: Selected Speeches of IBB*
   (n.p.: Precision Press, c. 1987), pp. 48–49.

10 Federal Republic of Nigeria, *The Constitution of the Federal Republic of Nigeria,
    1999*, Exclusive Legislative List, Second Schedule, Part 1, Item 68 (1999 Consti-
    tution).

11 See the table below for a summary of revenue-sharing formula (vertical)* since
    1981

Formula		Revenue	Allocation	(%)
(proposed and operational)	Federal government	State government	Local government	Special gunds#
1981	55	30.5	10	4.5
1989	55	32.5	10	2.5
1990	50	30	15	5

January 1992	50	25	20	5
June 1992–April 2002	48.50	24.00	20.00	7.50
May 2002 (Executive Order)	56.00	24.00	20.00	–
July 2002 (Executive Order)	54.68	24.72	20.60	–
RMAFC proposal (December 2002)	46.63	33.00	20.37	–

* On the horizontal plane RMAFC recommended (in December 2002) the following sharing formula: equality, 45.23 percent; population, 25.60 percent; population density, 1.45 percent; internal revenue generation efforts, 8.31 percent; landmass, 5.35 percent; rural roads/internal waterways, 1.21 percent; potable water, 1.50%; education, 3.00 percent; and Health, 3.00 percent.

\# The Supreme Court ruling in April 2002 nullified the allocation for special funds, which the federal government had previously monopolized.

See Theopilus Y. Danjuma, "Revenue Sharing and the Political Economy of Nigerian," J. Isawa Elaigwu, Paul C. Logams and Habu S. Galadima, eds., *Federalism and Nation Building in Nigeria: The Challenges of The 21st Century*, (Abuja: NCIR, 1994); *Vanguard* (Lagos), 22 February 2004, pp. 12–15; *Daily Trust* (Abuja), 9 January 2004, p. 2.

12 *Vanguard* (Lagos), 18 December 2003, pp. 1–2; *Daily Trust* (Abuja), 9 January 2004, p. 2.

13 *Daily Trust* (Abuja), 18 December 2003, pp. 1–2.

14 *This Day* (Lagos), 5 July 2004, p. 1.

15 The federal pyramid has the federal government at the apex and widens at the middle and lower levels as state and local governments act out their autonomy in governance. A hierarchical structure, as exists in unitary governments, would not provide for the autonomy of the various component units of the state.

16 This feeling came across strongly at the Global Dialogue on Federalism Roundtable on "Distribution of Powers and Responsibilities" held in Jos, Nigeria, on 15 September 2003.

17 Feeling captured from the roundtable, Jos, 15 September 2003.

18 See C.C. Phillips, *The Development of Nigerian Foreign Policy* (Evanston, IN: Northwestern University Press, 1964); Bolaji Akinyemi, *Foreign Policy and Federalism: The Nigerian Experience* (Lagos: Macmillan, 1986); Ibrahim A. Gambari, "Federalism and the Management of External Relations in Nigeria," *Publius: The Journal of Federalism* 2, 4 (December 1994): 113–124.

19 Billy J. Dudley, *Instability and Political Order: Politics and Crisis in Nigeria* (Ibadan: Ibadan University Press, 1973), p. 63. Also, in Nigeria, *Proceedings of General Conference on Review of Constitution* (Lagos: Government Printer, 1958), p. 218; also quoted in Tekana N. Tamuno, "Separatist Agitations in Nigeria," *Journal of Modern African Studies* 8, 4 (September 1970): 568.

20 Kalu Ezera, *Constitutional Developments in Nigeria*, 2nd ed. (Cambridge: Cambridge University Press, 1964), pp. 187–188; and Tekana N. Tamuno, "Separatist Agitations in Nigeria," pp. 560–572.

21 See detailed account in Mackintosh, *Nigerian Government and Politics*, p. 604; *Daily Times* (Lagos), 13 January 1963; *Daily Express*, 22 December 1964; *Daily Express* (Lagos), 30 December 1964.

22 Jonah I. Elaigwu, "Subnational Units and Political Developments in New States: An African Experience" (Ph.D. diss., Stanford University, 1976), p. 82.

23 Jonah I. Elaigwu, *Gowon: The Biography of a Solder-Statesman* (Ibadan: West Publisher Limited, 1985), p. 74.

24 Federal Government of Nigeria, *Report of the Constitutional Conference Containing the Resolutions and Recommendations*, vol. 2 (Abuja: National Assembly Press, 1995), p. 61.

25 Elaigwu, *Gowon*, 154.

26 Federal Government of Nigeria, "Constitution (Suspension and Modification) Decree (1966, No. 1)," in *The Laws of the Federal Republic of Nigeria* (Lagos: Government Printer, 1966), p. A3.

27 Ibid.

28 See Emergency Power Act, 1962.

29 L.O. Aremu, "Intergovernmental Relations in Nigeria: A Legal Overview, *Quarterly Journal of Administration* 14, 2 (1980): 137.

30 J.P. Mackintosh, *Nigerian Government and Politics* (London: Allen and Unwin, 1966); N.U. Akpan, *The Struggle for Secession, 1966–70* (London: Frank Cass, 1972); Abubakar Y. Aliyu, ed., *The Return to Civil Rule* (Zaria: Institute of Public Administration, 1983); Eme O. Awa, *Federal Government in Nigeria: A Study of Development of the Nigerian State* (Berkeley: University of California Press, 1964); Eme Awa, *Issues in Federalism* (Benin City: Ethiope Publishing Corporation, 1976).

31 See Jonah I. Elaigwu, "The Military and State Building: Federal-State Relations in Nigeria's 'Military Federalism,' 1966–1967," *Readings on Nigerian Federalism*, Bolaji Akinyemi, Patrick.D. Cole, and Walter Ofonagoro, eds. (Lagos: Nigeria Institute of International Affairs, 1976), pp. 155–182; Jonah I. Elaigwu, "Military Rule and Federalism in Nigeria," *The Foundations of Nigerian Federalism, 1960–1995*, vol. 3, J. Isawa Elaigwu and Rafiu A. Akinjide, eds. (Jos: Institute of Governance and Social Research, 2001), pp. 166–193.

32 Federal Republic of Nigeria, "Constitution (Miscellaneous Provision) (No. 2) Decree No. 27, 1967," in *The Laws of the Federal Republic of Nigeria*, pp. A133–137.

33 The Federal Republic of Nigeria, *Guidelines for Local Government Report* (Kaduna: Government Printer, 1976), para. 1.

34 For intergovernmental relations in Nigeria, see J. Isawa Elaigwu, "Intergovernmental Relations in Nigeria," *Indian Journal of Federal Studies* 2, 2 (June 2001): 65–78.

35 See Federal Republic of Nigeria, *Constitution of the Federal Republic of Nigeria, 1999*, Third Schedule, Part 1, Item C, Section 8(1b), for the Federal Character Commission's role in the implementation of the Federal Character Clause. For

detailed discussions of federal character, see Alex Gboyega, "Federal Character or the Attempt to Create Representative Bureaucracies in Nigeria," *International Review of Administrative Service* 50 (1984): 17–24; Eghosa E. Osaghae, "The Complexity of Nigeria's Federal Character Principle," *Journal of Ethnic Studies* 16, 3 (Fall 1988): 1–25; Peter Ekeh and Eghosa E. Osaghae, eds., *Federal Character and Federalism in Nigeria* (Ibadan: Heinemann, 1989).

36 The six zones adopted and the states allocated to each are:

North-Central	North-East	North-West	South-East	South-South	South-West
Benue	Adamawa	Jigawa	Abia	Akwa-Ibom	Ekiti
Kogi	Bauchi	Kaduna	Anambra	Bayelsa	Lagos
Kwara	Borno	Kano	Ebonyi	Cross River	Ogun
Nassrawa	Gombe	Katsina	Enugu	Delta	Ondo
Niger	Taraba	Kebbi	Imo	Edo	Osun
Plateau	Yobe	Sokoto		Rivers	Oyo
		Zamfara			

37 From the 2000 manpower statistics of federal ministries and extraministerial departments, 16.5 percent of the total federal workforce were from the North-Central geopolitical zone, 8.6% from the North-East, 9.4 percent from the North-West, 20.7 percent from the South-East, 15.8 percent from the South-South, 28.7 percent from the South-West, and 0.3 percent from the Federal Capital Territory. The North complained against domination of the federal civil service by the South despite its higher population. See Shuaibu Gimi "The Face of Marginalization: Yorubas Consolidate Dominance" in *Weekly Trust*, September 20–26, 2002, pp. 1–3.

38 *This Day,* 21 and 23 May 2004, p. 1; *Vanguard,* 28 May 2004, p. 14.

39 *Vanguard* (Lagos), 4 May 2000, p. 2.

40 Anambra State established a vigilante group, called "Bakassi Boys," to help combat crimes. *This Day,* Lagos, 18 August 2000, p. 13.

41 *Vanguard,* Lagos, 1 January 2004, p. 7.

42 *Punch,* Lagos, 7 July 2001, pp. 1 and 2.

43 *Vanguard,* Lagos, 23 August 1999, pp. 1 and 2.

44 *Vanguard,* Lagos, 9 March 2001, p. 1.

45 *Punch,* Lagos, 7 July 2001, pp. 1 and 2.

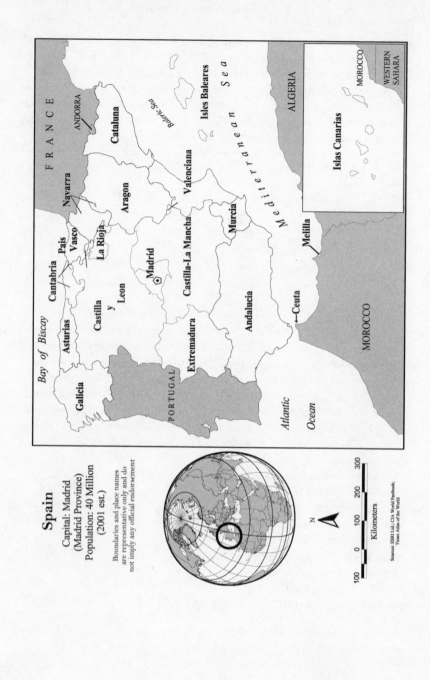

Spain

Capital: Madrid
(Madrid Province)
Population: 40 Million
(2001 est.)

Boundaries and place names
are representative only and do
not imply any official endorsement

N

100   0   100   200   300
Kilometers

Sources: ESRI Ltd.; CIA World Factbook;
Times Atlas of the World

Kingdom of Spain

ENRIC ARGULLOL AND XAVIER BERNADÍ

The Spanish Constitution of 1978 committed Spain to a form of territorial state organization (later referred to as "state of the autonomies") that, despite not having a federal name or nature, has allowed a decentralization of political responsibilities that is far superior to that of some nominally federal countries.[1] This peculiar model of political organization has probably not favoured the development of an authentic federal culture, nor has it sufficiently extended the value of territorial pluralism as a commodity to be protected and promoted. But it has made possible the greatest period in Spain's history, at least with regard to recognition of autonomy and self-government vis-à-vis the different parts of its territory.

The Spanish Constitution is an open text and it allows for quite different interpretations. The adopted interpretations have not favoured the expectations initially held in those territories with a deep desire for self-government (Catalonia, the Basque Country, and, to a lesser degree, Galicia). As a result, the period that began with the promulgation of the Constitution of 1978 can now be assessed as only a relative success. The political autonomy of the nationalities and regions that make up Spain has been recognized, but some of them still have not been harmoniously integrated into the Spanish state. This explains the strong divergences with regard to the desired state model – divergences that move between the defence of the status quo and demands for territorial power that go far beyond what is offered in the current system. Although in both Catalonia and the Basque Country separatist sentiment continues to be in the minority, the political demands of the nationalist forces have undoubtedly become increasingly strident, pointing more and more frequently to models of coexistence based upon the idea of true joint sovereignty or other such confederal models. These models would not seek to improve the present system but, rather, to replace it. Despite the fact that this prospect seems far off, there exists sufficient pressure to raise the possibility of an important reform of the system. This is described below.

THE FEDERAL CONSTITUTION IN ITS HISTORICAL
AND CULTURAL CONTEXT

Basic Social and Economic Features

Currently, Spain has a land area of 505,988 square kilometres and a total population of 43,197,684 inhabitants.[2] The vast majority of the population is indigenous and does not exhibit ethnic or racial differences. Although the Constitution only recognizes the existence of one nation (the Spanish nation, which is referred to as "the common and indivisible homeland of all Spaniards"), what is certain is that it also expresses a desire to protect all of the "peoples" of Spain, who are free to practise their cultures, traditions, languages, and institutions (Preamble). It also recognizes the right to autonomy of the "nationalities" and "regions" that comprise the nation (Article 2).

The clearly predominant, and official, language is Spanish; it co-exists with languages such as Catalan, Euskera, and Galician, which, in some regions, have co-official language status and are spoken by a significant portion of the population. With regard to religion, the strong establishment of Roman Catholicism and the close ties between state and Church have been transformed within a constitutional framework that affirms the non-denominational nature of the state. This allows the co-existence of Roman Catholics – both practising and non-practising (the latter being quite numerous) – with persons professing to have no religion.

The cultural situation in Spain is undergoing significant change as a result of immigration. After the emigration of many Spaniards for political reasons (after the Spanish Civil War in 1939) or for economic reasons (during the 1960s), Spain has become, like many other European countries, the destination of a significant flow of immigrants from Africa, Latin America, Asia, and Eastern Europe. In relative terms, the immigrant population is still not significant (given that it does not yet reach 10 percent of the total population), but its rapid increase in the last few years has had a great political and social impact.

Since the arrival of democracy in 1978, and with Spain's admission into the European Union in 1986, the nation has experienced marked economic development, with an overall rise in the standard of living, although it continues to have a significant unemployment rate (11.3 percent of the working population).[3] In 2002 the GDP rose to US$649,791,500,000, which signifies a gross national income per capita (former GDP per capita) of US$14,430. At present, the life expectancy at birth is seventy-eight years.[4]

Basic Political and Constitutional Features

In the 1970s Spain peacefully moved from a dictatorship to a democracy with a significant level of political consensus. This process, internationally considered to be an exemplary, ended with the approval of the Constitution of 1978. The Constitution was drawn up by a parliamentary commission created by the first democratic Parliament. The commission was made up of seven members representing the main parliamentary groups. Its final text was approved on 31 October 1978 by the House of Deputies and the Senate, ratified by a referendum of the electorate on 6 December, promulgated by the king on 27 December, and officially published on 29 December, at which time it became effective (in accordance with its final provision).

The Constitution attempted to respond to two basic and indivisible social demands: (1) the establishment of the rights and liberties of citizens living within a democratic institutional framework and (2) the recognition of the political autonomy of those territories/communities that were demanding it. The Constitution expressly attributes sovereignty to all Spanish people (Article 1.2) and is founded on the indissoluble unity of the Spanish nation. It also recognizes and guarantees the right to autonomy of the nationalities and regions that comprise the state as well as their solidarity with each other and the state (Article 2). In addition to establishing the foundation for the political decentralization of the state, the Constitution protects territorial pluralism (i.e., the personality and features of the societies established in each of the territories that comprise the state).

The Constitution states that Spanish is the only official language of the state and that all Spaniards must have enough knowledge of it to be able to use it in a social context (Article 3.1). With respect to the other languages (Catalan, Euskera, Galician), the Constitution indicates that they shall also be official in their respective Autonomous Communities (subfederal self-governing territorial units with political power) in accordance with their respective Statutes of Autonomy (regulations similar to those provided in a constitution). The Statutes of Autonomy of six of Spain's seventeen Autonomous Communities declare the official status of a language other than Spanish: this is the case for Catalan (Catalonia, the Valencian Community,[5] and the Balearic Islands), for Euskera (the Basque Country and part of Navarra), and for Galician (Galicia). As a result, a system of co-official languages exists throughout a great portion of Spain. The predominance of Spanish, however, impedes the achievement of perfect bilingualism, even though the autonomous institutions have developed policies for the promotion and standardization of their own co-official languages.

The co-official character of these languages and, therefore, the right of citizens to use them means that public institutions are obliged to serve people in the language of their choice. This also means that all legal and administrative documents have the same value in Catalan, Euskera, and Galician as they do in Spanish and that laws and other regulations shall be published in both Spanish and the co-official language in question.[6] But this system is provided only to those territories that have a system of official linguistic duality: constitutionally, the state is not obliged to publish its laws or to serve its citizens in a language other than Spanish. As a result, documents written in a language other than Spanish must be translated into Spanish whenever they are applied outside the Autonomous Community in which they originated. Despite all these measures, language remains one of the issues that arises frequently in political (although not social) conflicts.

The Constitution guarantees the ideological, religious, and cultural freedom of individuals and communities and affirms that the state shall have no denominational affinities. Historically, religion has divided Spaniards. For this reason the Constitution mandates that public authorities are to take into consideration the religious beliefs of all Spaniards and to maintain cooperative relationships with the Roman Catholic Church and other religious denominations.

The Constitution re-establishes the monarchy in the form of a parliamentary monarch, reserving a symbolic role for the crowned head. It ensures the horizontal division of powers through a parliamentary system of government based on a two-chamber legislative structure (the House of Deputies and the Senate),[7] the political preeminence of the executive, and the recognition of the independence of judicial power. Finally, it establishes a special jurisdiction through the creation of the Constitutional Court, a juridical institution responsible for ensuring the constitutionality of laws, territorial autonomy, the power distribution system, and the protection of the constitutional rights of citizens.

Effectively, the Constitution neither recognizes nor determines the political units that constitute the state: it does not establish a territorial "map" nor does it indicate what responsibilities or powers can be exercised by these units. The Constitution simply recognizes the right of territories to autonomy, assuming these territories function through Statutes of Autonomy, which are drawn up by their political representatives. The same occurs in relation to the number and the type of powers assumed by the new political entities. Thus this issue is reserved to the corresponding Statutes of Autonomy, which operate within the framework and limits imposed by the Constitution. The Constitution does not expressly establish the principle of federal (or institutional) loyalty, although this principle is implicit in the territorial organization of the state, as the Constitutional Court has repeatedly indicated.[8]

Logically, these constitutional design features can be explained through the country's history and in the concrete circumstances that surrounded the constitutional process. In the first place, we must remember that Spain, along with France, is one of the oldest countries of Europe, its origins dating back to the end of the fifteenth century. The state was constructed through the union of kingdoms, or independent Crowns – personal unions that allowed each political entity to maintain its own institutions and its particular form of government. However, tensions between centripetal and centrifugal pressures were resolved militarily in favour of the former, which allowed for the consolidation of the nation-state, unitary and centralized in nature, during the eighteenth century. The Constitution of 1931 rejected this model and recognized the right of the territories to accede to political autonomy; however, only Catalonia was able to exercise this right. The short life of the second Republic (1931–39) ended with a bloody civil war that gave way to forty long years of military dictatorship and totalitarianism. During this period the freedom of individuals and distinct groups was repressed with extreme firmness. That was why the move towards democracy was seen as an opportunity to recognize both types of rights (i.e., individual civil rights and collective territorial rights).

In the second place, we must also consider the importance given to political consensus when the constitutional text was drafted. The purpose of emphasizing consensus was to overcome the many fractures that had deeply divided Spanish society (monarchy-republic, State-Church, the system of territorial organization, and individual and collective rights) and to achieve a text that, without closing the door on various ideological options, would be adopted by all political forces. We must also remember that the Constitution was drawn up within precarious democratic conditions. Those who wrote it were under pressure from forces that had put up with the previous authoritarian regime and, in particular, from the military corps (a small faction of which was responsible for a frustrated coup d'état three years after the promulgation of the 1978 Constitution).

The alteration in the territorial structure of the state, which involved a clash between irreconcilable conceptions of the state, provoked great political controversy. As in the previous democratic period, constituents rejected the adoption of comparative constitutional models, particularly the federal model. Federalism was rejected by both the more centralist political forces, who considered it excessively rash and contrary to the unity of the nation and sovereignty, as well as by the majority of the regional political forces with nationalist leanings, who understood federalism as a process that inexorably leaned towards centralism and progressive political and social uniformity. They regarded federalism as being incapable of responding to the needs of those groups whose strong feelings of territorial identity precluded them from identifying with the nation as a whole. In addition, when the Constitution was written, the different regions demonstrated various levels of desire for self-government: this desire was strong in some and practically non-existent in others. However, in 1977–78 fourteen regions recognized a system of provisional autonomy, and this situation became difficult to reverse.[9]

The concurrence of these factors explains why the framers of the Constitution were not inspired by a general political theory or by a concrete ideological orientation, or, particularly, by one or another federal constitution from elsewhere. They tried to respond to specific problems with particular and pragmatic solutions. In many instances these were based on the democratic Constitution of 1931, and they were adopted by the greatest possible consensus. The end result was a constitutional text that is especially open and flexible, that encompasses many issues that lack definition, and that leaves many matters to future political and legislative decisions. The territorial autonomy issue, which is the most controversial, is also the least precisely defined. Some of the constitutional provisions, in particular those that provide an outline and establish principles, limits, and processes, are essentially transitory. The Spanish model of federalism cannot be explained without taking note of the importance of the Statutes of Autonomy and other regulations that have a quasi-constitutional value. Both types of regulations are approved by the state Parliament.

CONSTITUTIONAL AND STATUTORY DISTRIBUTION OF POWERS

The Role of the Statutes of Autonomy

The situation described above affected the distribution of powers between the state and the Autonomous Communities in a particular way. The constitutional design is neither exact nor complete. The Constitution lists the exclusive powers of the state (Article 149.1) but does not specify the powers of the Autonomous Communities; rather it transfers this determination to the provisions of the many Statutes of Autonomy. These statutes may assume all the powers not expressly attributed to the state by the Constitution, although without pushing certain explicit or implicit limits. As a result, it is not possible to understand Spain's power system, or the level of powers assumed by each entity, without understanding the concurrence of three types of regulations: the Constitution, the Statutes of Autonomy, and certain state laws to which the Constitution refers in order to frame the distribution of powers (e.g., laws pertaining to the "delimitation of powers," which are needed in areas such as public safety, the administration of justice, education, and the mass media).

The statutes and the laws pertaining to delimitation of powers lack constitutional status, but they are a necessary complement to the Constitution. For this reason, they, along with the Constitution, are considered to form part of the so-called "block of constitutionality" – the complex set of regulations that the Constitutional Court must consider in order to determine the validity or invalidity of state and/or Autonomous Community regulations.

The constitutional reliance on the Statutes of Autonomy in order to determine the powers of the Autonomous Communities has two main consequences. On the one hand, it lessens the guarantees and stability of such powers in comparison with state powers (which are directly guaranteed by the Constitution). On the other hand, it introduces the possibility of having a clearly asymmetrical power distribution. The Statutes of Autonomy can assume all the powers not reserved for the state, but they are neither obligated to do so nor must they do so in the same way, and this allows for a range of powers that may differ substantially among the Autonomous Communities.

The distribution system is characterized by its complexity and the originality of many of its options. These features prevent one from including the Spanish model among the usual theoretical articulations of federalism (e.g., dual, cooperative, executive, or competitive). Nonetheless, once one recognizes its peculiar features, the Spanish system of federalism can be defined as an "impure dual system." For, despite basing itself mainly on the idea of exclusivity, or division of powers, there are many areas that require the joint intervention of the state and the institutions of the Autonomous Communities. In a good portion of these areas or subjects, the Spanish system leans towards the German system of administrative federalism (e.g., execution of state legislation by the Autonomous Communities). Unlike in Germany, Austria, and Switzerland, however, in Spain such a solution does not have general application, nor does it, either explicitly or implicitly, constitute a constitutional principle.

In addition, the relationship between both spheres of power has been extended in a progressive way to the vast majority of areas of public intervention. The result has been a dynamic of intergovernmental relations not provided for by the Constitution (e.g., involving mixed agencies, collaboration agreements, joint investments or planning, and other technical features of cooperative federalism). In the end, and in a limited way, some solutions or practices could be considered to be similar to those produced in competitive federal systems. Consequently, the best way to describe the Spanish system is to say that it is based on the specific attribution of powers and responsibilities in each material field or subfield and its respective relationship to the different levels of government.

Retained State (Central Government) Powers

Overall, the distribution of powers reflects the existence of a political system in which centralization continues to predominate over decentralization. Effectively, in addition to the ability to modify the distribution of powers through constitutional reform,[10] the state can count on a collection of very important exclusive powers, both quantitatively and qualitatively (see below). Such powers grant great prominence to state institutions with respect to the regulation, intervention, and control of matters of the greatest political, economic, and/or social interest. Indeed, some constitutional provisions attributing power to the state have demonstrated a considerable capacity for penetrating areas of Autonomous Community jurisdiction.

In exceptional cases, the Constitution allows for the enactment of state laws in order to harmonize laws passed by the Autonomous Communities. It also attributes residual powers to the state, an option exercised in some, but not many, other federations. This can be explained as the process of a state devolving power to new political groups within it and thus achieving a form of decentralization.[11] The allocation of residual powers reveals that the powers of the Autonomous Communities have been devolved, while the powers of the state have not, with all of the consequences that these qualifications carry.

Despite all this, the current interpretation and practical application of the constitutional system entails weak, or low-intensity, autonomy. Yet, the autonomy recognized throughout the regions is not merely administrative but essentially political. The Autonomous Communities represent differentiated political communities, enjoy very strong organizational autonomy, and have democratically elected parliaments that exercise full legislative authority. The executive body is led by a president, who presides over the Autonomous Community and is the regular representative of the state – not in the sense of a prefect in France but, rather, in a symbolic sense (i.e., denoting that the Autonomous Communities are also part of the state).

Autonomous Community Powers

The Autonomous Communities count on numerous and significant powers in areas such as urbanism, local government, public safety, and the environment; they are responsible for the provision of such major public services as education and health; they administer a significant portion of public spending (close to 40 percent of the total) and, overall, have at their disposal a larger number of public workers than does the central government.

The power distribution system allows for decentralization, even carrying it to unexpected extremes, whether through interpretation or through the use of constitutional mechanisms for reassigning powers. Effectively, the open and amorphous nature of constitutional clauses allows for a drastic reduction in the scope of state powers without betraying either the wording or the spirit of the Constitution. In addition, as we shall see below, the constitutional text includes various mechanisms for devolving state powers towards the Autonomous Communities, without establishing precise material or functional limits.

Local Government

Decentralization also reaches the local level. The Constitution expressly indicates that the state must be organized territorially into municipalities, provinces, and Autonomous Communities,[12] and that all of these entities should enjoy autonomy with regard to the administration of their respective interests (Article 137). Logically, the (basically administrative) autonomy of the local entities is of less significance than is that of the Autonomous Communities. Constitutional references to local governments are rare but transcendental. Effectively, the Constitution expressly guarantees the autonomy of the municipalities, entrusting their government to democratically elected representatives of the population. It foresees the existence – necessary or optional – of some local intermediary bodies (i.e., provinces, regions, councils) and stipulates that all local entities should have sufficient financial resources to meet their responsibilities (Articles 140–142).

From these basic profiles, the concrete level of local government autonomy (institutional, organizational, and financial) is derived almost completely from the laws of the state and of the Autonomous Communities. Local bodies must generally rely on their "own" powers (i.e., those that are autonomous), but they can also exercise powers through delegation or by order of the state or the appropriate Autonomous Community. Nonetheless, the local level has rarely involved itself in indirect state or Autonomous Community administration. The overall position of local governments has experienced some important changes since 1978; for example, it now includes direct access to the Constitutional Court and a separate and specific system for large cities. However, the traditional weakness of local governments with regard to power and finances continues to generate a lively debate.

Understanding State versus Autonomous Community Powers

The list of powers exclusive to the state, important for a proper understanding of the Spanish system, does not constitute a good example of technical precision. Basically, it consists of an extensive, generic list of concerns arranged into thirty-two sections. It includes areas of public intervention, large sectors of the legal system, concrete legal institutions, infrastructure, and so on – all in a non-systematic way. Thus, the power of the state is extended to areas such as nationality; migratory movements; international relations; defence; judicial organization; public safety (the creation of autonomous policing bodies notwithstanding); legislation on all civil matters (the civil, regional, or special laws existing in some regions notwithstanding); legislation on labour, mercantile, criminal matters as well as on intellectual and industrial property and pharmaceutical products; foreign trade; international health and large parts of domestic health matters; large infrastructure of an interterritorial nature (highways, railroads, ports, airports, hydroelectrical facilities); shipping and air traffic control; and the basic system for protecting the environment, mines and energy, and mass media.

Other state powers, again due to their generic nature, can affect fields reserved to the Autonomous Communities. Examples of these are the state's power to ensure the equality of citizens in their exercise of their constitutional rights, its economic powers (such as coordinating economic activity and general finance), and its administrative powers.

The fact that the Constitution qualifies central powers as exclusive does not mean that the state enjoys a monopoly over all public functions. Although in certain areas (e.g., defence and immigration) such a monopoly does, in effect, exist, in other areas state power is limited to a legislative function (e.g., labour legislation and intellectual property law) or to determining the principles underpinning certain matters (e.g., the legal system behind public administration and environmental regulation). Therefore, the Spanish system is not based on the concept of exclusivity of powers in a strong, or "Belgian-style," sense; rather, the idea of *exclusive* powers is ambivalent. In some cases it is compatible with the existence of autonomous powers, although it is always limited to the development and/or execution of state legislation (i.e., *shared* powers).

The Statutes of Autonomy divided the powers of the Autonomous Communities into three different lists: (1) exclusive powers (both legislative and administrative), (2) powers limited to the development and execution of basic state legislation, and (3) powers restricted to the mere execution of state legislation. These three lists correspond to the three basic power distribution schemes in the Spanish system. Outside these lists both the Constitution and Statutes of Autonomy establish specific power relationships explainable by the particular nature of the matters affected (such as special complexity, the necessity of joint or concurrent actions, and the desire of Autonomous Communities to intervene in areas theoretically belonging to the state).

Initially, there were two different levels of autonomous powers as some Autonomous Communities were able to assume all the powers not reserved for the state, while others were restricted to limited powers regarding those matters mentioned in Article 148.1. In this way, two different rates of access to autonomy were established, depending upon the different traditions and motivations of each region.

Those Autonomous Communities (Catalonia, the Basque Country, and Galicia) that held an affirmative plebiscite on proposed Statutes of Autonomy were able to accede to the privileged system right away. Also in this was Andalucia, which had acceded to autonomy through a process that required a qualified majority in territorial initiative voting and in the system's final ratification. In different ways Navarra, the Canary Islands, and the Valencian Community achieved powers comparable to those of the first group of Autonomous Communities. However, the great asymmetry of power that separated these seven regions from the ten remaining ones was transitory.

The Constitution itself provided that, after five years, the "slow-route" Autonomous Communities would be able to increase their initial powers, which would be limited only by those reserved exclusively for the state, to reach the same status as that held by the other communities. This occurred after a delay of some years.[13] Once this process was completed, the powers of all the Autonomous Communities were substantially identical, despite the persistence of some differences explainable through reference to several particular causes. The provisions contained in Article 148 of the Constitution remain obsolete, but, according to the Constitutional Court, its list of powers may serve as a canon for interpreting the division of powers between the state and the Autonomous Communities.[14]

Mechanisms for Constitutional Flexibility

The Constitution completes the federal system described above by providing mechanisms that allow flexibility in the distribution of powers both in an ascending sense (i.e., harmonization laws) and in a descending sense (i.e., laws relating to the attribution, transfer, or delegation of state powers) (Article 150).[15] It also contains some closure clauses (e.g., the supremacy clause) relating to the resolution of regulatory conflicts and to the supplementary nature of state law with respect to the Autonomous Communities (Article 149.3).[16]

We would add that, in comparison with other federal systems, the Spanish system has more highly regulated mechanisms allowing for more flexibility with regard to redistribution of powers. In addition, these mechanisms may be utilized for the benefit of all of the Autonomous Communities, for the benefit of a few, or for the benefit of only one – a solution that allows for much power asymmetry.

The clause regarding the supremacy of federal law (paramountcy), which is present in the Constitutions of Australia, Argentina, Germany, Canada, the United States, and Switzerland, is also found in the Spanish Constitution. However, this clause is difficult to interpret since it holds that state laws "shall prevail, in case of conflict, over those of the Self-governing [Autonomous] Communities regarding all matters in which exclusive jurisdiction has not been conferred" upon the latter. The issue then becomes the determination – no less controversial – of what can be understood by the phrase "exclusively attributed to the Autonomous Communities." It is perhaps for this reason that this clause is seldom applied (except in cases where the state passes the normative principles and the Autonomous Communities develop them). The hypothesis that, when facing a conflict of laws, courts other than the Constitutional Court may make use of the supremacy clause has been firmly rejected by the latter, it being the only court statutorily empowered to control the constitutionality of legal provisions.[17]

The constitutional clause relating to the supplementary nature of state law has become problematic. This clause seems to cover the legal voids that existed during the founding period of the autonomous state, when the Autonomous Communities still had not legislated in many of the areas in which they had the power to do so. Nonetheless, since then, and based solely on this supplementary clause, the state has handed down new regulations regarding matters within the powers of the Autonomous Communities. However, the Constitutional Court has closed the door on such practices. It has affirmed that the supplementary clause constitutes a rule concerning the relationship between systems and not a universal rule pertaining to state powers. In other words, it is a rule that facilitates the application of the law but not its creation. Certain important authors have disputed this opinion;[18] we, however, firmly share it.[19]

The limitation of spending power has great importance in the Spanish system, as it does in any federal or compound system of government. In Spain this issue resulted in an important debate and often necessitates the intervention of the Constitutional Court, which recapitulated and consolidated its doctrine in Ruling 13/1992 of 6 February 1992. This ruling makes it clear that the state is not to exercise its spending power outside its area of legislative jurisdiction. Consequently, the state cannot use grants to recover powers at the expense of those of the Autonomous Communities. Nonetheless, reality has not always adapted itself to this constitutional doctrine.[20]

In practice, the doctrine of implied powers has not come into play with regard to resolving problems inherent in the distribution of powers. In theory, if a power is not expressly recognized then it does not exist. The exhaustive nature of the distribution of powers does not demand, nor does it ordinarily admit, the application of such a doctrine. However, the elasticity of specific state powers often allows for what amounts to the same thing. Even when the state does not count on an expressly recognized power, the residual clause can increase its jurisdiction whenever the equality of citizens, territorial solidarity, or the unity of the market may be affected by the exertion of an autonomous power. This may occur, for example, when an Autonomous Community exerts a power with extraterritorial effect. However, on this point the Constitutional Court's doctrine fluctuates between legitimating the state's intervention and upholding the powers of the Autonomous Communities.

LOGIC OF THE CONSTITUTIONAL DISTRIBUTION OF POWERS

The Spanish constitutional system is based on two principles, simultaneously enacted through Article 2 of the Constitution: the unity of the Spanish nation and the autonomy of the nationalities and regions. The distribution of powers must reconcile both principles and ensure their effective enforcement by attaining the equilibrium embodied in the Constitution. This equilibrium is not, however, absolute. In fact, as the Constitutional Court recalls, "it is clear that autonomy refers to a limited power, (that) autonomy is not sovereignty ... and given that each autonomous territorial organization is a part of it all, in no instance may the principle of autonomy be opposed to that of unity, but rather it is precisely within it where a true sense is reached."[21]

In other words, the principle of unity requires that the powers of the state enjoy a certain preeminence, since it is the state that has the primary responsibility of satisfying the general interest, identified in the Spanish case with unitary interests. The idea of the general interest is converted, in this way, into the basic criteria for distributing the powers among the state and the Autonomous Communities: the state must have the powers needed to preserve the unity of the system. However, the general interest criteria do not grant the state the power of disposition over the distribution of powers, nor do they permit an interpretation that allows state institutions to override the powers of the Autonomous Communities whenever they consider it necessary. The concept of general interest was applied at the time of the original distribution of the powers, not at a later stage. In other words, the Constitution has already translated the general interest into the concrete powers of the state; therefore the satisfaction of such interest is to be pursued through – and not despite – the constitutional distribution of powers.

The recognition of autonomy constituted a radical change in Spain. It assumed the substitution of the model of a strongly rooted unitary and centralized state with a model based on territorial pluralism and political decentralization. The magnitude of this change, the inertia of centralism, and the fear of something new explains the average Spaniard's distrust of the emergence of new political entities. It also explains the provision of multiple mechanisms to ensure unity as well as the numerous cautions that surround the exercise of autonomy.

Some of the techniques included within the Constitution are very much akin to federalism, while others are not. Since the Constitution maintains a unity of judicial power and restricts the powers of the Autonomous Communities in the exercise of their legislative and executive functions, the distribution of powers does not encompass all the classic powers of the state. Thus the Autonomous Communities have no independent judicial power.

In addition, the Constitution prohibits formal association among Autonomous Communities, limits the cooperation agreements that may be established among them to those with prior federal authorization, and allows for federal constraint in the event that an Autonomous Community does not meet its constitutional obligations or poses a serious threat to the general interests of Spain.[22] Should the central executive so request, offending laws and autonomous provisions could be brought before the Constitutional Court, which, in turn, could suspend them. This solution is hardly compatible with the political autonomy of the regional units, nor is it typical of relations between federal and state laws in other federations.

The more significant public powers are reserved for the state, whose powers are often clearly expansive in character. The lack of confidence in the Autonomous Communities reached the point at which the state was constitutionally granted the exclusive power to consult the people through referenda. This precaution allows the state to abort the legitimacy of any possible secessionist movement by issuing a call to the polls. Referenda like those that took place in Quebec are not legal in Spain if they do not have the prior authorization of the central institutions. As has been shown above, the regulation of residual and prevailing powers leans in favour of the state.

The Autonomous Communities are not able to participate either in state decision making or in appointing members of essential institutions such as the Constitutional Court or the General Council of Judicial Power.[23] Given that the Senate does not function as a real house of territorial representation, the communities cannot participate through this route either.

Within this framework, the defence of the interests of the Autonomous Communities has been effective only when state political parties need the collaboration of the nationalist forces located in the autonomous territories. However, in these instances the dialogue has been not so much between public institutions as between political parties – specifically, between the majority party in the central arena and the majority party in the concerned Autonomous Community. The compensation obtained by the latter is usually seen as the result of political blackmail and as a source of privileges and inequalities, which tends to be reflected in the next election. The result has generally been either greater electoral backing for the state party (thus freeing it from the further need to negotiate) or a change of the Autonomous Community's governing party. With respect to autonomy, a nationalist group's support for a state party may generate the false image that this group is the only defender of territorial interests. Even so, this collaboration invariably tends to translate into a decrease in electoral support for the local majority party. This is due to voter discontent with the terms of the political pact between the state and community majority parties, which are seen as not sufficiently sensitive towards autonomous interests.

Symmetry and Asymmetry

Some brief allusions to the debate over symmetry and asymmetry will serve to complete our discussion of the logic of the power distribution. At the outset, the Spanish model of federalism allowed great doses of organizational and power asymmetry; however, from this initial situation, and despite the survival of some outstanding elements of asymmetry, the distribution of powers has certainly moved progressively towards the equalization of all seventeen Autonomous Communities. Nevertheless, these communities continue to exhibit historical, linguistic, geographic (two communities are in archipelagos), political, legal, and economic differences. It is probably with regard to the economy that one sees the greatest differences among Autonomous Communities as two of them, the Basque Country and Navarra, enjoy their own privileged system of financing (the result of some historical arrangements sheltered by the Constitution).

The main sources of uniformity among the Autonomous Communities arise from the exercise of state powers, the integration into the European Union, the progressive importance of multilateral over bilateral relationships, and the fact that state political parties are often the same parties that govern the vast majority of the communities. The main sources of asymmetry arise mainly from particular constitutional provisions (e.g., different systems of financing), certain determinations of several Statutes of Autonomy (e.g., the existence of specific levels of local administration), a slightly superior number of powers in some Autonomous Communities (e.g., in matters such as language, civil rights, and/or the creation of their own police force), and/or the transfer of limited state powers to only one community (this is very rare).

In sum, the power and organizational asymmetry of the Autonomous Communities has definitely been reduced, but the multinational reality of the state obliges it to continue to maintain some asymmetrical regulations that, occasionally, continue to be significant.

EVOLUTION OF THE DISTRIBUTION OF POWERS

The distribution of powers between the state and the Autonomous Communities is established in the Constitution and in the Statutes of Autonomy. The reform of this framework could take us, logically, towards another power system. On this point the Constitution is not too rigid since strong majorities could achieve reform (i.e., amendment) through the passage of proposals in each central chamber, without the need for general referendum.[24]

Nonetheless, the Spanish Constitution has not been changed in this manner; however, this is not the case with the Statutes of Autonomy. On the one hand, most of the statutes that initially covered the Autonomous Communities with low levels of competence have been amended to allow those communities to reach the maximum level. On the other hand, current reform proposals pertaining to the so-called "historical" Autonomous Communities (especially Catalonia and the Basque Country) enjoy great political support in their territories and have certain possibilities of success.

As we have seen, the Constitution provided for several mechanisms to re-
adjust the distribution of powers, without the need for constitutional or
statutory reforms. However, these mechanisms have rarely been utilized
and then for purposes not always coincident with those initially foreseen.
Thus, the state gave all Autonomous Communities administrative powers
relating to cross-boundary transportation systems; it also transferred to Catalonia its functions relating to police control of vehicular traffic. Recently,
the state transferred to the Autonomous Communities limited regulatory
powers with respect to state taxes that had been ceded to them. These are
the most obvious examples of the utilization of the above-mentioned constitutional mechanisms, which have also been used to vary the powers of
some Autonomous Communities (as a preliminary step to the reform of
their statutes).

It is certain, however, that the current distribution of responsibilities
among the state and the Autonomous Communities could vary substantially through the use of constitutional mechanisms. One major constraint
on the use of these mechanisms is the constitutional requirement that
each use must be authorized by specific legislation passed by the state Parliament. The practical effect of this is to introduce a clear element of rigidity into a system that, on first glance, appears to be very flexible.

The distribution of financial responsibilities has also changed, and in a
very significant way, thanks to the successive reforms of the system of financing as it relates to Autonomous Communities. This did not require constitutional modification since the Constitution gave the state the authority to
implement this system. Through this method, it has been possible for the
state to cede a portion of the income taxes collected – initially 15 percent
and subsequently 30 percent – to the Autonomous Communities.

Apart from the exceptions noted above and a few others, it is clear that the
distribution of powers has moved towards progressively centralizing public
responsibilities in state institutions. This process has been driven by the successive executives that have governed Spain, and it has occurred mainly
when the governing party has had an absolute majority in Parliament.

The trend towards centralization has generated strong opposition in
some Autonomous Communities, and it constitutes one of the key explanations for the escalating power struggle that has taken place before the
Constitutional Court. To the disenchantment of the Autonomous Communities, we must also add the weak position of local governments, which
have been faced with the resistance of the state and the autonomous authorities to any increase in its level of powers and financing. At the root of
this problem lies the controversy surrounding the fiscal and legal dependence of local governments on the other levels of government.

Centralization must mainly be attributed to the fact that state institutions have broadly interpreted the functional and material scope of their

powers. The Constitutional Court has tended to accept this interpretation, although indicating that the Constitution allows equally for readings that favour the interests of the Autonomous Communities. One important factor has been the understanding given to the constitutional powers granted to the state concerning the "basic rules" (or framework rules) regarding any specific matter – a much extended power category. The Constitution does not define what should be understood by "basic rules" or by "basic legislation," and we are faced with very different initial interpretations. One interpretation is that the basic rules would be confined to the establishment of simple principles, through regulations in law, but would not be directly applicable on the ground without further legislation on the part of the Autonomous Community. However, the interpretation that has been imposed grants great leeway to the state Parliament's definition of basic rules. It allows a particularly exhaustive regulation of each matter affected, permits these rules to be set through administrative regulations, and even allows the rules to extend to administrative decisions. Even though the Constitutional Court has recognized the need for the Autonomous Communities to have sufficient room to further develop the state's framework legislation in order to adopt their own political options, the practical effect of this interpretation is to annul that capacity. This is seen, for example, in such cases as environmental law, local government organization, and administrative law.

Where the state is authorized to pass legislation, but where those laws are to be executed by the Autonomous Communities, state laws reserve certain actions of execution to the central institutions (e.g., the state grants administrative authorization to entities that preserve intellectual property; in many fields it is the state that manages subsidies). In addition, the Constitutional Court – faced with the silence of the Constitution on this point – has attributed jurisdiction for administrative regulation to the state. In this case, the Autonomous Communities can only pass administrative regulations that refer to organizational matters.[25]

The role of the Constitutional Court in the evolution of the system is ambivalent. In general, it is recognized that its doctrine has contributed to the centralization of the distribution of powers. Nonetheless, it must also be remembered that the Court only confirms the compatibility of the state's initiatives with the constitutional text: it does not close the door on other interpretations, which might be equally legitimate from a constitutional perspective. Basically, we can affirm that the Court has abandoned the possibility of establishing a general doctrine, preferring to lean towards a casuistic jurisprudence, and this has resulted in a complex system. Despite all this, we should point out that, on some occasions, its intervention has guaranteed the institutional role of the Autonomous Communities. For instance, this occurred in 1983, when the Court rejected the intention of the state legislature to redefine the whole system through a "harmonization law." Other cases include the Court's restrictive interpretation of such constitutional provisions as the residual clause and the supplementary clause, not to mention its quite rigorous doctrine regarding state spending power – all of which are discussed above.

The strengthening of central institutions is also the result of several factors that we can conventionally summarize under the idea of globalization. We refer mainly to the incorporation of Spain into the European Union but also to the growing importance of immigration and of information and communication technologies. The immigration phenomenon presents some radically different dimensions from those that were present when the Constitution granted exclusive powers to the state in this matter. The current situation clashes with the fact that the Autonomous Communities and local entities are the ones that are principally required to attend to the demands of the immigrant population in areas such as housing, education, and health care. Regarding information and communication technologies there are no direct provisions for powers. However, some state powers, such as the exclusive power over telecommunications, grant the state a clear preeminence in this new area.

Nonetheless, today the greatest threat to the powers of the Autonomous Communities comes from European institutions. The European Union has progressively increased its powers in areas originally entrusted to the Autonomous Communities. The Spanish Constitutional Court has ruled that admission to the European Community does not alter the internal distribution of powers with regard to executing or applying community policies – a general principle that it has not always been able to maintain. However, the problem persists with respect to ongoing decision making regarding European integration. The state and the Autonomous Communities have tried but thus far have failed to achieve the kind of cooperative process on European affairs – including the direct presence of the subnational governments before the institutions of the European Union – that has been achieved by the Belgian and German federal systems. This is, without a doubt, one of the greatest challenges faced today by the "state of the Autonomies."

PERTINENCE AND FUTURE OF POWER DISTRIBUTION

Although all predictions for the future are risky, it is always possible, in view of recent experience and current debates, to venture down some of the roads that the state model and its particular system of territorial distribution of political power might take.

One of the more generally held opinions is that the state of the Autonomies has been consolidated and is in relative equilibrium. This diagnosis obliges us to accept, as a first hypothesis, that nothing will substantially change in the short or medium term and that the state model will remain unaltered despite the existence of contrary pressures. The inverse hypothesis is equally admissible. One of the peculiarities of the Spanish model of federalism is that it may evolve in many and varied ways. Logically, the future will unfold according to the correlation of political forces that the citizens opt to establish at any given time.

Experience tells us that, in regard to the state model, the two large political parties (the conservative party [*Partido Popular*] and the Spanish Socialist Party [Partido Socialista], winner of the March 2004 election) do not substantially differ from one another. The state of the Autonomies has been deeply marked by two substantial agreements between those two large political groups: the Autonomous Agreements of 1981 and of 1992. The first related to the spread of autonomy throughout all the regions, and the second related to the equalization of the level of power for all Autonomous Communities.

Currently, the major political forces at the central level have begun to lay the foundations for a third agreement, known by the name of the "second decentralization," which favours a massive transfer of administrative responsibilities from the Autonomous Communities to the local government. In addition to controlling and dominating the evolution of the Spanish model, these agreements give evidence of the desire to channel it towards homogeneous solutions, with the state maintaining a preeminent position in all instances.

Until now, this centralist tendency has only been inverted – or counterbalanced – when the government does not have an absolute majority in the state Parliament and has been obliged to count on the political support of nationalist political forces, which are established only in some of the Autonomous Communities. On these occasions, political collaboration translates into an increase in powers for some or all of the Autonomous Communities as well as into an improvement of their institutional and financial positions. However, these improvements are a long way from meeting the expectations in some parts of these communities, which explains why the debate continues to be open and controversial. Today, this debate moves between those who consider the construction of the autonomous state to be complete, requiring only reinforcement and consolidation (especially through intergovernmental relations), and those who affirm that the current model is unsustainable and that it will fall into a structural crisis if deep changes are not introduced.

The defence of autonomous interests has occurred in the last few years and has involved several strategies. In the first place, some have demanded an improvement of the position of the Autonomous Communities within the frame of the existing system, "without touching" its basic institutional regulations (i.e., the Constitution and the Statutes of Autonomy). This could substantially change the model of power distribution.[26] The failure of this approach has reoriented the demand for reform of the Statutes of Autonomy, both in the Basque Country and in Catalonia as well as in other Autonomous Communities (such as Andalucia and the Valencian Community). In the first two instances, the desire to reform statutes has had broad support among "native" political forces and has been translated into some particularly ambitious first texts.[27] The possibilities for the success of these proposals are still uncertain, but they have increased notably thanks to the results of the 2004 general election and to the fact that the same party (the socialist) is now governing at the state level as well as at the Autonomous Community level (e.g., Catalonia). However, it is difficult to ensure the success of some of these proposals – mainly those from the Basque Country – because they are either in contradiction to the Spanish Constitution or demand an interpretation of the Constitution that differs completely from the current one.

If reform of the statutes fails or does not respond to present expectations, it is very likely that we will witness an increase in demands for greater autonomy or constitutional amendment – an option that has already begun to receive clear political and doctrinal support.[28] Having accepted the need to reform the Constitution, divergence persists regarding the scope of this reform. There is a largely majoritarian agreement in support of the "convenience" of modifying the constitutional provisions relating to the Senate, an institution that has little current use and that has not been able to exercise its theoretical constitutional function as a house of territorial representation. It would be hard to reform the Constitution only to modify the structure of the Senate, but it would also be difficult not to deal with this issue within the framework of a broad constitutional reform.

The demands for greater autonomy are varied and strong, and we can sort them into four broad areas. The first is the need to adapt the judicial system to the plural structure of the state, to ensure greater participation of the Autonomous Communities in the institutions and policies of the state, and to perfect vertical (state-Autonomous Communities) as well as horizontal (among the Autonomous Communities) institutional relations. The most important demand relates to the participation of the Autonomous Communities in the process of constructing the European Union. Certainly, some of these objectives could be reached through the constitutional reform of the Senate.

The second, and equally important, area involves the distribution powers. The Autonomous Communities want to increase their powers through a greater guarantee of those they already have as well as through the recognition of their right to intervene in areas currently dominated by the state. In the first case they advocate a new, restrictive interpretation of state powers (particularly those that allow the state to establish the "basic rules" for a specific matter) so that they may set their own policies fully and coherently. In addition, they demand that the state transfer or delegate to them the vast majority of the administrative functions that the former currently exercises in their territories – a proposal that would simplify administrative structures in favour of those Autonomous Communities sufficiently prepared to assume these new responsibilities. The pressure for an increase in powers is particularly strong in those areas that the Constitution has dealt with in a particularly restrictive way (such as the judicial power or the international activities of the Autonomous Communities) and in those areas that have progressively increased in importance since the adoption of the Constitution (such as immigration and information technologies).

The third area involves the financial system, with which the Constitution deals in a particularly open way. Here Autonomous Communities point to the need to increase the sufficiency of their resources, particularly through increasing their revenue autonomy in order to provide more guarantees of stability.

The fourth area involves respect for territorial pluralism. Here the Autonomous Communities demand that the different expressions of diversity within the state (language, traditions, culture, systems of civil law, political parties, etc.) not only be respected but also protected and promoted by state authorities, both in their organization and in their performance as well as through positive actions of an asymmetrical nature.

Finally, there is a need to improve the mechanisms of intergovernmental relations – an issue that has been the cause of several debates. These debates have concerned whether preference should be given to bilateral or multilateral relations as well as the constitutional limits of cooperative federalism. A number of Autonomous Communities feel that they have still not found a good fit within the overall state system. This has begun to lead to the perception that, after twenty-five years of the Constitution's being in force, Spain is again at a point of departure, that it is faced with the need to articulate a new system that harmonizes the unity of the state with the greatest possible respect for the autonomy and diversity of the territories that it comprises.

We foresee a long road that, at this stage, we can only walk along slowly, in unity and peace, through the introduction of changes (more or less profound) to our institutional system. In spite of everything, the success of this complex challenge does not depend so much on legal mechanisms as it does on dialogue and respect for pluralism.

NOTES

1 Traditionally, in Spain the term "state" refers not only to the overall system of
government but also to the central institutions. Thus it could be understood as
a synonym for "federation." The "parts" have been named "regions," or "auton-
omous communities." For general references on the Spanish system see Eliseo
Aja, *El Estado autonómico* [*The Autonomous state*], 2nd ed. (Madrid: Alianza,
2003); Eliseo Aja, ed., *El sistema jurídico de las Comunidades Autónomas* [*The Legal
System of Autonomous Communities*] (Madrid: Tecnos, 1985); Eduardo García de
Enterría, *Estudios sobre autonomías territoriales* [*Essays on Territorial Autonomies*]
(Madrid: Civitas, 1985); Jesús Leguina, *Escritos sobre autonomías territoriales*
[*Papers on Territorial Autonomy*], 2nd ed. (Madrid: Tecnos, 1995); Santiago
Muñoz Machado, *Derecho público de las Comunidades Autónomas* [*The Public Law of
the Autonomous Communities*], 2 vols. (Madrid: Civitas, 1982–84); Adolfo
Hernández, ed., *El funcionamiento del Estado autonómico* [*The Functions of the Au-
tonomous State*], 2nd ed. (Madrid: Ministerio de Administraciones Públicas,
1999).

2 The population information refers to 1 January 2003 and is available through
the Web site of the *Instituto Nacional de Estadística* [National Statis Institute],
<http://www.ine.es/inebase/cgi.axi> (accessed 26 June 2005).

3 Information provided by the Bank of Spain <http://www.bde.es/infoest/
e0202.pdf> accessed 26 June 2005).

4 Information obtained from World Development Indicators, <http://
devdata.worldbank.org/esternal/CPProfile.asp?SelectedCountry=
ESP&CCODE=ESP&CNAME-Spain&PTYPE=CP> (accessed 26 June 2005).

5 The Statute of Autonomy of the Valencian Community does not utilize the term
"Catalan" but, rather, "Valencian." There is great controversy – more political
than philological – over the unity and/or diversity of such languages. The linguistic differences are not abundant, nor do they impede the respective speakers from easily understanding each other. However, at the official (i.e., legal)
level, Catalan and Valencian are treated as distinct languages.

6 Eliseo Aja, *El Estado Autonómico* [*The Autonomous State*], 2nd ed. (Madrid:
Alianza, 2003), p. 14.

7 Both Houses comprise the Parliament, the constitutional institution that represents the Spanish people, exercises the legislative power of the state, adopts its
budget, and controls the actions of the government. The House of Deputies has
350 members who are elected by universal suffrage within a proportional
system of representation, in which the electoral constituency is the province
(a small administrative unit, not to be confused with the Autonomous Communities). The Constitution expressly states that the Senate is the "house of territorial representation." Voters of each province shall elect four senators by
universal suffrage. Autonomous Communities shall, in addition, appoint one
senator and a further senator for every million inhabitants in their respective

territories. However, in practice, the senators do not vote according to their territorial origin but, rather, according to their party affiliation. This fact prevents the Senate from accomplishing its constitutional function as a "House of territorial representation"; rather, it has become a house in which legislative initiatives are reviewed before their final adoption by the House of Deputies.

8 The first such affirmation of the court occurred in the early Ruling number 18/1982 of 4 May 1982. The principle of institutional loyalty has been recognized and developed by state legislation.

9 The first region that was conceded this system of provisional autonomy was Catalonia (5 October 1977). The last one to obtain it, barely two months prior to the enactment of the Constitution was Castilla-La Mancha (31 October 1978).

10 On this topic, see Santiago Muñoz Machado, *Derecho Público de las Comunidades Autónomas* [*The Public Law of the Autonomous Communities*], 2 vols. (Madrid: Civitas, 1982), pp. 344–345.

11 See the contributions of Professor Francis Delpérée in Enric Argullol Murgadas, ed., *Federalismo y Autonomía* [*Federalism and Autonomy*] (Barcelona: Ariel, 2004), pp. 89–90.

12 We use the term "municipalities" to refer to the basic level of local administration, without considering their size or population as "towns," "cities," "villages," and so on. The Constitution states that members of their government must be elected directly by universal suffrage. Provinces – and other smaller local entities – occupy a second level, situated between Autonomous Communities and municipalities. Basically, they cooperate with and provide aid and support to the municipalities. They also carry out functions delegated or transferred to them by the state or the Autonomous Communities. These governments are not directly elected by the population.

13 The majority political forces at the central, or national, level (the *Partido Popular* [Conservative Party] and the *Partido Socialista* [Socialist Party]) were inclined to frame this process in a prior and general agreement ("Autonomous Pacts of 1992") that, in an attempt to achieve the maximum rationality and uniformity, put off reforming the statutes in favour of transferring state powers only to those Autonomous Communities who were interested. The political solution adopted was strongly criticized by some authors because they understood that it was adjusted neither to constitutional provisions nor to the spirit of the system. See Santiago Muñoz Machado, "Los Pactos Autonómicos de 1992: La ampliación de competencias y la reforma de los Estatutos" [Autonomous Agreements of 1992: Extension of Powers and Statutes Reform], *Revista de Administración Pública* [*Public Administration Review*] 128 (May-August 1992): 85–105.

14 Ruling number 40/1998: "the content of art. 148.1 of the Constitution may be converted into interpretive criteria of art. 149.1 and of the corresponding precepts of the Statutes of Autonomy ... the Autonomous Communities may invoke art. 148.1, if not as an originating source of its powers, then at least

as an argument of a systematic nature in the interpretation of the precepts that make up its own block of the constitutionality."

15 The long and controversial Article 150 of the Constitution provides: "1. The parliament, in matters of state jurisdiction, may confer upon all or any of the Self-governing [Autonomous] Communities the power to pass legislation for themselves within the framework of the principles, bases and guidelines laid down by a state act. Without prejudice to the jurisdiction of the Courts, each enabling act shall make provision for the method of supervision by the Parliament over the Communities' legislation. 2. The state may transfer or delegate to the Self-governing Communities, through an organic act, some of its powers which by their very nature can be transferred or delegated. The law shall, in each case, provide for the appropriate transfer of financial means, as well as specify the forms of control to be retained by the state."

16 This constitutional provision states: "Matters not expressly assigned to the state by this Constitution may fall under the jurisdiction of the Self-governing Communities by virtue of their Statutes of Autonomy. Jurisdiction on matters not claimed by Statutes of Autonomy shall fall with the state, *whose laws shall prevail, in case of conflict, over those of the Self-governing Communities regarding all matters in which exclusive jurisdiction has not been conferred upon the latter. State law shall in any case be suppletory of that of the Self-governing Communities*" (emphasis added).

17 Different interpretations of this clause and its effects are studied in Julio C. Tejedor, *La garantía constitucional de la unidad del ordenamiento en el Estado autonómico: competencia, prevalencia y supletoriedad* [The constitutional guarantee of legal system unity in the Autonomous state: competence, prevalence and supplementarity] (Madrid: Civitas, 2000).

18 See Javier Barnés, "Una reflexión sobre la cláusula de supletoriedad del artículo 149.3 CE" [A reflection on the supplementarity of article 149.3 of the Spanish Constitution], *Revista Española de Derecho Administrativo* [*Spanish Review of Administrative Law*] 93 (January-March 1997): 83–97; and Eduardo García de Enterría, "Una reflexión sobre la supletoriedad del derecho del Estado respecto del de las Comunidades Autónomas" [A reflection about the supplementarity of the state law in relation to Autonomous Community law], *Revista Española de Derecho Administrativo* [*Spanish Review of Administrative Law*] 95 (July-September 1997): 407–15. Also, the magistrate Manuel Jiménez de Parga (later appointed President of the Constitutional Court) considered that the jurisprudence on these matters had a "constitutional" transcendence that implied "the de-configuration of the Autonomous state and the openness to the implementation of a federal model."

19 With the same opinion, see Iñaki Lasagabaster Herrarte, "La interpretación del principio de supletoriedad y su adecuación a los principios constitucionales rectores del Estado de las autonomías" [The interpretation of the principle of

supplementarity and its adjustment to the constitutional principles informing the Autonomous state] *Revista Española de Derecho Constitucional* [*Spanish Review of Constitutional Law*] 55 (January-April 1999): 43–76.

20 Eliseo Aja and Carles Viver Pi-Sunyer, "Valoración de 25 años de autonomía" [Evaluation of 25 years of autonomy] *Revista Española de Derecho Constitucional* 69 (October-December 2003): 69–114.

21 Ruling of 2 February 1981.

22 Article 155 of the Constitution provides that: "If a Self-governing Community does not fulfill the obligations imposed upon it by the Constitution or other laws, or acts in a way that is seriously prejudicial to the general interest of Spain, the Government, after having lodged a complaint with the President of the Self-governing Community and failed to receive satisfaction therefore, may, following approval granted by the overall majority of the Senate, take all measures necessary to compel the Community to meet said obligations, or to protect the above-mentioned general interest." This mechanism has to be understood as an exceptional solution, usable only on occasions of critical institutional conflict that simply cannot be solved in less dramatic ways.

23 The Constitutional Court consists of twelve judges. Of these, four are nominated by the House of Deputies, four by the Senate (with the same majority), two by the government, and two by the General Council of the Judicial Power. The General Council of the Judicial Power consists of the president of the Supreme Court (it is the highest judicial body in all branches of justice, with jurisdiction over the whole of Spain, except with regard to provisions concerning constitutional guarantees) and twenty other members. Of these twenty, twelve are judges and magistrates of all judicial categories; six are appointed by the House of Deputies and six by the Senate. Eight of its members are picked from among lawyers and other jurists of acknowledged competence and more than fifteen years of professional practice. Of these eight, four are nominated by Congress and four by the Senate.

24 The Spanish Constitution provides for two different amendment processes: the ordinary one, which demands strong majorities in each Chamber (a three-fifths majority of the House of Deputies and Senate or a two-thirds majority of the former if the latter only reaches an absolute majority) and ratification by referendum only when one-tenth of deputies or senators request it; and the exceptional one, which involves the approval of the reform principle by two-thirds of each House, the subsequent dissolution of Parliament and convocation of elections, the ratification of the new Parliament's decision to reform the Constitution, the approval of the text by two-thirds of each House, and the ratification of the reform by referendum. This last procedure must be followed when what is proposed is either the total revision of the Constitution or a partial revision that would affect the Preliminary Chapter (basic principles), fundamental rights and public liberties, and/or to the institution of the Crown.

25 For a copy of the doctrine of the Constitutional Court in this regard, see Ruling 103/1999, 3 June 1999, 4th legal principle (available at <www.tribunal-constitcional.es>).

26 This was the thesis that we maintained and tried to demonstrate in Enric Argullol Murgadas, *Desarrollar el autogobierno* [*Developing Self-Government*] (Barcelona: Peninsula, 2002).

27 In the case of Catalonia the proposals for the reform of the Statute of Autonomy prepared by four of the five parliamentary political groups can be read on the Web site for the *Observatorio de la Evolución de las Instituciones* [*Evolution of Institutions Observatory*] <http://www.upf.edu/obsei> (accessed 26 June 2005). See also the study prepared by an academic commission by order of the Autonomous Government: Antoni Bayona Rocamora, ed., *Informe sobre la reforma del Estatuto* [*Report on Statute reform*] (Barcelona: Generalitat de Catalunya [Government of Catalonia], 2003). In the case of the Basque Country, see the proposal formulated by the *Lehendakari* (president) of the Autonomous Community. This proposal is known as "Plan Ibarretxe" and is available, in English, on the following Web site: <http://www.nuevoestatutodeeuskadi.net/default.asp?hizk=ing> (accessed 26 June 2005).

28 In the realm of academics, the debate began with the work of Aja and Viver, "Valoración de 25 años de autonomía" ["Evaluation of 25 Years of Autonomy"], *Revista Española de Derecho Constitucional* 69 (October-December 2003): 69–114.

The need to reform the Constitution has been accepted and, nowadays, is clearly defended by the Spanish Socialist Party, which is currently in power. The rest of the political forces – including the conservative party (until now the principal opponent to this initiative) – also agree with this proposal.

SWITZERLAND

Capital: Bern
Population: 7.2 million (2002 est.)
Boundaries and place names are representative
only and do not imply any official endorsement.

N

0   30

Kilometres

GERMANY

AUSTRIA

LIECHTENSTEIN

ITALY

FRANCE

Schauffhausen

Basle-Country

Basle-Town

Jura

Solothurn

Argovia

Zurich

Thurgau

Outer Rhodes

Inner Rhodes

St. Gallen

Glarus

Schwyz

Zug

Luzerne

Nidwalden

Obwalden

Uri

Graubunden

Ticino

Neuchatel

Bern

● Bern

Fribourg

Vaud

Valais

Geneva

Swiss Confederation

THOMAS FLEINER

Switzerland's federal constitution, adopted in 1848 after a civil war, was a compromise that sought to accommodate both the liberals (mainly Protestants) promoting a unitary state and the conservatives (mainly Roman Catholics) defending the former Confederation. In addition, the Constitution had to accommodate the linguistic diversity among the four official language groups.[1] Based on a highly decentralized federalism, the Cantons (the constituent units of the federation) maintained their far-reaching original autonomy, now as self-rule within a federation, and continued to share their sovereignty with the federation. The constitutional concept of Switzerland's distribution of powers reflects a "bottom-up" construction of the federation and depends, finally, on the residual powers of the Cantons and, in some instances, even municipalities. As a logical consequence the Swiss Constitution does not distribute the powers between the Confederation and the Cantons in a final list, and it does not provide powers for the Cantons.[2] In principle it determines exclusively the powers delegated to the Confederation.[3] Where new powers are delegated to the federal government, they are formulated carefully so that, even within a delegated power, the Cantons still retain some part of their sovereignty. This chapter first addresses the basic constitutional principles behind Swiss federalism and the principal guidelines for the distribution of powers before taking a more in-depth look at the system of distribution of powers, including the autonomy of the Cantons and the specific powers of the Confederation, one of which (i.e., the fiscal system) has undergone important changes as a result of a referendum in late November 2004.

BASIC CONSTITUTIONAL PRINCIPLES[4]

The Historical-Cultural Context

The origins of Switzerland go back to the thirteenth century, but modern Switzerland was initiated by Napoleon's intervention in 1800 and properly started with the Constitution of 1848. With this Constitution the sovereign Cantons decided, after a civil war, to establish peace by forming a strongly decentralized federation, which was even – though in scientific terms wrongly – labelled a "Confederation."[5] Thus France, for a long time the only republican democratic neighbour, had a strong influence on the legal system of the Confederation and, in particular, on the legal systems of the French-speaking Cantons. The influence of Germany, another neighbour of Switzerland, gained strength in the second half of the twentieth century. Thus Switzerland is embedded in a civil law system of both French and German origin.[6]

Since the foundation of modern Switzerland the Constitution has only been totally revised twice, in 1874 and in 1999, respectively. In between those general revisions the Constitution has been partially revised more than a hundred times. Most of these revisions were intended to strengthen the powers of the federal government. In 1848, however, the main principle for the distribution of powers was to give to the Confederation the minimum of powers necessary to survive as a union of Cantons. The weakness of Swiss defence policy during the German-French war at the end of the nineteenth century was one of the principal reasons for constitutional change; that is, to provide a stronger federal government. The slogan of this revision was: "one army, one market and one law" (civil law and commercial law). The 1999 revisions have been promoted as a new edition of this slogan, intended to give the old Constitution modern wording without making any basic changes.

With regard to federalism, the clear tendency to more centralization has been balanced by increased opportunities for the Cantons to participate in the decision-making process at the central level, the point being to maintain the balance between shared rule and self-rule. The procedures for constitutional amendments and for a total revision of the Constitution differ slightly. However, as a general rule, in both cases the approval by simple majority of the National Council and the Council of the Cantons (the first and second chambers of the Federal Assembly, respectively) is required, as is the final ratification by the simple majorities of the people and of the Cantons (without any minimal quota as in some other countries). Constitutional amendments can be initiated either by the members of the Federal Assembly (Parliament), by the Federal Council (the Executive), or by 100,000 voters. If the amendments are initiated by the voters (a popular initiative), then the proposal must be submitted to a mandatory referendum of the people and counted both nationally and within their individual Cantons, even if the Federal Assembly rejects the proposal or makes a counterproposal. Thus the further centralizing of constitutional powers in the federal government was part of a continuous political process legitimated by the sovereign people (the majority of the voters of the Swiss people and the peoples of the Cantons). In the United States and other federations, and in the European Union, because the amendment procedure is so burdensome, the courts have a role in deciding the distribution of powers through interpreting the Constitution or the Union treaty. However, the Swiss direct democratic procedures provide a broad legitimacy to amendments, and, based on this legitimacy, their implementation has been generally accepted throughout the country. Thus distribution of powers in the Swiss Confederation may be regarded as being closer to the democratic wishes of the people than that provided in many other federations.

The Swiss Constitution has its roots in nineteenth-century liberalism. In particular, the cantonal constitutions installed after France's July revolution of 1830 have been shaped by modernity. With regard to individual rights, the federal Constitution adopted the ideology of negative individual rights (i.e., freedom from the state). The actual Constitution has an impressive catalogue of individual rights guaranteed by the federal court. However, the federal court has no power to protect individuals against the democratic majority of the legislature. The only legal protection against the violation of individual rights by the legislature is based in the International Treaties on Human Rights. International law is part of the law of the land and thus, based on international treaties, the courts can protect the human rights of individuals against the legislature.[7]

The Swiss concept of liberty has four dimensions: (1) liberty from the state (negative rights); (2) liberty within the state (democracy understood as a right of individual self-determination within the state); (3) liberty by the state (social rights with soft guarantees in the Constitution); and (4) liberty to the state (collective rights of language groups and religious communities [based on the principle of territoriality] and the right to autonomy of municipal corporations).

Switzerland first decided to install a federal system as a way of managing conflict between the two major Christian denominations: the Protestants and the Roman Catholics. The territorial borders of the religious communities and the language communities are only partially identical with the borders of the Cantons. In order to guarantee peace among the different religious communities the federal Constitution guaranteed individual freedom of religion at the federal level. However, this guarantee has not had the same impact as has the establishment clause of the United States Constitution. The Cantons retain the autonomy to decide on the relationship between church and state. As a consequence, in Switzerland there are at least four different systems regulating the relationship of church and state. The traditionally Protestant Cantons of Neuchâtel and Geneva basically aligned themselves with the concept of secularization used in formerly Roman Catholic France. The mainly Protestant German-speaking Cantons provided constitutional status for religious communities made up of citizens belonging to Protestant churches. The mainly Roman Catholic

Cantons provided religious associations of Roman Catholic citizens on the municipal level and privileged the Roman Catholic Church at the cantonal level (e.g., in primary and secondary education). The Cantons with both religious communities developed the concept of two different communities, with each having some kind of public status. Since the 1970s, and in particular since Switzerland ratified the European Convention on Human Rights, major developments have taken place on the cantonal level as the cantons now provide equal status for other religions (such as Judaism).

Another of Switzerland's important founding concepts is that of neutrality. The Swiss concept of neutrality was mainly a strategy to reduce, as much as possible, the influence of the country's big, culturally linked neighbours on its language communities. To the degree to which the neighbouring states respected this principle of neutrality, Switzerland could maintain its inner diversity. In order to avoid Switzerland breaking up along ethnic lines, the old (1848) Constitution prohibited Cantons from concluding political treaties with foreign countries or concluding interstate compacts that had political content. The present (1999) Constitution does not expressly prohibit such compacts as former enemies have, through a long nation-building process, become friendly adversaries.

In general, in order to reach a compromise between self-rule and shared rule, the drafters of the original federal Constitution agreed to leave as much power as possible at the cantonal level. Even the more than 100 twentieth-century amendments have been the result of a compromise between centripetal and centrifugal pressures. The interests of social justice, equal rights, and nation building have all promoted centralized decision making. However, minority interests (language or religion), conservative ideologies, and the desire to keep as much democratic local control as possible were pressures that promoted confederal solutions.

PRINCIPLE GUIDELINES FOR THE DISTRIBUTION OF POWERS

Direct democracy

Whoever examines the distribution of powers in Switzerland will notice, at first view, the country's astonishing difference from all other federal countries. While in most federal Constitutions the catalogue providing the distribution powers is short, plain, and clear, the Swiss Constitution provides a special and rather detailed article for each particular power (more than fifty articles with several sentences each)(see tables at end of chapter). Most of these articles not only grant general power to the federal government but also provide for the competences of the Cantons, which are to be respected by the federal legislature when it implements its power.

The main reason for this complexity is the system of direct democracy, which requires compromise for each new federal competence.

Swiss consensus democracy operates as a bottom-up process. This process starts with the self-determination of the individual and rises upwards through the levels of municipal, district, and cantonal communities before concluding at the federal (or even international or supranational) level. Decisions at the federal level should enable as many citizens as is possible (and efficient) to participate in the decision-making process. From this point of view, democracy can be considered as complementary to federalism as it enhances the principle of subsidiarity with regard to the distribution of powers. It provides an adequate distribution of powers not only between Confederation and Cantons but also between Cantons and municipalities. A thorough analysis of the distribution of powers determined in specific constitutional articles reveals, in almost any decision, the underlying concept of compromise between Cantons and federation, between the major parties, between the regions, and between the communities.

In Switzerland democratic procedures are not intended only to produce effective and legitimate decisions for Swiss society. In our multicultural society they must also function as tools for managing potential conflicts between the different communities. Our governmental system must be democratic, and democracy has priority over limited government as well as, to a certain extent, over the rule of law. This priority of democracy over other values of good government is due to the fact that, in Switzerland, all socio-cultural conflicts have always been resolved by the democratic decisions of the people rather than by constitutional principles or by the decisions of a constitutional court. For example, in many countries the conflict between the prohibition of abortion and freedom of choice has been decided by a constitutional court or by the supreme court; in Switzerland it has been decided by different democratic referendums.

The very fact that the Constitution can only be amended if the amendments are ratified by the majority of the people of the Cantons has a direct influence on the distribution of powers. All important social, technical, industrial, and international developments are disputed not through elections based on party programs but, rather, through constitutional amendments – either initiated by popular initiatives or by the federal government. New societal demands can often be answered only by assigning new constitutional powers to the federal government. Accordingly, all important constitutional amendments provide both the new federal powers and the basic guidelines that determine the aims, tools, and measures to be used by the federal legislature in implementing the new constitutional article. Thus, constitutional articles providing new federal powers often contain a description of the powers, their limits, the rights reserved to the Cantons, the goals to be achieved, and (often) the measures to be taken. In this way, the competences delegated to the federal government, and in particular to the federal legislature, are "earmarked." Very often the decision to delegate new powers to the federal government can only win the approval of the people if these specific powers are clearly limited and take special note of specific cantonal interests (such as those of the rural Cantons, the French-speaking Cantons, the export-oriented Cantons, the underprivileged Cantons, and so on).

Major social problems and developments have always resulted in initiatives drafted by concerned civil interest groups or parties. Since 1848, even though out of a total of 142 initiatives only eleven have been adopted while 131 have been rejected, most of the latter have had an impact on further constitutional developments. This is because either the Federal Assembly drafted a counterproposal or the idea in the initiative was later introduced in a government-sponsored constitutional referendum and was incorporated into legislation.

The fact that the Swiss Constitution does not provide for general emergency powers is another consequence of direct democracy. The Swiss people and the peoples of the Cantons would never accept the Federal Assembly or the Federal Council having general emergency powers. The only reference to "emergency" concerns the power of Federal Assembly to enact urgent legislation. In 1939, during the Second World War, the Federal Council was empowered by a unanimous Federal Assembly to enact all legislation necessary to protect Switzerland and its citizens. Thus it was decided, without any constitutional basis, that in cases of undisputed emergency all parties would agree to give the necessary power to the Federal Council. The Federal Council, though, must always remember that this power is not covered by the Constitution and that it applies only for the duration of the specific emergency.

Multiculturalism and Diversity[8]

We know that some constitutions are based on the homogeneity of the culture of their people, which enhances the cultural heritage of the country. A common language is often considered an essential element to guaranteeing homogeneity and democratic communication. Other states ignore culture as a nation-building factor. Their constitutions are based on a set of universal values uniting all citizens as political beings within a specific territory (e.g., France). Finally, immigration states (i.e., states that have arisen due to immigration) have to integrate the various cultures of diverse migrant peoples within one constitutional design. Often they exclude the cultures of indigenous peoples and unite the diversity of immigrants through integration based on common values (e.g., "the American Dream").

The Swiss Constitution has in fact tried to develop a special type of federal state – one that is developed and determined by its multicultural environment. This state is based on principles that have shaped the political culture of Switzerland, including the distribution of powers. The main aim of American and German federalism was to introduce vertical separation of powers in order to limit governmental power. In addition to this, through compromise Swiss federalism has had to accommodate the diversity of the union of sovereign Cantons. Taking cultural diversity seriously, the Constitution provides the Confederation with the general responsibility to promote cultural diversity within its delegated competences and, with regard to languages, to provide measures for the better mutual understanding of different language communities (Articles 2 and 70). Cultural sovereignty with regard to culture proper and to education (including university education) remains within traditional cantonal powers.

In the Swiss view a constitution that intends to take cultural diversity seriously cannot treat minorities as tolerated guests; rather, it must provide different cultural communities with proper constitutional status. Thus cultural communities have "state status," at least in terms of the constitution-making procedure, with the result that they accept their state as their homeland. Consequently, in principle, Switzerland provides for four official languages[9] – German, French, and Italian are on equal footing. Romantsch is an official language but not all legislation is translated into it. When a federal statute is implemented, each language is considered to be equal to the others. If there are different meanings or different interpretations, then each language has to be considered as an original and authoritative text. Public officials at the federal level express themselves in their own language; however, as officials, they are supposed to at least understand German, French, and Italian. Italian-speaking members of Parliament have a saying that demonstrates this: "For beauty they speak Italian; if they want the members of Parliament to listen, they speak French; but if they want to be understood, they speak German!" The National Council (lower house of the Federal Assembly) now requires simultaneous translations for plenary discussions. Similar arrangements are not provided for in the Council of States.

The question of official languages falls within cantonal jurisdiction. Bilingual Cantons provide an equal footing for two official languages, while the trilingual Canton of Grison does so for three (German, Italian, and Romantsch-Grisun). For a long time Romantsch had several idioms. Then, for financial reasons, the Canton of Grison began providing only one official translation per year: one year it would translate decisions into the Puter idiom and the following year into the Sursilvan idiom. Today the official language is Romantsch-Grisun, a "laboratory-made" idiom.

Cantonal competences to organize themselves according to their respective governmental systems, as well as according to their concept of local autonomy and their own judiciary, enabled the Cantons to continue their historic tradition as small democratic corporations. Their constitutions and their legal systems reflect their religions, their languages, and their international neighbourhoods as well as their rural, aristocratic, and commercial/corporate traditions.

The power of the Cantons to develop their own democratic vision has been essential in enabling their peoples to maintain their own "we"; that is, their own democratic communities (including their municipalities). Most democratic developments in Switzerland have been initiated in the Cantons. For example, the French-speaking Cantons began the trend of granting women the right to vote; this was followed by other Cantons and then by the Confederation. Only the last Canton (Appenzell Inner Rhodes) had to be forced by the federal court to recognize equal rights for women. In this case the court gave priority to the universality of equal rights over the collective right of a Canton to organize itself according to its own traditions. The Cantons, although integrated into a national-global market, differ to a great extent with regard to their democratic tools and with regard to their notions of how much power should be given to their municipalities.

From the Swiss perspective, a state that recognizes the political value of its different cultural communities (i.e., communities that are culturally but not politically united with their neighbour states) has to be based on a concept of multiple loyalties. The Swiss are politically loyal to the Confederation, the Canton, and the municipality, but they are culturally loyal to the cultural community of their kindred neighbour state. This multilevel loyalty is also reflected in the concept of citizenship. Swiss citizenship has a federal, a cantonal, and a municipal basis. On each level the political unit decides who will be accepted into the political community as a citizen. All three levels have to concur. Based on the principle of multiple loyalties, one must also consider the competences of the Cantons not only with regard to intergovernmental relationships within Switzerland but also with regard to relationships with other countries. The cultural cooperation of French-speaking Cantons with France and of Italian-speaking Cantons with Italy are essential for their development and, thus, for the development of the entire country.

The legitimacy of a state with cultural diversity can only be achieved if each cultural community considers the state as its own. This goal is attainable if the cultural community is convinced that its own cultural heritage is best developed within that particular political community. The state must not simply tolerate but also aim to promote such diversity. In Article 2 of the 1999 Constitution, the Confederation is mandated to promote cultural diversity. This gives the different branches of the federal government additional responsibility with regard to cantonal competences in the fields of culture, education, and religion. Moreover, according to Article 70, Paragraph 3, of the Constitution, the Confederation and the Cantons shall encourage understanding and exchange among the linguistic communities. And Paragraph 4 holds that the Confederation shall in addition "support the multi-lingual Cantons in the fulfillment of their particular tasks."

Swiss federalism is based on the principle of one person, one value; on the principle of one Canton, one sovereignty; and on the notion of equal Constitutional status. All Cantons enjoy the same rights notwithstanding their importance in terms of size, economy, and population. Switzerland is not an asymmetric federal state with regard to the Constitutional status of the Cantons; rather, it pointedly disrespects its actual asymmetry.

THE SYSTEM OF DISTRIBUTION OF POWERS

General Aspects: Autonomy of the Cantons

The Cantons must have the opportunity to make, finance, and implement those decisions that are relevant to their cultural development based on their cultural heritage. This includes decisions relating to education, the judiciary, administration, and the police. In fact, the legitimacy of a cantonal government is embedded in the historical, legal, constitutional, religious, and linguistic culture of its community; consequently, it can never depend on a centrally delegated legitimacy. Cantonal governments have the power to enforce law and order. The power of the police has its legal roots in the cantonal constitution and in the cantonal responsibility to guarantee the freedom and security of its people.

The most important power of Cantons and municipalities concerns their fiscal capacities. Cantons and municipalities decide on two-thirds of the state's income and expenditure. This fiscal capacity is based on the idea that the territorial units, which have the power and responsibility to perform and implement public justice, must also have the means to finance this public service through taxation. The federal government provides equalization payments in cases where some territorial units provide services for others; where, for specific geographical and demographical reasons, equal opportunities are not guaranteed; and where small units do not have the necessary resources to provide public services.

Based on their fiscal autonomy, the voters of the Canton and of the municipalities decide on the taxes that will provide the necessary income. Exceptionally, they fund public services through the raising of public debt or through federal grants. In addition, important new expenditures for projects such as roads, buildings, Olympic Games, and so on have to be submitted to a public referendum. Through these tools of direct democracy local accountability is safeguarded.

The development of Switzerland also depends to a great extent on the capacities of the Cantons to cooperate among themselves as well as with the federal government. For example, the new federal legislation on cooperation between cantonal and federal universities is based on a federal statute that can only be implemented if it is supported by a treaty of the Cantons that includes themselves as well as the federal government. Based on this treaty a new "super" agency, with power over the cantonal universities as well as over the federal technical universities, has been given the mandate to coordinate university development.

Within the limitations established by federal law, each Canton has the right to self-organization according to what is set down in its Constitution. The Cantons can decide on the organization and political structure of their territory as well as on how their institutions will be set up and how they will operate. They can limit their own cantonal powers or they can delegate some of these powers to municipalities. While the actual organization of the Cantons shows that there are several similarities among them as well as between them and the Confederation, there are, nevertheless, important organizational nuances.

The possibilities of the Cantons determining to whom they want to confer political rights are limited to the principles set down in a democratic constitution. The Cantons have the option of giving non-Swiss persons the right to vote and to be elected. They also have the authority to deprive citizens under guardianship of their political rights. In this respect, cantonal citizens are more powerful than are federal citizens. For instance, in the Cantons the citizens elect the members of the cantonal parliament and the cantonal government – and, in some cases, civil servants, teachers, and even judges. In addition, Cantons provide more means of direct democracy than does the Confederation. In most Cantons elections are decided by secret ballot. Very few Cantons (e.g., Appenzell Inner Rhodes and the Canton of Glarus) are still governed by an assembly of the people (*Landsgemeinde*).

Intercantonal Treaties and Cooperation[10]

Cantonal responsibilities have become more and more complex and interconnected. This complexity creates pressure to unify cantonal law and requires Cantons to strengthen their intercantonal cooperation. In order to prevent the transfer of powers to the federal level, the Cantons try to unify their laws through intercantonal treaties. According to Article 48 (1) of the Constitution, the Cantons may conclude intercantonal treaties known as concordats. These concordats cannot be contrary to constitutional or federal law, including those relating to the distribution of powers between the Federation and the Cantons, the interests of the Confederation, and the rights of other Cantons. The Confederation must be notified of all such concordats (Article 48 [3]).

Intercantonal treaties can regulate such subjects as administrative agreements or unifying legislation, and they can create common institutions. Political (I use the term in a narrow sense) intercantonal treaties are
prohibited because they endanger the political unity of Switzerland. Concordats can be concluded between two or more Cantons, and the Confederation can be party to the treaty and/or can participate in the common
institutions (Article 48 [2]). This provision is of relevance in areas where
the federal government and the Cantons have parallel powers. For instance, the Confederation is party to the concordat on the equivalence of
scientific degrees. Based on this concordat, the criteria for the equivalence
of high school diplomas were unified. The concordat may not transfer cantonal powers to the federal level, and the Confederation may only get
involved in areas where the Constitution indicates that federal power is appropriate. One must realize that these instruments for creating intercantonal or cantonal-federal cooperation have a tendency to restrict the scope
of citizen intervention. This is because often they can only be handled by
the executive branch of government.

A federation only exists on the basis of the solidarity of its partners. Along
with constitutionally instituted cooperation, Swiss federalism looks for complementary balance in a network of informal cooperation at all levels of
government and administration, including between labour unions and economic entities – the so-called "social partners." Due to its informal character
this network might not be apparent, but this comity of different partners is
most effective in establishing cooperation. The complexity of state tasks and
state obligations requires cooperation not only among magistrates and
elected authorities but also among civil servants of federal and cantonal administrations. This is the underlying philosophy of Article 44 of the Constitution, according to which the Confederation and the Cantons shall
cooperate and support each other in the fulfillment of their tasks.

According to Article 44 (2) the Cantons and the Confederation owe
each other mutual consideration and support and shall grant each other
administrative and judicial assistance. Article 47 requires the Confederation to respect cantonal autonomy. Moreover, disputes between the Cantons or between Cantons and the Confederation shall be resolved through
negotiation. Thus, in contrast to the German and other federal systems, in
the Swiss system disputes among Cantons and Confederation are seldom
resolved by court decision but, rather, by negotiation or by legislative or
constitutional amendments.

For example, ten years ago the people of the Canton of Basel Country-
side decided that Canton authorities should use all legal means in order to
prevent the construction of an atomic power plant in the neighbourhood
of the Canton. Some federal authorities, including the federal court,
would have considered such a legal mandate to be against the principle of

Bundestreue (loyalty to the federal state). However, the federal Parliament, when asked to approve this amendment (as is always the case with changes in cantonal constitutions), accepted it out of respect for cantonal sovereignty and popular democracy.

Since 1874, as a result of more than 140 constitutional amendments,[11] the originally extensive powers of the Cantons have slowly shifted to the federal level. Gradual integration into the European Union, along with bilateral treaties, may also have a centralizing effect on Swiss federalism. Taking these developments into account, the 1999 Constitution now mentions expressly: (1) the right of Cantons to participate in the foreign policy decisions of the federal government; (2) the general right to participate in internal federal legislation; and (3) the possibility for Cantons to regulate matters of general concern through international or intercantonal treaties.

The strengthening of the shared-rule principle has not led, as one might have expected, to a strengthening and widening of the powers of the second chamber; instead, this principle has been implemented by strengthening the possibilities for cantonal executive bodies to participate in federal decision-making processes. In order to participate in federal decision-making processes, cantonal executives have had to create a new body – one that represents all the cantonal governments. Thus, the widening of the shared-rule principle at the federal level has led directly to the establishment of the Council of Presidents (made up of the presidents of the Cantons), which in turn, has led to better cooperation between cantonal governments. The creativity of this cooperative (and executive) federalism is new, and may result in Switzerland having greater flexibility than it does now. For example, with regard to universities, the legislature has established a body – composed of representatives of cantonal governments and of the Federal Council – who must plan and establish strategies for developing federal and cantonal universities. With this new "superstructure" combining shared-rule and self-rule in the field of higher education, Switzerland is trying to meet the new challenge of a "European Space of Higher Education," as proclaimed in the Bologna-Declaration of 1999. There are also new tendencies, such as those in the field of professional education, that might lead to supracantonal cooperation on a regional basis.

It may well be that the new flexibility associated with intercantonal cooperation will lead to the establishment of real intercantonal bodies with specific democratic legitimacy – a legitimacy based on the citizenry and united by a specific functional focus (such as a school, hospital, or police region). Thus, Swiss federalism may produce new administrative bodies, new distinct regional parliaments and communities of voters, and new executive branches all united in order to efficiently fulfill specific tasks. Representative bodies with shared power could be supplemented by executive and administrative bodies with shared power. Still, the Federal

Assembly has a tendency, when creating new responsibilities, to impose specific systems of judicial administration on the Cantons.

The Supremacy Clause

According to the various systems of European continental law, the law forms a unity in which the Constitution, different treaties, and statutes, along with federal, cantonal, and municipal ordinances, are hierarchically classified. This is apparent in the German Basic Law as well as in the system adopted by the European Union. In Article 49 the Swiss Constitution determines that all levels of federal law take precedence over contrary cantonal law. According to this principle, even Federal Council ordinances take precedence over cantonal constitutional law. In addition, the Confederation has the duty to ensure that the Cantons respect federal law.

Article 49, Paragraph 1, of the Constitution, which provides for federal supremacy, also provides for the constitutionally guaranteed rights of citizen. In the case of a dispute between federal law and cantonal law, citizens may initiate public law action as a remedy in order to establish whether or not the latter contradicts the former. If there is a contradiction, then federal law prevails. However, federal authorities usually respect constitutionality – as the Constitution expects them to do.

Administrative Federalism and Enforcement

Contrary to the American and other systems of dual federalism, the Cantons implement federal law (i.e., administrative [*Vollzugs-*] federalism). Consequently, the federal administration is rather small in size and would not be capable of executing federal law by itself. While federal law binds the Cantons in terms of how they implement it, the Confederation must leave them as much leeway as possible and must shoulder the financial burden as well as take into account the particularities of each Canton (Article 46). Depending on the federal regulation, the Cantons have varying degrees of discretion in the execution of federal norms. Due to the diversity among Cantons with respect to size, topography, demography, and other structural elements, it is nearly impossible for the Confederation to take the particularities of the Cantons into account without granting them broad discretion.

Diversity and direct democracy at the cantonal level may be why the power of the federal government to enforce federal statutes within the Cantons is very limited. Historically, the Constitution was concerned mainly with conflict management rather than with enforcing federal laws within the Cantons. Swiss federalism has followed the European concept of administrative federalism. It is chiefly the responsibility of the Cantons to enforce federal law within cantonal territories. The Federal Council must control implementation; however, the tools with which it must work in order to do so are limited. Moreover, any particular federal competence to implement and enforce a law has to be determined by the appropriate statute. However, one potentially powerful tool remains: cantonal constitutions require the approval of the Federal Assembly. Thus, in the case of the emergence of the new Canton of Jura, the Federal Assembly did not approve a specific provision of the cantonal Constitution because it believed that it violated the principle of respect and tolerance, which is basic to any intergovernmental relationship. The offending provision in the proposed Jura Constitution mandated all cantonal authorities to influence the people of the Jura region in the neighbouring Canton of Bern to join the new Canton. One may note that, in the federal Constitution, this article has been deleted, but it remains in the cantonal Constitution!

Non-Promotion of Equal Living Conditions

Article 72 (2) of the German Basic Law provides for general federal legislative power to promote the standard of law necessary to the establishment of equal living conditions throughout the country. A similar provision is to be found in Article 130 of the Spanish Constitution, which provides that the "public authorities shall attend to the modernization and development of all economic sectors, particularly of agriculture, livestock raising, fishing, and handicrafts, in order to equalize the standard of living of all Spaniards." Modern constitutions generally require equal rights and equal opportunities, but not equal results.

The Swiss Constitution, however, guarantees neither equal opportunities nor equal results. Swiss federalism does *not* promote equality of living conditions among the Cantons. Diversity and autonomy can only be upheld if a certain degree of economic discrepancy among different Cantons – and even among different municipalities – is permitted. For the sake of the autonomy of the Cantons, Swiss federalism has always accepted this inequality. Equalization (of this sort) would mean centralization, and most Swiss people believe that this would imperil Switzerland's diversity.

With possible integration into the European Union, which promotes an open market based on equal opportunities, Switzerland may have to face a new era of federalism. Thus the Federal Assembly has already put into force a law guaranteeing equal opportunities with regard to Switzerland's internal market. According to this act, quite a number of cantonal legislative modifications would be required in order to ensure the eradication of intercantonal discrimination. However, according to evaluations based on Article 170 of the Constitution, most Cantons have not followed these federal requirements.

In a state with a fragmented society, the issue of equality pertains not only to individuals but also to the status of different cultural communities and religions. Equality of communities may often take priority over equality of individuals. This may be why the 1874 Constitution did not – and why the 1999 Constitution still does not – contain any provision guaranteeing equal opportunities among individuals or equal living conditions for all. Only the proposed constitutional amendment on equalization of finances (discussed below) provides, in Article 43, Paragraph 4, that basic state services must be equally available to all.

Spending Power

Unlike the United States, which accepts the general spending power of the federal executive, Switzerland can only give grants or subventions when explicitly empowered to do so by a federal statute. In addition, the federal legislature can only provide spending in a federal statute if this falls within the framework of federal government power. Unlike in Germany, in Switzerland the budget is not considered to be a statute. Thus the Federal Assembly cannot empower the Federal Council to make financial decisions through the budget. The budget is only considered to be a licence to spend if there is another general statute that provides a specific spending power with specific goals. Thus federal power cannot be indirectly enforced through general spending power, as it can in other federations.

SPECIFIC POWERS OF THE CONFEDERATION

Security

Switzerland has no professional army: its "army" is organized as a militia. Its main functions, due to the principle of neutrality, are the prevention of war, the maintenance of peace, the defence of the country, and the protection of the population. Furthermore, the Swiss army supports civil authorities in their efforts to repel serious threats to internal security as well as in other exceptional circumstances (Article 58 [2]).[12] According to Article 59, every Swiss man is required to perform military service. If a man refuses to comply with this fundamental obligation (*Dienstpflicht*), Article 81 of the Federal Military Penal Act allows for imprisonment of up to eighteen months. While alternative service is possible, it lasts longer than the military service. Military service is voluntary for Swiss women.

The use of the army is a federal matter. The Federal Council is entitled to take measures to secure the external security, independence, and neutrality of Switzerland (Article 185 [1]). According to Article 168 (1), during cases of external threat to national security, when a large contingent of troops may be assigned to combat, the Federal Assembly must elect the general and commander-in-chief of the Swiss army (Article 85 [1] of the Federal Military Act, SR 510.10). Until his/her election, however, the control of the military remains in the hands of the Federal Council, which is to use it on a provisional basis (Article 85 [2] of the Federal Military Act). Even after the general is elected, the Federal Council remains the supreme organ of the executive branch, giving the general his/her commission (Article 86 of the Federal Military Act). The general is elected only in case of, and only during the time of, major external threats to national security.

The federal Constitution does not provide a general police power for the Confederation. Article 57 conveys the responsibility for security jointly to the Cantons and the Confederation, which, within the frameworks of their respective constitutional powers, are responsible for protecting the population. Until now the people and the Cantons have regularly refused to empower the federal government with a specific police force that would enable it to guarantee law and order throughout the country. Unlike the United States (with the Federal Bureau of Investigation) and Germany (with the *Bundesgrenzschutz*), Switzerland has no specific police force available. When it is asked to provide specific protection, the Federal Council usually provides the army with a specific police task, although the army is composed of militia soldiers who have only limited professional training for specific police responsibilities. As the Cantons are responsible for protecting their citizens and for guaranteeing law and order, they have installed cantonal police, which often share responsibilities with municipal police (the municipalities also being responsible for protecting their citizens and for upholding law and order at the municipal level).

According to Article 52 (1), the Confederation shall protect the constitutional order of the Cantons. While primary responsibility for ensuring constitutional order lies with the Cantons (Article 57), if a particular Canton cannot ensure its own order, then the Confederation and the other Cantons are called upon to support it (principle of comity). This duty of support is based on Article 44 (1)-(2), which states that the Confederation and the Cantons shall support each other in the fulfillment of their tasks.

A *federal intervention* is foreseen when the inner order of a Canton is disturbed or threatened and cannot be protected by the Canton alone or with the help of other Cantons (Article 52 [2]). The Confederation will only intervene when the general support given to the Canton is not sufficient to reestablish the constitutional order and when the disturbance of the constitutional order does not emanate from a cantonal institution or agency. As a last resort, the Confederation will intervene with military force.

The territory of the Cantons is defined neither in the Constitution nor in other legal documents. At the time of the formation of the federation in 1848 cantonal territory was not disputed, and only those areas that, later, were subject to disputes and agreements have been defined in treaties or in court opinions. Nonetheless, the Confederation has the duty to protect the existence and territory of the Cantons (Article 53 [1]). Changes in the number of Cantons or in the redistribution of territory are only permissible in accordance with the constitutional procedure set down in Article 53 (2)-(3).

The Constitutions of 1848 and 1874, respectively, did not foresee the need for a procedure for territorial modifications. The rules that were recently introduced in Article 53 were developed according to the experience of the secession of the Jura territory from the Canton of Bern.

The current procedure for territorial changes includes as its main element the consent of the concerned populations. Article 53 distinguishes three different cases of modifications that concern the existence and territory of the Cantons. The modification can concern the total number of Cantons or it can change their status (Article 53 [2]). The number of Cantons can be increased or decreased, and the status of a Canton can be changed (e.g., by elevating a so-called half Canton to the status of a full Canton). In these cases the modification must be based on the consent of the populations concerned, of the Cantons concerned, and of the whole Swiss population. This procedure foresees a cascade of popular votes at the district and/or municipal level, at the cantonal level, and at the federal level, with the result being the highest possible legitimacy for the new boundaries. The creation of a new Canton needs the consent of: (1) the population inhabiting it, (2) the population inhabiting the Canton to which the territory formerly belonged, (3) the Swiss population as a whole, and (4) a majority of cantonal populations. Changes in the number and the status of the Cantons must fulfill the requirements of a constitutional revision because they entail amendments to the constitutional text (i.e., Article 1 in the case of enumeration of the Cantons, Articles 142 and 150 [2] in the case of a change of status).

Finally, Switzerland is one of the very few countries that has established a procedure for changing the structural composition of its federal units. If a part of the population were to want to secede from Switzerland, then this article might also become, by analogy, the legal ground for a secession procedure.

Foreign Affairs

Switzerland's foreign policy aims at alleviating world poverty, promoting respect for human rights, democracy, the peaceful coexistence of nations, and the preservation of natural resources (Article 54 [2]). The preceding provision outlines the various pillars of Swiss foreign policy, which are: (1) the relationship between Switzerland and Europe, (2) peace and security, and

(3) international development. Surprisingly, considering its importance to Switzerland, the Constitution does not expressly mention foreign trade policy (except for Article 101 [1], which grants to the Confederation the power to safeguard the interests of the Swiss economy abroad).

Foreign relations and treaty making are the prerogative of the sovereign state and are a federal matter (Article 54 [1]). However, the Cantons can participate in the preparation of foreign policy decisions that concern their powers or essential interests. In addition, the Confederation, in a timely manner, is to fully inform and consult with the Cantons. Furthermore, the position of the Cantons has particular weight whenever their powers are concerned. In these cases, the interested Canton will participate in international negotiations as appropriate (Article 55).

As a rule, relations between the Cantons and foreign countries are conducted by the Confederation on behalf of the Cantons. However, according to Article 56 (1), the Cantons are entitled to conclude treaties with foreign nations. The Constitution requires that: (1) the matter be within the scope of the powers of the Cantons (Article 56 [1]); (2) the treaty between one or more Cantons and a foreign nation is not contrary to the law or the interests of the Confederation or to the laws of other Cantons (Article 56 [2]); and (3) the Cantons inform the Confederation before the conclusion of a treaty (Article 56 [2]). The Cantons are allowed to deal directly with lower ranking foreign authorities (Article 56 [3] of the Constitution). In all other cases, the Confederation will act on behalf of the Cantons.

In the 1999 Constitution the element of cooperation (which is included in the shared-rule principle) has, as a compensation for diminished cantonal autonomy, gained in importance. In the context of foreign affairs, as noted, the Constitution underlines the role of the Cantons in the decision-making process as well as the relations between the Cantons and foreign nations. In accord with the concept of cooperative federalism, Article 55 (1) integrates the Cantons into the foreign policy decision-making process when their powers and essential interests are at stake. Additionally, in order to avoid centralization through foreign policy, the Federal Participation Act reconfirms the role of the Cantons in the federal foreign policy process, albeit without adding anything new to Article 55. Besides the right of the Canton to be timely and fully informed, and the obligation of the Confederation to consult with it (Article 55 [2]), the Constitution, as appropriate, grants the Cantons further participatory rights in international negotiations (Article 55 [3]).

As a result of the inadequate flow of information during the negotiations for entry into the European Economic Space in the 1990s, the Conference of the Cantonal Governments (*Konferenz der Kantonsregierungen*) was created by intercantonal agreement in 1993. The conference is not focused exclusively either on foreign policy or on European Union policy; rather, it aims to coordinate the decision-making process among Cantons so that they can exercise joint influence at the federal level. All twenty-six Cantons are members of the conference, and the vote of eighteen of them is sufficient to ratify a decision. Additionally, the conference sends a delegate to the European Union in Brussels. This delegate serves both to provide information to the conference and to augment its influence on the European Union.

Fiscal System

All three levels of government (federal, cantonal, and municipal) may raise taxes. The citizens pay about one-third of their taxes to each level of government. According to Article 127 (1) the general principles of taxation – particularly the circle of taxpayers, the object of the tax, and its calculation – shall be established by a statute submitted to a referendum.

In the areas of personal and corporate income tax, and corporate capital tax, the Confederation and the Cantons have concurrent powers; but here the federal government is very much the junior partner. The Constitution explicitly limits the federal government's power to raise income tax to 11 percent of the income of individuals (Article 128), and it limits value-added tax to 6.5 percent (Article 130). This is the outcome of different compromises between the Christian Democratic Party and the French-speaking Cantons, who are concerned with defending their autonomy. The limited federal value-added tax is a compromise between labour and business interests. Economic groups (including business) were interested in promoting equal opportunities and thus promoting equality through a value-added tax; labour, on the other hand, was interested in equalizing social disparities, which can only be achieved through a progressive income tax. Finally, populist parties were interested in plain and explicit constitutional competences as any constitutional amendment needs to be submitted to popular referendum. The federal power to levy direct taxes and the value-added tax expires in 2006 (Articles 13 and 14 Transitory Provisions). The federal government is therefore only accorded a provisional power in this case. Mainly due to these constitutional limitations, in Switzerland there is a comparatively low level of fiscal centralization.

Direct taxes are the most important aspect of cantonal and municipal tax revenue. According to Article 127 (3) intercantonal double taxation is prohibited, and the Confederation is to take the necessary measures to prevent it. Cantonal income tax is levied at one's place of residence. In order to prevent intercantonal double taxation corporate taxes are levied at the branches where the income was generated. This tax splitting favours fiscal competition. Within the limits of the federal Constitution, the

Cantons can decide on the type of taxes they levy, the tax base, the tax scale, the tax rate, and exemptions. Direct taxes, including federal taxes, are assessed and collected by the Cantons (Article 128 [4]). In some cases religious communities also have the right to levy taxes, which are then equally assessed and collected by the Cantons.

The Swiss taxation system has, inter alia, consequences with regard to tax inequalities among Cantons and municipalities. The global tax burden of a representative taxpayer differs decisively from one Canton to the other (57 to 131 index points by a mean of 100). Depending on their domiciles, citizens in one Canton may pay up to 2.5 times more taxes than do citizens of another Canton. The Constitution provides only a limited federal competence to harmonize the cantonal taxation system (Article 129 [2]). The tax scales, tax rates, and tax exempt amounts are decided either by a cantonal parliament or by popular cantonal referendum (without the intervention of the federal government or legislature). Federal harmonization can only concern tax liability, tax object, taxation period, and procedural and criminal taxation law.

Not only does the tax burden differ decisively among Cantons, but so does the Canton's financial capacity. The yardstick for measuring the financial capacity of the Cantons is established by federal regulations. It is based on a balancing of different indices, such as GDP per inhabitant, fiscal burden, fiscal revenue, and cantonal financial need. The financially weakest Canton has a 7.27 times lower financial capacity than does the financially strongest Canton.

Due to these differences, fiscal equalization has gained in importance. In Switzerland, fiscal equalization aims at giving the Cantons enough revenue to assure that they can provide a minimal – not an equal – level of services. In Article 46 (3) the Confederation is mandated to ensure equitable fiscal equalization. The basis for some fiscal equalization is provided in Article 135, which states that the Confederation is to promote fiscal equalization among the Cantons. When granting subsidies the Confederation is to take the revenue capacities of the Cantons and the special situation of the mountainous regions into account. Article 128 (4) provides that at least one-sixth of the amount raised through federal direct taxes is to be used for fiscal equalization among Cantons.

In October 2003 the Swiss Federal Assembly approved a fundamental new concept of fiscal equalization entailing important changes to the system. This concept was submitted to popular referendum in autumn 2004 and was accepted by the people (i.e., all Swiss voters, as a single constituency) and the Cantons (i.e., voters from each Canton, with the Canton as the constituency). The new equalization scheme is part of a broader reform to disentangle federal and cantonal responsibilities and, in the process, to provide a renewed basis for ensuring that fiscally weaker cantons can handle additional tasks. Basically, this proposal provides that the Confederation should only be responsible for tasks that Cantons can not fulfill themselves or that require uniform regulation. The objective is to ensure that the level of government (Confederation/Canton) that provides the service also pays the costs. In order to achieve these goals the federal government can decide that some intercantonal treaties of cooperation are mandatory for all Cantons. And, as part of the overall bargain, there would be an enhanced equalization fund.

Other Powers

As there is no general list for the distribution of powers it is only possible, through the appended table, to give a general idea of the distribution of powers in Switzerland. As already noted, each power delegated to the federal government requires a specific provision in the Constitution. The Constitution is divided into different titles. Title III deals with the relationship between the Confederation, the Cantons, and the municipalities. Chapter 3 of this title deals explicitly with the powers of the Confederation. It is divided into nine sections (Foreign Relations, Security, Culture, Environment, Transport, Energy and Communication, Economy, Social Security, and Foreigners). As noted above, the Constitution often delegates to the federal government not only a specific power but also the goals towards which this power should be directed. The system of distribution of powers follows the traditional concept, which distinguishes between exclusively federal, exclusively cantonal, and concurrent powers.

CONCLUSION

Swiss federalism is the result of a long historical process that has been shaped by different actors, institutions, and interests. Three major factors can be identified:

1 The presence of territorial units differing in terms of culture, language, religion, and democratic perception but forced to cooperate for economic and political reasons;
2 A constitution establishing the general principles of democracy and, through a bottom-up approach, dividing powers between the different levels of government; and
3 The extensive use of direct democratic (i.e., popular vote-based) tools as a way of conveying legitimacy to the constitutional and institutional expression of federal principles.

It is also important to stress that Switzerland must constantly seek the right equilibrium between its federalist commitment and the functional requirements of a modern state. This equilibrium cannot be fixed once and for all but, rather, must be the result of political contest.

A full understanding of federalism must therefore take into account how federal principles are put into practice and how they are lived every day. From time to time, such principles have to be adapted or even changed. In Switzerland the main works in progress are the reform of fiscal equalization and the allocation of tasks between the Confederation and the Cantons; intercantonal and transborder cooperation; and, in some Cantons, the drafting of new constitutions.

Will Switzerland be able to cope with globalization? Is Switzerland able to change? Federalism is a political formula that is flexible and that, consequently, is always changing and adapting. Thanks to the system of direct democracy and flexible federalism, Switzerland's capacity for adaptation is greater than many would expect. Direct democracy prevents extreme solutions, provides a high degree of legitimacy for changes, and guarantees that legal provisions will be implemented. If the challenge of European integration does not question these basic principles, which I do not think it will, then Switzerland should be able to adapt its system without losing its identity.

Finally, there is the unsolved problem of modern migration. Today, 20 percent of the people living in Switzerland are foreigners who do not have the right to participate in the democratic process. Can we still claim to be a democracy if we exclude one-fifth of the population? What, given our concepts of diversity and democracy, are our options for becoming more inclusive? Up until now, no acceptable answers have been found.

ANNEX

Table of the distribution of powers according to different fields of state activity[13]

Basic features and financial system

Field	Power	CO	SP	EF	Federal and cantonal						P	EC
					Legisl.		Implement.					
					EF	SH	EF	SH	EC	FC		
Basic Features												
	Residual Power	Art. 3	CA	N	N	N	N	N	N	N	N	Y
	Subsidiarity	Art. 42	FR	N	N	Y	N	Y	N	N	N	N
	Implementation of Federal Law	Art. 46	CA	N	N	Y	N	N	Y	Y	N	Y
	Supremacy of Federal Law	Art. 49	FR	Y	Y	Y	Y	Y	Y	Y	Y	Y
	Cantonal Constitutions	Art. 51	DE	N	N	N	N	Y	N	Y	N	Y
	Communes	Art. 50	AU	N	N	N	N	N	Y	N	N	Y
	Cantonal Existence	Art. 52	PO	N	N	Y	N	Y	N	N	Y	N
Financial System		CH3										
	Financial Management	Art. 126	BA	N	Y	N	N	N	N	N	Y	N
	Taxing Principles	Art. 127	N	N	Y	N	N	N	N	N	N	
	Direct Taxes	Art. 128	N	Y	YL	N	N	Y	N	Y	Y	N
	Harmonization of Taxes	Art. 129	N	N	N	YP	N	Y	N	N	N	N
	Value Added Tax	Art. 130	N	Y	YL	N	Y	N	N	N	N	N
	Consumption Tax	Art. 131	N	N	YC	N	Y	N	N	N	N	N
	Stamp and Withholding Taxes	Art. 132	N	Y	Y	N	Y	N	N	N	N	N
	Customs	Art. 133	FR	Y	Y	N	Y	N	N	N	N	N
	Financial Equalization	Art. 134	FR	Y	Y	N	N	Y	N	N	N	N

Foreign affairs, security, education, and culture

Relations with Foreign Countries		S1										
	Foreign Affairs	Art. 54	A	Y	N	N	N	Y	N	N	n	n
	Cantonal Relations with Foreign Countries	Art. 56	N	N	N	N	N	Y	N	Y	Y	N
Security National and Civil Defence		S2										
	Security	Art. 57	CR	N	N	Y	N	Y	N	Y	Y	N
	Army	Art. 60	N	N	Y	N	N	Y	N	Y	N	N
	Civil Defence	Art. 61	FR		Y	N	N	Y	N	Y	N	N
Education Research Culture		S3										
	Education	Art. 62	CA	N	YG	N	N	N	Y	N	N	Y
	Universities	Art. 63	CR	N	YG	N	N	Y	N	Y	P	N
	Professional Education	Art. 63	N	N	N	Y	N	Y	N	N	N	N
	Research	Art. 64	N	N	N	Y	N	Y	N	Y	Y	N
	Statistics	Art. 65	N	N	N	Y	N	Y	N	Y	Y	N
	Educational Needs of Adults and Young People	Art. 67	SU	N	N	YC	N	y	Y	Y	N	(Y)
	Sport	Art. 68	PR	N	N	Y	N	Y	N	N	N	N
	Culture	Art. 69	CA	N	N	PR	N	(y)	N	Y	N	Y
	Languages	Art. 70	RU	N		N	YO	N	N	N	YO	Y
	Cinema	Art. 71	EN	N	N	Y	N	Y	N	Y	N	N
	Church and State	Art. 72	CA	N	N	RU	N	N	Y	N	N	Y

Environment and public transport

Environment and Land Use Planning		S4										
	Sustainable Development	Art. 73	CP	N	N	Y	N	Y	N	Y	N	N
	Environment Protection	Art. 74	RP	N	N	Y	N	Y	N	Y	N	N
	Land Use Planning	Art. 75	CR	N	N	YP	N	N	Y	Y	N	N

	Water	Art. 76	RP	N	N	Y	N	Y	N	Y	N	N
	Forests	Art. 77	RP	N	N	Y	N	Y	N	Y	N	N
	Nature and Cultural Heritage	Art. 78	CA	N	N	YP	N	Y	N	Y	N	N
	Hunting and Fishing	Art. 79	N	N	N	YP	N	Y	N	Y	N	N
	Protection of Animals	Art. 80	RP	N	N	YP	N	Y	N	Y	N	N
Public Works and Transport		S5										
	Public Works	Art. 81	CI	N	N	Y	N	Y	N	Y	Y	N
	Road Traffic	Art. 81	N	N	Y	N	N	Y	N	Y	N	N
	National Highways	Art. 83	CP	ne	N	Y	N	Y	N	Y	N	BU
	Alpine Transit	Art. 84	RP	N	Y	N	N	Y	N	N	N	N
	Transport	Art. 87	N	FR	Y	N	N	Y	N	N	N	N
	Foot Paths and Hiking Trails	Art. 88	N	N	N	YP	N	Y	N	N	N	N

Energy, communication, and the economy

Energy and Communications		S6										
	Energy Policy	Art. 89	CP	N	YP	Y	N	Y	N	Y	N	N
	Nuclear Energy	Art. 90	N	N	Y	N	N	Y	N	Y	N	N
	Energy Transport	Art. 91	N	N	Y	N	N	Y	N	Y	N	N
	Postal and Telecommunication Services	Art. 92	FR	Y	Y	N	Y	N	N	N	N	N
	Radio, Television	Art. 93	CR	Y	Y	N	Y	N	N	N	N	N
Economy		S7										
	Gainful Private Economic Activity	Art. 95	N	N	N	Y	N	Y	N	N	N	N
	Competition Policy	Art. 96	N	Y	Y	N	Y	N	N	N	N	N
	Consumer Protection	Art. 97	CR	N	N	Y	N	Y	N	N	N	N
	Banking Insurance	Art. 98	N	Y	Y	N	N	Y	N	N	N	N
	Monetary Policy	Art. 99	N	Y	Y	N	N	Y	N	N	N	N
	Cyclical Economic Policy	Art. 100	FR	N	Y	N	N	Y	N	N	N	N
	Foreign Trade	Art. 101	FR	Y	Y	N	N	Y	N	Y	N	N

Maintaining Stocks of Essential Goods and Services	Art. 102	FR	Y	Y	N	N	Y	N	Y	N	N
Structural Policy	Art. 103	FR	N	N	Y	N	Y	N	N	N	N
Agriculture	Art. 104	FR	N	N	Y	N	Y	N	N	N	N
Alcohol	Art. 105	FR	Y	Y	N	N	Y	N	N	N	N
Games of Chance	Art. 106	FR	Y	Y	N	N	Y	N	Y	N	N
Weapons and Military Material	Art. 107	N	Y	Y	N	N	Y	N	Y	N	N

Social security, health, foreigners, and civil and criminal law

Housing, Work, Social Security and Health	S8										
Promotion: Construction, Access to Ownership	Art. 108	FR	N	Y	N	N	Y	N	Y	N	N
Leasehold	Art. 109	N	N	N	Y	N	Y	N	Y	N	N
Labour	Art. 110	N	N	N	Y	N	Y	N	Y	N	N
Old Age Survivors Disability Responsibility	Art. 111	EN	FR	Y	N	N	Y	N	Y	N	N
Old Age Survivors, Disability Insurance	Art. 112	mi	FR	Y	N	N	Y	N	Y	N	N
Pension Plans	Art. 113	PE	FR	Y	N	N	Y	N	Y	N	N
Unemployment Insurance	Art. 114	EN	FR	Y	N	N	Y	N	Y	N	N
Assistance to those in Need	Art. 115	CA	N	N	SU	N	Y	N	Y	N	Y
Family Allowance and Maternity Insurance	Art. 116	RP	N	N	RP	N	Y	N	Y	N	Y
Health and Accident Insurance	Art. 117	CR	Y	Y	N	N	Y	N	N	N	N
Protection of Health	Art. 118	CA	N	N	YT	N	Y	N	N	N	N
Procreation, Genetic Engineering involving humans	Art. 119	AP	N	N	Y	N	Y	N	Y	N	N

	Medical Transplants	Art. 119a	N	N	N	SU	N	Y	N	Y	N	Y
	Genetic Engineering (Non-Humans)	Art. 120	AP	N	N	Y	N	Y	N	Y	N	N
Foreigners	Establishment and Residence	Art. 121	N	FR	Y	N	N	Y	N	Y	N	N
Civil, Criminal Law		S10										
	Civil Law	Art. 122	N	FR	N	Y	N	Y	N	Y	N	N
	Aid to Victims of Criminal Acts	Art. 124	RC	N	N	Y	N	Y	N	N	N	N
	Weights, Measures	Art. 125	N	FR	Y	N	N	Y	N	N	N	N

NOTES

1 For statistical information about language and religion in Switzerland, please see: <http://www.bfs.admin.ch/bfs/portal/fr/index/themen/bevoelkerung/sprachen_religionen.html> (accessed 29 June 2005).

2 For the text of the Swiss Constitution, see: <http://www.admin.ch/ch/itl/rs/1/c101ENG.pdf> (accessed 29 June 2005).

3 See table annexed to this chapter.

4 For further discussison on this theme, see Thomas Fleiner and Lidija Basta Fleiner, *Allgemeine Staatslehre*, 3rd ed. (Heidelberg: Springer, 2004); and Thomas Fleiner, Nicole Toepperwien, and Alexander Misic, "Switzerland," *International Encyclopedia of Laws: Constitutional Law*, ed. André Alen (Deventer: Kluwer, 2004).

5 Officially Switzerland is still called a "Confederation" in French and Italian; the German word is "Eidgenossenschaft," which cannot be translated. In this chapter I always use the official term – "Confederation" even though I'm speaking of what, technically, is a "federation." The phrase "the Confederation" refers to the federal (or central) government.

6 Reverdin Olivier, *Introducing Switzerland* (Lausanne: Development of Trade, 1967).

7 Jonathan Steinberg, *Why Switzerland?* (Cambridge: Cambridge University Press, 1976).

8 Raoul Blindenbacher and Arnold Koller, eds., *Federalism in a Changing World* (Montreal: McGill-Queen's University Press, 2003); Telford Hamish, "Federalism in Multinational Societies: Switzerland, Canada and India," *Mapping Canadian Federalism for India*, ed. Rekha Saxena (Delhi: Konark, 2002), p. 52.

9 Kenneth D. McRae, "Precepts for Linguistic Peace: The Case of Switzerland," *Language and the State: The Law and Politics of Identity*, ed. David Schneiderman

(Cowansville: Editions Y. Blais, 1991), p. 167; Grin François, "Language Policy Developments in Switzerland: Needs, Opportunities and Priorities for the Next Few Years," *Revue Suisse de Science Politique* 3: 108–113.

10 Nicolas Schmitt, *The Foreign Relations of Swiss Cantons within the Frame of the New 1999 Swiss Constitution* (Fribourg: PIFF, 2000), p. 165.

11 <http://www.admin.ch/ch/d/pore/va/index.html> (accessed 28 June 2005).

12 Unless otherwise indicated, references to articles in this section are from the 1999 Constitution.

13 Explanations and abbreviations for the distribution of powers table:
Column 1 indicates the different fields of powers according to Chapter 2 of the Constitution; Column 2 labels the power and Column 3 indicates the article in the Constitution. Column 4 gives the abbreviations for specific goals and obligations that the Confederation has to observe when using the specific power. Column 5 indicates whether the federal power is exclusive, and it also indicates where the federal government does not have an exclusive power but does have a primary responsibility to legislate. The next six columns indicate the distribution of legislative, executive, and judicial power between the Confederation and the Cantons. In some cases the federal government has the exclusive legislative power, but implementation may be shared between it and the Cantons. In some cases the Confederation and the Cantons share legislative power. The last column indicates the power of the courts. In most cases federal laws are implemented by the Cantons. Although cantonal administrative courts control implementation, in the final instance the federal court can control cantonal administrative decisions. The possibility of the federal court controlling cantonal jurisdiction is indicated by the penultimate column.

ABBREVIATIONS

A	Aims of Foreign Policy: Independence, prosperity, welfare, alleviation of poverty, human rights, democracy, peace, natural resources
AP	Abuse Protection
AU	Guarantee of Autonomy
BA	Financial Balance
BU	Build and Construct
CA	Primary Cantonal Responsibility
CC	Civil and Criminal Law, Weights and Measures
CI	Common Interest
CI PR	Civil Law and Civil Procedure
CO	Constitution
CP	Cooperation Responsibility of Confederation and Cantons
CR	Coordination Responsibility
CR LA	Criminal Law and Procedure

CH	Chapter
CP	Federal Power only based on a Constitutional provision
DE	Guarantee of Democratic System
EC	Exclusive Cantonal
EF	Exclusive Federal
EN	Ensure an adequate social security provision
FC	Implementing Administrative Decisions is controlled by cantonal administrative courts but, finally, is under the jurisdiction of federal administrative courts
FR	Primary Confederal Responsibility
MI	Pension must be sufficient to cover basic living expenses
NE	National Network
N	No
n	no, with exceptions
P	Parallel Powers of Confederation and Cantons
PE	Company Pensions Plans together wit the old age insurance should permit to maintain previous standard of living
PO	Protection
PR	Responsibility to promote
PROF	Professional Education
RC	Common Responsibility of Cantons and Confederation
RP	Responsibility to protect
RU	Responsibility for common understanding
S	Section
SECU	Social Security (Age, Disability)
SH	Shared Power
SU	Supplement Cantonal Measures
SP	Special Obligation
SU DE	Sustainable Development
STA	Statistics
VI	Aid to Victims of Criminal Acts
Y	Yes
y	yes, with exceptions
YC	Limited to specific products
YL	Limited to exact value
YP	Limited to principles
YO	Restricted to the use of official languages
YT	Limit to its powers for food, drugs, organic material etc; fighting contagious diseases, protection against ionising radiation
yc	May only complement Cantonal measures
YG	Limited to federal grant

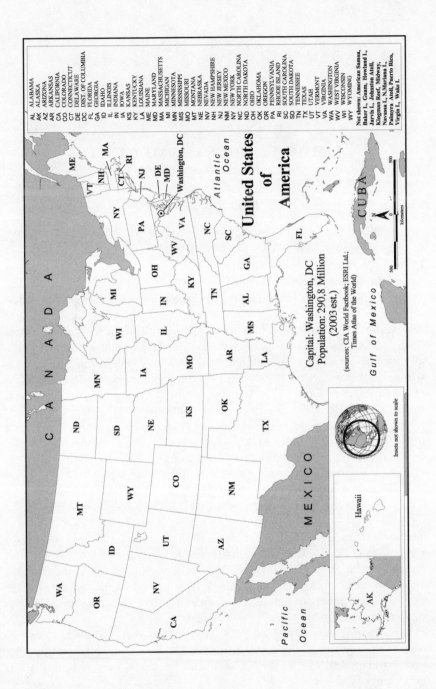

United States
of
America

Capital: Washington, DC
Population: 290,8 Million
(2003 est.)

(sources: CIA World Factbook; ESRI Ltd.;
Times Atlas of the World)

Not shown: American Samoa,
Baker I., Guam, Howland I.,
Jarvis I., Johnston Atoll,
Kingman Reef, Midway,
Navassa I., N.Mariana I.,
Palmyra Atoll, Puerto Rico,
Virgin I., Wake I.

AL	ALABAMA
AK	ALASKA
AZ	ARIZONA
AR	ARKANSAS
CA	CALIFORNIA
CO	COLORADO
CT	CONNECTICUT
DE	DELAWARE
DC	DIST OF COLUMBIA
FL	FLORIDA
GA	GEORGIA
ID	IDAHO
IL	ILLINOIS
IN	INDIANA
IA	IOWA
KS	KANSAS
KY	KENTUCKY
LA	LOUISIANA
ME	MAINE
MD	MARYLAND
MA	MASSACHUSETTS
MI	MICHIGAN
MN	MINNESOTA
MS	MISSISSIPPI
MO	MISSOURI
MT	MONTANA
NE	NEBRASKA
NV	NEVADA
NH	NEW HAMPSHIRE
NJ	NEW JERSEY
NM	NEW MEXICO
NY	NEW YORK
NC	NORTH CAROLINA
ND	NORTH DAKOTA
OH	OHIO
OK	OKLAHOMA
OR	OREGON
PA	PENNSYLVANIA
RI	RHODE ISLAND
SC	SOUTH CAROLINA
SD	SOUTH DAKOTA
TN	TENNESSEE
TX	TEXAS
UT	UTAH
VT	VERMONT
VA	VIRGINIA
WA	WASHINGTON
WV	WEST VIRGINIA
WI	WISCONSIN
WY	WYOMING

CANADA

MEXICO

CUBA

Atlantic Ocean

Gulf of Mexico

Pacific Ocean

Washington, DC

kilometers

Insets not shown to scale

Hawaii

AK

United States of America

ELLIS KATZ

In the United States the distribution of powers and responsibilities is better understood as a delegation of powers by the Constitution to the federal government than as a full distribution of powers between the federal government and the states. Rather than listing and separating the powers of the national and state governments, the Constitution of the United States delegates certain specified powers to the federal government and reserves all other powers, unless prohibited, to the states. This approach to the distribution of powers and responsibilities reflects the peculiar historical circumstances that led to the writing of the Constitution, the framers' overriding concern with the protection of liberty, and the state of political science at the end of the eighteenth century. It has led to an overlapping of powers and responsibilities in the actual operation of contemporary American federalism, creating unique patterns of cooperation and conflict between the national government and the states.

OVERVIEW OF THE AMERICAN FEDERATION

The American federation is composed of fifty states, a federal district (Washington, D.C.), fourteen territories (American Samoa, Guam, the Northern Marianas, Puerto Rico, the Virgin Islands of the United States, and nine small, largely uninhabited islands and atolls in the Pacific Ocean), and numerous federally recognized Indian (i.e., aboriginal) tribes on Indian reservations.

Each American state enjoys equal constitutional status. Each is equally represented in the U.S. Senate, and each has equal authority to frame its own government, enact its own laws, and create its own system of local government.

The District of Columbia (often referred to as Washington or Washington, D.C.) is subject to control by the Congress, but the latter has delegated a great deal of home rule to a locally elected mayor and council. The District of Columbia has an elected, non-voting observer in the House of Representatives but is not represented in the Senate. There have been a number of unsuccessful attempts to gain full representation for the District of Columbia in both the House of Representatives and the Senate. Since the enactment of the Twenty-Third Amendment in 1961, residents of the District of Columbia can vote for presidential and vice-presidential electors.

Relations with territories are governed by statutes and agreements. They differ from one territory to another, with the largest territories generally enjoying the most self-government. Puerto Rico, the largest territory, has rejected both independence and statehood in three referendums, apparently preferring to keep its status as a commonwealth. Puerto Rico has a non-voting observer in the House of Representatives, but residents of Puerto Rico cannot vote in presidential elections.[1]

Relations with the Indian Tribes are governed by statutes and treaties. Indians living on reservations enjoy considerable autonomy. Tribal governments are permitted to adopt constitutions, regulate their internal affairs, hold elections, and enforce their own laws. Generally, federal law prohibits the states from taxing or regulating tribes or extending judicial power over them. Off the reservation, however, individual Indians are usually subject to the same state laws as are any other state residents.

Demographic Profile

In the year 2000 the population of the United States was 285,230,516, making it the third most populous country in the world. Its landmass of 9,629,091 square kilometres ranks third (after Russia and Canada) among the countries of the world. Its per capita GDP of $36,200 also ranks third (after Bermuda and Luxembourg).

Because there is no official census of religion, one can only estimate the number of adherents to various organized religions. A majority of the population of the United States is Christian. Between 75 percent and 85 percent of the population identify themselves as Christian, about one-third Roman Catholic and two-thirds Protestant. The 160 million or so Protestants are divided into at least 220 different denominations. Estimates for the number of Jews range between 2.8 million and 5.0 million. Estimates for the number of Muslims vary considerably, but they tend to cluster around 3 million. There are close to 2 million Buddhists and 1 million Hindus. No other religion approaches 1 million adherents.

The United States is approximately 84.0 percent white (Caucasian), 12.5 percent African American, and 3.5 percent Asian. In the 2000 Census, approximately 7 million Americans identified themselves as biracial. The United States has a growing Hispanic population, estimated in 2000 at almost 13 percent. Approximately 2.5 million individuals identify themselves as Native Americans, or Indians.[2] There is no official language in the United States, although there is a political movement to have English declared the official language. English is by far the most widely spoken and understood language, although about 20 percent of Americans report that they speak some language other than English in their homes.

There is considerable variation in the population diversity from one region of the country to another. For example, African Americans tend to live in the South or in the larger cities of the Northeast and Great Lakes region, while most Hispanics live in California, the Southwestern states, and in Florida and Texas. Many Asian Americans live in California, Oregon, and Washington, the three American states that border on the Pacific Ocean.

THE FEDERAL CONSTITUTION IN HISTORICAL-CULTURAL CONTEXT

The United States began as thirteen separate British colonies along the Atlantic seacoast, from what is now the State of Maine to present-day Georgia. All of the colonies were founded during the seventeenth century. There was considerable self-government in the colonies, and all of them had written charters. Some had constitutions adopted by the colonists themselves. Until the 1760s the United Kingdom ruled the colonies with a loose hand, dealing with individual colonies as the need might arise.

The French and Indian Wars of 1754–63 and the changes in British policy that followed had a profound impact upon the colonies. Britain gradually developed a colonial policy and began treating the colonies as a unit rather than as individual entities. British colonial policy had a dual impact, creating both an American identity and an American interest. Ultimately, this led to a complete break with Great Britain when the Continental Congress adopted the Declaration of Independence in 1776. Plunged into a war of independence, the former colonies, now sovereign states, sought some political arrangement to coordinate their war effort. The solution was the Articles of Confederation and Perpetual Union, first proposed in 1776 but not adopted until 1781. Taken together, the Declaration of Independence and the Articles of Confederation constitute the first American Constitution. Under the Articles of Confederation the general government did not have any power over individual citizens: it dealt only with the individual states that composed the confederation. Even at that, the Confederation operated primarily by the voluntary consent of the states, having no real authority to enforce its resolutions. Furthermore, the general government had no authority to deal with internal affairs. Its authority was confined to certain external tasks of general interest – diplomacy, war, and common defence, for example.

During the period between 1781 and 1788 the United States was a fully functioning constitutional polity. Between 1776 and 1780 eleven of the thirteen former colonies adopted republican constitutions,[3] and the states were linked together first under the Second Continental Congress and then under the Articles of Confederation. This structure was sufficient for the successful prosecution of the War of Independence but proved inadequate to the challenges of the postwar period as all the old state rivalries and jealousies re-emerged. First, trade among the states was difficult because each state adopted protectionist legislation and issued its own currency. Second, some of the states were characterized by considerable political and economic instability so that, at least in the eyes of the political elites, property was threatened, economic development was uncertain, and liberty was in jeopardy. Third, there were real military threats to the United States. Great Britain still had troops in the United States as well as in nearby Canada, and Spain controlled navigation on the lower portion of the Mississippi River. Finally, the new United States could not be taken seriously in international affairs and was unable to secure loans or enforce its treaties.

George Washington, James Madison, Alexander Hamilton, and others called for a strengthening of the bonds of union among the states in order to address these problems. After an unsuccessful meeting in Annapolis, Maryland, in 1786, delegates from twelve of the thirteen states[4] assembled in Philadelphia, Pennsylvania, in the summer of 1787 "to deliberate on all measures necessary to cement the union of the states and promote their permanent tranquillity and security."

The story of the American Constitutional Convention is well known[5] – large states versus small states, southern slave states versus northern free states, and, perhaps most important, advocates of a centralized (or consolidated) government versus proponents of states-rights who favoured no more than a modified version of the Articles of Confederation. The solution to all of these conflicts was the invention of modern federalism, an entirely new system of governance that was neither unitary nor confederal. The new federal government was to have only those powers delegated to it by the Constitution; all other powers, unless prohibited, were to remain with the states. Under the Articles of Confederation the central government's powers were also delegated – but by the states themselves, and they could be withdrawn by the unanimous consent of the states. This type of delegation remains the essence of confederal forms of government. However, the proposal at Philadelphia in 1787 broke new ground by protecting the central government's powers in a Constitution that could not be changed without the consent of the central representative institutions.

The new national government was to operate directly on individuals within its limited sphere of delegated powers. Consequently, the framers thought there had to be effective limits on national power in order to prevent it from exceeding its authority. For this reason the framers of the American Constitution divided power between the executive and the legislature and, within the legislature itself, between the House of Representatives and the Senate.

The original U.S. Constitution is better understood as a delegation of powers to the national government than as a distribution of powers between the national government and the states. Under the Articles of Confederation, almost all authority remained with the thirteen sovereign states; very limited power was delegated to the weak national government. The Constitutional Convention of 1787 created a stronger and more complete national government and endowed it with more powers than the national government had under the Articles. Nevertheless, the new national government was to have only those powers granted to it by the Constitution. All other powers, unless prohibited, remained with the states, just where they had been under the Articles of Confederation and even earlier. Thus, the Constitution does not grant powers to the states.[6] The Constitution merely delegates certain limited, albeit very important, powers to the national government and leaves all others (except where prohibited) where they were before – with the states. In fact, the Constitution recognizes this explicitly. Amendment X to the Constitution (adopted in 1791) provides: "The powers not delegated to the United States by the Constitution, nor prohibited by it to the States, are reserved to the States respectively, or to the people."

The delegates to the Convention approved a draft constitution in September 1787. This was submitted to special ratifying conventions in each of the states for their consideration. While some states ratified the Constitution quickly and with little debate, opposition surfaced in such crucial states as Massachusetts, New York, and Virginia. While there were numerous objections to the proposed constitution, the opposition soon focused on the lack of a bill of rights, a feature contained in most existing state constitutions. In fact, North Carolina, when first presented with the Constitution, rejected it because it did not contain a bill of rights. To counter this growing opposition, the Constitution's proponents promised to add a bill of rights as soon as the document was ratified. With this promise, the Constitution was ratified in 1788, and ten amendments – the Bill of Rights – were added to the Constitution in 1791.

CONSTITUTIONAL DISTRIBUTION OF POWERS AND RESPONSIBILITIES

The Constitution, as written and ratified, creates a system of dual federalism in which both the national government and the states are sovereign in their respective spheres of competence. Over time, as the role of the national government has expanded, the actual operation of the American federal system became more interactive and cooperative in nature.

In the early days of the American republic most governmental functions remained with the states. Daniel Elazar, in examining the actual operation of the American federal republic during its earliest years, has concluded that, "for the first two generations under the Constitution, the United States resembled a confederation almost as much as it did a federation."[7] For at least the first fifty years of its operation, it operated in a very decentralized manner.[8] Today, however, American federalism is much more centralized than it once was.

Powers of the Federal Government

Article 1, Section 8, of the Constitution delegates eighteen specific powers to the Congress of the United States. Almost all of these powers deal with commerce, foreign affairs, or military affairs. Among the most important of these powers are (1) the power to "collect Taxes ... to pay the Debts and provide for the common Defence and general Welfare of the United States," and (2) the power to regulate commerce "with foreign Nations, and among the several States, and with the Indian Tribes" – both powers that the federal government did not have under the Articles of Confederation. In addition, the very last provision of Section 8 empowers Congress "to make all Laws which shall be necessary and proper for carrying into Execution the foregoing powers." This "elastic clause" is quite different from a parallel provision in the Articles of Confederation, which provides that the states retain all power "not *expressly* delegated to the United States."[9] The Congress is granted many other important powers by Section 8, such as exclusive authority over copyright, bankruptcy, and patents, but it has been through the broad interpretation of the power to tax and spend and the power to regulate interstate and foreign commerce that the role of the federal government has expanded so tremendously.

One continuing question is whether the powers delegated to the federal government are exclusive or concurrent. Sometimes when the Constitution delegates a power to the federal government it explicitly denies the same power to the states. For example, Article 1, Section 8, Paragraph 5, gives the power to "coin money" to the federal government, and Article 1, Section 10, Paragraph 1, prohibits the states from coining money. There are several examples of this sort, but, by and large, whether a delegated power is exclusive or concurrent is often ambiguous, and it has been left to the U.S. Supreme Court to decide the issue on a case-by-case basis. Even when the Court finds that a power is concurrent, it may hold that the exercise of that power by the federal government preempts the field, precluding state regulation of the

same subject matter. In enacting legislation Congress sometimes states its intention to preempt the field. It may even authorize the administration to
preempt a specific policy area, either in whole or in part.

State and Local Autonomy

Both the federal government and the states have a high degree of autonomy. The states write their own constitutions, usually through popularly
elected constitutional conventions and usually requiring ratification by the
voters at the polls. State voters, of course, elect their own public officials.
There are no federally appointed "governors" within the states. With few
exceptions, the states have wide latitude in structuring their governments
in ways that are in keeping with their own traditions and needs.

Starting in the 1960s many states used their constitutional authority to
modernize their legislative, executive, and judicial institutions. During the
first half of the twentieth century many state legislatures met only every
other year for a limited number of legislative days. Individual legislators
were poorly paid and had little or no staff support. Since the 1960s, however, many states have provided for annual legislative sessions, increased
legislative pay, and professional staff support.

Two changes, both adopted in response to popular pressure, are especially noteworthy. First, some states – especially those western states most
influenced by the Progressive movement in American politics – adopted
the direct initiative, a system under which voters, by collecting signatures
on a petition, can place an issue directly on the ballot to be voted upon by
the citizenry at the next election. If passed by the voters, the initiative becomes state law just as if it had been enacted through the normal legislative
process. Thus, twenty-four states now have some system of what has come
to be called direct democracy. Second, seventeen states now have term limits, under which the number of years an individual can serve in the state
legislature is strictly limited, usually to eight years. Sixteen of these seventeen systems of term limits were enacted by the initiative process.

Many states have also used their constitutional authority to modernize
and strengthen their executives, their governors. With the exception of
that of Massachusetts, the earliest state constitutions were wary of executive
power and created very weak governors. Beginning about 1965 most states
strengthened their governors in order to enable them to provide public
and legislative leadership. Governors were given four-year terms, their powers of appointment were increased, and their control over the state budget
was strengthened. Using their enhanced constitutional authority, state governors have become important policy leaders and have taken the initiative
in formulating new programs in education, welfare, economic development, and criminal justice.

The states have also modernized their judiciaries. Historically, state court systems were a hodgepodge of structures, created and financed by both state and local governments. Many states did not have intermediate appellate courts, and state supreme courts were often overwhelmed by thousands of appeals. During the 1970s and 1980s many states streamlined the structure of their court systems, developed state-wide personnel systems for court employees, increased state funding, created administrative offices for the courts under the control of the state supreme court, and centralized rule-making authority in the state supreme court. State supreme courts were given *certiorari* jurisdiction, thus enabling them to have discretion over the cases they heard and therefore to decide only the most important cases that arose under state constitutions or state law. Many state supreme courts have been very active in protecting individual rights and liberties, often holding that their state constitutions protect rights that go beyond those protected by the U.S. Constitution. State supreme courts have the final say on the interpretation of state constitutions and state laws.[10]

The political context in which these state governmental institutions operate has also changed. Before the 1960s the legislative districts in many states were apportioned in such a way as to favour rural constituencies and to underrepresent urban and suburban ones. In 1964 the U.S. Supreme Court ruled that this sort of malapportionment violated the Equal Protection Clause of the Fourteenth Amendment to the U.S. Constitution, and it held that state legislative districts had to be equal in population – the principle of one person, one vote.

Compliance with the Supreme Court's decision brought about a fundamental change in state politics. State legislative districts were redrawn to more accurately reflect urban and suburban populations, and the states were forced to address the concerns of urban and suburban voters. Reapportionment – along with the federal Voting Rights Acts, 1965 – brought a new breed of political activists into state politics. Legislators were younger and better educated, and the proportion of women, African Americans, and Hispanics increased significantly. In 2000, of the 7,424 members of the fifty state legislatures, almost 1,500 were women, 520 were African American, and 150 were Hispanic.

The second important political change since the 1960s has been the increase in competition between Republicans and Democrats (i.e., the two major and overwhelmingly dominant political parties in the U.S. political system) in many states. From the 1860s to the 1960s the political parties each had a regional base, the Democrats in the South and the Republicans in New England and the Midwest. The states of these regions were so dominated by their respective parties that candidates from the minority party had little real chance of winning elections. Demographic, economic, and political changes, however, increased party competition, so that by the year

2000 in many states either party had an almost equal chance of winning
any given state-wide election. The closeness of the 2000 presidential election in Florida is a good example of this increased party competition.

In addition, the federal Voting Rights Act brought about increased voter
turnout by African American and Hispanic voters. Their increased participation has led to an increase in the number of minority candidates winning elections. For example, by 1992, 4,557 African American and 1,908
Hispanics were serving in elected city council and county offices throughout the country. Women also were elected to local offices in increasing
numbers. In 1975 there were only thirty-five female mayors in America's
larger cities; by 1995 that number had increased to 178.

The territorial autonomy of the states is guaranteed by Article IV, Section 3, of the U.S. Constitution, which requires the approval of both the
Congress and the states involved before any state boundaries can be altered.[11] Article V of the Constitution guarantees that the equal representation of every state in the U.S. Senate shall not be deprived without consent
of the state.

The states also have substantial fiscal autonomy. They cannot tax imports
or exports,[12] or use their tax policy to place an undue burden on interstate
or foreign commerce, or tax the instrumentalities of the federal government. Otherwise, they generally have great discretion in taxation. In 2003
forty-five states had general sales taxes[13] and forty-one had broad-based
personal income taxes. Together these taxes account for approximately
70 percent of all state tax revenue. Other state taxes typically include taxes
on alcoholic beverages, gasoline and tobacco, and inheritance taxes. States
that produce oil, natural gas, and coal often use severance taxes (taxes on
the extraction of these natural resources). Most states also generate revenue from various fees (such as for automobile registration) and from lotteries. Most states have constitutional requirements for the submission of
balanced budgets. States, however, do borrow money for major capital expenditures. The states alone are responsible for repayment of these debts;
the federal government has no legal responsibility to step in if a state is on
the verge of default.

While there is relatively little constitutional coordination between state
and federal tax policy, the states are affected by federal tax law. For example, some states tie their own income and inheritance tax rates to the federal Internal Revenue Code. In 2001 the federal government lowered both
of these tax rates, causing a corresponding decrease in state tax rates and a
reduction in state tax revenues. Furthermore, when Congress eliminated
the deductibility of state sales taxes for federal tax purposes, the states were
implicitly encouraged to rely more heavily on income taxes since state income taxes retained their deductibility.

State taxation is also affected by tax competition among the states. Because the states compete with each other for citizens and business investments, they cannot allow their total package of taxes to get too much higher than those of the other states. In 2002 state tax burdens, expressed as a percentage of personal income, ranged from a high of 13.6 percent in Maine to a low of 7.6 percent in New Hampshire.[14] Throughout the United States the average total burden of all state taxes was 10.2 percent. Thirty-six of the fifty states fell into the range between 9 percent and 11.9 percent.

State tax and spending policies are also influenced by a substantial federal program of grants-in-aid. By 2002 federal grants-in-aid to state and local government exceeded $350 billion distributed through more than 600 different programs. In 2003 federal grants-in-aid constituted almost 25 percent of state revenue. While federal grant-in-aid-programs reach almost all areas of public policy, including such traditionally local concerns as police protection and education, the two largest federal programs, by far, are for social welfare and health care. Under these federal programs the states merely pass through federal funds to individuals. According to the most recent estimates, more than 60 percent of federal grant-in-aid funding is dedicated for payments to individuals.[15] Unlike other federations, almost all of the transfer funding from the U.S. federal government to the state and local governments is categorical or conditional. There are few general or unconditional transfer programs (see further discussion below).

Congress often uses the incentive of financial aid to encourage the states to develop and administer programs that are high on the agenda of Congress. Even without federal funding, Congress and the courts can sometimes compel the states to develop and administer programs, especially in the name of civil rights. For example, recent federal legislation requires mandatory HIV testing of newborn babies, making the public streets accessible to the handicapped, and the regular testing of school children in mathematics and reading. In 1995 Congress passed the Unfunded Mandate Reform Act, which attempts to limit the power of the federal government to enact unfunded mandates of this sort. The federal government, however, has no general authority to compel the states to implement or to administer its programs.[16]

Local government – cities, towns, counties, and special districts – are not mentioned in the Constitution. Local government is a matter for the states. In legal theory, local government is wholly a creature of the state. Local governments' institutional structures are defined, their responsibilities are delineated, and their powers of taxation are all derived from state government. In fact, it is the state government that gives local governments the breath of life, without which they could not even exist. Whatever legal theory might say, the political reality is that U.S. cities and towns often enjoy a high degree of autonomy and independence. This is true for several reasons. First, in some cases, towns and local communities preceded state government. Connecticut, for example, was created as little more than a federation of local communities. Furthermore, local governments are well represented in state legislatures and have been able to achieve a considerable degree of independence through the legislative process. About half the states provide what is called "home rule" for local governments. For example, under Pennsylvania's constitutional provision for home rule, local government "may exercise any power or perform any function not denied by this Constitution, by its home rule charter, or by the General Assembly." Home rule provides some degree of flexibility for local governments. Finally, local governments have become participants in the complex web of intergovernmental relationships that have developed in the United States since the 1960s.

LOGIC OF THE CONSTITUTIONAL DISTRIBUTION OF POWERS AND RESPONSIBILITIES

The framers of the American Constitution were concerned with individual liberty, or what the Declaration of Independence calls "life, liberty and the pursuit of happiness." The American experience taught that liberty could be threatened both by distant, unaccountable government (the United Kingdom) on the one hand, and by local government that, while democratically elected, too often reflected majoritarian passions and short-term selfish interests, on the other hand. While democracy was a necessary condition for the protection of rights, it could itself degenerate into the tyranny of the majority. In *Federalist Number 10*, James Madison articulates the view that rights are better safeguarded in an extended republic, in which the existence and representation of many interests would encourage a more deliberative decision making in which the public good and the rights of the minor party are protected. At the same time, the framers recognized that the consolidation of power in the hands of some distant, federal government could degenerate into imperial rule, itself a threat to the public interest and individual rights. The solution was federation, in which the states would continue to be responsible for most domestic policy making. At the same time, a strong national government was necessary to deal with national concerns, such as interstate commerce and foreign and international affairs.

The logic of this analysis suggests dual federalism, based on the dual sovereignties of the states and the national government. While some scholars argue that the United States operated in this dual manner during its early development, others suggest that there was more overlap in the actual operations of the state and federal governments than the dualistic model suggests. Whatever the merits of these historical arguments, the actual functioning of modern American federalism is clearly better characterized as cooperative. By the latter half of the twentieth century there was scarcely a policy area in which the federal government, the states, and even local government were not involved. Because federal laws are the supreme law of the land, and because of the federal government's very substantial financial resources, some argue that the federal government has become so dominant that contemporary American federalism is no longer cooperative but, rather, has become permissive, with the states exercising only those powers *permitted* to them by the federal government.[17] Certainly federal-state relations are more coercive than they were during the 1950s. Since the late 1960s American federalism has become characterized by considerably expanded federal power over the states, as reflected in increased federal preemption of state law and federal encroachments on state tax bases, and by the federal government compelling and pressuring states to comply with federal policies through mandates, regulations attached to grants-in-aid, and court orders.[18]

EVOLUTION OF THE CONSTITUTIONAL DISTRIBUTION OF POWERS AND RESPONSIBILITIES

Constitutional Amendments

The U.S. Constitution has been amended twenty-seven times. While all of these amendments have some impact upon the constitutional distribution of powers and responsibilities, some have had very substantial impact.

The Tenth Amendment, adopted in 1791, makes explicit what had been implicit in the original Constitution; namely, that all powers not delegated to the federal government by the Constitution, nor prohibited to the states, are reserved to the states. The Tenth Amendment was often used by the U.S. Supreme Court during the first third of the twentieth century to limit the reach of federal power under both the Interstate Commerce Clause and the Taxing and Spending Clause.[19] This position was abandoned beginning in 1937 as the Court upheld President Franklin D. Roosevelt's New Deal and subsequent federal regulatory and social welfare legislation.[20] There are a few Supreme Court decisions in the 1990s, however, in which the Supreme Court has invoked the Tenth Amendment to invalidate federal legislation.[21]

The Eleventh Amendment was adopted in 1798 to overturn the Supreme Court's 1793 decision in *Chisholm v. Georgia*, which had held that a state could be sued in federal court by a citizen of another state without its consent. The Eleventh Amendment reverses this holding by providing that the federal courts lack jurisdiction to decide a case "commenced ... against

one of the United States by Citizens of another State." In the 1990s and
early 2000s the U.S. Supreme Court cited this provision of the Eleventh
Amendment to limit the authority of the federal government to empower
individuals to sue a state for an alleged deprivation of rights.[22]

Of the three Civil War Amendments, the Fourteenth has had the most
impact on the distribution of powers and responsibilities in the American
federal system.[23] Section 1 of the Fourteenth Amendment (1) defines
both federal and state citizenship, matters on which the original Constitution had been silent; (2) prohibits a state from making any law "which
shall abridge the privileges or immunities of citizens of the United
States"; (3) prohibits a state from depriving "any person of life, liberty, or
property, without due process of law"; and (4) prohibits a state from denying "to any person within its jurisdiction the equal protection of the
laws." Section 5 of the Amendment gives Congress "power to enforce this
article by appropriate legislation." By and large the Fourteenth Amendment is concerned with protecting rights – both of individuals and of corporate entities – against state encroachment. During the latter part of the
nineteenth century and the first third of the twentieth century, the U.S.
Supreme Court used the Fourteenth Amendment (especially the due
process clause) to protect property rights against state regulation. More
recently, the Court has invoked the same due process clause to invalidate
state laws and practices that it found to violate individual rights protected
by the Fourteenth Amendment. The Court has been equally vigorous in
using the Fourteenth Amendment's equal protection clause to protect
the rights of racial minorities, women, the handicapped, linguistic minorities, resident aliens, and other groups. Furthermore, Congress has often
used its authority under Section 5 of the Fourteenth Amendment, and
similar provisions in the Thirteenth and Fifteenth Amendments, to enact
such important civil rights laws as the Civil Rights Act, 1964, and the
Voting Rights Act, 1965. The federal role in affirmative action, in school
desegregation, in promoting the rights of the handicapped, and in bilingual education are all founded on Congress's authority under Section 5.
The Fourteenth Amendment has brought about a fundamental change
in the nature of American federalism and has added to both the federal
government's powers and its responsibilities.

The Sixteenth Amendment, adopted in 1913, empowers the federal government to enact income taxes, and it has also had a substantial impact on
the expansion of federal power. The federal income tax, while originally
levied at a low rate and applied only to those with high incomes, has become a broad-based federal tax that generated almost $1 trillion in reve-
nues by 2001. These revenues are used to finance a substantial program of
grants-in-aid to state and local governments.

While federal grants-in-aid in some form have always been part of the American federal system, the modern system can be traced to the presidency of Republican Dwight D. Eisenhower (1953–61). Building upon a bipartisan consensus of support for cooperative federalism, the federal government established a federal-state partnership for the building of the nation's interstate highway system.[24] By 1960 the national government distributed almost $7 billion in intergovernmental transfers. While the federal grant-in-aid system expanded during the 1950s, by the end of that decade, approximately 70 percent of the funds still went for four purposes: highways, aid to the aged, aid to dependent children, and employment security. Over 90 percent of the funds went to state governments.

During the 1960s the grant-in-aid system expanded tremendously, both in terms of the amount of federal funds and the number of programs. By 2000 the federal grant-in-aid system had grown to more than $350 billion distributed through more than 600 different programs. They reach almost all areas of public policy, and awards are given both to states and to local units of government, creating a vastly more complex web of intergovernmental fiscal, administrative, and political relationships than existed forty years earlier.

Other amendments have also been important. The Seventeenth Amendment (1913) provides for the direct election of U.S. senators. Presumably, this weakens the representation of the states in the Senate since, under the original Constitution, senators were appointed by their respective state legislatures.[25] One notes, however, that the amendment fixed what had already become the practice in a number of states. The Eighteenth Amendment (1919) prohibits "the manufacture, sale, or transportation of intoxicating liquors," and it makes clear that both "Congress and the several States shall have concurrent power to enforce this article by appropriate legislation." The Twenty-First Amendment (1933) repeals the Eighteenth Amendment but also provides that "the transportation into any State ... of intoxicating liquors, in violation of the laws thereof, is hereby prohibited."[26]

Judicial Interpretation

The U.S. Supreme Court has played a major role in the allocation of powers and responsibilities in the United States.[27] In the early years of the American Republic, the U.S. Supreme Court, under the leadership of Chief Justice John Marshall, used its authority to enhance federal power. For example, in *McCulloch v. Maryland* (1819), the Court upheld the chartering of a national bank despite the fact that there was no clear authority in the U.S. Constitution for the federal government to issue bank charters. The Court maintained that the constitutional grants of authority to the federal government should be broadly interpreted and that the elastic clause of Article I, Section 8, expanded rather than restricted national power. Five years later, in *Gibbons v. Ogden*, the Court took an exceptionally broad view of Congress's power to regulate interstate commerce, maintaining that the commerce power "is complete in itself, may be exercised to its utmost extent, and acknowledges no limitations other than are prescribed in the Constitution." Furthermore, the Marshall Court sometimes used its power of judicial review to invalidate state legislation that threatened property rights.[28]

Beginning in the 1880s the Supreme Court took a narrower view of federal authority, often holding that federal attempts to regulate economic affairs violated the Tenth Amendment to the Constitution by invading areas reserved to the states.[29] During the latter half of the nineteenth century and the first third of the twentieth century, the Court also took a narrow view of state authority to regulate economic affairs, ruling that such state regulations deprived individuals of their liberty without due process of law, a violation of the Fourteenth Amendment.[30]

The Court maintained its narrow view of federal and state authority during the first term of Franklin D. Roosevelt's New Deal presidency (1933–37), but with Roosevelt's overwhelming re-election victory in 1936 and the threat of his court packing plan,[31] the Court again reversed course and began to uphold the exercise of federal authority under both the interstate commerce clause and the taxing and spending clause of the Constitution.[32] Similarly, the Court upheld state economic regulatory legislation against challenges that it violated the due process clause of the Fourteenth Amendment.[33] On the other hand, the Court often struck down state legislation when it appeared to conflict with either federal laws or with the need for the free flow of interstate commerce.[34] In addition, the Court began to invalidate state laws and practices where they violated individual rights protected by the due process and equal protection clauses of the Fourteenth Amendment. Beginning especially in the 1950s, the Court invalidated both federal and state laws because they violated the Bill of Rights, bringing about a "revolution in rights and liberties" in the United States.[35]

This dual standard of a permissive attitude towards economic regulation and a restrictive attitude towards laws that infringe upon individual rights and liberties has continued until the present time. There are some recent decisions, however, in which the Court has held that there are limits to federal authority under the interstate commerce clause[36] and that some state economic regulatory legislation, especially in the area of environmental protection, is invalid because it constitutes a taking of private property without just compensation in violation of the Fifth Amendment (made applicable to the states by the due process clause of the Fourteenth Amendment).[37] In recent years the Court has, by and large, maintained its defence of such individual rights as freedom of speech, press, assembly, and religion. In 2003 the Court went even further, invalidating a state law against sodomy, maintaining that it was protected by a right to privacy implicit in the concept of liberty as that term is used in the Fourteenth Amendment.[38]

Finally, as discussed more fully below, the Supreme Court has, since the *Garcia* case of 1985, drawn back significantly from judicial review of federal legislation on the grounds of federalism (i.e., that it may encroach on state jurisdiction); instead, it has ruled that state interests are better protected through political institutions, particularly Congress.

Overview of Historic Trends

Several historic social and economic forces have shaped American federalism over the past 200 years: the purchase of the Louisiana Territory from France in 1803 and the subsequent opening of the American west, the Civil War, large-scale immigration during the late nineteenth and early twentieth centuries, industrialization and urbanization, the Great Depression and President Franklin Roosevelt's New Deal programs of the 1930s, the Second World War and the Cold War that followed it, technological changes, and globalization. While these events increased the role of the federal government in the American federal system, all governments – federal, state, and local – do more than they did 200 years ago. All governments are involved in making and implementing public policies in areas unknown to the American founders. In the context of American federalism, this has meant the intergovernmentalization of public policy. Increasingly, policies are not in the exclusive domain of any one government but, rather, involve actors from all planes of government. Thus, dual federalism has come to be replaced by cooperative federalism as the paradigm for understanding the actual operation of the system. While there is a general trend for the federal government to be the most important actor in many policy areas, the role and relative influence of the actors varies from one policy area to another, from one issue to another, and even from one state to another.

MAINTENANCE AND MANAGEMENT OF THE DISTRIBUTION OF POWERS AND RESPONSIBILITIES

American federalism is characterized by both cooperation and conflict. The period of the New Deal through the 1950s was the high point of cooperative federalism. The states and the federal government usually agreed on policy goals, and the states were intimately involved in the implementation of programs. With the Great Society programs of the mid-1960s federal-state relations became more conflicted. The Democratic administration of President Lyndon B. Johnson was suspicious of the states' willingness to support its anti-poverty and civil rights initiatives, and it began to channel federal funds directly to the cities and other units of local government, bypassing the states altogether. In addition, most new federal grant-in-aid programs emphasized categorical (conditional) grants, which gave the states and cities little discretion in how the federal funds were used, compared with broad-purpose bloc grants favoured by the states. Third, the number of federal programs increased dramatically, reaching many policy areas that were traditionally the exclusive responsibilities of the states. While there have been several efforts to "reform" the federal system, especially under Presidents Richard M. Nixon and Ronald Reagan, the pattern of cooperation and conflict continues.

Cooperation and conflict are built into the division of powers and responsibilities created by the U.S. Constitution. The powers and responsibilities of the federal and state governments are concurrent and overlapping and require cooperation. At the same time, federal and state political leaders often have different priorities and perspectives, bringing about conflict in the actual exercise of power. Since the mid-1960s there has been relatively little conflict over the substance of federal policy initiatives. Most state political leaders have come to accept the broad scope of federal authority and rarely challenge the exercise of federal power. States do not always seek to maintain their prerogatives and frequently are quite willing to accept federal policy leadership and federal funds. Conflict is much more about the manner in which federal power is exercised.

First, while most federal aid programs are in the form of narrowly focused categorical grants, the states generally prefer broad bloc grants, which give them more flexibility. Second, even when bloc grants are used, the states maintain that federal funding is inadequate. Third, since the 1980s the federal government has relied increasingly on mandates rather than on grant programs to accomplish its objectives. Fourth, the states maintain that they are not adequately represented in the formulation of federal programs and are simply assigned roles in their implementation. Finally, congressional legislation often preempts a field and precludes state action in the same policy area.

One consequence of the increased intergovernmentalization of American public policy is that it is sometimes difficult for the citizenry to know who is accountable for policy failings. State and local officials tend to blame the federal bureaucracy, while federal officials claim that state and local efforts are inadequate. Second, while one of the traditional strengths of American federalism is that local officials are accountable to local constituencies, when local programs are funded from federal sources, local officials may become more accountable to their funding providers in Washington, D.C., than to their constituents.

Conflict Management

American federalism has developed several mechanisms to manage the conflict that is characteristic of the system. These mechanisms are legal, political, and administrative. Except for the judiciary, all of these mechanisms are extraconstitutional. Some are informal while others are institutionalized.

Many American presidents have taken a substantial interest in federalism, and several have attempted to reform the federal system of grants-in-aid in response to pressures from the states. In recent years most presidents have appointed a special assistant for intergovernmental affairs and charged him or her with pursuing the president's intergovernmental agenda and with hearing issues raised by the states. Generally, however, efforts at federalism reform did not generate much interest among the citizenry, and no American president – Republican or Democrat – has let his belief in federalism stand in the way of his policy preferences.

State governors are often articulate spokespersons for state interests in the distribution of powers and responsibilities in American federalism. Individually, governors, working with the state's congressional delegation, can have an impact on how specific federal programs are structured and implemented. In addition, at least thirty-two states have offices in Washington to lobby Congress and the executive branch when their state's vital interests are affected by pending legislation or administrative action.

Collectively, the governors are organized into the National Governors Association (NGA). The NGA's main office is in Washington, D.C., and it attempts to present a unified position on issues that affect state interests. Because of the diversity of the states, the NGA works on a consensus principle and takes stands on issues only when there is near unanimity among the governors. Also because of this diversity, the governors are organized into two partisan organizations, the Democrat Governors Association and the Republican Governors Association, and a number of regional organizations, such as the Western Governors Association, the Southern Governors Association, the Coalition of Northeastern Governors, and the Midwestern Governors Conference.

The normal process of legislation in the U.S. Congress often involves conflict and debate about the extent of federal and state powers. Nevertheless, the trend over the past fifty years has been for Congress to expand federal authority, often at the expense of the states. At the same time, individual members of both the House of Representatives and the Senate are sensitive to local interests, to supporting special projects, to devising funding formulas, and to sponsoring legislation in support of state and district needs. In addition, many individual members of Congress are responsive to the needs of state and local officials, and will often intervene with the federal bureaucracy on behalf of local interests.

Members of state legislatures are organized into the National Conference of State Legislatures (NCSL), which lobbies Congress and the federal executive on behalf of state interests. Because of the diversity of its membership, it is often difficult for the NCSL to take a united stand on issues.

While the role of the U.S. Supreme Court is especially crucial, all federal courts play an important role in resolving federal-state conflicts. While these conflicts sometimes raise constitutional issues regarding the proper exercise of federal or state authority, they are even more likely to involve questions of statutory interpretation or the legality and appropriateness of administrative procedures. In recognition of the important role of the courts in resolving federal-state conflicts, the State and Local Legal Center was created in 1983 to help prepare state attorneys for their court appearances and to submit *amicus* briefs in federalism cases.[39] The states have become much more active in defending and promoting their interests through litigation and have had some significant victories in recent years.

Beginning in the 1970s state-federal judicial councils were formed in most of the states and were charged with the responsibility of maintaining continuing communication on all joint problems and of mitigating the friction between state and federal courts. While these joint councils addressed some practical problems, such as the coordination of court calendars, few exist today. The National State-Federal Council was created in 1992, but that body also lapsed into desuetude. State judges, however, continue to serve on the major committees of the federal Judicial Conference. The Federal-State Jurisdiction Committee of the Judicial Conference is especially relevant because it is primarily concerned with developing recommendations about legislation affecting state and federal jurisdiction, and it attempts to promote state-federal judicial cooperation generally.[40]

Far more important for the resolution of federal-state judicial conflict is the National Center for State Courts (NCSC), which brings together the Council of [State] Chief Justices (CCJ), the Conference of State Court Administrators (COSCA), and other state trial and appellate judges, and which provides information to Congress and the federal judiciary on issues of concern to state judiciaries.

The U.S. Advisory Commission on Intergovernmental Relations, which had been created in 1959 to monitor federal-state relationships and to make recommendations for their improvement, had its funding eliminated from the federal budget in 1996, effectively ending its existence. According to one observer, "Clearly, the perception of a need for general purpose intergovernmental specialists had waned in Washington, D.C."[41] Even so, however, most federal agencies responsible for administering domestic programs have institutionalized mechanisms for state and local input into their rule-making and other decision-making processes.

While American political parties focus more on winning elections than on issues, both Republicans and Democrats have, from time to time, articulated concern with the distribution of powers. The Republicans, especially in the 1980s and early 1990s, advocated a diminished federal role and the devolution of responsibilities to the states. The Democrats, while often campaigning on the basis of new federal policy initiatives, have also advocated a reform of the federal grant-in-aid system so as to give states more discretion in policy implementation. Even so, neither political party has let its interest in federalism stand in the way of its policy preferences. Both Republicans and Democrats have supported new federal programs that have the effect of diminishing state power.

The distribution of powers and responsibilities in the American federal system is affected by two types of interest groups. First, as noted already, state and local officials are organized into a variety of associations that seek to promote their interests in national policy making. The major players in this intergovernmental lobby are the "Big Seven" – the National Governors Association (NGA), the National Conference of State Legislatures (NCSL), the U.S. Conference of Mayors (which represents larger cities), the National League of Cities (which represent smaller cities), the National Association of Counties, the Council of State Governments (CSG), and the International City Managers Association (ICMA).[42] Given the diversity of interests they represent, while they can sometimes reach a consensus on broad principles, they tend to pursue their own interests on more detailed policy questions. Other state officials are also organized into associations that lobby in the national arena when their interests are affected. Examples include the National Association of [State] Attorneys General, the Council of Chief State School Officers, the Council of [State] Chief Justices, and the American Association of State Highway and Transportation Officials.

Other interest groups affect the distribution of powers and responsibilities through their normal lobbying activities. For example, Mothers against Drunk Driving (MADD) lobbies in both the federal and state arenas to advance its goal of reducing the practice of driving a motor vehicle while under the influence of intoxicating beverages. MADD had won several victories in state legislatures when it turned to the federal government in 1984 to get Congress to enact a law reducing federal highway funds to states unless they raised the age for the purchase of alcoholic beverages to twenty-one.[43] In 2003 MADD used the same strategy to lobby Congress to enact a law that would reduce a state's federal highway funds unless it adopted a 0.8 blood alcohol standard to determine intoxication.

Because American federalism is a non-centralized matrix rather than a decentralized hierarchy,[44] the national government has no generalized role in monitoring or supervising the states. At the same time, if a state accepts federal funds for specific programs, federal officials may monitor the administration of the programs and hold the state accountable for how the funds are expended. In addition, if a state official violates some prohibition of the U.S. Constitution, or fails to comply with some valid federal law, then the offending state official may be sued in federal court. Courts can order compliance and even find that a non-complying state official is in contempt of court. Finally, both state and federal officials can be (and are) indicted for violation of the criminal law. There have been many federal prosecutions and convictions of state and local officials for such crimes as bribery, corruption, and obstruction of justice.

The states have little recourse for alleged violations of the Constitution by federal officials. The principle remedy is political, although states may and do bring legal actions against federal officials. The doctrine of nullification, by which a state claimed it could nullify the operation of a federal law it believed unconstitutional, was always controversial and was thoroughly discredited by the American Civil War.

ADEQUACY AND FUTURE OF THE DISTRIBUTION OF POWERS AND RESPONSIBILITIES

Whether the actual distribution of powers and responsibilities is consistent with the design of the original Constitution is, of course, arguable. According to James Madison in Federalist No. 45, "The powers delegated ... to the federal government are few and defined. Those which are to remain in the State governments are numerous and indefinite. The former will be exercised principally on external objects ... The powers reserved to the several States will extend to all the objects which ... concern the lives, liberties, and properties of the people, and the internal order, improvements, and prosperity of the State." The scope of federal activities has expanded tremendously, and the sharp distinction between federal and state roles suggested by Madison has become blurred. While there are some who conclude that the actual functioning of American federalism is no longer consistent with the values embedded in the original Constitution, there are others who claim that the U.S. Constitution is a living document, broad enough to be interpreted and adjusted to the needs of each generation.

To a considerable extent, contemporary American federalism depends on both strong states and a strong federal government. Every federal system is challenged by both centrifugal and centripetal forces. If either the central government or the states are weak, then the federal union is threatened by disintegration on the one hand or by excessive centralization on the other hand.

The weak American federal government was challenged by the centrifugal forces of state and regional diversity many times during the nineteenth century, culminating in the American Civil War. Buttressed by victory in the war, the subsequent constitutional amendments, westward expansion, and rapid industrialization, the federal government of the twentieth century was much stronger than was that of the nineteenth century.

Similarly, some argue that the American federal union was challenged by excessive centralization during the period between the 1930s and the 1960s. Beginning in the 1960s most states developed broad-based and relatively stable revenue systems, modernized their governmental institutions, created modern and professional administrations, and became more representative of their populations. By the 1980s the states were generally strong and representative constitutional polities with the financial and political resources necessary to play an important policy-making role within the context of American federalism.

Contemporary Issues

By way of conclusion one may note briefly that the actual distribution of powers and responsibilities in the American federal system is likely to be affected by three contemporary challenges: one constitutional, one political, and one international.

Beginning in 1937 the U.S. Supreme Court began to interpret the interstate commerce powers of Congress so broadly that its authority seemed unlimited. In fact, from 1937 through 1995, there was only a single instance in which the Court held that Congress had exceeded its delegated powers,[45] and even that decision was reversed nine years later.[46] Furthermore, in 1985 the Court seemed to suggest that questions of the scope of federal power should be resolved through the political process rather than through constitutional litigation.[47] In 1995, however, the Court invalidated the federal Gun-Free School Zones Act, 1990, as going beyond Congress's power under the interstate commerce clause.[48] This decision, and a number of other decisions supporting the states, was decided by a vote of five-to-four, so whether it marks the beginning of the end of the Court's sixty-year pattern of upholding the exercise of federal authority or whether it is a temporary aberration will depend on future appointments to the Supreme Court and on political dynamics generally.

Second, until the 1960s U.S. representatives and senators were generally closely tied to their states' political parties. The decline of American political parties, however, has weakened this linkage, and members of Congress have become much more subject to the pressures of nationally organized interest groups. As a consequence, Congress is less reflective of state interests and more likely to enact legislation in response to perceived national demands, often expanding federal authority and reducing state power.

Finally, the United States is a signatory to both the North American Free Trade Agreement (NAFTA) and the World Trade Agreements (WTO), the latter including the General Agreement on Tariffs and Trade (GATT). These trade agreements are binding international obligations, which the United States must fulfill regardless of its internal political arrangements. According to one observer, "the trade pacts create a wide range of new limits and duties for state and local government."[49] While the impact of NAFTA and the WTO has thus far been relatively minor, these agreements carry within them a significant potential impact on the distribution of powers and responsibilities in the American federal system.

NOTES

1 The American Electoral College system apportions electoral votes for the president and vice-president among the states. Because Puerto Rico (as well as the other territories) is not a state, it has no electoral votes.

2 About 800,000 Indians live on reservations, mostly in the western part of the United States. The largest Indian tribe is the Navajo, with about 250,000 members and a reservation of 17 million acres.

3 Connecticut and Rhode Island continued to function under their colonial charters until they replaced them with constitutions in 1818 and 1842, respectively.

4 Rhode Island refused to send a delegation to the convention.

5 For a good telling of that story, see Catherine Drinker Bowen, *Miracle at Philadelphia: The Story of the Constiutional Convention, May-September 1787* (Boston: Little, Brown and Company, 1966).

6 The Constitution does, of course, empower the states to participate in the new federation by appointing presidential electors, selecting U.S. senators, conducting federal elections, and so on. In addition, the Constitution places limits on the power of the states (especially in Article I – "No State shall enter into any Treaty, Alliance, or Confederation ...") and imposes new obligations on them (especially in Article IV – the rendition of fugitives from justice).

7 Daniel J. Elazar, "Confederation and Federal Liberty," *Publius: The Journal of Federalism* 12, 4 (Fall 1982): 13. For a similar conclusion, see Jack Rakove, "The Legacy of the Articles of Confederation," *Publius: The Journal of Federalism* 12, 4 (Fall 1982): 45–66.

8 See Ellis Katz, "The Development of American Federalism, 1763–1865," *The Federal Idea: A History of Federalism from the Enlightenment to 1945*, Andrea Bosco, ed. (London: Lothian Foundation Press, 1991), pp. 39–50.

9 Thirty-one years after the Constitution was written, Chief Justice John Marshall pointed out this difference in holding that the Constitution's "Necessary and Proper" clause leads to an expansive, rather than a restrictive, view of federal powers. See *McCulloch v. Maryland*, 17 U.S. [Wheat.] 316 (1819).

10 The U.S. Supreme Court has been very deferential to state court interpretations of state constitutions and state laws. See, for example, *Michigan v. Long*, 463 U.S. 1032 (1983), holding that, where a state case is decided wholly on the basis of a state constitution or statute, the United Supreme Court will not review it. For interesting discussions of this "new judicial federalism," see *State Constitutions in the Federal System* (Washington: U.S. Advisory Commission on Intergovernmental Relations, 1989); and *Annals of the American Academy of Political and Social Science* 496 (March 1980).

11 Boundary disputes between states are settled by the U.S. Supreme Court.

12 "Except," according to Article I, Section 10 of the Constitution, "what may be absolutely necessary for executing its inspection Laws."

13 A contemporary controversy concerns the authority to tax Internet sales. In 1998 Congress enacted the Internet Tax Freedom Act, imposing a temporary moratorium in state sales taxes on the sale of goods or services transacted electronically through the Internet. The moratorium was extended by subsequent legislation. State officials claim that this ban costs the states $13 billion in tax revenues each year, an amount that will grow as Internet sales grow.

14 Excluding Alaska, which gets most of its revenue from oil royalties. The tax burden in Alaska in 2002 was 6.3 percent of personal income.

15 John Kincaid, "The State of U.S. Federalism, 2000–2001: Continuity in Crisis," *Publius: The Journal of Federalism* 31, 3 (Summer 2001): 1–69. See also, John Kincaid, "De Facto Devolution and Urban Defunding: The Priority of Persons Over Places," *Journal of Urban Affairs* 21, 2 (Spring 1999): 135–167.

16 See *Printz v. United States*, 521 U.S. 98 (1992), invalidating a federal requirement that local officials conduct background checks on gun purchasers.

17 This is the view of Michael D. Reagan and John G. Sanzone, *The New Federalism* 2nd ed. (New York: Oxford University Press, 1981).

18 The term "coercive federalism" was coined by John Kincaid. See John Kincaid, "From Cooperation to Coercion in American Federalism: Housing, Fragmentation and Preemption, 1780–1992," *Journal of Law and Politics* 9 (Winter 1993): 333–433; and John Kincaid, "From Cooperative to Coercive Federalism," *Annals of the American Academy of Political and Social Science* 509 (May 1990): 139–152.

19 See, for example, *Carter v. Carter Coal Company*, 296 U.S. 238 (1936); and *United States v. Butler*, 297 U.S. 1 (1936).

20 Examples include *National Labor Relations Board v. Jones and Laughlin Steel Corporation*, 301 U.S. 1 (1937); *Steward Machine Company v. Davis*, 301 U.S. 548 (1937); *Wickard v. Filburn*, 317 U.S. 349 (1958); and *Heart of Atlanta Motel v. United States*, 379 U.S. 241 (1964).

21 See, for example, *United States v. Lopez*, 514 U.S. 549 (1995).

22 For an interesting analysis of this recent development, see Susan Gluck Mezey, "The U.S. Supreme Court's Federalism Jurisprudence," *Publius: The Journal of Federalism*, 30 (1–2) (Winter/Spring 2000): 21–38.

23 The Thirteenth Amendment abolishes slavery, and the Fifteenth Amendment forbids the denial of voting rights on the basis of race.

24 The federal highway program actually got its start in 1921, but it was greatly expanded during the 1950s.

25 See Jay Bybee, "Ulysses at the Mast: Democracy, Federalism, and the Sirens' Song of the Seventeenth Amendment," *Northwestern University Law Review* 91 (1977): 500. Ralph A. Rossum argues that "Post-Seventeenth Amendment federalism differs dramatically from the federalism of the framers." See his "Constitution of the United States," *Encyclopedia of American Federalism*, Joseph A. Marbach, Ellis Katz and Troy Smith, eds. (Westport, CT: Greenwood Press, forthcoming).

26 Nevertheless, in *South Dakota v. Dole*, 483 U.S. 203 (1987), the U.S. Supreme Court held that the Twenty-First Amendment did not prohibit Congress from denying federal highway funds to states that failed to raise the minimum age for the purchase of alcoholic beverages to twenty-one.

27 For a detailed analysis of the role of the U.S. Supreme Court in the allocation of powers and responsibilities, see Ellis Katz, "The U.S. Supreme Court and the Integration of American Federalism," *Fédéralisme et Cours Suprêmes/Federalism and Supreme Courts*, Edmond Orban, ed. (Montréal: Les Presses de l'Université de Montréal, 1991), pp. 35–58.

28 Article I, Section 10, prohibits the states from passing any law "impairing the Obligation of Contracts." The Marshall Court used this provision to invalidate state legislation in several important cases, such as *Fletcher v. Peck*, 6 Cranch 87 (1810); and *Dartmouth College v. Woodward*, 17 U.S. [4 Wheaton] 518 (1819).

29 See, for example, *United States v. E.C. Knight Company*, 156 U.S. 1 (1895); and *Hammer v. Dagenhart*, 247 U.S. 251 (1918).

30 The leading decision is *Lochner v. New York*, 198 U.S. 45 (1905).

31 After his re-election in 1936, Roosevelt promoted legislation that would have allowed him to appoint an additional justice to the Supreme Court for every justice that was then over seventy years of age. While Roosevelt said that this was necessary because the Court had fallen behind in its work, everyone knew that his real motive was to add additional justices who would be more sympathetic to his New Deal.

32 *National Labor Relations Board v. Jones and Laughlin Steel Corporation*, 301 U.S. 1 (1937); and *Steward Machine Company v. Davis*, 301 U.S. 548 (1937).

33 See, for example, *West Coast Hotel Company v. Parrish*, 300 U.S. 379 (1937).

34 Decisions include *Southern Pacific Company v. Arizona*, 325 U.S. 761 (1945); *Dean Milk Company v. City of Madison*, 340 U.S. 349 (1951); and *City of Philadelphia v. New Jersey*, 437 U.S. 617 (1978).

35 A good sourcebook for this development is Henry J. Abraham and Barbara A. Perry, *Freedom and the Court* (New York: Oxford University Press, 1994).

36 The leading decision is *United States v. Lopez*, 514 U.S. 549 (1995).

37 See, for example, *Nollan v. California Coastal Commission*, 483 U.S. 825 (1987); and *Lucas v. South Carolina Coastal Council*, 505 U.S. 1003 (1992).

38 *Lawrence v. Texas,* 123 S. Ct 2472; 156 L.Ed. 508 (2003).

39 For a discussion of the effectiveness of the State and Local Legal Center, see John Dinan, "State Government Influence in the National Policy Process," *Publius: The Journal of Federalism* 27, 2 (Spring 1997): 129–142.

40 The activities of these state-federal judicial councils are chronicled in the *State-Federal Judicial Observer,* published by the Federal Judicial Center in Washington, D.C.

41 Bruce D. McDowell, "Advisory Commission on Intergovernmental Relations in 1996: The End of an Era," *Publius: The Journal of Federalism* 27, 2 (Spring 1997): 123.

42 CSG and ICMA do not lobby but are considered part of the "Big Seven."

43 The law was upheld by the U.S. Supreme Court in *South Dakota v. Dole,* 483 U.S. 203 (1987) over South Dakota's challenge that the law exceeded Congress's spending power and violated the Twenty-First Amendment.

44 For a discussion of the distinction between non-centralization and decentralization, see Daniel J. Elazar, *Exploring Federalism* (Tuscaloosa, AL: University of Alabama Press, 1987).

45 *National League of Cities v. Usery,* 426 U.S. 833 (1976).

46 *Garcia v. San Antonio Metropolitan Transit Authority,* 469 U.S. 528 (1985).

47 In *Garcia v. San Antonio Metropolitan Transit Authority,* 469 U.S. 528 (1985), Justice Harry Blackmun, writing for the majority, commented that "we are convinced that the fundamental limitation that the constitutional scheme imposes on the Commerce Clause to protect the 'States as States' is one of process rather than one of result," suggesting that that the interests of the states are better protected by their representation in Congress than by any constitutional limits drawn by the Supreme Court.

48 *United States v. Lopez,* 514 U.S. 549 (1995).

49 Conrad Weiler, "Free Trade Agreements: A New Federal Partner?" *Publius: The Journal of Federalism* 24, 3 (Summer 1994): 113–134

Comparative Conclusions

RONALD L. WATTS

INTRODUCTION:
A FUNDAMENTAL FEATURE OF FEDERATIONS

The essential characteristic of federations is that they are composed of two (or more) orders of government operating within a constitutional framework, with one order providing *shared rule* through common institutions for certain specified purposes and with the other order (or orders) providing regional or local *self-rule* through the governments of the constituent units for certain specified purposes. Thus, as the foregoing chapters in this volume make clear, a constitutional distribution of legislative and executive authority, responsibilities, and finances among the general and constituent unit governments constitutes a fundamental, indeed defining, aspect in the design and operation of all these federations.

In comparing the distribution of powers within the federations analyzed in this volume four preliminary observations stand out. First, while a constitutional distribution of authority, responsibilities, and finances among the orders of government is a fundamental feature common to all these federations, there is enormous variation with regard to the constitutional form and scope and to the operation of the distribution of powers. There is no single ideal model; rather there are many practical variations. The historical pressures affecting the allocation of functions to one order of government or another have varied. The form and scope of the constitutional distribution of authority have also differed. In some federations powers are assigned to the constituent units symmetrically, in others, in order to take account of particular circumstances in different constituent units, the allocation is asymmetrical. There are variations in the relative roles of the orders of government in different policy areas and in the provisions for intergovernmental interaction. The financial arrangements and the degree of reliance on intergovernmental financial transfers also vary. There is also considerable variation in the degree of centralization and non-centralization (or decentralization) of powers and in the degree of intergovernmental cooperation or competition among governments within federations.

Second, within each federation there is considerable difference between the constitutional form and the operational reality of the distribution of powers. In most cases political practice and processes have transformed the way the constitution has operated. Here the Global Dialogue on Federalism process, on which the chapters in this volume are based, is particularly helpful. The country roundtables, involving an exchange of views between practitioners and academics, helped to bring theory, constitutional law, and actual practice together. Furthermore, the subsequent international theme conference that followed the country roundtables provided a comparative context for the authors of the individual chapters.

Third, while in each of the federations there is a constitutional allocation of specific powers to each government, overlaps and intergovernmental interdependence have proved inevitable in virtually every federation. This interdependence requires a variety of processes and institutions in order to facilitate intergovernmental collaboration. But here too there is much variation from federation to federation regarding the degree and character of such intergovernmental collaboration and the balance struck between independence and interdependence of governments. For instance, Germany and Mexico are marked by closely interlocked relationships while Canada and Belgium lean in the opposite direction.

Fourth, as the final sections of the individual chapters indicate, virtually all contemporary federations are currently experiencing pressures to adjust their distribution of powers in order to meet changing and new conditions. The current context of globalization, with its emphasis on market economics, the benefits of decentralization, and security, requires a rebalancing of centralization and non-centralization and of collaborative and competitive federalism. With this has come recognition that the actual operation of federations should not be understood in terms of rigid structures for the division of powers but, rather, as evolving processes enabling reconciliation of internal diversity within their respective federal frameworks.

INFLUENCE OF THE HISTORICAL AND CULTURAL CONTEXT

To understand the factors that have shaped the distribution of powers in each federation requires an examination of the historical and cultural context that has led to its original creation, that influenced the drafting of its constitution, and that continued to influence the subsequent operation of the federation. A common feature of the federations examined in this volume is the simultaneous existence of two sets of powerful motives: (1) those seeking united action for certain purposes and (2) those seeking the autonomy of the distinctive constituent units of government for other purposes. This feature has in each case expressed itself in the constitutional distribution of powers between a federal government (for those purposes shared in common) and the constituent units of government (for those purposes related to the expression of distinctive regional identities and interests).

As the preceding chapters make clear, however, the specific form and allocation of the distribution of powers has varied according to the nature of the common interests and the diversity peculiar to the particular society of each federation. Different geographic, historical, economic, security, demographic, linguistic, cultural, intellectual, and international factors, and the interrelation of these, have been significant in contributing to the particular strength of the motives for union and for regional identity and, therefore, have affected the specific distribution of powers in each federation. Generally, the more territorial homogeneity within a society, the greater the powers allocated to the federal government. Generally, the sharper the diversity, particularly where linguistic and cultural differences are deep-rooted, the greater the relative autonomous powers assigned to the constituent units of government. Switzerland, Canada, and Belgium provide classic examples of the latter. The constitutions of Canada and Belgium have also tended to emphasize the exclusivity of powers rather than shared or concurrent powers. In some cases, however, where territorial social diversity and fragmentation is strong, it has been considered desirable, as in Canada and India initially, and in Spain, to give the federal government sufficiently strong, and even overriding, powers to resist possible tendencies to balkanization.

The process by which a federation is established also affects the character of the distribution of powers. Where the process of establishment involves the aggregation of previously distinct units giving up some of their sovereignty to establish a new federal government, the constitutional distribution of powers usually takes the form of specifying the new limited set of exclusive and concurrent federal powers, with the residual (usually unspecified) powers remaining reserved to the constituent units. The United States, Switzerland, and Australia are classic examples of this. By contrast, where the creation of a federation involves a process of devolution from a formerly unitary state, the reverse arrangement is often the case, with the powers of the regional units of government being specified and the residual authority remaining with the federal government, as in Belgium and Spain. Some federations, such as Canada and India, grew out of a combination of processes of aggregation and devolution, and in both cases their constitutions list specific exclusive federal, exclusive provincial or state, and concurrent powers, and the residual authority is assigned to the federal government. As well, in those instances in which there have been previous periods of military or authoritarian rule, such as in Brazil, Mexico, and Nigeria, this has left a relatively centralized distribution of powers. Nevertheless, in these cases in order to express the change from the previous centralized authoritarian regime, the distribution of powers has at least been given the form of defining federal exclusive and concurrent powers, with the residual powers being assigned to the states.

Another factor affecting the character of the constitutional distribution of powers is the influence of earlier models. The example of the United States was consciously in the minds of the constitution drafters in Switzerland, Australia, Germany, Brazil, and Mexico, while in India the Government of India Act, 1935 – itself patterned on the Canadian model – had a strong influence upon the Constituent Assembly shaping the new Constitution of 1950.

Note should be taken of three other sets of significant factors. One is the period in which the constitutional distribution of powers was drafted. The eighteenth century and nineteenth century constitutions of the United States, Switzerland, and Canada distributed powers in fairly general terms. By the onset of the twentieth century the Australian constitutional distribution of powers was more detailed and included references to such new subjects as labour arbitration. The newer federal constitutions of the latter half of the twentieth century go even further, including minutely detailed lists of powers and extensive provisions for intergovernmental institutions and processes. An example is the three lists (exclusively federal, concurrent, and state) of powers in the Seventh Schedule of the Indian Constitution, which contain 97, 47, and 66 entries, respectively, or the very finely detailed distribution scheme in the Swiss federal Constitution of 1999.

The prevalence of a common law tradition (as in the United States, Canada, Australia, India, and Nigeria) or of a civil law tradition (as in the European and Latin American federations such as Switzerland, Germany, Belgium, Spain, Brazil, and Mexico) has had a strong bearing on how the constitutional law is applied and interpreted. A number of chapters emphasize this and the resulting more limited scope for judicial review in federations with a civil law legal tradition.

Finally, a factor that has some impact upon the form and operation of the distribution of powers is the character of the legislative and executive institutions. This particular aspect of federations will be dealt with much more fully in the third volume of the Global Dialogue on Federalism, but it is relevant here. Whether these institutions are presidential-congressional in form (as in the United States and the Latin American federations) or essentially parliamentary in form (as in most of the other federations) affects the diffused or fused way in which the assigned legislative powers are handled within each level of government and, therefore, the character of

interactions between governments. In this respect Switzerland's system of
collegial executives at both federal and cantonal levels contributes to the
uniqueness of its operation.

CONSTITUTIONAL DISTRIBUTION OF LEGISLATIVE AND EXECUTIVE AUTHORITY

Variations in Non-Centralization

Although in federations the basic features of the distribution of legislative
and executive authority are typically embodied in the constitution, the orientation and character of this distribution varies from federation to federation.
There has, for instance, been considerable variation in the degree of centralization, decentralization, and non-centralization in the constitutional distributions of powers. Here two preliminary points need to be made. First, the
concepts of decentralization and non-centralization are closely related but
have different connotations. Some analysts prefer to use the term "non-
centralization" rather than "decentralization" on the grounds that the latter
implies a hierarchy with power flowing from the top or centre, as occurs in
decentralized unitary systems, whereas the former implies a constitutional
dispersion of power with limited central authority, thus better representing
the character of the distribution of powers in federations.[1] While the term
"decentralization" is the one used most extensively in this volume, with regard to federations "non-centralization" may be a more accurate word. In
any case, the distinctive character of federal decentralization needs to be
kept in mind.

Second, while in ordinary language we may loosely compare differing
degrees of decentralization within federations, the comparative measurement of decentralization is actually a complex issue.[2] To begin with, it is
necessary to distinguish different forms of decentralization: legislative,
executive and administrative, and financial. These do not necessarily correspond with each other. For example, the Swiss federation is more centralized in terms of legislative jurisdiction than is Canada, but it is more
non-centralized in terms of administration, finances, and the requirement
of cantonal participation in federal decision making. Furthermore, within
each of the categories of legislative, executive, and financial jurisdiction
the degree of decentralization of different subject areas may vary. Thus a
given federation may be more centralized than other federations in some
matters while less centralized in others.

Difficult as it is, therefore, to arrive at a precise overall ranking of decentralization and non-centralization among federations because of the variety
of relevant indices that have to be taken into account, some broad overall
generalizations can be reached on the basis of a review of these various

indicators.[3] Three federations – Switzerland, Canada and Belgium – appear to be the most non-centralized. India, although it has some centralist elements, would appear to rank next, given the significant devolution of autonomous revenues and expenditures that has occurred during the past half-century. The United States and Australia, which began as strongly non-centralized federations, have both evolved a considerably expanded role for their federal governments. Germany is relatively centralized in legislative and fiscal terms, but this is moderated by the extensive devolution of the responsibility for administration and expenditures. The remaining federations examined in this volume are marked by relatively greater central dominance, with Brazil, Spain, Nigeria, and Mexico in ascending order of centralization.

One other major difference in the character of the constitutional distribution of powers is that between those federations where this relates to two orders of government and those where it relates to three. In the former, governments at the state level are usually given the power to devolve jurisdiction to local governments as they see fit; in the latter, the constitution expressly recognizes a third order of local and municipal governments. The United States, Canada, Australia, Belgium, and Spain fall in the former category, while Brazil, Germany, India (as a result of major constitutional amendments), Mexico, Nigeria, and Switzerland fall in the latter.

Variations in the Form of the Distribution of Legislative Authority

In most federations some areas of responsibility are assigned exclusively to one level of government or the other, but the extent of these varies greatly. In Canada, originally in Switzerland (but somewhat less so under the 1999 Constitution), and more recently in Belgium, most areas of responsibility were assigned exclusively to either the federal or the constituent unit legislatures. By contrast to these three federations, in the United States and Australia the powers assigned exclusively to the federal legislature are much more limited, and most federal powers are identified as shared concurrent powers. In Germany, India, Brazil, Mexico, and Nigeria the exclusive jurisdiction assigned to the federal legislature is more extensive, but the distribution of powers in each of these federations includes large areas of concurrent jurisdiction. The form of the Spanish distribution of powers is distinctive. The Constitution lists the exclusive powers of the central government but transfers the determination of the powers of the Autonomous Communities (regions) to separate Statutes of Autonomy. Under these, despite an emphasis upon exclusivity in the assignment of powers, in practice many areas have required joint governmental intervention.

Jurisdiction over residual matters not otherwise listed or specified in the constitution has been assigned in each federal constitution to the legislature of one level of government or the other. In most federations, especially those created originally by a process of aggregating previously separate units, the residual power has remained with the federating units. Examples of this are the United States, Switzerland, Australia, Germany, Brazil, Mexico, and Nigeria. In some federations, however, usually where devolution from a preceding – more centralized – unitary regime has occurred, the residual authority has been left with the federal government. Examples are Canada, India, Belgium, and Spain, although in the case of Belgium the governments have formally agreed to reformulate the constitutional distribution of powers so that the residual authority lies with the devolved units (it should be noted that this has not yet been implemented).

The significance of the residual authority is related to the number and comprehensiveness of the enumerated lists of legislative powers in the constitution. The greater the enumeration of specific powers the less significant the potential scope of the residual power. Thus, in federations such as Canada and India, where the constitutions set out three comprehensive lists of exclusive federal, exclusive provincial, and concurrent jurisdiction, the assigning of the residual authority has been relatively less significant. By contrast, in federations such as the United States, Switzerland, Australia, Germany, Brazil, Mexico, and Nigeria, where the state jurisdiction has not been enumerated and has simply been covered by a substantial unspecified residual authority, the latter is highly significant. In most of these federations the assignment of significant residual authority to the states was intended to symbolically underline their autonomy and the limited nature of the exclusive and concurrent powers transferred by the constitution to the federal legislature. It is worthy of note, however, that in practice in most of these federations there has been a tendency for the courts to read the maximum "implied powers" into the constitutionally specified federal authority at the expense of the scope of the unspecified residual state powers. This has contributed over time to the progressive expansion of federal powers in these federations. Paradoxically, in such federations as Canada and India, where the centralist founders enumerated what were intended to be limited specific provincial or state powers, the courts have in practice tended to read those powers broadly, thus limiting the expansion of federal authority.

In a few federations the constitution provides the federal government with specific override, or emergency, powers enabling it to invade or curtail what would otherwise normally be state constitutional powers. These arrangements reflect the fears of their founders over the prospects of potential balkanization or disintegration. Among the federations reviewed in this volume Canada and India provide examples of such arrangements. The Canadian Constitution continues to include some such federal powers. These include the powers of reservation and disallowance of provincial legislation; the declaratory power relating to public works in the national interest; and the peace, order, and good government clause as interpreted by the courts. However, in practice, over the past half century almost all of these federal unilateral powers have fallen into disuse. On the other hand, the extensive emergency powers embodied in the Indian Constitution of 1950 have, in fact, been frequently used over the past fifty years (although there is now growing political pressure to limit their use).

Relationship between Distributions of Legislative and Executive Authority

In some federations, particularly those in the Anglo-American and common law traditions, such as the United States, Canada (with the exception of criminal law), and Australia, each order of government has been assigned executive responsibility in the same fields for which it has legislative authority. Although derived from different traditions, the Belgian distribution of power also closely ties the allocation of executive powers to the allocation of legislative jurisdiction. There have been several reasons for favouring such an arrangement. First, it reinforces the autonomy of the legislative bodies. Second, it gives each government the authority to implement its own legislation, thereby assuring that the legislation is not meaningless. Third, in such federations as Canada and Australia, where the "Westminster" principle of parliamentary executives being responsible to their legislatures has been adopted, it is only if legislative and executive jurisdiction coincide that the legislature can exercise its control over the body executing its laws.

In some federations, most notably in Germany but also to a considerable extent in Switzerland, there are constitutionally mandated and entrenched provisions for splitting the legislative and executive jurisdictions in a particular area between different orders of government. In the German case this has led to a high degree of legislative centralization coupled with the very decentralized administration of much federal legislation carried out by the Länder. Another example is the case of India, where all federal legislation enacted in an area of concurrent jurisdiction is specified in the Constitution as the administrative responsibility of the states. This sort of arrangement enables the federal legislature to lay down uniform legislation while leaving it to be applied by state or cantonal governments in ways that take into account varying regional circumstances. However, such a bifurcation of legislative and executive responsibilities does, in practice, require extensive collaboration between the levels of government.

In practice, however, the contrast between these two approaches is not quite as sharp as the constitutional provisions might suggest. Even in those federations where legislative and executive responsibilities constitutionally coincide, federal governments have often delegated considerable responsibilities for federal programs to constituent unit governments, often by providing persuasive financial assistance through grant-in-aid schemes. Nevertheless, there are differences in the degree to which overlapping responsibilities have led to intergovernmentalization. As the chapter on the United States indicates, intergovernmentalization there has become almost total, while this has been much less the case in Belgium, with its emphasis on exclusive jurisdictions. But even in the latter case some intergovernmental agreements have been necessary.

Scope of Legislative Jurisdiction Allocated

Important as differences in the form of the constitutional distribution of authority are in determining the degree of governmental autonomy and non-centralization within federations, the assignment of particular functions and powers to each order of government is also significant.

Broadly speaking, in most federations international relations, defence, the functioning of the economic and monetary union, major taxation powers, and interregional transportation are placed under federal jurisdiction. Social policy (including education, health services, social welfare, and labour relations), maintenance of law and security, and local government are usually assigned to the constituent unit governments. Parts of these areas, however, especially those relating to social services, are often shared, as are the areas of agriculture and natural resources. Despite this general pattern, there is considerable variation in the specific allocations within different federations depending on the degree of emphasis placed upon common action or upon non-centralization as well as upon the impact of particular circumstances.

Some subject matters have proven particularly troublesome. Foreign affairs is an example. In many federations a sweeping federal jurisdiction over foreign affairs and treaties has sometimes been used to override jurisdiction that would otherwise belong to the governments of the constituent units. In a few federations, however, the federal treaty power is limited by the constitutional requirement that, where treaties affect the jurisdiction of the constituent unit governments, consultation must occur (and sometimes consent must be obtained). In the case of Canada, as a result of judicial interpretation of the Constitution, a treaty related to a field of provincial jurisdiction can only be implemented if the required measures (including legislation) are undertaken by the provincial legislatures or governments. In the case of Germany such treaties require the endorsement of a majority of votes in the Bundesrat, which is composed of delegates of the Land governments; since 1993 the German Basic Law has required extensive Länder consultation or agreement with regard to European Union matters. Two of the most recent federal constitutions, that of Belgium

(1993) and Switzerland (1999), assign to their respective constituent units a major role in the conduct of foreign relations or require their extensive consultation regarding foreign policy decisions.

The increased interrelation of economic and cultural policy in the contemporary world has made the resolution of multiethnic issues within federations more complex than it was in the past. The original simple Canadian solution of 1867, which consisted of centralizing control of economic policy but assigning responsibility for cultural distinctiveness and related social programs to the provinces, has been complicated by two developments. One is the greatly increased cost of social policies requiring federal financial assistance and the other is the realization by regionally concentrated ethnic groups that their distinctiveness depends not just upon cultural policy but also upon being able to shape economic policies regarding their own welfare. A further complication is that different ethnic groups are never completely demarcated in territorial terms. Consequently, any distribution of powers has to take account of the need to protect minorities within minorities by placing constitutional limits upon state or provincial governments regarding their policies towards internal minorities.

As the foregoing chapters make clear, economic policy and social policy are two areas in which one usually finds extensive activity on the part of both federal and constituent unit governments. With regard to economic policy, states, provinces, and Cantons are concerned to ensure the economic welfare of their own citizens and to develop policies related to their own particular economic interests. In some cases this has produced a highly competitive situation among governments within federations. It has also sometimes led to states or provinces establishing offices in foreign countries to encourage both trade and investment – a pattern found in the United States, Canada, Australia, and Germany. With regard to social policy, including health, education, and social services, the primary constitutional responsibility is generally assigned to the constituent unit governments. In some cases such standards are provided in federal framework legislation. Often program costs and pressures for federation-wide standards of public service have led to extensive federal financial assistance and, hence, influence. And where constituent units have welcomed such federal financial assistance, it has frequently proven to be a Trojan horse for federal dominance.

DISTRIBUTION OF FINANCES

Significance of the Allocation of Financial Resources

The fourth volume of the Global Dialogue on Federalism will deal in detail with the financial arrangements in federations. Nevertheless, for two main reasons some reference to the allocation of financial resources is relevant to this volume: (1) the distribution of financial resources enables or constrains governments with regard to the exercise of their constitutionally assigned legislative and executive responsibilities; and (2) taxing powers and expenditure authority are themselves important instruments for affecting and regulating the economy.

Allocation of Revenue and Expenditure Powers

Most federations specify in their constitutions (or, in the case of Belgium and Spain, in special legislation) the revenue-raising powers of the two orders of government. The major taxing powers usually identified are customs and excise, corporate income taxes, personal income taxes, and various sales and consumption taxes. A common characteristic of the allocation of fiscal powers is that the majority of revenue sources are assigned to the federal government, although in Canada, Switzerland, and the United States (although to a lesser extent) the constituent unit governments have considerable taxing powers of their own in such fields as personal income taxes and sales and consumption taxes. In some other federations, where the levying and collecting of major taxes are concentrated in the federal government, there are constitutional stipulations for the sharing of the proceeds of these federal taxes with the states. Germany and India are prime examples of this pattern, but such arrangements exist in a number of other federations as well. Three factors have contributed to the frequent concentration of the major taxing powers in federal governments. The first involves the fact that the concentration of resources in the federal government is necessary if it is to perform the redistributive role usually expected of it. The second involves the influence of Keynesian theories concerning the need for federation-wide policies pertaining to economic stability and development. Such theories were particularly prevalent at the time many of the current fiscal arrangements were developed. The third factor involves the promotion of tax harmonization and mobility for the purposes of economic union.

In addition to taxation another source for government fundraising – public borrowing – has usually been open to both orders of government. In some cases, however, foreign borrowing is placed under exclusive federal jurisdiction in order to prevent constituent unit action from undermining the credit worthiness of the federation (e.g., India, Mexico, Nigeria, and Spain). A unique arrangement with the same objective was Australia's 1928 establishment of the intergovernmental Loan Council, which had the power to make decisions that were binding on both levels of government.

Broadly speaking, the constitutional distribution of expenditure powers in each federation corresponds to the combined scope of the legislative and administrative responsibilities assigned to each government. Three points should be noted, however. First, where the administration of a substantial portion of federal legislation is constitutionally assigned to the governments of the constituent units (as in Switzerland, Germany, and India), this has usually resulted in these units being responsible for substantially larger expenditure responsibilities than legislative responsibilities. The need for substantial federal transfers, either in the form of shared federal tax proceeds or in the form of unconditional and conditional grants, has, therefore, been a typical feature of these systems. Second, expenditure requirements of different areas of responsibility vary considerably. Thus, such responsibilities as health, education, and social services usually prove to be high-cost functions when compared to those relating more to regulation than to provision of services.

Third, in most federations the constitution does not impose strict limits on government expenditures, restricting them to specified legislative and administrative jurisdictions. In most cases governments have usually been taken by the courts to possess either explicitly or implicitly a constitutional *general* spending power.[4] This has enabled federal governments to provide grants to states and to use these grants to influence state government policies in areas outside federal jurisdiction. For their part, although typically with much lower expenditures, constituent unit governments use their general spending power to fund trade and promotion offices in foreign countries even when they have no constitutionally specified jurisdiction in external affairs. The recognition of a general unrestricted spending power provides some flexibility in the operation of governments within a federation; however, if this power is used extensively by a federal government, then it may become a device for federal dominance. There are some cases, however, in which a federal constitution does restrict spending in areas not within the government's constitutionally specified legislative or administrative jurisdiction. Belgium provides a notable example, generally limiting expenditures to areas of constitutionally assigned jurisdiction. In Germany the federal exercise of spending in areas of Land jurisdiction requires the approval of the Bundesrat, which is composed of Land delegates. And in Switzerland both long-held traditions and the constitutional provisions referring to collaboration between federal and cantonal governments (Articles 44–6) have led to the avoidance of unilateral federal decisions regarding federal spending in areas of cantonal jurisdiction.

Consequent Need for Financial Transfers

Because in federations it is generally necessary to allocate the major taxing powers to the federal governments in order to facilitate an effective economic union – and to allocate major expenditure responsibilities in such expensive fields as health, education, and social services to the constituent unit governments in order to facilitate administrative effectiveness – in virtually every federation there is an imbalance between the allocations of revenue capacity and of expenditure responsibilities. In most federations this has resulted in the need for substantial transfers from the federal to the constituent unit governments, although the extent of the imbalance to be corrected varies according to the precise constitutional allocations of taxing powers and expenditure responsibilities. These transfers take several forms. One of these is revenue sharing, which involves the transfer of all or part of the proceeds of certain federal taxes, as in Germany, Switzerland, India, Spain, Brazil, Nigeria, and Australia (in the latter case since the institution of the Goods and Services Tax [GST]). Another is the use of substantial unconditional or semi-conditional block grants. This was the predominant form of transfer in Australia prior to the establishment of the GST and continues to be the predominant form in Canada as well as India. A third form of transfer is the use of specific-purpose conditional grants. These are used extensively in the United States, Switzerland, Germany, Australia, Mexico, Spain, and, to a lesser degree, India and Brazil. The importance of these intergovernmental transfers is illustrated by the fact that, as a percentage of total constituent unit government revenues, in 2000–01 federal transfers in total constituted 72.8 percent in Spain, 46.0 percent in India, 45.3 percent in Australia, 43.8 percent in Germany, 30.0 percent in Brazil, 29.6 percent in the United States, 24.8 percent in Switzerland, and 19.8 percent in Canada.[5]

A further complication in the allocation of revenue powers and expenditure responsibilities arises from horizontal imbalances among the federated units within federations. Differences among units regarding the capacity to raise revenues from the same taxes or regarding the costs of providing the same services are often a source of political resentment. Consequently, in order to enable all units within a federation to provide their citizens with generally comparable services without having to exact excessively different tax rates, most federations have established formal schemes for "equalization" transfers. The United States is, in this respect, a significant exception. The form and scope of equalization transfers and the processes involved in their periodic adjustment vary considerably, and an in-depth analysis of these phenomena will be offered in the fourth volume of the Global Dialogue on Federalism.

The generally prevailing pattern of concentrating taxation powers in the federal government and of relying on intergovernmental financial transfers to balance the cost of the responsibilities assigned to the constituent units raises a number of issues. One is the difficulty of fostering accountability when taxation and expenditure responsibilities reside at different levels of government. There is also the need to avoid the sense of dependency that arises from relying too heavily upon financial transfers. Closely related to this is the need for incentives to encourage lower levels of government to exercise what taxation powers they do have rather than to rely upon transfers. Yet another issue is the danger that the autonomy of the receiving government will be undermined in cases where a substantial portion of federal transfers are discretionary and conditional in nature.

RATIONALE FOR THE DISTRIBUTION OF POWERS AND RESPONSIBILITIES

Each of the preceding chapters examines whether the particular distribution of powers in a specific federation is based on a fundamental logic or is mostly the outcome of political bargaining and interest group compromises. From the examples examined it would appear that the latter has been a strong element in virtually all cases. Nevertheless, out of the process of negotiation some logical rationale for the distribution of jurisdiction embodied in the constitution has often emerged. One of the clearest examples of this is to be found in the Report of the Drafting Committee and its chairperson's presentation to the Constituent Assembly of India. There the various compromises are woven into a clear explanation of the need for a strong Union government (for economic and security reasons) as well as the need to accommodate India's diversity. Similarly, pronouncements by the founding constitution drafters of other federations often set out the need for a strong and effective federal government while at the same time ensuring that there is sufficient decentralization and, indeed, noncentralization to ensure autonomous regional jurisdiction over those policies particularly important for local self-government and distinctiveness.

It is noteworthy that, while the specific distribution of powers in each federation is the product of its own particular circumstances, not infrequently the drafters are influenced either positively or negatively by preceding examples. In many respects the makers of the 1848 Swiss Constitution took into account the experience of the United States (e.g., the form of the distribution of powers and the Senate) but were determined to avoid concentrating power in the president. Canadians, who were creating a new federation just when the United States was emerging from a horrendous civil war, deliberately tried to avoid what they perceived as a too weak American federal government. On the other hand, the Australians preferred the U.S. model to the Canadian due to the former's decentralized distribution of powers. Later federations have had even more models to consider. For instance, the Constituent Assembly of India included in its deliberations three volumes of constitutional precedents from other countries. But useful as these models have been, ultimately, federations have had to devise solutions to their own particular situations, sometimes coming up with interesting innovations (e.g., the Belgian distribution of powers).

One issue that distinguishes some federations from others involves whether the constitutional distribution of legislative and executive powers should apply uniformly (i.e., symmetrically) to all the federated units or whether there should be variations (i.e., asymmetry) to take into account the different circumstances or particular requirements of some constituent units.

In a majority of federations, including the United States, Switzerland, Australia, Germany, Mexico, and Nigeria, the formal constitutional distribution of legislative and executive jurisdiction applies symmetrically to all the full-fledged member states.[6] In some other federations, however, significant variations among the full-fledged units (arising from different intensities in pressures for regional autonomy, sharp differences in linguistic, religious, or ethnic composition, or major variations in economic situation or geographic size and population) make necessary the provision of constitutional asymmetry in the jurisdiction assigned to full-fledged constituent units.[7] Belgium, Spain, and India are examples of this. The Canadian constitutional distribution of powers is fundamentally symmetrical in form, but there are some unique provisions relating to Quebec, and, in practice, this asymmetry is extended in a number of ways.[8]

Clearly, where there is asymmetry in the constitutional jurisdiction assigned to the constituent units within a federation, this has introduced greater complexity. Nevertheless, it would appear that some federations have found that the only way to accommodate sharply varying intensities in the pressures for political autonomy has been to resort to asymmetry in the constitutional assignment of jurisdiction. The most notable cases involve the "double asymmetry" embodied in the Belgian federation, the cases of the northeastern states and Jammu and Kashmir in India, and the situation of Quebec in Canada. In some other cases, asymmetry is justified as a transitional arrangement accommodating regions at different stages of political development. The justification of the arrangements for the Autonomous Communities in Spain provides an example of this rationale. In some cases, as in Canada and Spain, pressures for asymmetry have induced contentious counter-pressures for greater symmetry. These suggest that there may be limits to constitutional asymmetry beyond which extreme asymmetry may become dysfunctional. On the other hand, it would also appear that, on balance, the recognition of constitutional asymmetry has in some cases provided the only effective way to accommodate major differences among constituent units.

Another issue is the extent to which the constitutional distribution of powers emphasizes either a system of shared powers and responsibilities and, with that, the interaction between orders of government (cooperative federalism), or the independent and exclusive operation of the dual orders of government (dualist federalism). Virtually all federal constitutions recognize some areas of exclusive jurisdiction for each order of government (either enumerated or residual) and some areas of concurrent jurisdiction, but there is wide variation in the extent of the exclusive and the extent of the concurrent jurisdictions.

The advantages of assigning responsibility exclusively to one level of government or the other would appear to be twofold. It reinforces the autonomy of that government and it makes clear which government is accountable for policy in that area. In practice, however, even where most powers are assigned exclusively to one level of government or the other, experiences such as those of Switzerland, Canada, and Belgium indicate that it is virtually impossible to define watertight compartments of jurisdiction and that, therefore, some jurisdictional overlaps and some intergovernmental interaction are unavoidable. This has, in practice, softened the exclusivity of the allocated powers even where they have been emphasized.

The recognition of the inevitability of overlaps in many fields has, in some federations, led to extensive areas of concurrent legislative jurisdiction being allocated in their constitutions right from the beginning. Examples are the United States, Australia, Germany, India, Brazil, Mexico, and Nigeria. This contrasts with Canada, for instance, where the areas of concurrent jurisdiction are relatively limited. Originally, the only constitutionally specified areas of concurrent jurisdiction in Canada were agriculture and immigration, to which have been added, by constitutional amendments, old age pensions and benefits and the export of non-renewable natural resources, forest products, and electrical energy.

Concurrency has a number of apparent advantages. It provides an element of flexibility in the distribution of powers, enabling constituent unit legislatures to pursue their own initiatives until such time as the subject becomes one requiring federal action. Frequently, federal legislatures use areas of concurrent jurisdiction to legislate federation-wide standards, leaving regional legislatures and governments room to legislate the details and to deliver the services in a manner sensitive to local circumstances. Indeed, in Germany (and, in some respects, in Spain, Mexico, and Brazil) there is a special constitutional category of jurisdiction establishing federal powers to enact "framework legislation" in certain fields, leaving the Länder to fill out these areas with more detailed laws. In addition, in Germany a 1969 constitutional amendment added a category of "joint tasks," in which the federal government would participate in the discharge of certain specified Länder responsibilities.

Concurrent lists of legislative powers also avoid the necessity of the constitution enumerating complicated minute subdivisions of individual functions to be assigned exclusively to one level of government or the other. Such subdivisions of responsibilities are likely, over time, to become

obsolete and hence restrictive. Again, however, one has the notable exception of Switzerland, where the recent constitutional revisions have
brought such minute distinctions up-to-date.

Normally, where concurrent jurisdiction is specified, the constitution
also stipulates that, in cases of conflict between federal law and unit law,
the former prevails. Thus, areas of concurrent jurisdiction are, ultimately,
potential areas of federal jurisdiction. One notable exception occurs in
Canada, where old-age pensions are placed under concurrent jurisdiction
but where, in cases of conflict, provincial law prevails over federal law. This
has enabled the Province of Quebec to preserve its own pension system
while the other provinces accept a federal pensions jurisdiction.

EVOLUTION OF THE CONSTITUTIONAL
DISTRIBUTION OF POWERS

Federations are not static organizations and, over time, the distribution of
powers in each has to adapt and evolve to respond to changing needs and
circumstances and the development of new issues and policy areas. Thus,
for instance, federations established during the eighteenth or nineteenth
centuries have subsequently had to work out which governments should be
responsible for environmental and energy issues. But the need to adjust
and adapt the constitutional distribution of powers requires finding a balance between flexibility and rigidity. Ease of adjustment to the distribution
of powers runs the danger of undermining the sense of security of minorities and regional groups, whose concerns made the adoption of a federal
system necessary in the first place. But too rigid a distribution of powers,
while assuring the constitutional protection of regional and minority interests, may make effective response to changing circumstances difficult. In
seeking this balance federations rely on four processes, although in varying
degrees: formal constitutional amendments, judicial interpretation and review, intergovernmental financial adjustments, and intergovernmental collaboration and agreements.

Formal constitutional amendment is one major process that enables constitutional distributions of powers to evolve over time. In most federations,
in order to ensure a continued balance between the federal and regional
orders of government, the constitutional distribution of powers is not uni-
laterally amendable by either order of government and requires formal
adoption not only by the federal legislature (sometimes, as in the United
States, Mexico, and Nigeria, by special majorities) but also by a significant
proportion of the constituent units. The latter may be signified by referendum (as in Switzerland and Australia), by legislatures (as in the United
States, Canada, India, Mexico, and Nigeria), or by instructed delegates in
the federal second chamber (as in Germany). Three federations – Belgium,

Brazil, and Spain – depart from the requirement of some form of assent from the constituent units; instead, they require special majorities and special processes in the federal legislature for amendments to the constitutional distribution of powers.

While all these various procedures for formal constitutional amendments introduce some element of constitutional rigidity, the actual degree of rigidity varies enormously in practice, depending upon such factors as the extent to which amendment proposals are minor or comprehensive in scope, the degree of conservatism prevalent in the political culture, and the extent of interparty cohesion or the dominance at both levels of a single party. Thus, despite almost identical processes for constitutional amendment in Switzerland and Australia, over a century some 100 partial constitutional revisions were adopted in Switzerland, while over the same period only eight of forty-four proposed amendments were adopted in Australia. The amendment procedure in the United States is also relatively rigid: the first ten amendments were made in 1791, and over two centuries later there have been only seventeen further constitutional amendments. In Canada, too, the formal process for amending the constitutional distribution of powers (established in 1982) has proved to be quite rigid. The amendment procedures in some other federations, such as Germany, India, Mexico, and Nigeria, have in practice proved to be less rigid. Of the three federations that do not require assent of the constituent units but that require special majorities and processes in the federal legislature, the Brazilian procedure has proved to be remarkably flexible; however, in Belgium and Spain the political strength of the distinct communities makes their amendment procedures less flexible than might be expected.

Judicial interpretation and review is more important in the evolution of the distribution of powers in those federations (such as the United States, Canada, and Australia) where the constitutional amendment procedures are rigid. Judicial interpretation also plays an important role in other federations in the common law tradition, such as India and Nigeria. As noted in the chapters on Switzerland, Brazil, Mexico, and Spain, these federations, which are in the civil law tradition, rely much less upon judicial review for the adaptation of the distribution of powers. Nevertheless, in both Germany and Belgium the constitutional courts play a significant role in relation to the distribution of powers.

One important process for adding flexibility to the distribution of powers and responsibilities over time involves intergovernmental financial arrangements. Invariably, the processes for adjusting these are more flexible in practice than is the constitutional enumeration of legislative and executive jurisdiction. This adjustment was found to be necessary because the values of revenue sources and the costs of expenditure responsibilities change significantly over time. Federations have, therefore, needed to establish processes and institutions to facilitate the regular adjustment of intergovernmental financial transfers. In those federations characterized by a separation of legislative and executive powers within each order of government (such as the United States, Switzerland, Brazil, and Mexico), the primary arena for making such adjustments to the financial arrangements is the federal legislature (in the Swiss case advised from time to time by ad hoc commissions).

In the other federations characterized by fused parliamentary executives, the primary arena is that of "executive federalism," involving intergovernmental negotiations between the executives representing the federal and regional units of government. In a number of these, special independent expert commissions are entrusted with the primary task of determining and adjusting the distributive formulae for finances. Examples are the Commonwealth Grants Commission in Australia, the quinquennial Finance Commissions provided for by the Constitution in India, and the Revenue Mobilization, Allocation, and Fiscal Commission established by the Nigerian Constitution. In addition to these formal processes for adjusting financial arrangements, in most federations the widespread use of federal grants-in-aid to the governments of the constituent units provides a means not only for assisting these units to undertake costly responsibilities but also for the federal government to influence policy in matters not constitutionally assigned to it. Such grants have provided flexibility and have encouraged intergovernmental cooperation, although sometimes at the price of federal domination.

A fourth process affecting the evolution of the distribution of powers and responsibilities is the practice of intergovernmental cooperation, as such. Without requiring formal constitutional amendment, such practices as interdelegation of legislative responsibilities, administrative cooperation and joint action, and formal intergovernmental agreements enable various federations to respond to changing needs and circumstances without formal constitutional amendments. A later volume of the Global Dialogue on Federalism will deal fully with such processes.

In some cases emergency powers that enable the federal government in times of emergency, or special constitutional provisions designed to facilitate flexibility in particular matters (such as the creation of new states), contribute to flexibility. India provides prime examples of both types of arrangements.

Also, it is worth noting that, in some federations (such as the United States, Australia, Germany, Brazil, Mexico, and Nigeria), the evolution of the distribution of powers has, over time, displayed a general trend towards the reinforcement and expansion of federal powers. In some of these federations this has been the result of a consolidation of the unifying forces within the federation (or what some would refer to as nation building). In others it has been the result of a dominant political party or of periods of authoritarian rule. Furthermore, the changing importance of different powers and responsibilities, particularly those relating to the global economy and international trade, have also had an influence. But increasing centralization is not a universal trend among federations. Canada, India, and Belgium have, over time, clearly experienced a marked trend towards greater decentralization, reflecting the strength of the diverse communities of which they are composed. While in some respects Switzerland has become more centralized over the past century and a half, it still retains a high degree of non-centralization, as is illustrated by its 1999 Constitution. Spain, since the adoption of its 1978 Constitution, has undertaken major devolutionary development. Nevertheless, in comparative terms it remains relatively centralized.

MAINTENANCE AND MANAGEMENT OF THE DISTRIBUTION OF POWERS

Impact of Interdependence

A major feature in the operation of the distribution of powers in federations is the inevitable interdependence between governments and the need for intergovernmental cooperation. In practice the different orders of government have to treat each other as partners. This requires extensive consultation, cooperation, and coordination between governments within federations. The institutions and processes for intergovernmental collaboration serve two important functions: (1) conflict resolution and (2) a way of adapting to changing circumstances.

One important element of intergovernmental relations occurring extensively in all federations is the great variety of informal direct communications (e.g., by letter, telephone, etc.) between ministers, officials, and representatives of different governments. In addition to these informal interactions, most federations have developed a range of more formal institutions to facilitate intergovernmental collaboration. These usually take the form of a variety of standing and ad hoc meetings involving ministers, legislators, officials, and agencies of different governments. A noteworthy feature in federations with parliamentary institutions, where the first ministers and cabinet ministers tend to predominate within each order of government, is the prevalence of what has come to be known as "executive federalism," in which governmental executives (ministers and their officials) provide the main channel for intergovernmental negotiations and collaboration. The institutions and processes of executive federalism usually develop pragmatically rather than by constitutional requirement. In such federations as Australia, Canada, Germany, and India frequent

meetings of officials, ministers, and first ministers are particularly important, providing institutional processes for consultation, negotiation, cooperation, and, on occasion, joint projects. On the other hand, sometimes
these meetings are also the arena for intergovernmental confrontation
and conflict.

Among contemporary federations executive federalism is most extensively developed in Germany and Australia. In Germany, the Bundesrat
serves as a central focus for a wide range of intergovernmental executive
interaction. In 1992 Australia established the Council of Australian Governments (COAG) to oversee the extensive intergovernmental ministerial
councils that had already developed. A particular objective of COAG is to
make the Australian economic union more effective.

Extensive interaction between governments has not been limited to parliamentary federations, however. In federations where there is a separation
of legislative and executive powers within each government, channels for
intergovernmental relations tend to be more dispersed. In such federations as the United States, Switzerland, Brazil, Mexico, and Nigeria a variety of channels between executives, administrators, and legislators, often in
crisscrossing patterns, can be observed. A notable feature of these federations is the widespread lobbying of federal legislators on the part of various
state and cantonal representatives. The 1999 Swiss Constitution also includes numerous provisions requiring intergovernmental consultation and
collaboration in a wide range of matters.

In such federations as Germany and Switzerland, where there are constitutional requirements that a considerable portion of federal legislation
must be administered by the states or Cantons, the need for close intergovernmental relations is especially accentuated. In Germany this has been a
major factor contributing to the "interlocking federalism" for which that
federation is noted.

In virtually every federation intergovernmental relations have both vertical and horizontal dimensions. In addition to federal-unit relations, inter-
unit relations are usually extensive. These often deal with cross-boundary issues affecting neighbouring states or provinces concerning, for example,
jointly shared rivers, transportation routes, or environmental issues. In addition there are efforts by regional groups of units to cooperate on issues of
regional concern. Sometimes inter-unit collaboration is extended even
more broadly to encompass all the units within a federation in order to
avoid resorting to the centralizing impact of transferring responsibility for
shared problems to the federal government. This approach is sometimes referred to as "federalism without Washington" or "federalism without Bern."

The inevitable and unavoidable interdependence of governments within
federations and the resulting need for intergovernmental collaborative institutions and processes has led, within most federations, to an emphasis upon

"cooperative federalism." As noted earlier, the extent of this varies greatly, from those where duality and exclusivity of powers are strongly emphasized to those where the emphasis is on shared and concurrent jurisdiction.

Cooperative federalism has both benefits and costs. It often contributes to the reduction of conflict and facilitates coordination. When, however, it becomes "interlocking federalism" (where action can only occur if both orders of government agree) to the extent experienced, for example, in Germany, it may lead to what has been called the "joint decision trap." This can reduce the autonomy and freedom of action of governments at both levels and can lead to general policy inertia.[9] Furthermore, where executive federalism predominates, it may limit the role of legislators in negotiations. In some instances, too, where the main instrument for inducing cooperation is the employment by the federal government of extensive conditional grants, it may become a form of "coercive" or "collusive" federalism leading to federal government dominance.[10] Nevertheless, virtually every federation, even those such as Canada and Belgium (which have emphasized exclusivity in the assignment of jurisdiction), have found that it is impossible to isolate the activities of the different levels of government. Consequently, given the unavoidability of overlaps of jurisdiction, some degree of cooperative federalism in the form of intergovernmental collaboration has proved necessary.

There remains, however, the question of at what point such intergovernmental cooperation may, if excessive, limit or undermine the opportunity for flexible and autonomous action by each order of government. Advocates of competitive federalism suggest that competition between governments within a federation may actually produce beneficial results for citizens. Albert Breton argues that, just as competition in the economic realm produces superior benefits when compared to monopolies or oligopolies, so competition between governments serving the same citizens is likely to provide those citizens with better service.[11] He equates cooperative federalism with collusion between governments serving their own interests rather than those of their citizens. But while competitive federalism may contribute to maintaining the duality in the distribution of powers, it must be conceded that, taken to excess, it can lead to intergovernmental conflict and acrimony and can have a divisive impact upon a federation. This is illustrated by the experiences of Canada, Belgium, and Brazil. As with all partnerships, it would appear that, in maintaining and managing the distribution of powers in federations, a blend of both cooperation and competition is likely, in the long run, to be the most fruitful.

Key Actors and Institutions

In addition to the executives and legislatures, a number of other actors and institutions play key roles in maintaining and managing the distribution of powers in federations. These include the electorates, the courts, political parties, and interest groups, although their relative significance varies from federation to federation.

A fundamental question is whether electoral or judicial processes should be the primary means for resolving disputes and conflicts over the distribution of powers and responsibilities. Most federations have, in fact, relied on a combination of these processes. Ultimately, through periodic elections that occur within each level of government in federations, the electorates have the opportunity, where there is a conflict between governments, to express and support their preferences by voting parties in or out of office at each level of government. Consequently, in defending or advocating changes to the distribution of powers, the political parties and interest groups play an important role. For example, where the same party dominates governments at both levels for an extended period – as in the early years of the Congress in India and the lengthy period of Partido Revolucionario Institucional party dominance in Mexico – the dividing lines between federal and state politics are blurred and the federal government tends to dominate. On the other hand, the recent fragmentation of the Indian party system, with federal governments composed of coalitions of state parties, has imposed restraints upon the dominance of the federal government. In addition to political parties, interest groups have played an important part in managing the distribution of federal powers, tending to support governments whose constitutional jurisdiction coincides with their own particular objectives.

In the case of Switzerland, in addition to participating in elections at each level of government, the electorate plays a major direct role in maintaining and managing the distribution of power through the processes of the legislative referendum and the initiative. In the former process, any federal legislation that is challenged by 50,000 citizens or eight Cantons must be submitted to a direct popular vote in a referendum. As a result, the referendum process becomes the adjudicative process for ruling on the validity of federal legislation. An interesting by-product of this constitutional procedure is that, in order to reduce the risk of a successful challenge through the legislative referendum process, the maximization of interparty compromise within the federal government and legislature has in practice been induced. The initiative process adds a further opportunity for the electorate to influence the distribution of powers and responsibilities.

In many federations, especially those in the common law tradition, courts play a major role in maintaining the distribution of legislative and executive authority. In this role the courts perform three functions: (1) impartial constitutional interpretation, (2) adaptation of the constitutional distribution of powers to changing circumstances (especially where constitutional amendment is difficult), and (3) resolution of conflicts between governments over their respective powers. Two types of courts whose purpose is to determine constitutional jurisdiction may be found among federations. One is the "supreme court," which serves as the final adjudicator in relation to all laws, including the Constitution. Examples of this type of court may be found in the United States, Canada, Australia, Mexico, India, Brazil, and Nigeria. The other is the "constitutional court," which specializes in constitutional interpretation. Examples of this type of court may be found in Germany, Belgium, and Spain. A third type of court is unique to Switzerland. There the Federal Tribunal may rule on the validity of cantonal laws but not on the validity of federal laws (the latter being determined through legislative referendum).

The significance of judicial review in maintaining the constitutional distribution of authority, as already noted, varies enormously. In the United States, Canada, Australia, Germany, India, and Belgium it plays a very important role. It plays a more minor role in Mexico, Brazil, and Spain.

CURRENT AND FUTURE ISSUES

Federations are not static structures; rather, they are dynamic and evolving systems. Consequently, any analysis of the distribution of powers and responsibilities within them must see them in this context. The final sections of the preceding chapters on individual federations examine current issues relating to the distribution of powers and likely future responses to changing circumstances and challenges.

It would appear that, in terms of the degree of equilibrium achieved by their respective distributions of powers and responsibilities, the federations examined in this volume can be placed into two broad groups: (1) those in which an equilibrium is yet to be established and (2) those in which some equilibrium has been achieved (even though there still remain issues to be resolved).

In the first group are Belgium, Brazil, Mexico, Nigeria, and Spain. The constitutional structure in most of these countries is relatively recent and the balance in each of them between the appropriate levels of centralization and non-centralization appears to be relatively fragile.

In the case of Belgium, following five stages of devolution over the past thirty-five years, it is not yet clear whether an equilibrium has been established or whether it will undergo further devolution, transforming it into a basically confederal form. And in Brazil it appears that the 1988 Constitution has yet to achieve equilibrium. This is apparent from unbalanced financial arrangements, which have resulted in a "fiscal civil war," and the failure to address regional and social disparities. Although federalism is clearly seen by Brazilians as the model of government best able to reconcile the pressures for both small and large polities, it would appear that

further modifications to the distribution of powers will be needed in order
to address the social and regional inequalities within the federation. Mexico, after experiencing the expansion of federal powers during most of the
twentieth century, now faces pressures for devolution. It has yet to achieve
a regional counterbalance to its federal powers, however. The 1999 Nigerian Constitution is very recent, but the manner of its establishment and
the impact of the lengthy periods of military rule that preceded it have
meant that Nigeria's distribution of powers does not reflect the current
pressures for significant decentralization. A major issue, therefore, is how
to achieve a significant measure of decentralization without undermining
the effectiveness of the federal government.

Spain is continuing to seek a balance between the pressures for asymmetry and symmetry in the powers and responsibilities of the Autonomous
Communities in general as well as to accommodate the strong demands for
greater devolution on the part of Catalonia and the Basque Country
(among others). There are also issues involving a "second decentralization" to the local government entities and the need for improved intergovernmental relations.

The other six federations have, by comparison, achieved relative equilibrium in their distribution of powers and responsibilities, although in each
there are significant current issues of concern. The United States has existed
for more than two centuries and, over that period, its federal powers have expanded substantially; however, it still operates under the original Constitution, which means that the states remain relatively strong. Nevertheless,
there are three contemporary challenges related to the distribution of powers in the United States: (1) the likely impact of the changing composition
of the Supreme Court, which plays such a predominant role in interpreting
the constitutional distribution of powers; (2) the declining impact of state
political parties and interests within Congress; and (3) the limits imposed on
state and local governments by membership in the North American Free
Trade Agreement and other international trade agreements.

The new Swiss Constitution of 1999, which followed three decades of
deliberations, managed to avoid substantial and controversial reforms.
Indeed, it consisted largely of modernizing the language of the older Constitution and bringing the equilibrium in federal and cantonal powers
(which had evolved over the previous century and a half) up to date.
Some issues, however, have remained. These include reform of the financial equalization arrangements, some refinement in the allocation of tasks
between the federal government and the Cantons (along with arrangements for intercantonal and transborder cooperation), and the revision of
some cantonal constitutions.

Although marked by a considerable expansion of federal powers, especially in terms of fiscal capacity, the Australian distribution of powers – over

a century marked by economic crises and two world wars – appears to have evolved to the point where it is serving Australia well. Among the current and prospective issues affecting the distribution of powers are the likely emergence of the Northern Territory to full statehood (probably requiring some asymmetrical arrangement), responding to global economic and legal pressures, and the impact of the prospective transformation to a republican form of government.

In Canada, too, the distribution of powers has proved relatively flexible over nearly a century and a half, including periods of economic crisis and two world wars. In this case, however, the Constitution has enabled the transformation of a relatively centralized federation into one of the most decentralized in the contemporary world. Among the issues facing Canada in the immediate future are: (1) improving the role and effectiveness of city and local governments and of Aboriginal self-government; (2) developing processes for responding to unexpected shocks and emergencies; (3) improving intergovernmental cooperation to meet citizens' needs in such fields as health care; (4) responding to the challenges of the global and North American economy; and (5) accommodating the pressures for a more distinctive role for Quebec within the federation.

For half a century the German political reality with regard to the distribution of authority has more or less corresponded to constitutional law, establishing an interlocking relationship between the orders of government. However, in the past decade there have been increasing pressures to enable greater governmental initiative at both levels through introducing an element of disentanglement that would lead to less centralization. Also important are the issues of reforming the intergovernmental financial arrangements and of moderating the impact of European integration upon the German federal structure.

In India, the Union model of distribution of authority has shown considerable resilience and flexibility over more than half a century. As in Canada, in India an originally relatively centralized distribution of powers has been able to adapt to a more decentralized pattern through relying upon consensus via coalition governments at the federal level as well as by turning to intergovernmental forums as a response to the deep diversity marking Indian society. This trend continues to raise many issues relating to the distribution of powers – issues that have recently been addressed by several important commissions. A major current issue is the need to make more genuinely effective the movement begun in 1992 to develop local government as a full-fledged third order of constitutional government in India.

In a number of federations a major current and prospective issue is the impact of membership in suprafederal organizations on the internal distribution of powers. This is major issue in Germany, Belgium, and Spain, who are negotiating their position within the European Union, and it is a factor in Swiss reluctance to approve membership in that body. While the North American Free Trade Agreement is a much looser free trade organization than is the European Union, the United States, Canada, and Mexico feel its impact upon the relative roles of federal and state/provincial governments.

One other issue that is having an impact on contemporary federations involves the relationship between democracy, federalism, and multiculturalism. In Switzerland, with its multicultural context, the processes of direct democracy have, in practice, encouraged consensus politics. By contrast, in the largely bicommunal political context of Belgium, direct democracy is studiously avoided due to fears that it would accentuate the country's bipolarization. Elsewhere, the use of institutions of direct democracy is limited. In the United States some states have adopted processes of direct democracy, but these have not been extended widely, nor have they been applied at the federal level. In Canada, the tendency for executive federalism to involve closed-door intergovernmental negotiations has frequently been criticized as fundamentally "undemocratic," but beyond efforts to ensure greater overview of these processes on the part of legislatures and their committees, there has been little reform. On the one hand, there is considerable public pressure for more effective cooperation between governments; on the other hand, a currently significant trend shows a substantial number of provinces undertaking major reviews of the electoral process.

It is clear that, in all the federations examined in this volume, the issue of the appropriate distribution of powers and responsibilities between orders of government has been of fundamental importance to their character and operation. It is also clear that it will continue to be a lively topic of discussion among their politicians, government officials, and citizens as they attempt to respond to changing circumstances and new challenges.

NOTES

1 Daniel J. Elazar, *Exploring Federalism* (Tuscaloosa: University of Alabama Press, 1987), pp. 34–6.
2 For a fuller discussion see Ronald L. Watts, *Comparing Federal Systems*, 2nd ed. (Montreal and Kingston: McGill-Queen's University, 1999), pp. 71–80.
3 Ibid., 79.
4 Ronald L. Watts, *The Spending Power in Federal Systems: A Comparative Study* (Kingston: Institute of Intergovernmental Relations, Queen's University, 1999), pp. 56–58.
5 Derived from a working paper, R.L. Watts, *Autonomy or Dependence: Intergovernmental Financial Relations in Eight Countries* (Kingston: Institute of Intergovernmental Relations, Queen's University, 2005).

6 In some of these federations, federal territories or peripheral associated states and federacies are treated differently, however.

7 Robert Agranoff, ed., *Accommodating Diversity; Asymmetry in Federal States* (Baden-Baden: Nomos Verlagsgesellschaft, 1999).

8 David Milne, "Equality or Asymmetry: Why Choose?" *Options for a New Canada*, eds. R.L. Watts and D.M. Brown (Toronto: University of Toronto Press, 1991), pp. 285–307.

9 Fritz Scharpf, "The Joint Decision Trap: Lessons from German Federalism and European Integration," *Public Administration* 66 Autumn (1988): 238–278.

10 John Kincaid, "From Cooperative to Coercive Federalism," *Annals of the American Academy of Political and Social Science* 509 (May 1990): 139–152. Compare: Martin Painter, *Collaborative Federalism: Economic Reform in Australia in the 1990s* (Melbourne: Cambridge University Press, 1998).

11 Albert Breton, "Supplementary Statement," *Report of the Royal Commission on the Economic Union and Development Prospects for Canada*, vol. 3 (Ottawa: Supply and Services Canada, 1985), pp. 486–526. See also Vincent Ostrom, *The Political Theory of the Compound Republic: Designing the American Experiment* (Lincoln: University of Nebraska Press, 1987).

Contributors

ENRIC ARGULLOL MURGADAS is administrative law professor at the Universidad Pompeu Fabra, director of the *Observatorio de la Evolución de las Instituciones*, and member of the Legal Advisory Commission of the Autonomous Government of Catalonia. Among other positions, he was dean of the Faculty of Law of the Universidad Autónoma de Barcelona, member of the Catalonia Advisory Board, and vice-chancellor of the Universidad Pompeu Fabra (1990–2001). His main fields of research revolve around federalism, organization of territory, and urbanism – areas in which he has published several papers and doctrinal studies. Recently, he led the comparative study *Federalismo y autonomía* (2004).

XAVIER BERNADÍ GIL is administrative law professor (senior lecturer) at the Universidad Pompeu Fabra, coordinator of the *Observatorio de la Evolución de las Instituciones*, and official on-leave of the Senior Administrative Body of the Autonomous Government of Catalonia. He was also advisor of the *Instituto de Estudios Autónomicos* for the Catalonian government. His research activity focuses on federalism and, in particular, on executive federalism and the repercussions of communication and information technologies on the distribution of powers.

DOUGLAS M. BROWN is assistant professor, Department of Political Science, St. Francis Xavier University, Antigonish, Nova Scotia; and fellow and former director, Institute of Intergovernmental Relations, Queen's University, Kingston. His main interest is in Canadian and comparative federalism and intergovernmental relations, where he has over twenty-five years experience as a practitioner and an academic analyst. He is also the author and editor of over thirty publications. His most recent book is *Market Rules: Economic Union Reform and Intergovernmental Policy-Making in Australia and Canada* (2002).

HUGUES DUMONT received his doctorate in law from the Université catholique de Louvain and his *candidat* diploma in philosophy from the Facultés universitaires Saint-Louis. He is dean of the faculty of law and a professor at the Facultés universitaires Saint-Louis (Brussels), where he teaches constitutional law and legal theory. His publications include *Le pluralisme idéologique et l'autonomie culturelle en droit public belge* (1996). He recently co-coordinated two books: *Autonomie, solidariteit en samenwerking* (2002); and *Les dix-neuf communes bruxelloises et le modèle bruxellois* (2003).

ISAWA ELAIGWU is professor emeritus of political science at the University of Jos and president of the Institute of Governance and Social Research in Jos, Plateau State, Nigeria. He obtained his first degree from the Ahmadu Bello University, Zaria. He holds a master's and a doctorate from Stanford University, USA. He served as director general and chief executive of the National Council on Intergovernmental Relations in Abuja from 1992 to 1996. He also served as chairperson of the Board of Trustees for the United Nations Institute of Training and Research. He has many publications to his name, both internationally and within Nigeria.

THOMAS FLEINER is a full professor of constitutional and administrative law and director of the Institute of Federalism at the University of Fribourg, Switzerland. Professor Fleiner's current areas of interest include theory of the modern state and comparative government, federal and cantonal administrative and constitutional law, and comparative administrative and constitutional law. Professor Fleiner, with Professor Lidija Basta Fleiner, has recently published a new and revised edition of *Allgemeine Staatslehre* (*General Theory of Political Government* (2004), an English translation of which will be published in 2006). His book *What Are Human Rights?* has been published in Chinese (1999), English (1999), German (1995), French (1999), Portuguese (2003), Russian (1997), Serbian (1996), and Spanish (1998).

MANUEL GONZÁLEZ OROPEZA is a tenured faculty member at the Law School and Institute of Legal Research from the National University of Mexico. He has been a member of the National Research System of Mexico since its foundation. He holds a doctorate degree in law from the National University of Mexico and a master's degree in Political Science from the University of California at Los Angeles. He has written books and articles about the federal system in Mexico, comparative law, and state constitutional law. He has been a visiting professor at various universities in Mexico, the United States, and Canada.

ELLIS KATZ is professor emeritus of political science at Temple University, Philadelphia, and a fellow of the Center for the Study of Federalism at the Meyner Center for the Study of State and Local Government at Lafayette College, Easton, Pennsylvania. He is the author or editor of several books, including *American Models of Revolutionary Leadership* (1992), *Ethnic Group Politics* (1969), *Federalism and Rights* (1993), and *State Constitutions in the American Federal System* (1987). His articles have appeared in publications both in the United States and in other countries, including Brazil, China, India, Mexico, Russia, Spain, and Yugoslavia. He is currently working on the two-volume *Encyclopedia of American Federalism* to be published in 2006.

JOHN KINCAID is the Robert B. and Helen S. Meyner professor of government and public service, and director of the Meyner Center for the Study of State and Local Government at Lafayette College, Easton, Pennsylvania. He is the editor of *Publius: The Journal of Federalism*, the editor of a series of books on the governments and politics of the American states, and an elected fellow of the National Academy of Public Administration. He is the former executive director of the U.S. Advisory Commission on Intergovernmental Relations, Washington, D.C., and author of various works on federalism and intergovernmental relations.

NICOLAS LAGASSE has a bachelor of law degree and is a researcher at the Facultés universitaires Saint-Louis, Brussels. He is a parliamentary assistant with the Belgian House of Representatives, and he studies problems relating to the development of Belgian federalism.

CLEMENT MACINTYRE is senior lecturer in politics at the University of Adelaide, South Australia. He has worked on British and Australian politics and political history. He was recently chair of the Panel of Experts appointed by the South Australian government to advise on state constitutional reform, is a former editor of *Legislative Studies*, and is a member of the Australian Association of Constitutional Law. Clement Macintyre and John Williams are editors of *Peace, Order and Good Government: State Constitutional and Parliamentary Reform* (2003).

AKHTAR MAJEED is a professor of political science and is director of the Centre for Federal Studies at Hamdard University in New Delhi, India. He has taught at the Universities of Allahabad and Aligarh, has been a visiting professor at the University of Illinois at Urbana-Champaign, and is on the faculty that oversees the on-line program on federalism at Transcend Peace University. His recent publications include: *Federalism within the Union* (2004), *Nation and Minorities* (2002), *Constitutional Nation-Building: Half a Century of India's Success* (2001), and *Coalition Politics and Power-Sharing* (2000). He is editor of the biannual *Indian Journal of Federal Studies*.

GEORGE MATHEW is founding director of the Institute of Social Sciences, New Delhi. He is now specializing in local governments, decentralization, and gender equity. Born in Kerala (1943) he took his doctorate in sociology from the Jawaharlal Nehru University, New Delhi. He was a visiting fellow of the University of Chicago, South Asian Studies Centre (1981–82), and visiting professor at the University of Padova (1988) and the University of Trent (2005). He was awarded a Fulbright Fellowship in 1991 and has participated in international conferences on religion and society, political process and democracy, and human rights.

MARTIN PAPILLON is completing a Ph.D. in political science at the University of Toronto and is a research associate with the Canadian Policy Research Networks. He also worked as a policy analyst with the government of Canada in the Privy Council Office, Intergovernmental Affairs. His current research focuses on federalism in multinational societies and the development of treaty federalism and Aboriginal-federal-provincial intergovernmental relations in Canada. He has published articles on these and related topics in, among others, *Politics and Society*, the *International Review of Canadian Studies*, *Lien Social et Politiques*, and a number of edited volumes.

MARCELO PIANCASTELLI has a bachelor's from the Federal University of Minas Gerais, a master's degree from the University of Manchester, and a doctorate in economics from Kent at Canterbury, where he taught economic development at the graduate level. He is former associate professor of economics at the Federal University of Minas Gerais, where he was chief economist at the State of Minas Gerais Finance Secretariat, and coordinator of the stabilization program agreement with the International Monetary Fund, and deputy secretary of the Brasilian treasury. Presently he is the director of public finance and regional studies at the Institute of Applied Economic Research in Brasília.

HANS-PETER SCHNEIDER is professor emeritus in constitutional and administrative law at the University of Hanover. In 1987 he was a member of the Constitutional Court of Lower Saxony; in 1992 he was director of the Institute for Federal Studies at the University of Hanover; in 1993 he was a member of the Constitutional Court of Saxony; in 1998 he was vice-president of the International Association of Centres for Federal Studies; in 2003 he was an expert for the Joint Commission for the Modernization of the Federal System. He has written more than 250 books and articles on matters of constitutional law, legal theory, and public administration.

RICHARD SIMEON is professor of political science and law at the University of Toronto. A life-long student of federalism, he was director of the

Institute of Intergovernmental Relations at Queen's University, Kingston (1976–83), and research coordinator, federal institutions, for the Canadian Royal Commission on the Economic Union (1985). Among his publications are *Federal-Provincial Diplomacy* (1972); *State, Society and the Development of Canadian Federalism* (with Ian Robinson, 1991). His current focus is on federalism and institutional design in divided societies. In 2004 he was elected a fellow of the Royal Society of Canada.

MARC VAN DER HULST is head of the Legal Service of the Belgian House of Representatives and teaches constitutional law at the Vrije Universiteit Brussel. He serves on the editorial committee of the journal *Chroniques de droit public* and has written a number of articles on constitutional law as well as two books on parliamentary law: *Het federale Parlement* (1994) and *Le mandat parlementaire* (2000).

SÉBASTIEN VAN DROOGHENBROECK received his doctorate in law from the Facultés Universitaires Saint-Louis and his bachelor's degree in philosophy from the Université Catholique de Louvain. He is a researcher at the Fonds National de la Recherche Scientifique and teaches constitutional and human rights law at the Facultés Universitaires Saint-Louis (Brussels). His publications include *La proportionnalité dans le droit de la Convention européenne des droits de l'Homme. Prendre l'idée simple au sérieux* (2001) and, in collaboration with Olivier De Schutter, *Droit international des droits de l'Homme devant le juge national* (1999)

RONALD L. WATTS is principal emeritus and professor emeritus of political studies at Queen's University. He is a fellow and former director of the Institute of Intergovernmental Relations at Queen's University. He was president of the International Association of Centres for Federal Studies (1991–98) and is currently a member of the Board of the International Forum of Federations. He is a former board member and chairman of the Research Committee of the Institute for Research on Public Policy. He has worked for over forty years on the comparative study of federal systems and on Canadian federalism. His most recent book is *Comparing Federal Systems* (2nd ed. 1999). He became an officer of the Order of Canada in 1979 and was promoted to Companion of the Order of Canada in 2000.

JOHN WILLIAMS is a reader in Law at the Australian National University, Canberra. His research areas include constitutional law, Australian legal history, intergovernmental relations, and human rights. In 2003 he was the country coordinator for the Australian global dialogue workshop. He is a council member of the Australian Association of Constitutional Law.

Participating Experts

We gratefully acknowledge the input of the following experts who participated in the theme of Distribution of Powers and Responsibilities in Federal Countries. While participants contributed their knowledge and experience, they are in no way responsible for the contents of this book.

Ursula Abderhalden, Bundesamt für Justiz, Switzerland
Eleael Acevedo Velásquez, Congreso del Estado de Morelos, Mexico
Christy Adokwu, Benue State Government, Nigeria
Josá Rosas Aispuro Torres, Ayuntamiento de Durango, Mexico
Fareed Amin, Government of Ontario, Canada
Carlos Araújo Leonetti, Universidade Federal de Santa Catarina, Brazil
Glauco Arbix, Instituto de Pesquisa Econômica Aplicada, Brazil
Enric Argullol, Universitat Pompeu Fabra, Spain
Balveer Arora, Jawaharlal Nehru University, India
Solomon Asemota, Alliance for Democracy, Nigeria
Fabricio Augusto de Oliveira, Brazil
Luis Aureliano Andrade, Universidade Federal de Minas Gerais, Brazil
Carlos Báez Silva, Poder Judicial de la Federacion, Mexico
Earl M. Baker, Pennsylvania State Senate (former), United States
John Bannon, Government of South Australia (former), Australia
Javier Barnés, Universidad de Huelva, Spain
José Barragán Barragán, Instituto Federal Electoral, Mexico
Martín Bassols, Congreso de los Diputados, Spain
Antoni Bayona, Generalitat de Catalunya (former), Spain
Isabel Benzo, Presidencia del Gobierno, Spain
Xavier Bernadí Gil, Universitat Pompeu Fabra, Spain
Teresa Bhattacharya, Government of Karnataka (former), India
Raoul Blindenbacher, Forum of Federations, Switzerland
Thomas Bombois, Université Catholique de Louvain, Belgium

Paul Boothe, University of Alberta, Canada

Raphael Born, Université Catholique de Louvain, Belgium

Francisco Borrás Marimon, Instituto Nacional de Administración Pública, Spain

Albert Breton, University of Toronto, Canada

César Camacho Quiroz, Senado de la República, Mexico

Ronaldo Camillo, Governo do Brasil, Brazil

Gilson Cantarino, Governo do Estado do Rio de Janeiro, Brazil

Beniamino Caravita de Toritto, Osservatorio sul Federalismo e i processi di governo, Italy

Pran Chopra, India

Sujit Choudhry, University of Toronto, Canada

David Cienfuegos Salgado, Poder Judicial de la Federacion, Mexico

Jan Clement, Raad van State, Belgium

Fabiano Core, Governo do Brazil, Brazil

Luis Cosculluela, Universidad Complutense Madrid, Spain

Sulamis Dain, Universidade Federal do Estado do Rio de Janeiro, Brazil

Rui de Britto Álvares, Fundação do Desenvolvimento Administrativo, Brazil

Pierre-Olivier De Broux, Facultés Universitaires Saint-Louis, Belgium

Armand de Mestral, McGill University, Canada

Jean-Thierry Debry, Université de Liège, Belgium

Xavier Delgrange, Conseil d'État, Belgium

Donald Dennison, Forum of Federations, Canada

Hugues Dumont, Facultés Universitaires Saint-Louis, Belgium

Richard Eckermann, Bezirksregierung Lüneburg, Niedersachsen, Germany

Maureen Egbuna, Intercellular Nigerian Limited, Nigeria

J. Isawa Elaigwu, Institute of Governance and Social Research, Nigeria

Robert Ezeife, Association of Local Government of Nigeria, Nigeria

Patrick Fafard, Government of Canada, Canada

Jeffrey Featherstone, Center for Sustainable Communities, United States

Alexander C. Fischer, Universität Heidelberg, Germany

Thomas Fleiner, Université de Fribourg, Switzerland

Michel Frédérick, Governement du Québec, Canada

Bernie Funston, Northern Canada Consulting, Canada

Peter Gahan, Government of Victoria, Australia

Habu Galadima, University of Jos, Nigeria

Juan Carlos Gómez Martínez, Tribunal Superior de Justicia del Distrito Federal, Mexico

Juan Luis González Alcántara y Carrancá, Tribunal Superior de Justicia del Distrito Federal, Mexico

Manuel Gonzalez Oropeza, Universidad Nacional Autónoma de Mexico, Mexico

Vanessa Gore, Australia

Peter Graefe, McMaster University, Canada

Rachael Gray, Australia

Laura Grenfell, University of Adelaide, Australia
José de Jesús Gudiño Pelayo, Suprema Corte de Justicia de la Nación, Mexico
Virgilio Guimarães, Governo do Brazil, Brazil
Jim Hancock, South Australian Centre for Economic Studies, Australia
Tom Henderson, National Center for State Courts, United States
Meenakshi Hooja, Government of Rajasthan, India
Rakesh Hooja, Government of India, India
Paul Huber, Regierungsrat des Kantons Luzern (former), Switzerland
Siraj Hussain, Hamdard University, India
Jordi Jané, Congreso de los Diputados, Spain
Priscilla Jebaraj, CNBC India, India
Nirmal Jindal, Delhi University, India
Nelson Jobim, Corte Suprema do Brazil, Brazil
Hayden Jones, Tasmanian State Government, Australia
Sindhu Joy, University of Kerala, India
Subhash C. Kashyap, Parliament of India (former), India
Ellis Katz, International Association of Centers for Federal Studies, United States
Markus Kern, Université de Fribourg, Switzerland
Arshi Khan, Hamdard University, India
John Kincaid, Lafayette College, United States
Jutta Kramer, Universität Hannover, Germany
Nicolas Lagasse, Facultés Universitaires Saint-Louis, Belgium
Harvey Lazar, Queen's University, Canada
J. Wesley Leckrone, Temple University, United States
Oryssia Lennie, Western Economic Diversification Canada, Canada
Geoff Lindell, University of Adelaide, Australia
Bruno Lombaert, Facultés Universitaires Saint-Louis, Belgium
Augustin Macheret, Université de Fribourg, Switzerland
Clem Macintyre, University of Adelaide, Australia
Akhtar Majeed, Hamdard University, India
Ignasi Manrubia, DEA, Spain
Jospeh Marbach, Seton Hall University, United States
George Mathew, Institute of Social Sciences, India
Stephen McDonald, University of Adelaide, Australia
Ully C. Merkel, Australia
Mônica Mora, Instituto de Pesquisa Econômica Aplicada, Brazil
Jacqueline Muniz, Governo do Brazil, Brazil
Francesc Muñoz, DEA, Spain
Alhaji Ghali Na'abba, National Assembly, Nigeria
Adam Nagler, Government of Ontario, Canada
A.S. Narang, Indira Gandhi National Open University, India
Amy Nugent, University of Toronto, Canada
Nurudeen A. Ogbara, National Association of Democratic Lawyers, Nigeria

Ajene Ogiri, Benue State Government, Nigeria
Georg-Berndt Oschatz, Bundesrat (former), Germany
Sam Oyovbaire, TAS Associates, Nigeria
Martin Papillon, University of Toronto, Canada
Arijit Pasayat, Supreme Court of India, India
Tom Pauling, Government of Northern Territory, Australia
Malte Pehl, Universität Heidelberg, Germany
Anna Peliano, Instituto de Pesquisa Econômica Aplicada, Brazil
Marcelo Piancastelli de Siqueira, Instituto de Pesquisa Econômica Aplicada, Brazil
Patricia Popelier, Universiteit Antwerpen, Belgium
Sérgio Prado, Universidade Estadual de Campinas, Brazil
Michael Prince, University of Victoria, Canada
Ranjita Rajan, India
C. Rangarajan, XIIth Finance Commission, India
A.K. Rastogi, Government of India, India
David Renders, Université Catholique de Louvain, Belgium
Fernando Antonio Rezende da Silva, Fundação Getulio Vargas, Brazil
Christian E. Rieck, Humboldt-Universität zu Berlin, Germany
Horst Risse, Bundesrat, Germany
Marcial Rodríguez Saldaña, Ayuntamiento de Acapulco, Mexico
Eduard Roig, Universitat de Barcelona, Spain
Géraldine Rosoux, Université de Liège, Belgium
Ash Narain Roy, Institute of Social Sciences, India
Cheryl Saunders, University of Melbourne, Australia
Rekha Saxena, University of Delhi, India
Annemie Schauss, Université Libre de Bruxelles, Belgium
Stephen L. Schechter, Russell Sage College, United States
Hans-Peter Schneider, Universität Hannover, Germany
Jean-Claude Scholsem, Université de Liège, Belgium
Brad Selway, Federal Court of Australia, Australia
Sandeep Shastri, International Academy for Creative Teaching, India
Kenneth Shear, Philadelphia Bar Association, United States
Richard E.B. Simeon, University of Toronto, Canada
Julie Simmons, Guelph University, Canada
M.P. Singh, Delhi University, India
Ajay K. Singh, Hamdard University, India
Santosh Singh, Institute of Social Sciences, India
Jennifer Smith, Dalhousie University, Canada
Troy E. Smith, Drury University, United States
Saifuddin Soz, Parliament of India, India
Nico Steytler, University of the Western Cape, South Africa
Kumar Suresh, Hamdard University, India
Johan Swinnen, Gouvernement fédéral, Belgium

Bruce Tait, Government of Alberta, Canada
G. Alan Tarr, Rutgers University, United States
Victor Tootoo, Government of Nunavut, Canada
Joaquim Tornos, Generalitat de Catalunya, Spain
Dircêo Torrecillas Ramos, Fundação Getulio Vargas, Brazil
Paola Torres Robles, Instituto para el Desarrollo Técnico de las Haciendas Públicas, Mexico
François Tulkens, Facultés Universitaires Saint-Louis, Belgium
Judy Tyers, Government of Victoria (former), Australia
Bala Usman, Ahmadu Bello University, Nigeria
Clemente Valdez Sánchez, Mexico
Marc Van der Hulst, Belgische Kamer van Volksvertegenwoordigers, Belgium
Sébastien Van Drooghenbroeck, Facultés Universitaires Saint-Louis, Belgium
Damien van Eyll, Gouvernement fédéral, Belgium
Jeroen Van Nieuwenhove, Raad van State, Belgium
Patrick van Ypersele, Chambre des Représentants, Belgium
Manu Vandenbossche, Universiteit Brussel, Belgium
Ricardo Varsano, Instituto de Pesquisa Econômica Aplicada, Brazil
Clara Velasco Rico, Universitat Pompeu Fabra, Spain
M.N. Venkatachaliah, National Commission to Review the Working of the Constitution, India
Michael Vethasiromony, Government of Kerala, India
Joan Vintró, Parlament de Catalunya, Spain
Carles Viver, Institut d'Estudis Autonòmics, Spain
Donatienne Wahl, Conseil de la Région Bruxelles-Capitale, Belgium
Ronald Watts, Queen's University, Canada
Conrad Weiler, Temple University, United States
Paul Weizer, Fitchburg State College, United States
Fiona Wheeler, Australia National University, Australia
John White, Saskatchewan Institute of Public Policy, Canada
John Williams, University of Adelaide, Australia
Mark Winfield, Pembina Institute for Appropriate Development, Canada
Vicente Y Pla Trevas, Presidência da República, Brazil
Farah Abdullah Yasmin, India
Lars Zimmermann, Aspen Institute Berlin, Germany

Index